Twilight of the Merkel Era

Twilight of the Merkel Era

Power and Politics in Germany after the 2017 Bundestag Election

edited by

Eric Langenbacher

NEW YORK • OXFORD
www.berghahnbooks.com

Published in 2019 by
Berghahn Books
www.berghahnbooks.com

Originally published as special issues of
German Politics and Society, volume 36, numbers 1 & 2.

Library of Congress Cataloging-in-Publication Data

Library of Congress Control Numzxber: 2019942496

British Library Cataloguing in Publication Data

A catalogue record for this book is available from the British Library

ISBN 978-1-78920-264-9 hardback
ISBN 978-1-78920-265-6 paperback
ISBN 978-1-78920-266-3 ebook

Contents

List of Illustrations

Tables

Figures

••• INTRODUCTION •••

MERKELDÄMMERUNG

Eric Langenbacher

Liminal Germany

The last few years in Germany, like elsewhere in the West, have been a bit strange. On the surface, everything seems to be going rather well. The economy has been chugging along with the country having the largest trade surplus in the world for three years. Unemployment is at near-record lows and real wages have been increasing.[1] State finances are solid–budgetary surpluses have been used to reduce the debt-to-GDP ratio. In light of this economic strength, even though it took nearly six months to form a new government after the September 2017 Bundestag elections, few seemed to notice. Various crises bubbled up periodically, but nothing has been too dramatic. Syria? Brexit? Trump? The Alternative for Germany (AfD)? The diesel scandal? Chancellor Angela Merkel would always be there to take care of things.

Much, however, had been brewing underneath the surface. Expectations were mounting for increased spending on domestic social programs, affordable housing, and infrastructure after years of relative austerity. Responses to the simmering external challenges that had been put on hold for much of 2017 and 2018 because of the election campaign and the caretaker government had to be formulated. Despite hopes from some quarters that the British will pull back from the 2016 decision, Brexit in some form will likely happen during the current parliamentary term. Given the possibility of a transitional phase or delay, it is uncertain how much of a negative impact this will have on the German or European economy–but negative it will be at one point.[2] Illiberal eastern European governments in places like Hungary and Poland need to be more vigorously confronted, and the new pop-

Notes for this section begin on page 32.

ulist government in Italy with its budget-busting spending plans needs to be handled. Presidents Vladimir Putin of Russia, Recep Tayyip Erdoğan of Turkey, and, ever-the-wild-card Donald Trump in the U.S. (despite much wishful thinking) are not going away any time soon. Indeed, Putin's warmongering against Ukraine was ratcheted up in late 2018. Trade restrictions (including tariffs announced by Trump in March 2018 with more threatened) and a deleterious transatlantic trade war are possible.

Looming in the background was the most dramatic event of the last parliamentary term–the migration crisis, which peaked in 2015 when Merkel modified policy and opened Germany's borders to over a million asylum seekers, refugees, and other migrants. Despite some incidents such as the attacks on women in Cologne at New Year's 2016, many observers have concluded that the country's efforts to integrate these newcomers have thus far been reasonably successful.[3] Nevertheless, migration and integration remain huge issues, not the least because they have spurred a backlash, specifically the empowered right-radical Alternative for Germany party and a wave of right-wing, xenophobic demonstrations such as in Chemnitz at the end of August 2018 and some violence.[4]

More structurally, many have observed that Germany's power has been rising for years. Notable instances include imposing policy preferences on other EU member states during the Eurozone crisis and the migration crisis in 2015. Millions of people are waiting to see if Germany is going to take on a bigger leadership role abroad–if it can or will help to fill the vacuum of shrinking American leadership. Nevertheless, the country has continued to deny its newfound influence and has shrunk from more conventional power projection as with the 2011 decision not to support allied efforts to oust Gaddafi in Libya. Despite some increases, it cannot even bring itself to commit 2 percent of GDP to defense spending–despite a budget surplus. It is the ever-reluctant hegemon. Yet, as much as Germans might not want to take up the mantle of leadership, the alternative–a power or leadership vacuum could be much worse with proliferating bad actors filling the void and doing substantial damage to the regional and global interests of Germany and the liberal democratic community more broadly. Until now, the country has been able to delay a reckoning or a clear acknowledgement of the reality of its increased power, as well as the obligations that come with accepting such a role. It is a kind of luxury to take your time, deciding not to decide. Germany's liminal moment is, however, coming to an end.

This long-anticipated reckoning is now at hand as the Merkel era winds down. Merkel herself probably sensed her weakened position ever since her party's lackluster result in the 2017 election–if not already earlier with the fallout from her policies during the height of the migration crisis. At the age of sixty-four, she is currently the third-longest serving postwar chancellor with over thirteen years in power and was Christian Democratic Union (CDU) party leader for the better part of two decades, until she announced that she would not stand again for this office at the December 2018 CDU Party Congress.[5] She might last as chancellor until the next scheduled elections in 2021, but this is unlikely once the new party boss consolidates her position over the course of 2019. Merkel's party and the country are preparing for who will come next and what kind of leadership the country needs or wants.

Certainly, the Federal Republic has had many other moments of transition with a *fin de siècle* feeling. The waning years of Chancellors Konrad Adenauer in the early 1960s and Helmut Kohl in the mid 1990s come immediately to mind. Nevertheless, something feels different currently. At those previous transitional moments, there was a clear, exciting (to many at least) alternative–leaders who articulated a novel vision, or joint project–younger politicians like Willy Brandt and Gerhard Schröder with vigor and momentum. This time, however, there is nothing and no one like that in the wings of the major parties. The current crop of CDU and SPD politicians largely preaches more of the same–only with a different face and perhaps better management at the margins. This, of course, disregards the Alternative for Germany–which has had momentum, but with a pessimistic, dystopian, and retrograde vision–as well as the Green Party, which surged over the course of 2018. Nevertheless, no one seems to want to articulate a clear vision for the country, continent, or world for which so many have been calling. It is indeed the twilight of Merkel (*Merkeldämmerung*), but what dawn (*Morgenrot*) is on the horizon? These are the issues surrounding the 2017 Bundestag election and its aftermath that this edited volume confronts.

The Campaign

As expected, the campaign was short on drama, although it was perhaps not quite as boring as the last few. There were two big developments in the nine months before election day in September 2017. First was the saga of Martin Schulz and his Social Democratic Party (SPD). A prominent social democratic politician in the European Parliament–a MEP from 1994 to 2017 and parliamentary president from 2012 to 2017 (although also involved in the domestic party leadership), he was selected as SPD chancellor candidate in January 2017, and then replaced Sigmar Gabriel as party leader in March of that year. He seemed like an ideal choice–experienced but not sullied by a leadership role in the Red-Green or later grand coalition governments. Unlike prominent ministers or parliamentary leaders, this would allow him to criticize the out-going government and differentiate the SPD from Merkel's CDU. At first, Schulz had massive support within the party and the electorate. In fact, he was elected party chair with an unprecedented 100 percent of the delegates and (re-elected with 82 percent in December 2017).[6] Polling from February to April 2017 had the party at or above 30 percent–at one point even with or slightly ahead of the CDU.[7]

But, from May 2017 onwards the party began to slip in the polls. Its electoral program was full of classic social democratic themes, emphasizing justice (*Gerechtigkeit*) for all. Full employment, more jobs as part of union-negotiated wage agreements, more European governance, eliminating gender pay differences, and continuing a humane, but Europeanized migration policy were all in there.[8] Observers considered these campaign messages to be lackluster, although better than the vague 2013 slogan ("Das Wir entscheidet"–"the we decides" for readers who had forgotten). Common posters included "Time for more justice. Time for Martin Schulz" or a picture of a woman with the message "whoever works 100 percent, should not earn 21 percent less."[9]

Moreover, this emphasis on social justice and inequality did not resonate strongly with voters. The party tried to pivot towards a focus on migration and integration closer to election day, but this was too little too late. The many compromises that came with almost continuous governing for fifteen of the last nineteen years had taken a toll–as has competition from the other leftist and populist parties. Numerous SPD politicians expressed frustration that so many of their issues had become policy (e.g., minimum wage), but that Merkel typically got all the credit.

The second big campaign development was the strengthening of the AfD–despite all of the factional in-fighting and the leadership carousel. It had barely missed the 5 percent threshold in 2013 when it was a more Euroskeptic party and seemed to be on a downward trend after that. Then, the migration crisis and Merkel's August 2015 decision to admit over a million people into the country brought the AfD roaring back. It had also done quite well in Landtag elections. At the time of the 2017 Bundestag election, it was in every state parliament except for Bavaria and Hesse, and entered those parliaments as well after the October 2018 elections in those states. All polls in the months before the Bundestag election had the party well over the 5 percent threshold. Thus, the success of the AfD and its entrance into the Bundestag–the first new party to do so since reunification (excluding the transformation of the Party for Democratic Socialism (PDS) into the Left Party in 2007)–was no surprise.

The AfD ran a highly professional campaign–help from the U.S. (Harris Media, which worked for the Trump campaign)[10] and perhaps Russia did not hurt. Their electoral program had the expected right-populist elements with a German twist: more referendums, less lobbying, no more Euro. They advocated for a foreign policy based on interests, eliminating public support for wind energy, and social conservatism ("gender ideology is unconstitutional," "children need fathers and mothers"). Above all, they called for migration and multiculturalism to be minimized or stopped with slogans such as "Deutsche Leitkultur statt 'Multikulturismus,'" "Africa can't be saved in Europe," and "Islam does not belong to Germany."[11]

Unlike the other parties that had unified messaging campaigns throughout the country, the AfD micro-targeted its slogans and posters quite effectively in different states and types of communities albeit with a coordinated theme: "Trau dich Deutschland!" (Germany, dare yourself!). Deep in the eastern German state of Saxony-Anhalt, their posters proclaimed that the constitution had to be protected from Merkel ("Grundgestez vor Merkel schützen!")–referencing a conspiratorial right-wing belief that Merkel's decision to admit the refugees and migrants in 2015 was unlawful.[12] In Bavaria, most of the posters went for the Christian Social Union's (CSU) jugular: "Wir halten, was CSU verspricht" (We'll deliver what the CSU only promises). An especially controversial poster depicted the legendary postwar CSU leader proclaiming "Franz Josef Strauss würde AfD wählen" (Franz Josef Strauss would vote for the AfD). In Berlin, by contrast, ads depicted two white women in swimsuits with the text: "Burkas?" Wir steh'n auf Bikinis" (Burkas? We prefer bikinis). Another had a picture of women in traditional regional costumes, proclaiming: "Burkas? Wir stehn' mehr auf Burgunder" (Burkas? We prefer Burgundies) or "Bunte Vielfalt? Haben wir schon" (Colorful diversity? We already have it). One poster depicted a pregnant white woman with the text: "Neue Deutsche?" Machen wir selber" (New Germans? We'll do that ourselves). Belying their denials of right-radicalism, they constantly parroted such themes and images. There was an image of a male same-sex couple holding a non-white baby with the "new German" message. Another contained an image of a piglet, proclaiming "Der Islam? Paßt nicht zu unserer Küche" (Islam? Doesn't fit into our kitchen).

As for the other small parties, the liberal Free Democratic Party (FDP) garnered wide praise for its campaign performance. Its young (thirty-eight at the time of the election) party leader since 2013, Christian Lindner, was an especially exhilarating stump speaker, who seemed to hit a chord with many voters. As one psychologist concluded: "There was a real love for Lindner … The FDP's candidate is seen as a modern TV star, even like a kind of 007, who can engender change. A kind of dream team is the result: the proven Merkel and a mini German Macron that gives her a helping hand."[13] The party's campaign platform diverged some from classically liberal emphases on lower taxes, although abolishing the solidarity surcharge (known as the "Soli" and put in place in the early 1990s to pay for the costs of reunification in eastern Germany) and fostering entrepreneurship were mentioned. Instead, a variety of reforms to the state administration, education, and the European Union were highlighted. The most attention, however, was devoted to digitalization and preparing for the next phase of economic development.[14] This last theme permeated their ads and posters, which heavily profiled Lindner in various GQ model poses–black-and-white, in a suit and no tie, or suit jacket off. Messages included "Vererben wir nicht Schulden sondern Chancen" (We should not bequeath debts, rather chances), "Bildung: Unser Jugendwort des Jahres" (Education: our youth word-of-the-year); "Digital First: Bedenken Second" (Digital first, reservations second), and "Die Digitalisierung ändert alles. Wann ändert sich die Politik?" (Digitalization is changing everything. When will politics change?).[15]

The Green's pink and green advertisements with the yellow sunflower logo were somewhat memorable and certain better than the warped cardboard posters and forgettable messages of the 2013 campaign. Playing with Willy Brandt's famous phrase, one poster stated: "The Environment is not everything. But everything is nothing without the environment" (Umwelt ist nicht alles. Aber ohne Umwelt ist alles nichts)[16] Others included "Nobody gets more from less Europe" (Von weniger Europa hat keiner mehr), "Healthy food does not come from a sick nature" (Gesundes Essen kommt nicht aus einer kranken Natur"), and, striving for middle class votes "There should not be an 'or' between the environment and the economy" (Zwischen Umwelt und Wirtschaft gehört kein oder).[17] The Left Party utilized the same kinds of ads as in previous campaigns (at least there is brand consistency) with a unified message centered on respect. Examples included "Respeckt: Rente mit Niveau" (Pensions at a high level); "Miete und Energie Bezahlbar für alle" (Rent and energy affordable to all); and as a reminder of the SPD's earlier alleged policy sell out of poorer Germans "Respekt: Mindest-Sicherung statt Hartz IV" (A guaranteed minimum income instead of Hartz IV).[18]

Finally, the CDU's effort disappointed. Unlike 2013, when the campaign fetishized images of Merkel and her hands (the famous *Raute*), the CDU/CSU de-emphasized the chancellor this time around. It appeared that she was perceived as a liability at least for advertising purposes. Indeed, never a fan of campaigning, she was even more absent than usual from the campaign trail. One of her last big rallies in Munich was marked by protests and heckling. The CDU also "innovated" with a gimmicky campaign venue in central Berlin full of interactive, digital displays ("the pulse of the German economy" replete with a large beating heart) and high-tech information touting the party's successes, especially with the economy. This "accessible and interactive platform" (*das begehbare Programm*) did not really work and must have cost a fortune.[19]

The Christian Democrats' campaign platform rested on touting previous achievements and a record of good management. Given their good–even exemplary–stewardship of the economy, one could understand why the party made this choice. Indeed, such an economic record is what politicians' dreams are made:

Table 0.1: German Economic Performance, 2009-2019

Year	Real GDP Growth Rate (%)	Budget Deficit/ Surplus (% GDP)	Public Debt (% GDP)*	Unemployment Rate (harmonized)
2009	-5.56	-3.23	75.38	7.64
2010	3.95	-4.22	84.68	6.97
2011	3.72	-0.96	83.98	5.83
2012	0.69	-0.03	86.52	5.38
2013	0.60	-0.14	81.50	5.24
2014	1.93	0.33	81.92	4.99
2015	1.50	0.64	77.89	4.63
2016	1.86	0.82	74.70	4.13
2017	2.54	1.20**	71.67	3.60***
2018	2.29		68.66	3.73****
2019	1.90			3.66****

Sources: http://www.oecd-ilibrary.org/economics

* https://knoema.com/vuuebne/germany-government-debt-forecast-2015-2020-and-up-to-2060-data-and-charts

** https://tradingeconomics.com/germany/government-budget *** November 2017.

**** projections: https://www.statista.com/statistics/375209/unemployment-rate-in-germany/

In their planned government platform for 2017-2021 they listed goals such as good jobs and fair pay, strengthening internal security, pushing for free trade, and fostering innovation and digitalization (obviously a big buzzword in this political cycle).[20] Otherwise the slogans were "For a Germany in which we live well and happily" (Für ein Deustchland in dem wir gut und gerne leben) and, simply, if a little heavy-handed: "Successful for Germany" (Erfolgreich für Deutschland).[21]

In sum, the campaign was a relatively short, low-drama affair. The eventual outcome was mooted for a while, or at least since the SPD started its slide in the early summer and the AfD's support ticked upwards. The television debate between Schulz and Merkel in early September had the two candidates mostly agreeing–one newspaper's headline even read "Two Candidates, One Opinion."[22] Again, the SPD candidate had a real problem trying to differentiate his party from a government of which it was a part. There were some interesting exchanges about the refugee crisis, but overall concurrence. Notably, Merkel made it clear that large numbers of migrants would likely not be admitted in the future, but stood by her 2015 decision.

Two final notes about the campaign are pertinent. First, the term *Wutbürger* (enraged citizen) frequently surfaced. Although this was an older formulation (2010 word-of-the-year), it seemed to capture the mood of much of the electorate in 2017.[23] Indeed, there was a pervasive sense that segments of the population (especially men and eastern Germans) were quite angry and vocal with expressions of their bitterness–especially regarding migration/integration, the fast pace of demographic and cultural change, but also about stagnant incomes and growing inequality despite the good economy over the last decade. Again, this was not just a German peculiarity–similar sentiments in most western countries have been observed and help to explain the rise in support for various populist movements.

Second, in a surprising move given her years of opposition, Merkel allowed the Bundestag to vote on same-sex marriage in late June 2017. The Greens, followed quickly by the FDP and SPD proclaimed earlier that month that legalizing same-sex marriage would be a condition of any coalition agreement with the CDU/CSU. On 27 June, Merkel unexpectedly indicated that she would allow a vote of conscience in the Bundestag (where party discipline does not apply). Three days later on 30 June, a two-thirds majority of deputies voted for marriage equality, although 75 percent of CDU/CSU caucus (225 deputies) including Merkel herself voted no versus every single SPD, Green, and Left Party member who voted for the legal change. For the record, some prominent CDU/CSU members who voted for marriage equality included Ursula von der Leyen, Peter Altmaier, Jens Spahn, and Peter Tauber. Merkel's maneuver eliminated a sticking point to eventual coalition negotiations and neutralized a potential wedge issue for the "hot" phase of the campaign. Incidentally, a very large majority of the German population (75 percent and even 73 percent of CDU supporters) supported marriage equality at that time.[24]

An Uncertain Outcome

Unlike the campaign, election night on 24 September 2017 was rather more exciting. The banner headlines were the entrance of the AfD with 12.6 percent of the vote and ninety-four seats (13.3 percent) of the total. Despite surveys long predicting its entrance into parliament, the AfD over-performed its polling averages, ended up winning three direct mandates in southeastern Saxony, and became the third-largest fraction in the new parliament. In light of the eventual grand coalition (GroKo), it is also the largest opposition party–a position that provides a degree of power and leverage–control of the parliament's influential budget committee (Haushaltsauschuss) for example. The FDP also had a good night with 10.7 percent of the vote and 11.3 percent of the seats. Lindner was definitely one of the winners and gave a stellar performance in the televised *Elefantenrunde* of party leaders right after the election was called (Merkel looked tired, Schulz belatedly showed some spunk, the Green Katrin Göring-Eckhardt was impressive; everyone teamed up on the AfD participant, Jörg Meuthen). The Liberals' eighty seats were not enough combined with the CDU/CSU total to form a repeat of the 2009-2013 center-right coalition. The Greens and Left did slightly better than in 2013, but did not significantly increase their support.

Participation was up almost 5 percent from 71.5 percent of the electorate in 2013 to 76.2 percent. The use of postal ballots continued to rise to 28.6 percent from 24.3 percent in 2013 and 9.4 percent in 1990, largely driven by an increase in voters living abroad, especially in Switzerland and other EU member states. Older voters disproportionally preferred the two catch-all parties. Men expressed a greater preference for the AfD (16.3 percent to 9.2 percent of women), FDP, and Left Party, whereas women disproportionally supported the CDU/CSU and Greens. Support for the SPD was even from a gender perspective.[25]

The governing catch-all parties (*Volksparteien*) had a bad night. They ended up 2 to 5 percent below where they were averaging in polls in the weeks and months before election day.[26] Pollsters did record a rather precipitous drop in support just in the days before the vote–to the benefit of the smaller parties, particularly the AfD, which went from a longer-term average of 7 to 10 percent up to over 12 percent. There is no clear explanation for why this late-breaking development occurred. Some argued that certain media outlets had increased coverage of issues like migration, crime, and integration, which then boosted the salience of these concerns and thus support for the AfD. No one observed substantial meddling by the Russians or other actors. Some commentators even noted that there was more intervention from U.S. right-wing actors than from Russia.[27]

Table 0.2: Bundestag Election Results, 2017 and 2013

	2017 Percent 2nd Vote	Seats	Percent Seats	2013 Percent 2nd Vote	Seats	Percent Seats	Percent 2nd Vote Change (2017 v. 2013)	Percent Seat Change (2017 v. 2013)
CDU/CSU	33	246	34.7	41.5	311	49.4	-8.5	-14.7
SPD	20.5	153	21.6	25.7	193	30.6	-5.2	-9
FDP	10.7	80	11.3	4.8	-	-	+5.9	+11.3
Greens	8.9	67	9.4	8.4	63	10.0	+0.5	-0.6
Left	9.2	69	9.7	8.6	64	10.2	+0.6	-0.5
AfD	12.6	94	13.3	4.7	-	-	+7.9	+13.3
Others	5	-		6.2*	-	-		
		709			631			

Source: Bundeswahlleiter
* in 2013 All <5 %=15.7%

The decline of the two *Volksparteien* has been on-going for decades, but was temporarily masked by the anomalous 2013 election result. With the demise of the FDP and the near miss from the AfD that year, a record high over 15 percent of the vote went to parties below the 5 percent threshold. This artificially inflated the parliamentary delegations of the parties that did make it over the threshold, particularly the two catch-all parties. But, in 2017, the longer-term decline continued. The CSU went from 7.4 to 6.2 percent of the national vote, but from 49.3 to 38.8 (a 10.5 percent decline) in Bavaria, the only state in which it competes. CDU support fell from 34.2 to 26.8, a 7.4 percent decline. Put differently, both the CDU and CSU lost over a fifth of their 2013 support level. At 20.5 percent, the SPD had its worst outcome since 1949 or 1890 when it got 19.8 percent (in May 1924 it achieved 20.5 percent, and November 1932 20.4 percent). It lost 21 percent of its 2013 support. To be just a bit melodramatic, the party has not seen such a poor electoral performance since Chancellor Otto von Bismarck's Anti-Socialist Laws were in place before 1890!

Figure 0.1: SPD Share of the Vote since 1890

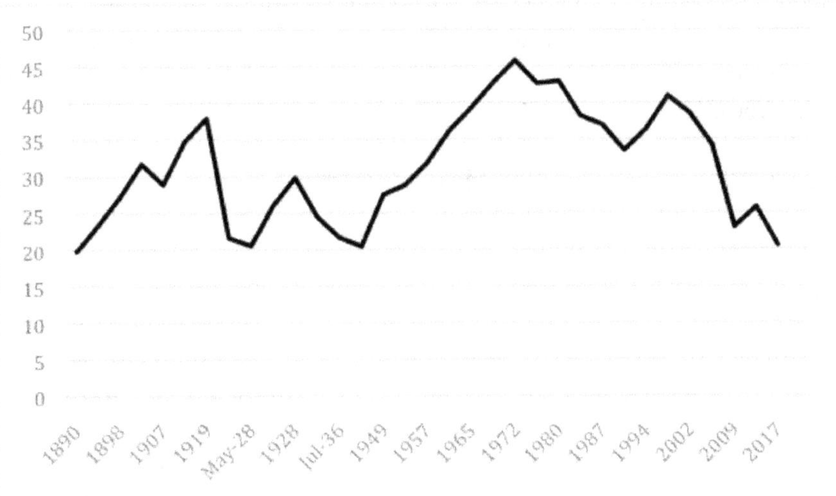

Sources: https://www.bundestag.de/blob/190454/782a532c7e19aa9cd5119e62ca77a260/wahlen_kaiserreich-data.pdf; https://www.bundestag.de/blob/190456/f8d637d1039a06a614cff0264f8b5d10/reichstagswahlergebnisse-data.pdf; Bundeswahlleiter

The nineteenth electoral period (2017-2021) will have the most fragmented Bundestag in the post 1949 period, with six party fractions and seven parties (differentiating between the CDU and CSU, which are legally distinct parties but always caucus together). According to the effective number of party calculation,[28] the parliament now has 4.64 effective parties based on seats (5.07 based on votes)–a figure not seen since the Weimar Republic. Even the first election of 1949, when a new party system was emerging, produced only 3.53 effective parties based on seats. This is cause for concern because the country is rapidly approaching the extreme (rather than moderate) multiparty category. Given the almost six months without a new government, it is evident how difficult this fragmentation is making coalition formation. Moreover, two fractions–the ideologically radical Left Party and the AfD–are currently not considered acceptable coalition partners (*koalitionsunfähig*). Together they comprise almost a quarter of the Bundestag (23 percent) and with 163 seats between them, have more than the SPD. No wonder it is difficult for the four mainstream fractions to form a coalition when a government needs 50 percent of the seats, but can work with only about 75 percent of the total. This is reminiscent of postwar Italy where the Christian Democrats (DC) ruled seemingly in perpetuity because 20-40 percent of the legislature was controlled by antisystem parties (communist or neofascist). This was also a recipe for endemic corruption, which led eventually to the dramatic demise of the colloquially deemed "First Republic" in the early 1990s. Another parallel would be Austria, with its long history GroKos (forty of seventy-three years since 1945, but twenty-three of the last thirty-one years), which empowered the right-populist Freedom Party.

Figure 0.2: Effective Number of Parties Based on Votes and Seats over Time

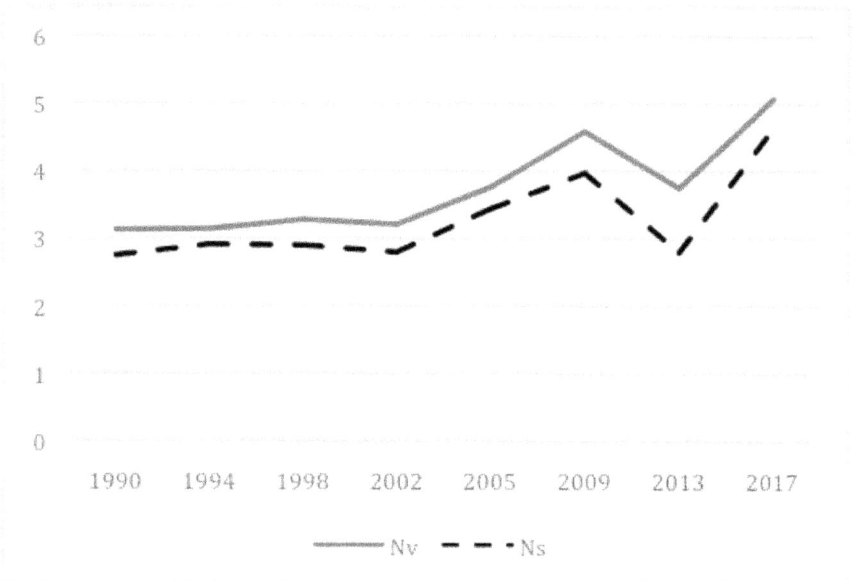

6
5
4
3
2
1
0
1990 1994 1998 2002 2005 2009 2013 2017
Nv Ns

Unsurprisingly, electoral volatility has also increased considerably as of late and is now well beyond the 8.6 long-term average.[29] Yet, note that the increase has really only been marked since the early 2000s. The decline of the SPD and the splintering of the left was largely a consequence of neoliberal Red-Green government policies in the early 2000s. Ironically, these reforms contributed greatly to putting the economy on a better footing, ending the declinist "sick man of the euro" narrative, and laying the basis for the export boom of the last decade. Given the strong economy and public finances, one would think that the parties presiding over this situation would benefit and volatility would be moderate. But, that was not the case.

One driver of increased volatility is the increasing propensity of voters to split their first (constituency) and second (party list) vote. Although the trend goes back to the 1980s, it has really taken off since reunification and especially this century. A record 27.3 percent of voters split their ballots, a boon to the smaller parties, especially the Greens and FDP. In fact, 56 per-

Figure 0.3: Volatility Based on Votes and Seats over Time

30
25
20
15
10
5
0
1990
1994
1998
2002
2005
2009
2013
2017
Votes
Seats

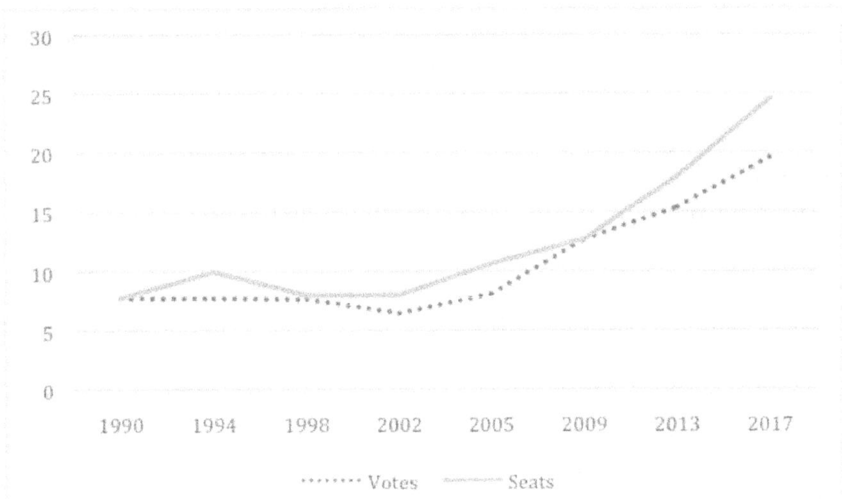

cent of those who gave their second vote to the Liberals, chose another party with their first vote–likewise for 48 percent of Green voters. This unprecedented incidence of tactical voting behavior shows declining loyalty at least to the two catch-all parties.

Figure 0.4: Vote Splitting over Time

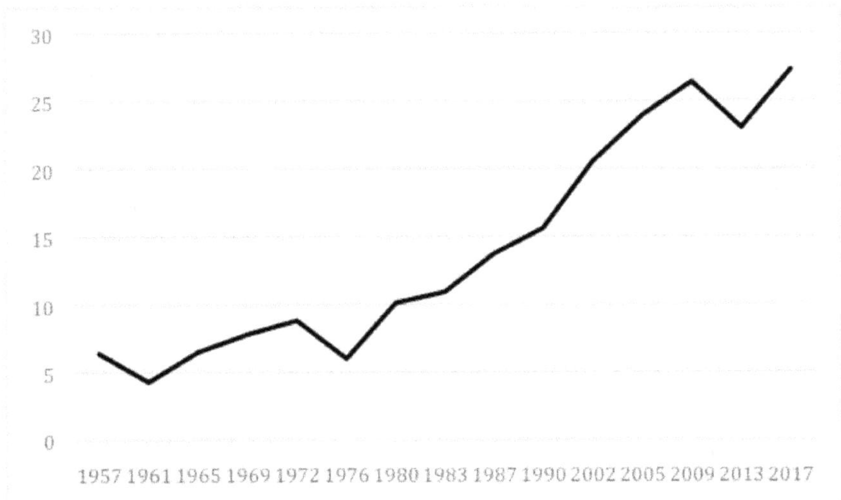

30
25
20
15
10
5
0
1957 1961 1965 1969 1972 1976 1980 1983 1987 1990 2002 2005 2009 2013 2017

Source: Bundeswahlleiter

The size of this Bundestag is also massive–the largest German parliament ever. This is due to the 111 extra seats–forty-six overhanging (*Überhangmandaten*) and sixty-five compensatory mandates (*Ausgleichmandaten*). The number of overhanging mandates has increased considerably over time and especially since reunification as the number of parties gaining parliamentary representation has increased from the three that were typical from the 1960s to the 1980s. The change to the electoral law required by the Constitutional Court just before the 2013 election has made matters much worse with the addition of compensatory mandates to allow for even closer vote-seat correspondence.[30] According to the cube root rule of the population to determine the ideal size of a legislature, the Bundestag should have a mere 436 members. There are deleterious consequences of having such an oversized chamber–it makes it too easy to represent niche preferences and decreases the ability of parties to aggregate interests and formulate overarching legislative agendas.[31] Moreover, these additional deputies will cost taxpayers an extra euro 51 million over the duration of this parliamentary period.[32]

Figure 0.5: Overhanging and Compensatory Mandates Over Time

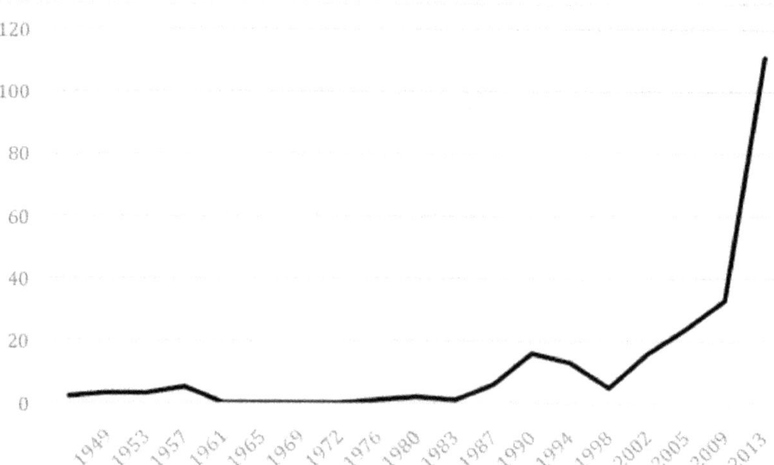

Long an exemplary mixed member proportional electoral system, combining single member constituencies with closed list proportional representation, the system has evolved into an over-engineered mess. Even the sacrosanct 5 percent electoral threshold–which has done much over the decades to disincentivize small, often radical parties–might also be in jeopardy. The Federal Constitutional Court invalidated a 3 percent hurdle for European Parliament elections in 2013 and some Land courts have done likewise for local elections.[33] Such a development would further exacerbate the splintering of the Bundestag. It might be time to contemplate changes along the more majoritarian lines of Britain or France in order to engineer an advantage for larger parties. Germans would have to accept the price of lower proportionality and fewer parties gaining validating parliamentary representation.

These developments–increased volatility and the splintering of the Bundestag–represent a rather novel political context for government formation. Postwar and earlier postunification electorates were not renowned for radical course shifts and suddenly changing preferences. Things evolved slowly, even glacially and governing coalitions remained in power for long periods of time. Since 1949, the Federal Republic has had only eight chancellors. By contrast, over the same period of time, the United States has had thirteen presidents, the UK has had fourteen prime ministers, and France has had eight presidents (and seventeen prime ministers) since 1959. In fact, the only time in almost seventy years that German voters have thrown the rascals out and completely replaced a government (complete partisan alteration) was 1998. All other changes in government have been partial with a coalition partner being replaced with another, but one remaining in power (as in 1966, 1969, 1982, 2005, 2009, 2013, and 2017).

But, the fragmented Bundestag and the shrunken catch-all parties means that the traditional coalition options are not possible. Previously, one of the catch-call parties would govern with a smaller ideologically affiliated partner, as the SPD did with the FDP from 1969-1982 and then with the Greens from 1998-2005 or the CDU with the FDP from 1982-1998 and 2009-2013. This time, such an option was mathematically impossible, so Merkel initially looked to form a three-party "Jamaica" coalition–named after the colors of the Jamaican flag and the traditional colors of the German parties–CDU/CSU (black), Greens, and FDP (yellow). This attempt, however, fell apart before it was even fully negotiated, scuttled by the FDP at the end of November 2017 after several weeks of exploratory talks (*Sondierungsgespräche*). Reports pointed to an inability to agree on migration (specifically family reunification), as well as Green demands to move more quickly away from coal power. Lindner proclaimed that "It is better not to govern than to govern wrongly."[34] "Jamaica-Aus" (Jamaica failure) was selected the word of the year–just ahead of "Ehe für alle" (marriage for all).[35] The FDP has taken a reputational and polling hit (currently down in the 8-9 percent range). There is even a new word: *lindnern*–to lindner, to back out at the last minute with the whiff of treachery and bad faith.[36]

Thus, another grand coalition was the only possibility besides a minority government, which is deeply taboo and has never been attempted in Federal Republic, or new elections. In fact, minority governments in other parliamentary democracies have been surprisingly resilient. But, Germany is not Sweden and the dynamics of minority government are harder to accommodate in such a large country with its clout in Europe and abroad. Despite Schulz's deep reservations (he had stated that the election result rejected another grand coalition) preliminary talks started in January 2018 and formal negotiations were concluded in early February, and then voted on by SPD party members. Despite intense opposition particularly from young Socialist (Juso) leader Kevin Kühnert, 66 percent of the 450,000 or so SPD party members (including 24,000 new members just since 1 January) endorsed the agreement via postal ballot. The new government was installed in mid-March 2018.[37]

Table 0.3: Merkel's Fourth Cabinet (2018-)

	Ministry/Title	Party
Angela Merkel	Chancellor	CDU
Heiko Maas	Foreign Office	SPD
Olaf Scholz	Finance/Vice Chancellor	SPD
Horst Seehofer	Interior	CSU
Ursula von der Leyen	Defense	CDU
Peter Altmaier	Economics	CDU
Hubertus Heil	Labor and Social Affairs	SPD
Katarina Barley	Justice and Consumer Protection	SPD
Jens Spahn	Health	CDU
Anja Karliczek	Education and Research	CDU
Julia Klöckner	Food and Agriculture	CDU
Andreas Scheuer	Transportation and Digital Infrastructure	CSU
Gerd Müller	Economic Cooperation and Development	CSU
Franziska Giffey	Family, Seniors, Women and Youth	SPD
Svenja Schulze	Environment, Nature Conservation and Nuclear Safety	SPD
Helge Braun	Chancellery Office	CDU

There are substantial personnel changes in Merkel's fourth cabinet even though the governing parties remain the same. In fact, only Merkel, Müller, and von der Leyen remain in the same positions. Several in-coming ministers have changed portfolios (Altmaier from the chancellery to economics, Maas from justice to the foreign office). Some have returned after several years away from the federal cabinet (Scholz, Seehofer). But, the vast majority are brand new, albeit often with deputy ministerial

(Staatssekretär) or regional/local political experience (Braun, Giffey, Heil, Karliczek, Klöckner, Scheuer, Schulze, Spahn–Barley also has less than one year of experience). Some surprise departures include Thomas de Maiziere (a Merkel confidant), Brigitte Zypries, Hermann Gröhe, Barbara Hendricks, and, above all, Sigmar Gabriel–who was SPD party leader until March 2017 and vice chancellor in the last coalition. After January 2017 when he moved from the economics to the foreign ministry, he was often more popular than Merkel herself. In another development, the interior ministry is being beefed up for Seehofer, taking up competences in building and *Heimat* (homeland)–although no one seems to know what this latter competence really means. A little more than half of the cabinet is comprised of women, and there is one other eastern German (Giffey) besides Merkel.

Initial reactions saw the partisan distribution of ministries as a major victory for the SPD, which received six out of sixteen portfolios, including the powerful finance ministry, the foreign office, labor, and justice. The influential tabloid, *Bild Zeitung* even ran a headline: "Chancellor at any price: Merkel gifts the government to the SPD" (Kanzlerin um jeden Preis: Merkel schenkt der SPD die Regierung). The SPD probably needed this to successfully sell the agreement to its members. Content-wise, the agreement was characterized as "expansionary continuity" with the parties agreeing to use a good portion of the budget surplus on programs like increased child benefits, pensions, and subsidies for (affordable) housing. There will also be an investment in broadband for all. The Soli tax will be eliminated for all but the top 10 percent of taxpayers. Refugees will be capped at 200,000 per year and family reunification will also be limited to 1,000 per month.[38]

Moving beyond Merkel

As relieved as so many were with the new coalition agreement, it took almost six months after the election to achieve–the longest postwar Germany has gone with a caretaker government. Presiding over all of this was Angela Merkel, leading her fourth government (including three grand coalitions) since first assuming office in 2005.

Merkel has dominated German and European politics for most of this century. Her style has been quite different from other chancellors and global leaders. She exemplifies "leading from behind" with a more self-effacing and behind-the-scenes style–never dominating or hogging the limelight like so many of her largely vanquished (male) rivals. She is not particularly charismatic and does not appear to enjoy retail politics, campaigning, or interacting with voters or the press. Moreover, she has never really been about the "vision thing." She has seemed especially exhausted since the election–and actually since the pushback on her 2015 decision to open the country's borders to the wave of refugees.

Merkel has greatly influenced, even transformed the CDU, as many scholars have noted.[39] Indeed, the policy areas in which the CDU has shifted is notable–from family policy, to same-sex marriage, to energy and environmental policy. Admittedly, when it comes to fiscal policy, the CDU has stayed true to conservative principles–the "schwarz-null" of no new state borrowing, the constitutional amendment to limit deficits, and the achievement of budget surpluses over the last few years are big successes from a conservative perspective. Mention should also be made of German pressure having effects on EU, specifically Eurozone member states to follow a similar path.

This, though, was largely the achievement of Wolfgang Schäuble, the long-serving finance minister (2009-2017) and before that in various ministerial roles from 1984 to 1991 and 2005 to 2009, as well CDU/CSU caucus chair from 1991 to 2000 and CDU leader from 1998 to 2000. But, due to his election as president of the Bundestag in October 2017, he will not be part of the next government. At seventy-six, he is rapidly approaching the twilight of his long and influential public career. Indeed, Schäuble's transition from positions of real policy influence and power is a huge milestone and loss for Merkel, who has worked with (and sometimes against) him for her entire political career. In one regard, this transition is almost as symbolically significant as the death of Helmut Kohl–Merkel's first political mentor–in June 2017.

Many observers believe that Merkel has social democratized (although she would rather say "modernized") the party and brought it firmly into the center, if not the center-left of the political spectrum. Others believe that all things considered, Merkel has made the party ideologically murky and amorphous. She is renowned for waiting until the last minute to commit to a policy course–widely deemed the "Merkel method."[40] This is captured in the neologism *merkeln*–to merkel, meaning to dawdle or dither, be wishy-washy, reveal no opinion or position, and wait until the last possible moment to decide.[41] In most instances and for many years, such tactical methods have worked for her–while also garnering a lot of criticism at home and abroad. Nevertheless, it has left the party lacking a coherent strategy, identity, or platform in the eyes both of many voters and CDU party members. The party's right flank has also been exposed to new competitors–a situation that the AfD has exploited.

As noted above, Merkel herself and all political observers acknowledged her weakened position after the 2017 election. But, she soldiered on and seemed to recover her standing sufficiently by the time the new coalition was in place in March 2018. Always savvy and looking towards the future, she installed many new, younger, and largely loyal faces in the new cabinet, even if she gave up supporters such as Gröhe and de Maiziere. She retained allies like Altmaier and von der Leyen, the returning defense minister. Although long perceived to be Merkel's preferred successor, von der Leyen had never been very popular within the party or the electorate, and had seemingly lost Merkel's support. Moreover, in February 2018, Merkel installed another younger loyalist, Annegret Kramp-Karrenbauer (widely referred to as AKK) as CDU secretary-general, the position from which Merkel herself began her takeover of the party in 1998.

After a few relatively placid months, the new government started to wobble and Merkel's position deteriorated once again. The CSU was responsible for most of these tensions as it maneuvered before the state elections in Bavaria in October. In March 2018, the party installed a new minister-president Markus Söder, as Seehofer quit to run the federal Interior Ministry–albeit remaining party leader until he decided in November 2018 to step down in January 2019.[42] The party decided to take on the right-populists through its own rightward turn, for example decreeing the installation of crosses in government offices in Bavaria and through Seehofer pushing the older, provocative formulation that "Islam does not belong to Germany," although he backtracked by the end of the year.[43] Over the course of the summer, Seehofer almost brought the government down twice, first over migration policy and then over his responses to the controversial statements of Hans-Georg Maaßen, the head of the domestic security agency.[44] An even bigger blow to the chancellor came at the end of September when the CDU/CSU caucus in the Bundestag surprisingly voted to replace the long-time parliamentary group leader (since 2005) and close Merkel ally Volker Kauder with the younger Ralph Brinkhaus (a finance and budgetary expert). All understood that this was a vote of nonconfidence in Merkel's leadership.

Then, in October 2018 came the greatly anticipated state elections in Bavaria and Hesse, perceived as a kind of midterm or referendum on the national government. In Bavaria on 14 October, the result was not nearly as bad for the CSU as feared when they achieved 37.2 percent, which was 2 to 4 points better than the last pre-election polls showed, but down from the 47.4 percent it won in 2013. The SPD did worse than expected with a paltry 9.6 percent. The Greens had an excellent night at 17.5 percent (although a little less than polling had predicted), dominating in the cities where they picked up their first ever direct mandates in Munich and Würzburg. The FDP scraped in at 5.1 percent (the Left did not make it over the threshold). Finally, the AfD secured 10.3 percent and the Free Voters 11.5 percent (+2.5). On 28 October in Hesse, the CDU gained only 27 percent (down from 38.3 percent in 2013). The SPD lost almost 11 percent coming at 19.8, the same number as the surging Greens. The AfD received 13.1 percent just slightly more than its result at the 2017 Bundestag election.

The next day, Merkel announced that she would not run again for the Christian Democratic party chair in December. She stated her intent to continue as chancellor, but added that this was her last term. This unexpected announcement immediately unleashed what had long been a repressed power struggle for control over the governing party. Unlike previous changes in party leadership such as Kohl in 1973 or Merkel in 2000 in which the machinations took place behind closed doors and the candidate was consensually endorsed at the party congress, there was an unprecedented five-week public campaign for the position.[45] A series of regional fora, endorsements for the candidates from party big wigs (like Schäuble openly advocating for his "friend" Friedrich Merz[46]), and much politicking occurred.

Three serious candidates emerged. First was Jens Spahn, installed as the health minister in the current government (in an example of Merkel keeping her enemies closer). Long scheming behind the scenes, he vowed to move the party back towards the right, for instance, advocating a reimplementation of military service and totemically stating that Islam does not belong to Germany. Born in 1980 and hailing from populous North Rhine-Westphalia, Spahn is a devout Catholic and would make history being the first openly gay leader of a major country.[47] A well-known Merkel critic, he vowed to create a very different CDU. Nevertheless, party members perceived him as rather inexperienced, opportunistic, and maladroit–at one point stating that recipients of the much criticized (by the left) Hartz IV welfare programs were not really poor.[48]

Second was Annegret Kramp-Karrenbauer, the former minister president of the Saarland from 2011 to 2018 who is considered a younger (fifty-six) version of Merkel herself and someone who will likely maintain the chancellor's more centrist vision for the party, including on migration policy.[49] Indeed, she has even been described as "Mini Merkel."[50] Nevertheless, she has differentiated herself from the chancellor by noting that the party needs more "fire," expressing concerns about same-sex marriage as well as dual citizenship, and wanting to more vigorously reach out to youth. She cleverly used her new position as general secretary to re-organize personnel in party headquarters and travel the country in a "listening tour" in conjunction with revisions to the party platform, which no doubt also provided excellent networking opportunities.

Finally, there was Friedrich Merz, who returned to political prominence after a sixteen-year hiatus. The sixty-three-year-old was pushed out as parliamentary caucus leader by Merkel back in 2002. In 2007, he returned to the private sector as a corporate lawyer and member of several boards, even leading the board of directors of Blackrock Germany, the world's largest asset management company. He struggled at times, for example, awkwardly announcing that he earns over a million euros (gross) per year, amassing a modest fortune (including a private jet), but still considers himself to belong to the "upper" middle class (*gehobene Mittelschicht*). He stands for fiscal and social conservatism–wanting to simplify the tax code and being credited with coining the "Leitkultur" concept around the turn of the millennium. He would not just take the party to the right, but would be a lightning rod for all old-guard conservatives who have been sidelined by Merkel over the years. Merz represents the old-boys-club CDU–upper middle-class, religious, and very western. He was considered a member of the much-ballyhooed, all-male "Andenpakt" group of Christian Democratic politicians including Roland Koch and Günther Oettinger, both of whom openly endorsed Merz. Merz represents a return to the past. It is almost as if he wants to abolish the Merkel era, wiping the last fifteen years from the history books.[51]

For most of the campaign period, Kramp-Karrenbauer led Merz in the polling. At the end of November, she was ahead 38 to 29 percent, with Spahn a distant third (6 percent).[52] Nevertheless, there were many undecided delegates, Merz performed quite well at the various regional fora, and many prominent conservatives publicly supported him. But, in the end, on 7 December in Hamburg, the delegates narrowly selected Kramp-Karrenbauer over Merz in a run-off with 52 percent (571/999) of the votes.[53] This result represents continuity with Merkel's leadership–and probably ensures the chancellor at least another year in power. The CDU almost immediately gained about 3 percent in the polls and the fevered political atmosphere subsided just in time for the holidays.

Parties in Flux

To a degree, parties are always in flux, depending on the popularity or predilections of leaders, the vicissitudes of public opinion, the frequency of crises, and the ever-more competitive environment for votes. This moment in German politics, however, is unique for creating a situation in which virtually every party is in a challenging state.

The SPD stands out for being in an especially treacherous position. For years, no one has known what the party stands for. The years of governing co-responsibility (in government as a senior or junior coalition partner for seventeen out of twenty-one years since 1998) have taken a toll. It has never really been able to live down its neoliberal Hartz IV/Agenda 2010 reforms of the early 2000s, which alienated many leftist voters but laid the basis for the subsequent economic boom years. The party has also been a poor competitor against other actors. Willie Paterson has pointed out that the Social Democrats already had two epochal failures: not having integrated the Greens in the 1980s and then failing to absorb the PDS/Left in the 1990s and early 2000s. It has lost votes to Merkel's more centrist CDU and is now threatened by the AfD in many regions. It is quite possible that the rise of the AfD will be more lethal to the SPD than to any other party, including the CDU and CSU. As Jakob Augstein recently argued, the SPD was competitive when it was clearly the party of the "little guy" (*kleiner Mann*).[54] Having long ago lost this identity (perhaps when it embraced neoliberal reforms), the AfD is increasingly the mouthpiece for this segment of the electorate. In fact, AfD leader Alexander Gauland has consistently profiled the party in this manner.[55] Fears that the SPD is losing its *Volkspartei* status have been voiced repeatedly. Its horrible 20 percent result at the 2017 Bundestag election and erosion to 18, 17, and 15 percent in early 2019 polls are existential red flags. Its support among workers has tanked from 49 percent of this group in 1998 to a record low of 23 percent in 2017.[56]

Instability in party leadership is both cause and consequence of these poor election results. Since 1999 (just before Merkel took over the CDU), there have been eight party chairs, including one-year stints by Franz Müntefering (two) and Schulz, but just over seven years under Sigmar Gabriel from 2009-2017, which was the longest tenure since Willy Brandt from 1964 to 1987. In April 2018, Schulz gave up the party chair to Andrea Nahles, who continued to run the party's Bundestag fraction. The first woman leader in over 150 years, she is associated with the party's left wing (in contrast to Gabriel), having risen to prominence as a critic of Schröder's

Agenda 2010. She was also minister of labor and social affairs in the last government, was secretary general of the SPD from 2009-2014, and took over as SPD fraction leader in the Bundestag after the September 2017 election. Tactically, this move signaled to the SPD base and the larger electorate that the party will move back into a more leftist position going forward. Nahles appeared to be a good choice for the party because she articulates a more leftist vision and could be more effective in countering the Christian Democrats because she is outside of the current government.[57]

But, besides promoting a woman to the top job, there is no clear path forward for the party. Every option–moving left, remaining centrist, embracing some populist policies–has vociferous proponents and detractors. Admittedly, there was widespread agreement that a spell in the opposition was the best thing for the party. But, the extremely divided Bundestag after 2017 and the inability of Merkel to create a Jamaica coalition, left the country with few other options besides another GroKo. SPD leaders–at first reluctantly–rose to the occasion. All other options were worse–tolerating a minority government would have meant voting with the CDU/CSU on most bills in the absence of any impact on policy. Early elections would likely see their share of the vote decline even more if polling is to be believed. That said, the SPD has not completely imploded at the state level. Seven of sixteen current minister presidents are Social Democrats and they are in governing coalitions in eleven states. Although it lost control of North Rhine Westphalia and Schleswig-Holstein in 2017, the party's performance was not abysmal. Also, it has done a decent job of promoting up-and-comers to cabinet-level positions–Scholz, Heil, Manuela Schwesig, and Barley come to mind.

Nevertheless, 2018 was even more brutal than 2017 for the party. The results in Bavaria (9.6 percent) and Hesse (19.8 percent) were abysmal. In national polls, it is as low as 14 percent, below the Greens and the AfD, and the lowest level of support ever recorded for the party.[58] Nahles has not been able to turn things around and is losing support internally. The only saving grace is that almost all political attention was devoted to Merkel's slow retreat from the national stage and the power struggle within the CDU.

The Greens had struggled over the last few electoral cycles–at their peak around 2010 and 2011 they were polling about 20 percent, at one point more than the SPD. Commentators were even talking about them as the new leftist *Volkspartei.* A subpar 2013 result and an only slightly better 2017 one put such speculation aside. Of course, the Greens have been liminal since their founding. Their lingering 1970s new-leftist tendencies have often made them their own worst enemy. Constant leadership, ("speakership") flux–well-known leader Cem Özdemir lost his leadership spot in early 2018–and the never-ending battle between Realo and Fundi factions, as well as some fringe policy positions (the pedophilia matter that infected the 2013 campaign) are not ways to embrace a national, *Volkspartei* identity.

But, this trajectory changed considerably for the better over the course of 2018, culminating in 17.5 percent of the vote in Bavaria, 19.8 percent in Hesse, and 19 to 23 percent in national polls–well ahead of the SPD and at one point not far behind the CDU. The Greens are currently represented in all but two state parliaments and are in governing coalitions in nine states (leading Baden-Württemberg under Winfried Kretschmann's centrist leadership since 2011). The Greens have clearly benefitted from their opposition status at the national level, a consistent ideological profile (liberal on migration and social issues, more centrist on the economy), a crop of exciting, young-ish leaders like Robert Habeck nationally and Tarek al-Wazir in Hesse and Katharina Schulze in Bavaria, and, arguably, the increased salience of their core environmental platform (in the face of the worst drought for fifty years in 2018).[59] The continued implosion of the SPD has greatly benefitted the party, although it has also poached many voters from the CDU/CSU.

It is an open question if the Greens can continue this upward trajectory. If the Social and Christian Democrats recover, there will be fewer voters for the Greens to attract. Joining a federal coalition–either a Jamaica constellation (without Merkel), or after the next Bundestag election–will depress their oppositional profile and will alienate voters, as the inevitable cost of wielding power. They could also take a hit due to the on-going challenges (spiking consumer energy prices) implementing the much-vaunted energy transition (*Energiewende*), a signature Green issue. Their multicultural and pro-immigration stance will never attract AfD supporters and other conservatives. Green supporters are typically better-educated, middle-class westerners, which are also a finite segment of the electorate. Moreover, many Green leaders have currently moved to the center, even trying to re-appropriate traditionally conservative concerns like patriotism and *Heimat*–possibly alienating their more leftist base. Finally, the party has been benefitting from a "backlash to the backlash" effect, i.e., a response to the successes of the AfD, but this is likely temporary. Indeed, by early 2019, the party was in the 18-20 percent range. Still, this is a party to watch over the next electoral cycles.

The Left Party–like the PDS before–continues to be plagued by similar strains. In this case, however, there has always been the tension between ideological extremism and a more pragmatic eastern German identity. This latter aspect is now threatened by the popularity of the AfD in large swaths of the former East Germany and the fact that the AfD may be taking away the protest component of the Left's support. Moreover, the Left Party is increasingly dominated by westerners and their concerns. With polls showing about the same level of support as the party achieved at the 2017 election, party leader Sahra Wagenkencht has tried to jump-start momentum by advocating for a new leftist movement "Aufstehen" (rise up) with some populist elements intended to attract voters who defected to the AfD. But, this effort has generated substantial friction within the party and has not gained much traction with voters.[60]

Despite seemingly unstoppable momentum (15 to 18 percent in most late 2018 polls, but down to 12-14 percent in early 2019), the AfD also has its challenges. Headlines around the world rightfully emphasized that the entry of the party into the Bundestag marked the first time since the Nazi era that right-wing, far-right, extreme-right, right-populists (the jury is out regarding the best moniker) had achieved this feat. There was some angst that it was 1933 all over again.[61] Yet, the Germans are late to this game–the list of European countries with a sizeable right-populist party is long–and there is, of course, Brexit and Trump elsewhere in the West. From this perspective, the rise of the AfD could be seen as a kind of normalization of German politics. Some have even argued that the AfD could be good for German democracy by shaking up the stultifying consensus between the two *Volksparteien*.[62]

It is important to understand where the AfD got its votes in 2017. Of its 5.88 million votes, 1.28 million (22 percent) came from previous non-voters; 740,000 (13 percent) from the 2013 "other" category, which included parties such as the Pirates and right-radical NPD; 430,000 (7 percent) from the Left; 500,000 (8.5 percent) from the SPD; and about 1 million (17 percent) from the CDU. Yet, note that the CDU lost the majority of its 2013 voters to the FDP (1.3 million, 26 percent of the FDP's total). Of the voters who fled the SPD, the most (500,000) went to the AfD (430,000 to FDP; 400,000 to Greens and 380,000 to the Left).[63] Thus, it is not the case that the AfD benefitted solely from disgruntled right-wing or center-right voters. Moreover, it did particularly well in eastern Germany. With 22.5 percent of the vote there, it was the second-largest party behind only the CDU at 28.2 percent and ahead of the Left (17.4 percent) and the SPD (14.3 percent).[64] Like similar parties elsewhere, it did much better with men than women–gaining 26 percent of the eastern male vote.

The success of the AfD, however, should not be over-interpreted. There has been extensive pushback from all other quarters of the political spectrum. This was symbolized by the "guerilla" art installation of a replica of Berlin's Monument to the Murdered Jews of Europe on a property adjacent to the eastern German home of prominent AfD politician Björn Höcke, who had deemed the original a "monument of shame."[65] The political and social norms against right-radicalism are still largely operative.[66] In future elections, many AfD voters could return to their previous choices or fall back into the non-voting category. True, the AfD brought a campaign sophistication that eluded most of the other parties.[67] But, in future elections, competitors will emulate these tactics and neutralize this advantage.

Moreover, there were contingent factors that will not recur. After twelve years of Merkel, some voter fatigue set in. Merkel's strategy of "social democratizing" the CDU also has generated a cost. At one point, however, Merkel, a favored target of the AfD ("Merkel muss weg"), will indeed be gone, depriving the party of this key line of attack. From another perspective, the AfD's success was simply the political price the establishment had to pay for Merkel's controversial decision in late summer 2015 to open the borders to the wave of migrants that entered Europe that year. Again, this policy shift was successful (more or less), humane, practical (Germany needs immigrants), but also hugely controversial in light of the sheer scale–and cost– of the challenge. Survey after survey showed that AfD voters were animated overwhelmingly by migration and related issues–but, not just AfD voters. Exit polls showed that the most important issue cited by all voters was "refugees and integration" at 44 percent, followed distantly by social injustice at 20 percent.[68] Given just how contingent AfD support was on the salience of this issue, it will be challenging for the party to maintain such a level of support as that issue recedes in importance. Balancing among the many disparate groups of supporters will likewise be challenging.

I do not want to downplay the AfD's insidiousness. Like other right-populists they have parroted the same us/them, pure/impure, anti-pluralistic rhetoric and engaged in Islamophobia and xenophobia.[69] There is more than enough fake right-wing news, although the German authorities have been much more vigilant about this than other governments, getting Facebook, for example, to verify and curate content that could be classified as hate speech.[70] The AfD also has some extreme and bizarre policies on natalism, families, or homosexuality that likely will not resonate too widely. Even their own voters do not like party leaders like Gauland, Alice Weidel, Meuthen, or Frauke Petry (who left the party shortly after the election). Recently, there have been serious allegations of shady and possible illegal campaign donations from abroad that have enveloped Weidel as well as Gauland.[71] Worryingly, this might not affect the AfD's core supporters. As Daniel Ziblatt has noted: ""Around the world, populist authoritarians claim that because 'the system' is corrupt anyway, the leaders' own corruption should be seen as a kind of virtuous one that will operate on behalf of the people."[72]

Nevertheless, even the AfD is in a liminal place–and has been since its inception. Will it embrace right-radicalism or "merely" right-populism? Will it tolerate Holocaust-deniers, neo-Nazis, racists, and xenophobes? Or will it moderate and endeavor to take on *Volkspartei* status–what some have deemed a new "national socialism?"[73] Will it continue to be a protest movement or will it routinize and institutionalize? Will it become yet another eastern German identity party or will it strive for truly national appeal? Will it tend towards anti-immigrant xenophobia or euroskepticism? Will it actually deliver policy for the *kleiner Mann*? Will it continue to have extreme leadership instability and flux?

Finally, the FDP has challenges. The party has a history of surging and falling rather dramatically–14.6 percent in 2009 (its best result ever), to 4.8 percent in 2013 (losing all its seats in the Bundestag), and back to 10.7 percent in 2017. By the end of 2018 and early 2019, it is polling was lackluster–a little below its 2017 result at 7 to 10 percent. It received only 5.1 percent (+1.8) in Bavaria and 7.5 percent (+2.5) in Hesse. Lindner had a great campaign in 2017, projecting an image of a strong, dynamic and youthful leader–but so did Guido Westerwelle in 2009. It is risky to invest so much attention in the charisma and personality of one individual party leader, who will inevitably falter. Lindner and his party took a hit after breaking off the Jamaica coalition talks in late 2017, and their polling has not really recovered. They also have been out-maneuvered by the Greens in many contexts, allowing the latter to channel the dual backlashes to the governing parties and the AfD. Moreover, if the CDU moves to the right after Merkel, the FDP could lose its neoliberal policy differentiation and the advantage (and voters) that comes with occupying this policy space.

The Contributions

At this moment of political transition and given the importance of Germany to European and global politics, leading academics have come together in this edited volume to provide their insight into the current and future trajectory of the country.[74] The book begins with Frank Decker and

Philipp Adorf's examination of the party system, in which they note that the Bundestag shifted to the right overall in 2017. A certain symmetry has now emerged in a new six-party system with three parties of the left (SPD, Greens, Left) and, now, three also on the right (CDU/CSU, FDP, AfD). After analyzing the factors that led to the election result, the authors examine the new coalition formation environment. It will take a while for the parties to adapt to the novel options: grand coalitions as in Austria, a partisan divide-spanning coalition of the center, or a Scandinavian model with coalitions from one political camp, but tolerated by an extremist party. The arrival of right-wing populism on the political stage has set many dynamics in motion, not the least of which is a necessary recalibration of the catch-all parties.

Alexander Beyer and Steven Weldon examine the media environment of the campaign to test the hypothesis that the media were responsible for the rise and success of the AfD. Based on an examination of the published content from the four most popular online media outlets, the AfD did indeed receive a disproportionate share of coverage, especially in the last phase of the campaign. Moreover, these outlets clearly reinforced the salience of migration issues in the weeks before election day, which strengthened the AfD. Yet, analysis of Google search data shows that these media were largely following public sentiment–that is, more frequent reporting on such issues was a response to demand for such stories.

Louise K. Davidson-Schmich delves into LGBTI issues during the campaign. After recounting the evolution of LGBTI rights in Germany, she analyzes the parties' positions on a range of issues deemed important by this community, including marriage and family rights, anti-discrimination measures, health, and everyday acceptance. The Left and Green parties were the most supportive across almost all issue areas with the CDU/CSU and especially the AfD the least. Overall, the campaign ignored the vast majority of these issues with the big exception of marriage equality, which was achieved in June 2017 through an open vote of the Bundestag. An important finding was the agency of a critical actor, in this case veteran Green politician Volker Beck, who had diligently campaigned for this right over many years. Next, Joyce Mushaben analyzes gender images in the presentation of Angela Merkel over four campaigns. Mushaben delves into the many stereotypes that women politicians have to traverse and how these affected, and, at times, disadvantaged Merkel over the years. This environment led her to overtly downplay the gender dimensions of her leadership, while allowing her to achieve much positive change under the surface.

Turning to the parties, Clay Clemens looks at the CDU/CSU's lackluster election campaign. Concluding that it was "ambivalent"–as manifested by the result on election day–he highlights several reasons such as internal disagreements over Merkel's "modernization" of the CDU and more general pro- and anti-Merkel camps within the party; continued fallout from her 2015 decision on migration; a campaign strategy that bizarrely bred complacency among many supporters while mobilizing skeptics; and tactical mistakes. Clemens highlights the deep internal division over strategy: the "Merkelianers'" preference to compete for the center versus opponents' position that a battle between the partisan camps (*Lagerwahlkampf*) would be the only successful path–a strategic disagreement left unresolved on election day. One might also add that sub-par campaign messaging did not help. One key slogan was "For a Germany in which we live well and gladly," which was then transformed into an awkward and widely mocked hashtag #fedidwgugl.

Andreas M. Wüst analyzes the situation of the SPD and the new grand coalition. After looking at some of the reasons for the SPD's poor performance on election day, the author outlines the twisted road the party took to agree to a continuation of the grand coalition. A detailed analysis of the coalition agreement shows just how many social democratic priorities were adopted especially in social policy–although the party was not able to push through its preferences on migration-related issues. The chapter concludes by noting the risks to the coalition partners and the German party system more generally of continuing such consensual governments in perpetuity. David Patton looks at the smaller parties and the race for third place in 2017. He outlines both structural and contingent factors behind the unprecedented success of the niche parties. Indeed, he finds that each of the four smaller parties focused on a specific issue space–the Greens on the environment, the Left party on social justice, the AfD on immigration, and the FDP on education, deregulation, and taxes. One especially interesting finding is how the Left Party is now dominated by western elements. Patton concludes by noting that government formation has not yet caught up with the more fragmented and pluralistic nature of the party system.

Because the rise of the AfD has caused so much consternation in Germany and abroad, we have included several chapters on this new party. First, Matthias Dilling tackles the issue of whether the rise of the AfD really is the threat to the Christian Democrats that so many have proclaimed. Through an analysis of the parties' campaign manifestos, as well as sophisticated statistical analyses, he concludes that contrary to popular belief, the AfD does not really threaten the CDU/CSU. Its ideology has veered overall far to the right of the conservatives, but is also a hodgepodge of disparate ideological fragments. More importantly, its voter base is extremely heterodox and it will be hard-pressed to keep all constituencies satisfied over the medium and long term. Meanwhile, David Art notes that the party's breakthrough electoral result–largely due to Merkel's policy on refugees–shows that the strategy of containment of the far right no longer works as it once did. Despite the establishment's continued efforts to combat the party, the AfD is rapidly normalizing, as right-populist parties have throughout Europe in recent years. That said, Art does think it is plausible that the party could implode just like many right-wing precursors in previous decades. If it does not, however, the ramifications of the AfD's institutionalization will be felt far beyond Germany's borders.

Lars Rensmann begins his chapter by noting that founded just five years ago, the Alternative für Deutschland (AfD) represents the biggest opposition party in the German parliament. In light of this success, he addresses three questions in European comparative perspective: What is the nature of the AfD as a relevant political party in the Bundestag? What explains the AfD's rise? And what is the party's behavior and impact in parliament and thus on German politics in general? Examining party platforms over four years, Rensmann first identifies programmatic shifts that have turned the AfD from a single-issue anti-Euro party into the first radical right-wing (populist) party in the German parliament since the Nazi era–yet a party similar to other electorally successful actors of this party family in parliaments across Europe. Second, electoral results and survey data show that the political radicalization of the AfD, which continues while in parliament, has not undermined the party's appeal. To the contrary, initial electoral success and radicalization have been mutually reinforcing factors in the AfD's development. This reflects, third, a deepened polarization of political culture and party competition that is further advanced by the AfD's antagonizing strategies in parliament and mirrors European trends. The electoral support of the party's evolution towards radical right populism make it likely that the AfD seeks to transform politics in and beyond the Bundestag, and German political culture at large. In so doing, the party follows its European counterparts' strategic orientations and partakes in the Europeanization of a sociocultural "counter-revolution."

Samuel Salzborn also analyses the young AfD's recent development, focusing on antisemitism within the party–something the party would prefer to keep out of public debate. By investigating its treatment of antisemitism, Nazism, and the politics of remembrance, Salzborn shows that the AfD has the features of a far-right party, to a much clearer extent than might be guessed from its media image, particularly inside Germany. Next, Jonathan Olsen focuses on eastern German voters, and in particular the fortunes of the Left Party and the AfD in that region. Even though many headlines proclaimed the weak results of the two catch-all parties and the rise of the AfD, the collapse of the Left party's vote in eastern Germany was just as consequential–it has now become a more nationalized party of the radical left. Meanwhile, the AfD has poached the protest vote and is rapidly becoming the new eastern German identity party. Olsen goes on to compare and contrast the populist elements in both parties, concluding that although there is some overlap, the AfD is clearly much more populist than the Left Party is or ever was–effectively tapping into the disaffected, anti-establishment sentiment of much of the eastern electorate.

Looking beyond the country's borders, Steve Szabo provides a sober assessment of the new coalition's foreign policy. The likely situation is an international environment with as many if not more challenges than in previous years, including Turkey, Russia, and the Transatlantic relationship, as well as lingering issues with France and the European Union. These challenges, however, will be met with less capacity than in previous governments. Many relevant policy portfolios are now occupied by the coalition partners, meaning that internal disagreements within the government will result in feeble policy responses. Merkel herself is weakened and will be less able to assert influence from the chancellery. All of this likely means that the new grand coalition will be transitional and that real policy change and robust policy responses will have to await the next government and a generational turnover in leadership.

Finally, Christian Schweiger's chapter is a rather critical take on Germany's dominant leadership role in the European Union in recent years. German leadership since the Euro Crisis, including policy decisions during the refugee crisis of 2015, have greatly contributed to the severe legitimacy issues within the EU today. Schweiger faults German leadership for empowering right-populist parties throughout the continent and contributing quite a bit to the Brexit decision in 2016. He thinks Merkel must focus on creating a more inclusive agenda for the European Union through rebuilding relationships with France and Central European countries, especially Poland. If a more consensual approach is not achieved, the further disintegration of the EU is a distinct possibility.

ERIC LANGENBACHER is a Teaching Professor and Director of the Honors Program in the Department of Government, Georgetown University. Recent publications include *The German Polity*, 11th edition, co-authored with David Conradt (Lanham, 2017) and *Mapping Comparative Politics: Power and Legitimacy* (Thousand Oaks, forthcoming 2020). He is also Managing Editor of *German Politics and Society*, which is housed in Georgetown University's BMW Center for German and European Studies.

Notes

1. https://www.destatis.de/DE/ZahlenFakten/GesamtwirtschaftUmwelt/Verdienste Arbeitskosten/RealloehneNettoverdienste/RealloehneNettoverdienste.html, accessed 2 December 2018. I would like to thank the IASGP and DAAD for organizing yet another outstanding study tour around the 2017 Bundestag election. I would also like to thank Georgetown University's BMW Center for German and European Studies for continued research support.
2. Eric Langenbacher, "Tschüss Perfidious Albion: German Reactions to Brexit," *German Politics and Society*, 35, no. 3 (2017): 69-85.
3. http://www.spiegel.de/international/germany/integrating-refugees-in-germany-an-update-a-1147053.html, accessed 28 November 2018.
4. https://www.verfassungsschutz.de/de/arbeitsfelder/af-rechtsextremismus/zahlen-und-fakten-rechtsextremismus, accessed 28 November 2018.
5. If Merkel serves as chancellor until just before Christmas 2019, she will overtake Konrad Adenauer's fourteen years and thirty days. I think it is unlikely that she will surpass Helmut Kohl's record sixteen years, twenty-six days.
6. https://www.zdf.de/nachrichten/heute/abstimmung-ueber-spd-vorsitzenden-100.html, accessed 31 January 2018
7. https://www.wahlrecht.de/umfragen/dimap.htm, accessed 31 January 2018.
8. https://www.welt.de/politik/deutschland/article167574916/Das-ist-das-SPD-Wahl programm-im-Ueberblick.html, accessed 1 February 2018.
9. https://www.welt.de/debatte/kommentare/article168792096/Das-ganze-Elend-der-deutschen-Politik-in-einem-Bild.html, accessed 1 February 2018.
10. https://www.stern.de/politik/deutschland/von-trump-zur-afd–wie-eine-us-agentur-den-wahlkampf-aufmischen-will-7599188.html, accessed 3 February 2018.
11. https://www.afd.de/wp-content/uploads/sites/111/2017/08/AfD_kurzprogramm_a4-quer_210717.pdf, accessed 31 January 2018.
12. http://www.zeit.de/politik/deutschland/2016-01/angela-merkel-fluechtlingspolitik-verfassung, accessed 3 February 2018.
13. http://www.spiegel.de/international/germany/germans-ahead-of-the-vote-i-ve-never-seen-so-much-hate-a-1165684.html, accessed 3 February 2018.
14. https://www.fdp.de/sites/default/files/uploads/2017/08/07/20170807-wahlprogramm-wp-2017-v16.pdf, accessed 31 January 2018.
15. http://www.wz.de/home/politik/inland/bundestagswahl/wahlplakate-im-experten check-die-fdp-angesagte-totgesagte-1.2505604; http://www.rp-online.de/politik/deutsch land/bundestagswahl/die-fdp-verstoesst-2017-eigentlich-gegen-jede-wahlplakat-regel-aid-1.7076012, accessed 31 January 2018.
16. https://www.gruene.de/ueber-uns/2017/unsere-kampagne-zur-bundestagswahl-darum-gruen.html, accessed 31 January 2018.
17. Ibid.

18. https://www.die-linke.de/wahlen/kampagne/, accessed 31 January 2018.
19. https://www.cdu.de/haus, accessed 29 January 2018.
20. https://www.cdu.de/system/tdf/media/dokumente/170816-kurzfassung-regierungs programm.pdf?file=1, accessed 1 February 2018.
21. https://www.cdu.de/artikel/plakate-zur-bundestagswahl, accessed 29 January 2018
22. http://www.rp-online.de/politik/deutschland/bundestagswahl/tv-duell-2017-zwei-kandidaten-eine-meinung-aid-1.7058072, accessed 1 February 2018.
23. See note 13.
24. https://www.welt.de/newsticker/news1/article166052867/Umfrage-Drei-Viertel-der-Deutschen-fuer-Ehe-fuer-alle.html, accessed 5 February 2018.
25. https://www.destatis.de/DE/PresseService/Presse/Pressekonferenzen/2018/Repr_Wahlstatistik_2017/Statement_ReprWStat_PDF.pdf?__blob=publicationFile, accessed 20 February 2018.
26. See note 7.
27. https://www.usatoday.com/story/news/world/2017/09/20/meddling-germany-election-not-russia-but-u-s-right-wing/676142001/; https://www.the-american-interest.com/2017/10/17/russian-propaganda-germany-effective-think/, accessed 31 January 2018.
28. The formula is $N=1/(p^2)$; where p is the proportion of seats or votes for each party.
29. The formula is $Vt= \frac{1}{2} (P(t-1) - Pt)$; where Vt is volatility at any given year compared to the last election; Pt is the party's vote or seat share (percent) in the current time period; and Pt-1 is the vote or seat share (percent) in the last election. For the hundred-year average volatility of 8.6, see Stefano Bartolini and Peter Mair, *Identity, Competition, and Electoral Availability: The Stabilisation of European Electorates 1885-1985* (Cambridge, 1990), 100.
30. https://www.bpb.de/politik/wahlen/bundestagswahlen/163311/das-neue-wahlrecht?p=all, accessed 3 February 2018.
31. On the cube root rule, see Rein Taagepera, *Predicting Party Sizes: The Logic of Simple Electoral Systems* (Oxford, 2007).
32. https://www.focus.de/finanzen/videos/reichstag-platzt-aus-allen-naehten-so-viele-abgeordnete-wie-noch-nie-was-kostet-uns-steuerzahler-der-xxl-bundestag_id_7635560.html, accessed 1 February 2018.
33. http://www.rp-online.de/nrw/staedte/duesseldorf/die-kleinen-parteien-feiern-das-ende-der-sperrklausel-aid-1.7219169, accessed 10 March 2018.
34. http://www.dw.com/en/german-election-preliminary-coalition-talks-collapse-after-fdp-walks-out/a-41445987, accessed 3 February 2018.
35. http://www.dw.com/en/political-buzzword-jamaika-aus-is-german-word-of-the-year-2017/a-41711361, accessed 3 February 2018.
36. http://www.faz.net/aktuell/feuilleton/debatten/meierei-die-neue-wortschoepfung-lindnern-15306755.html, accessed 4 February 2018.
37. https://www.tagesspiegel.de/politik/newsblog-zum-spd-mitgliedervotum-spd-will-minister posten-paritaetisch-besetzen/21029416.html, accessed 9 March 2018.
38. https://www.economist.com/blogs/kaffeeklatsch/2018/02/loveless-marriage?cid1=cust/ddnew/email/n/n/2018027n/owned/n/n/ddnew/n/n/n/nna/Daily_Dispatch/email&etear=dailydispatch, accessed 7 February 2018.
39. See Joyce Marie Mushaben, *Becoming Madam Chancellor: Angela Merkel and the Berlin Republic* (New York, 2017); Sarah Wiliarty, *The CDU and the Politics of Gender in Germany: Bringing Women to the Party* (New York, 2010).
40. http://www.spiegel.de/international/germany/german-coalition-talks-everyone-loses-a-1179358.html, accessed 3 February 2018.
41. https://www.theguardian.com/world/2015/aug/04/angela-merkels-influence-now-extends-to-german-slang-merkeln, accessed 4 February 2018.
42. http://www.spiegel.de/politik/deutschland/csu-horst-seehofer-will-innenminister-bleiben-a-1237977.html, accessed 3 December 2018.

43. https://www.dw.com/en/seehofer-tells-islam-conference-muslims-are-a-part-of-germany/a-46489983, accessed 3 December 2018.
44. See https://www.zeit.de/politik/ausland/2018-06/horst-seehofer-union-asylstreit-angela-merkel; https://www.theguardian.com/world/2018/sep/11/germany-security-agency-hans-georg-maassen-explain-claims-far-right-videos-chemnitz, accessed 30 November 2018. Maaßen contested media reports about right-radicals "hunting" down non-white people in Chemnitz at the end of August. Seehofer tried to move Maaßen into another leadership position, but massive pushback led to Maaßen's forced retirement (which he then blamed on a conspiracy of radical left-wing forces).
45. https://www.ardmediathek.de/ard/player/Y3JpZDovL2Rhc2Vyc3RlLmRlL3Jlc G9ydGFnZSBfIGRva3VtZW50YXRpb24gaW0gZXJzdGVuL2JlYjMzMjljLThiND ctNGE0OC1hMjQ5LTJmNzFkOTJhYjMxOQ/der-machtkampf-wer-folgt-auf-merkel, accessed 3 December 2018.
46. http://www.spiegel.de/politik/deutschland/cdu-wolfgang-schaeuble-wirbt-oeffentlich-fuer-friedrich-merz-a-1241943.html, accessed 4 December 2018.
47. Iceland, Belgium, Luxembourg, Serbia, and Ireland have already had gay heads of government. In Germany, openly gay Guido Westerwelle (FDP) was the vice-chancellor and foreign minister between 2009 and 2013.
48. https://www.handelsblatt.com/politik/deutschland/nach-hartz-iv-aussagen-kritik-aus-der-cdu-jens-spahn-hat-den-bezug-zur-lebenswirklichkeit-verloren/21058884.html, accessed 4 December 2018.
49. http://www.spiegel.de/international/germany/search-for-merkel-successor-leads-to-kramp-karrenbauer-a-1190391.html, accessed 2 February 2018.
50. http://www.bild.de/politik/inland/landtagswahlen-saarland-2017/darum-bangt-merkel-um-mini-merkel-50981516.bild.html, accessed February 4, 2018.
51. https://www.zeit.de/politik/deutschland/2018-10/merkel-nachfolge-cdu-vorsitz-annegret-kramp-karrenbauer-friedrich-merz-jens-spahn; http://www.spiegel.de/politik/deutschland/friedrich-merz-und-der-cdu-vorsitz-millionaer-der-mitte-a-1239073.html, accessed 30 November 2018.
52. http://www.forschungsgruppe.de/Aktuelles/Politbarometer/; https://www.welt.de/politik/deutschland/article184885298/Forsa-Umfrage-Jeder-Dritte-findet-Merz-unangenehm-nur-jeder-Fuenfte-haelt-AKK-fuer-fuehrungsstark.html, accessed 4 December 2018.
53. https://www.faz.net/aktuell/politik/liveblog-kramp-karrenbauer-ist-neue-vorsitzende-der-cdu-15929379.html, accessed 8 January 2019.
54. http://www.spiegel.de/politik/deutschland/spd-und-grosse-koalition-das-macht-die-afd-zur-volkspartei-kolumne-a-1189124.html, accessed 2 February 2018.
55. https://www.stuttgarter-zeitung.de/inhalt.interview-mit-afd-bundesvize-gauland-die-afd-will-als-partei-der-kleinen-leute-punkten.f915c96e-4687-4f28-9b5c-596fbc15cf2b.html, accessed 2 February 2018.
56. http://www.zeit.de/politik/deutschland/2017-09/wahlverhalten-bundestagswahl-wahlbeteiligung-waehlerwanderung, accessed 4 February 2018.
57. http://www.spiegel.de/international/germany/how-merkel-has-fundamentally-changed-german-politics-a-1191422.html, accessed 7 February 2018.
58. https://www.wahlrecht.de/umfragen/, accessed 30 November 2018.
59 https://www.nytimes.com/2018/11/27/world/europe/germany-greens-merkel-election.html, accessed 30 November 2018.
60. http://www.spiegel.de/politik/deutschland/sahra-wagenknecht-und-ihre-aufstehen-bewegung-war-s-das-schon-a-1237724.html, accessed 1 December 2018.
61. https://www.nytimes.com/2017/09/29/opinion/german-election-afd.html, accessed 2 February 2018.
62. Hans Kundnani, "Why the AfD Could Be Good for German Democracy: Will It Bring an End to the CDU-SPD Consensus?" *Foreign Affairs*, 2 November 2017, accessed 2 February 2018.

63. https://www.welt.de/politik/deutschland/article168989573/Welche-Parteien-die-meisten-Stimmen-an-die-AfD-verloren.html, accessed 29 January 2018.
64. https://www.focus.de/politik/deutschland/bundestagswahl_2017/wahlergebnisse-2017-so-haben-die-bundeslaender-bei-der-bundestagswahl-gewaehlt_id_7631289.html, accessed 4 February 2018.
65. https://www.theguardian.com/world/2017/nov/23/protesters-holocaust-memorial-far-right-german-politician-afd, accessed 2 February 2018.
66. David Art, *The Politics of the Nazi Past in Germany and Austria* (New York, 2006).
67. There were reports about Trump campaign aides coming to help–and suggesting slogans like "Germany for the Germans," which even AfD leaders rejected.
68. https://interaktiv.morgenpost.de/analyse-bundestagswahl-2017/, accessed 4 February 2018.
69. Jan-Werner Müller, *What is Populism?* (Philadelphia, 2016).
70. https://www.theatlantic.com/international/archive/2017/11/germany-facebook/543258/, accessed 4 February 2018.
71. http://www.spiegel.de/politik/deutschland/afd-spendenaffaere-alice-weidel-muss-sich-ihrer-fraktion-erklaeren-a-1239183.html; http://www.spiegel.de/international/germany/billionaire-backing-may-have-helped-launch-afd-a-1241029.html, accessed 1 December 2018.
72. Quoted in https://www.washingtonpost.com/blogs/plum-line/wp/2018/11/30/trumpism-is-rotten-to-its-core-and-the-stench-of-corruption-and-failure-is-everywhere/?utm_term=.d4504e131957, accessed 1 December 2018.
73. http://www.spiegel.de/politik/deutschland/afd-die-rechtspopulisten-und-dernationale nationale-sozialismus-kolumne-a-1191417.html, accessed 5 February 2018.
74. These contributions were previously publishing over the course of 2018 in *German Politics and Society* in two special issues (Spring and Summer 2018) devoted to the 2017 Bundestag election and its consequences, as well as several from the Autumn 2018 issue.

··· Chapter 1 ···

Coalition Politics in Crisis?

The German Party System Before and After the 2017 Federal Election

Frank Decker and Philipp Adorf

Shift of the Political Balance of Power to the Right

Following the elections to the nineteenth Bundestag, parties had to cope with a newfound shortage of space. Previously, all four parliamentary party groups were able to claim one of the building's corner towers as their own. Now six groups were fighting for the best spaces. The refusal of the Christian Democratic Union/Christian Social Union (CDU/CSU) and Social Democratic Party (SPD) to reform the country's current electoral law, moreover, meant a few hundred-additional people (both members of parliament and employees) had to be accommodated somewhere as the size of the Bundestag expanded beyond its regular number of seats from 598 to 709. And in the plenary hall itself, the seats on the far right that had previously been filled by the Free Democrats (FDP) before their parliamentary exit in 2013, were now given to the Alternative for Germany's (AfD) parliamentary group whose members thus sit merely a few feet away from the government bench.[1]

The parliamentary entry of the Alternative for Germany does not merely mark another break in the country's party system, but also constitutes a watershed moment for Germany's postwar democracy. After the National Democratic Party's (NPD) narrow failure to enter parliament in 1969 (winning 4.3 percent of the vote that year), right-wing extremist parliamentarians will for the first time since the 1950s take their seats in the federal parliament–in the same building that had served as the stage and backdrop for the rise of the Nazi party between 1925 and 1932. At the same time, the parliamentary emergence of right-wing populism in Germany represents a kind of European "normalization," as ideologically similar parties have

Notes for this section begin on page 55.

become established actors across virtually all neighboring countries.[2] Why Germany appeared to be immune to such developments before 2013 continues to pose a difficult question, even with the luxury of hindsight.[3]

The AfD's success has once again moved the party system's center of gravity to the right–in a substantial manner. While the three left-of-center parties (SPD, Greens, and PDS/The Left) enjoyed a comfortable lead in the combined share of the vote in the three elections of 1998, 2002, and 2005 over their opponents of the CDU/CSU and FDP, the balance of power reversed for the very first time in 2009–before the emergence of the AfD. In 2013, the three parties of the right (now including the AfD) already possessed a lead of around 8 points over the left-of-center camp (51.0 to 42.7 percent). The latter's numerical majority in parliament was owed to the narrow failure of both the FDP and AfD to cross the five-percent-threshold. In 2017, the three right-of-center parties combined to win 56.2 percent of the vote as their counterparts on the left only managed a combined share of 38.6 percent.

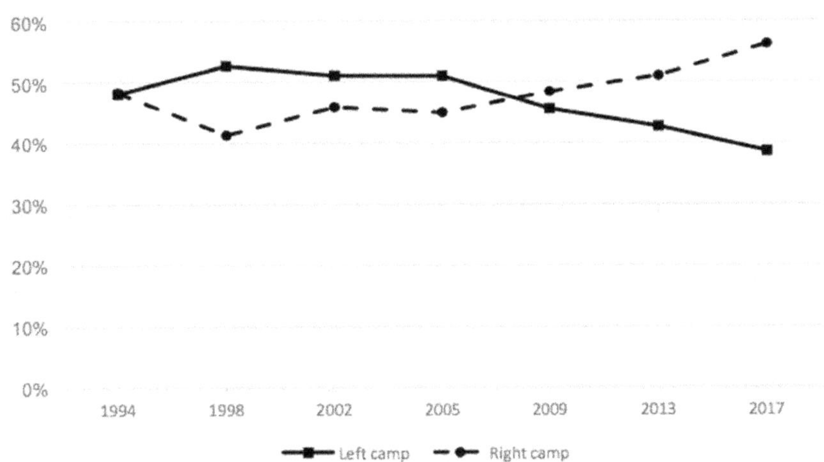

Figure 1.1: Combined Vote Shares of the Left-of-Center (SPD, Greens, PDS/The Left) and Right-of-Center Parties (CDU/CSU, FDP, AfD) in Federal Elections since 1994

This asymmetrical distribution of the vote is now, however, met with a newfound structural symmetry. With the left camp having been composed of three parties since reunification, as one of its actors–the Party of Democratic Socialism (PDS)/Left–continues to be regarded as a rather problematic if not unacceptable coalition partner,[4] the AfD's emergence has created a similar constellation on the right. The SPD's dubious pleasure of facilitating the rise of new and viable parties within its own ideological camp while governing the country (as was the case with the Greens in the late 1970s and after 2004 with the establishment of an all-German Left Party) has for the very first time also befallen the Christian Democrats. Franz Josef Strauß's famous dictum that no democratically legitimate party was to be allowed to emerge to the right of the CDU and CSU has been rendered null and void by the AfD's widespread success. This major transformation will also come to at least partially define future judgments regarding the "Merkel era."

Both the dramatic losses of the Christian democratic sister parties as well as the ability of the right-wing populists to come in third cannot hide the fact that the CDU/CSU once again comfortably secured first place over the SPD (for the third time since 2009). The conservative lead over its social democratic competitor decreased only marginally from 15.8 percentage points in 2013 to 12.4 points last year (see figure 1.3). This is only more remarkable in light of the fact that the SPD's nomination of Martin Schulz as its candidate for the office of chancellor in January of 2017 provided the party with an auspicious start to the election year. The subsequent surge in support that catapulted it beyond the 30 percent barrier in the polls for the first time in a decade and allowed it to once again credibly contest first place in the country's party system was to be short-lived though. Disappointing results in the Saarland state election, where the SPD failed to oust the governing CDU state premier, already put the party back on a losing path in March 2017 before defeats in Schleswig-Holstein and the party's heartland of North Rhine-Westphalia in particular brought about a collapse in support.

Why did the election eventually unfold the way it did? Without assigning an order of significance, the following factors determined the outcome of the vote:

Crisis: Angela Merkel's frequently repeated sentence that we were living through "tumultuous times" was also to be interpreted as a hint to the electorate that in such a challenging environment, it was best to leave the government in the hands of a nationally and internationally experienced crisis manager. The chancellor benefitted from her widely perceived role as an "anchor of stability" as Germany's most important European partners (France, the United Kingdom, and Italy) all saw their governments or heads of government replaced in short succession while Americans opted to select an erratic "anti-politician" in the form of Donald Trump as president.

Good economic growth: Merkel's aura as Europe's most powerful head of government not the least rested on Germany's continued strong economic growth, a factor that her party was also able to contrast with the economic "malaise" present in other countries. According to exit polls from Forschungsgruppe Wahlen, 62 percent of voters considered the state of the economy to be good (compared to 46 percent in 2013). The CDU/CSU was furthermore once again able to improve upon its position as the most trusted party on economic matters, widening the gap between itself and the SPD, whose own criticism of a severe lack in public investments largely went unnoticed.

Perceptions of competence: Concerning policy areas that represent the SPD's core brand of "social justice" and were put at the center of its campaign, voters either placed lower (pensions and education) or just marginally higher levels of trust (family policy and taxes) in the Social Democrats than they did in their conservative counterparts. Even more damaging was the continued dominance of the topic of migration and refugees where the SPD trailed the CDU/CSU by a significant margin. This also applied to the issues of crime and domestic security.

Candidate: Contrary to Peer Steinbrück, the SPD's 2013 candidate for the chancellery who never really embodied the party's program, Schulz appeared to be a–at the very least potentially–good candidate. After the initial honeymoon, Schulz revealed two decisive weaknesses, however. On the one hand, he lacked an apparent hunger for power, both within his own party as well as towards Chancellor Angela Merkel, while also failing to exhibit the necessary leadership capabilities for the job. On the other hand, he was neither willing and/or capable of freeing the SPD from its responsibilities as the junior coalition partner and cast the party as a genuine alternative to the CDU/CSU. The issue of social justice was, for example, addressed in a far too tepid manner while proposals related to Europe were more or less buried deep within the party manifesto. Schulz's experience as a leading EU politician would have made him the perfect spokesperson for precisely this topic.

Campaign: Schulz's weaknesses as a candidate ultimately came to the fore because of a poorly planned out campaign that was rife with a number of inexcusable technical mistakes. Schulz's predecessor as party leader, Sigmar Gabriel, bears a significant part of the blame for this. Instead of waiting until January to forgo his own candidacy, Gabriel should have settled on Schulz at a much earlier date, in the process allowing the entire party to prepare in a more thorough manner for the election. A lack of coordination between the two carried over into the election campaign itself. In what would prove to be a fatal mistake, the party decided to remove Schulz from the media spotlight for two months in the wake of his initial meteoric rise rather than keeping the general public occupied with a steady stream of information related to both Schulz and the SPD. The explanations provided for this decision–a desire to neither pre-empt the formulation of a party manifesto nor "disrupt" the state election campaign in North Rhine-Westphalia–illustrate a complete lack of a strategic plan on the part of the SPD.

New Competition: A closer look at the movement of voters reveals virtually no vote transfer between the CDU/CSU and the SPD. The number of electoral districts won by both parties also remained largely unchanged compared to 2013: 231 for the CDU/CSU and fifty-nine for the SPD, whereas four years earlier the respective numbers stood at 236 and fifty-eight. The Christian Democrats primarily lost voters to both the FDP and AfD–in other words, parties within their own camp–while the SPD's losses were equally distributed among the other parties (Left, Greens, FDP, and AfD). Right-wing populist competitors, therefore, also drive down the social democratic vote. In eastern Germany in particular, these changing voting patterns have hurt the Left Party which has as a result been relegated to third place behind the CDU and AfD in the region.

No viable coalition of the left or prospect of obtaining power: Immediately following the 2013 election, the SPD already announced it would no longer categorically rule out any form of cooperation with the Left Party. A subsequent rapprochement between the two failed to materialize, however. The outcome of the 2017 Saarland state elections–in which both the SPD and Left Party combined to lose 4.3 points–once again illustrated the general public's lack of support for a red-red-green coalition. The SPD could therefore only achieve its electoral goal of regaining the chancellery by becoming the strongest party, an objective that became little more than a fantasy following the poor showing in North Rhine-Westphalia. Subsequent discussions concerning the future federal government therefore revolved around the question whether the SPD would join another grand coalition as junior partner or if a black-green-yellow "Jamaica" coalition of the CDU/CSU, Greens, and FDP would be formed at the federal level for the very first time. This may have encouraged potential social democratic voters in west Germany in particular to throw their support behind the Greens or the Left in the final days of the campaign. While the latter suffered massive losses in the east, it managed to increase its share of the vote in the western part of the country by 1.8 points to 7.4 percent.

The fact that poll after poll indicated a comfortable CDU/CSU lead over their Social Democratic opponents undoubtedly contributed to voters abandoning both catch-all parties as the election drew closer. A strategy of "asymmetrical demobilization" that had been employed to great success by the CDU in both 2009 and 2013 would this time around come back to haunt the Christian Democrats themselves. The inability to deemphasize the issue of migration played a significant role as well. While the rise of the SPD's numbers in the wake of their nomination of Schulz boosted hopes that a close race between the top two parties would perhaps even push the AfD below the 5 percent threshold, the SPD's inability or reluctance to provide a credible and clear political alternative to their conservative opponents ultimately played into the hands of the right-wing populists, particularly in the waning weeks of the campaign.[5] The question (also related to the media's role) remains, however, to what extent a sounder strategy could have shifted attention away from the refugee topic towards socioeconomic questions.

The Successful Establishment of the Right-wing Populist Alternative for Germany

Until the emergence of the AfD, both right-wing populist and extremist actors were only able to celebrate sporadic success at the ballot box in the Federal Republic. After both the first and second waves of right-wing extremism in the early 1950s and late 1960s quickly faded away, a third wave began to surface at the beginning of the 1980s, constituting a constant feature of the political world since. None of the German right-wing extremist and populist actors nonetheless exhibited the ability to permanently establish themselves within the country's political system. Among the right-wing populist actors that ultimately vanished are the Statt Party from Hamburg, the Bund Freier Bürger (Association of Free Citizens) as well as the Schill Party which also had its roots in Hamburg. The most prominent right-wing extremist actors that have intermittently been able to enter regional parliaments are the NPD and the German People's Union (DVU), with the latter eventually joining the former. Having been established as a far-right conservative splinter off the CSU in the early 1980s, the Republikaner quickly transformed themselves into a right-wing populist force under the leadership of Franz Schönhuber, as subsequent years saw an ever-increasing incorporation of right-wing extremist elements into the party's ideology and organizational structure. After a string of impressive results in a variety of state elections, the party disappeared into electoral oblivion in the mid 1990s as quickly as it had emerged a few years earlier.

Why did right-wing populist sentiments fail to translate into political success for parties espousing such views for such a considerable period of time? Explanations such as the Christian Democrats' success in politically integrating the right fringe of society until the early 2000s as well as an absence of political discussions surrounding immigration policies only provide a partial answer.[6] In particular, as the weakness of right-wing populist parties in the 1990s coincided with an upsurge in other forms of right-wing extremism: from intellectual movements–assembled under the banner of the "New Right"–and xenophobically motivated far-right violent crimes that sometimes took on the form of outright terrorism, to the more recently practiced types of action inspired by the historically leftist "fun" or "communication guerilla" that have been appropriated and adopted by the Identitarian Movement as well as Dresden's PEGIDA movement, which began organizing anti-immigration street protests in 2014.[7]

The escalation of the refugee crisis in the fall of 2015, ultimately served as an unexpected catalyst for the AfD's rise just a few weeks after the exodus of several prominent members of its more moderate wing around co-founder Bernd Lucke had thrown the party into disarray. The assertion made by some that the AfD might have disappeared altogether without this "gift" (Alexander Gauland) does not hold up to closer scrutiny, especially when assessing the developments that triggered the party's genesis in the first place. The party, on the one hand, filled a void that had been opened by the actions and programmatic shifts of the governing center-right parties of the time (the CDU/CSU and FDP), as both the eurozone rescue policies as well as a more liberal approach on sociocultural matters by the CDU constituted the primary political openings for the AfD to exploit. On the other hand, the party already possessed a remarkable degree of organizational strength by the summer of 2015 as a result of previous electoral achievements which allowed it to withstand the split.[8]

Scholars are divided on whether the rise and success of right-wing populism is attributable to socioeconomic or sociocultural conflicts.[9] This debate is reflected within the sociological research of the AfD. While one side sees its voters as the typical losers of globalization or modernization, the other side stresses that the party's biggest support can be found precisely among those that do not suffer from economic hardships. This attempt to clearly distinguish and contrast economic and cultural factors appears somewhat contrived–it is the interaction and reciprocal reinforcement of the two that accounts for the explosive nature of these conflicts. This is particularly true concerning immigration. Right-wing populist actors have, after all, obtained far better electoral results in western and northern Europe than in the south, not least because of the interplay between a high share of a non-native population and the presence of a traditionally comprehensive welfare state.[10] The fact that the latter constitutes the most impor-

Table 1.1: AfD Election Results since 2013 (in percent)

	Federal Elections	Elections to the European Parliament	State Elections
2013	4.7		Hesse 4.1
2014		7.1	Brandenburg 12.2 Saxony 9.7 Thuringia 10.6
2015			Hamburg 6.1 Bremen 5.5
2016			Baden-Württemberg 15.1 Rhineland-Palatinate 12.6 Saxony-Anhalt 24.3 Mecklenburg-West Pomerania 20.5 Berlin 14.2
2017	12.6		Saarland 6.2 Schleswig-Holstein 5.9 North Rhine-Westphalia 7.4 Lower Saxony 6.2
2018			Bavaria 10.2 Hesse 13.1

tant safeguard against the possible downsides of globalization only makes this tension more relevant.[11]

Most threats that could jeopardize the AfD's survival are homemade. The party's short history has once again illustrated why right-wing challengers have a harder time establishing themselves in Germany than they do in other European countries.[12] All fledgling parties face the threat of falling victim to their own organizational incompetence as party officials and members lack both experience and professionalism. Furthermore, the party has to confront the restrictive conditions and environment any political newcomer encounters in the Federal Republic. The primary challenge undoubtedly continues to be the stigmatization of far-right sentiments as a result of the nation's Nazi legacy. Parties like the AfD, which attempt to present a more moderate face, are always used by right-wing extremist elements as a vehicle to overcome said stigmatization. This entails inevitable conflicts about how to handle unwanted supporters, resulting in discussions that invariably threaten to ruin the party's internal cohesion and public reputation.[13]

The dominance of the migrant issue in recent years has drawn even more people from the far-right fringe into the AfD. This is not just the case in the east of the country where parts of the party openly espouse racist and antidemocratic positions. The AfD's increasing inability (or unwillingness) to credibly distance itself from the far right is exemplified by the party's handling of the leader of its Thuringia state branch, Björn Höcke. Both Lucke and his successor as leader, Frauke Petry, failed in their endeavor to expel Höcke from the party's ranks. Höcke, who continues to maintain ties with NPD associates of the New Right and whose public speeches frequently employ a rhetoric reminiscent of Germany's darkest historical chapter, also received some support from the more moderate wing in his attempts to stave off his expulsion. What brought the two together was a shared opposition to Petry. After having been relegated to the sidelines during the 2017 campaign as a result of an increasingly high-handed manner of running the party, Petry herself eventually decided to leave the party just days after its surprisingly strong federal election result of 12.6 percent.

A look at the demand side paints a more promising picture for the right-wing populists. The sentiments that spur support for the AfD can probably best be described by the paired feelings of "anxiety" and "uneasiness." Anxiety is linked to the socioeconomic state, related to fears about a loss of prosperity, whereas uneasiness is associated with feelings of cultural alienation and the demise of a familiar social order and its moorings.[14] Both motives combine to form the desire of limiting government services and benefits to the own, native population ("welfare chauvinism.")[15]

That fears related to non-natives are not always highest in places home to the largest concentration of foreigners is nothing new–neither is the finding that far-right sentiments have spread to the heart of society in those areas. The AfD's electoral performance in the east–where it won around twice as many votes as it did in the west–lends further support to this conclusion. At the same time, results such as these illustrate the political-cultural parallels in place between the former German Democratic Republic and other postcommunist societies in central Europe. Having said that, two thirds of all AfD voters live in the west of the country. Above average results were obtained both in the prosperous southern states of Baden-Württemberg and Bavaria, as well as in the Social Democratic heartland of the Ruhr region, the economic state of which leaves much to be desired. Among voters that the AfD captured between 2013 and 2017, 30 percent had a center-right partisan background while 20 percent supported the left-of-center camp in 2013. Moreover, the party did quite well among voters that had previously stayed home on election day, while also siphoning some votes off other smaller parties. This mobilization contributed to a narrowing socioeconomic turnout gap that had already been present in previous state elections.

Even the most optimistic voices doubt that the AfD will exit the various parliaments it has entered during the next slew of elections. The current combination of supply and demand factors provides the party with a favorable environment, at least in the medium term. Regarding the demand side, decisions made in 2015 and 2016 related to the migration crisis and subsequent

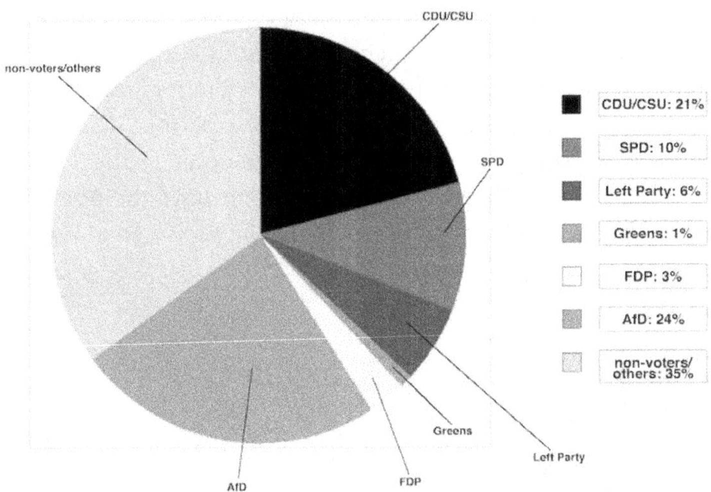

Figure 1.2: 2017 AfD Voters' Electoral Choices in 2013
Source: Forschungsgruppe Wahlen.

challenges concerning the deportation of migrants whose asylum claims have been rejected and the associated "strain" on the country's welfare system due to the remaining refugees present the AfD with plenty of policy openings. With regards to the supply side, the AfD's success at the ballot box (having entered fourteen of Germany's sixteen state parliaments as of early 2018) will allow it to utilize the immense state funds that are made available to parties with parliamentary representation. The party also profits from the structural change that the rise of social media has set off within the general media landscape.[16] The tools of social media communication provide the AfD with the ability to directly address potential voters and circumvent traditional media outlets, all while the latter are branded as part of the despised establishment.[17]

Taking a Political Cue from Austria, the Netherlands, or Scandinavia? The Impact of the Changing Party System on the Formation of Coalitions and the Government

What consequences does the establishment of the AfD within the country's political party system have on the process of forming a coalition and government? From the perspective of the Christian Democratic sister parties, surprisingly little has changed. Since the AfD–as has been illustrated–also acquired votes from the left, it has become even more difficult (if not impossible) for the SPD to obtain a majority beyond the CDU/CSU. In that sense, the rise of right-wing populism protects the Christian Democrats' strategic position of power, in so far as no governing majority can relegate the CDU/CSU to the opposition benches. The flip side of this development is an inability on the part of the conservatives to obtain a governing majority of their own with just their traditional coalition partner, the FDP. Instead, this alliance now requires another ally from the other political camp, either the SPD or the Greens. Painful compromises that have the potential to further alienate the party's base appear inevitable in such a coalition context.

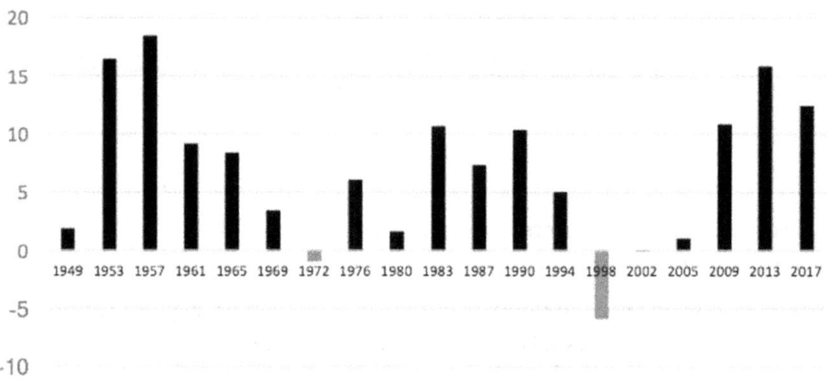

Figure 1.3: Gap Between the Vote Share Won by the CDU/CSU and the SPD, 1949-2017*

* positive value indicates higher CDU/CSU share; negative value indicates higher SPD share

The effects of the transformation of Germany's party system on the coalition formation process are made readily apparent by developments within Germany's sixteen states. Along with the increasingly rare instances of outright CDU or SPD majorities, twelve or–if you include the different senior/junior coalition partner dynamics–fifteen different coalition arrangements have governed since the 1990s.[18] In addition, the PDS/Left Party has tolerated two SPD and SPD/Green minority governments in Saxony-Anhalt and North Rhine-Westphalia. At the time of the official start of Merkel's third grand coalition (March 2018), just six coalition state governments with members from one political camp (made up of two or three parties) remained in office, in contrast to nine coalitions that required alliances beyond the traditional political divide. Among those were four CDU-SPD or SPD-CDU coalitions (Saxony, Saarland, Lower Saxony, Mecklenburg-West Pomerania) two CDU-Green or Green-CDU coalitions (Hesse, Baden-Württemberg), one "traffic light" coalition made up of the SPD, Greens, and FDP

(Rhineland-Palatinate), one "Jamaica" coalition between the CDU, FDP, and Greens (Schleswig-Holstein) along with a "Kenya" coalition comprised of the CDU, SPD, and Greens (Saxony-Anhalt).

Table 1.2: Coalition Arrangements in Germany's States since the 1990s

Intrapolitical Camp Coalition of Two Parties	Cross-political Camp Coalition of Two Parties	Intrapolitical Camp Coalition of Three Parties	Cross-political Camp Coalition of Three Parties
CDU/CSU-FDP	CDU/CSU-SPD SPD-CDU/CSU (mostly grand coalitions)	CDU/CSU-FDP-Schill	SPD-Greens-FDP (traffic light)
SPD-Greens	CDU/CSU-Greens Greens-CDU/CSU	SPD-Left Party-Greens / Left Party-SPD-Greens	CDU/CSU-FDP-Greens (Jamaica)
SPD-Left Party	SPD-FDP	SPD-Greens-SSW (Danish or coast coalition)	CDU/CSU-SPD-Greens (Kenya)

Comparisons between the coalition types found at the German state level and patterns present at the national level in Europe's multiparty-systems, indicate that the three dominant models of the latter are also represented within the former:

> (1) Grand coalitions of the Austrian type are the first model.[19] They have been the primary manner of forming governments at the federal level since 2005, with their combined share of the vote however only crossing the two-thirds mark in 2005 and once again in 2013. At the state level, this extent of popular support can currently only be found in Lower Saxony and the Saarland.
>
> (2) The second model is made up of centrist coalitions that span the traditional political divide and are comprised of at least three parties of the political center. Parties located at the left or right fringes are excluded. This model, a staple of Belgian and Dutch coalition governments, can be found in the traffic light, Jamaica, and Kenya coalitions at the German state level. The federal Jamaica coalition would actually have been comprised of four parties if one considers the CDU and CSU to be separate entities.
>
> (3) The third model are coalitions limited to one political camp that are tolerated or supported by a fringe party.[20] This model dominates Scandinavian politics but has been emulated at the German state level, as mentioned, in only a few exceptional instances. Whenever the exclusion of a fringe party has been overcome, governing parties have preferred to establish a formal coalition agreement. Except for a coalition in the city-state of Hamburg between the CDU, FDP and Schill Party in 2001 that failed to survive a single legislative term, all of these arrangements have been found on the left (Mecklenburg-West Pomerania, Berlin, Brandenburg, and Thuringia).

One remarkable feature of the most recent federal election proved to be that in its wake all three models were floated as possible coalition arrangements. Plans for a Scandinavian model were, however, merely of a theoretical nature, in no small part because the proponents of a minority government lacked an understanding of its character and mode of operation. After all, their proposals did not envision a minority government comprised from within one political camp that relied on the toleration by a fringe actor. A minority government of the left tolerated by the Left Party would, of course, have fallen well short of a majority to begin with. On the other side of the partisan divide, the prospect of a center-right minority government tolerated by the AfD never appeared to be a credible alternative as any sort of cooperation with the AfD remains beyond the pale. Instead, the supposed solution was to be an arrangement in which a CDU government or coalition received the support of one or more parties from the other political camp, "ideally" with ever-changing alliances to pass legislation depending on the policy topic of the day, a model that was also presented as raising parliament's stature vis-à-vis the government. The SPD's primary proponent of this design–usually endorsed by journalists without a hint of criticism–was Malu Dreyer, one of the party's deputy leaders and state premier of Rhineland-Palatinate. In hindsight, however, her primary role probably was to lay the groundwork for and legitimize the SPD's about-face on the matter of reentering a government with the CDU/CSU, in particular in an attempt to soften the party base's opposition to this reversal.

The Arduous March Towards Another Grand Coalition

On election night, few could foresee the momentous watershed moment the AfD's entry represented. Protracted or failed coalition negotiations had always been regarded as feature of the political environment of other countries–most recently for example Belgium and the Netherlands–whose months-long search for a government not infrequently elicited pity among German political observers. Any reasons for hubris have disappeared though in the wake of the Jamaica failure. After it had already taken three months to form a grand coalition following the 2013 election, 2017 left Germany with a caretaker government for almost half a year. This also had Europe-wide consequences as France's dynamic President Emmanuel Macron seized the opportunity to compensate for his country's recent decline in clout and relevance at the European level by placing himself at the very center of European politics while Merkel continued to be preoccupied with domestic matters.

Table 1.3: Duration Between Federal Election and Swearing-in of Government since Reunification

Election	Number of Days Between Federal Election and Swearing-in of Government	Government
1990	47	CDU/CSU/FDP
1994	32	CDU/CSU/FDP
1998	30	SPD/Greens
2002	30	SPD/Greens
2005	65	CDU/CSU/SPD
2009	31	CDU/CSU/FDP
2013	86	CDU/CSU/SPD
2017	171	CDU/CSU/SPD

Source: Datenhandbuch zur Geschichte des Deutschen Bundestages, Chapter 6.7, Regierungsbildung, 2017.

As the Social Democrats categorically ruled out another grand coalition just minutes after the polls had closed, a Jamaica alliance between the CDU/CSU, FDP, and Greens remained as the sole viable option. Such a partial governmental change appeared justified from a democratic point of view. While both catch-all parties continued to control a majority of seats, the CDU/CSU and SPD had lost 8.6 and 5.2 percentage points respectively, obtaining their smallest combined share of the vote in the history of the Federal Republic (see Figure 1.4). Both of the prospective new governmental parties, the FDP and Greens, had on the other hand increased their share of the vote by 5.9 and 0.5 points respectively. The SPD was, moreover, able to justify its decision as an act of "political" if not even "national responsibility" as the AfD was placed to take over the role of largest opposition party.

Exploratory talks between the Jamaica parties, which essentially already took on the form of semi-official negotiations, proved to be slow-moving. This could first of all be traced back to an almost unbridgeable gulf on core policy matters like climate protection or refugees, where reconciling the Green position with those of the FDP and CDU/CSU was always going to prove hardest, in particular as the CSU opted for a tougher stance on migration. At the same, both the CDU and FDP were unable to reestablish a trusting relationship. Feeling pushed to the sidelines during negotiations, the Liberals increasingly worried that they would once again be deprived of oxygen by their larger coalition partner as had been the case during their previous coalition between 2009 and 2013.[21] The FDP had entered that particular alliance with its best-ever result only to be ejected from parliament for the very first time four years later. Behind the scenes, the Free Democrats had probably hoped for talks to break down over a disagreement between the Greens and CSU on the topic of refugees and migration. As a compromise between the two began to emerge, however, the FDP saw no option but to announce its own departure from coalition talks.

With pressure from the Christian Democrats and an increasingly worried Federal President Frank-Walter Steinmeier subsequently mounting, the SPD was forced to reassess its opposition to another grand coalition. The decision by the party executive to enter exploratory talks with their Christian Democratic counterparts opened a major internal rift.[22] It was the party's youth wing (the Young Socialists) in particular that gave voice to the internal opposition to once again joining Merkel in government. As the SPD failed in its attempts to push through a variety of ideological core objectives in initial talks, such as the introduction of a single public health insurance scheme or a hike in the top income tax rate, the party leadership needed the promise of additional amendments[23] to any final coalition agreement to win over a majority of delegates (56.4 percent) during a special party conference that determined whether to enter official coalition negotiations–a serious blow to the already wounded party chair Schulz.

That despite these major headwinds, support among SPD members for the final coalition agreement turned out to be considerably stronger than the party leadership had expected (66 percent approved of the arrangement in a referendum with a turnout of 78.4 percent) can be traced back to a number of reasons. First, members were aware of the gravity their decision carried–a negative verdict could very well have called the party's existence into question as the infighting of the previous weeks had already coincided with steady downward trajectory in the SPD's polling numbers (from around 21 percent in mid November to 17 percent by early March). Second, the media's commentary regarding the agreement painted a rather favorable picture for the SPD. Assessments of the final deal concluded that–as in 2013–the SPD had obtained policy concessions well beyond what was to be expected given its electoral atrophy. This also applied to the allocation of ministries. While retaining both the Foreign and Labor Ministries, the SPD was able to also secure the powerful finance portfolio that had previously been controlled by the CDU. And third, Schulz eventually decided against following through with his plan to join the Merkel government as foreign minister, a move which had caused a fair degree of consternation among the base.[24]

The Social Democrats were thus able to combine their less-than-enthusiastic entry into government with a (partial) reorientation at the very top. Gabriel, who had just a year earlier relinquished his role as party leader and candidate for the chancellery to Schulz in exchange for the post of foreign minister,[25] was snubbed by the new leadership around Andrea Nahles and Olaf Scholz, finding himself out of a job. High approval ratings and a virtually flawless performance in office could not compensate for the bad reputation Gabriel had garnered within his own party as a result of his undisciplined and sometimes abrasive behavior towards other fellow Social Democrats. His seat at the cabinet table was taken by the previous Merkel government's justice minister, Heiko Maas. Designated party leader Nahles also retained her leadership post within the SPD's parliamentary party group, while Scholz assumed the offices of finance minister and deputy chancellor.

Arguments within the Christian Democratic sister parties in the wake of their worst result since 1949 were not as dramatic but nonetheless still substantial. Most notably, all other debates were overshadowed by doubts even within the CDU's own ranks concerning the future of a chancellor whose own position appeared more precarious than ever before. Notwithstanding these internal rumblings, Merkel's position appeared, at least initially, to be bolstered by the potential formation of a new governing alliance. To begin with, the previously untested Jamaica model promised a fresh start for a party and chancellor that had already been in power for twelve years. At the same time, internal disagreements between the sister parties concerning refugees and immigration had been laid to rest before coalition talks began by agreeing on a compromise of a flexible cap of allowing no more than 200,000 refugees annually into the country, a number that was subsequently in principle also backed by both the Greens and FDP, as well as the SPD.

The failure of the Jamaica negotiations only confirmed Merkel's poor track record of handling (potential) coalition partners, a trait she had already exhibited towards the Free Democrats during their first coalition between 2009 and 2013. Following the conclusion of negotiations with the SPD, Merkel was even accused of having been taken advantage of by her future coalition partner. With regards to the distribution of ministries, the SPD's share was actually in line with its electoral results (as it obtained six compared to the CDU/CSU's nine posts). Instead, Merkel's Bavarian sister party received an undue number of three ministerial posts, including the particularly important Interior Ministry.[26] Said department was taken over by Horst Seehofer, allowing the veteran politician to stay at the center of the country's political stage even after having lost his previous post of Bavarian state premier to his unloved rival Markus Söder.

With the October 2018 Bavarian state election in mind, Seehofer wasted no time in offering a tougher stance on domestic security and migration policies, all with the intent of driving down AfD-support by re-occupying more conservative positions. Acting against the explicit wishes of the chancellor, Seehofer's announcement of his intention to turn back refugees coming into the country from Austria brought an end to the fragile peace between the

CDU and CSU on the topic and plunged the country into a three-week-long government crisis in June of 2018. All three governing parties sustained substantial losses in state elections in Bavaria and Hesse. In response, Merkel announced her decision to not stand for another term as party leader. Shortly after having been selected by Merkel for the post of the CDU's general secretary, Annegret Kramp-Karrenbauer managed to narrowly come out on top in the leadership contest against the preferred choice of the party's conservative wing, Friedrich Merz. In doing so, Kramp-Karrenbauer has become the front runner to succeed Merkel as chancellor.

Outlook

The outcome of the 2017 federal election offered another premiere in the history of the Federal Republic: for the first time a grand coalition will continue to remain in office. The torturous path towards the formation of a new government that forced both partners to put aside the outcome they had preferred in the immediate aftermath of the vote, has entailed a more inauspicious start compared to 2005 and 2013. An ominous sign of the mutual lack of trust exhibited by both partners is the stated goal–also noted in the coalition agreement but missing from previous ones–to take stock of the state of the coalition at the halfway point of the legislative term. This should by no means be interpreted as a potential emergency exit but serves as an indicator that all concerned parties are subjected to enormous pressure after

Figure 1.4: Combined CDU/CSU and SPD Vote Share in Federal Elections 1976-2017 (in percent)

their historically poor election results. Chancellor Merkel's third grand coalition will therefore likely feature even more internal disagreements than the two previous iterations (2005–2009 and 2013–2017).

The SPD is faced with the most daunting challenge. The claim, frequently voiced by opponents of another grand coalition, that the thankless role of junior coalition partner bears the primary responsibility for the party's dire state, denotes a certain degree of autosuggestion. Admittedly, it will nonetheless be difficult to square the promise of a fundamental Social Democratic regeneration with the constraints of governing. This is even more challenging as the SPD is finding it increasingly difficult to credibly occupy positions within the two primary conflict dimensions of the party system. Concerning the topic of immigration and integration, the party has to grapple with the simple fact that potential burdens are primarily shouldered by the lower third of society, in other words the SPD's electoral base. And on socioeconomic and welfare-related questions, the party is inevitably confronted with its own welfare and labor market reforms that have widened the gap between the rich and poor even further.[27]

Recovering the party's working-class base is made even more difficult if not impossible by the emergence of a new challenger, the AfD.[28] This will be especially true, if Germany's right-wing populists emulate their European sister parties and abandon economically liberal positions in favor of a more socially populist or protectionist profile.[29] Virtually all social democratic avenues to power would then be blocked. If left-of-center majorities are a thing of the past, the SPD's sole hope would be to overturn the positions of senior and junior partners in a grand coalition by once again overtaking the CDU/CSU as the strongest party. As polls from the beginning of the election year illustrated, this appears possible given the right circumstances and in conjunction with a compelling policy plan and persuasive political team–but not particularly likely.

The CDU/CSU also needs to tread carefully in the new six-party system. If the party is forced to adopt a moderate course in a grand or centrist coalition, it will find it nearly impossible to sharpen its conservative profile or pursue a more nationally minded agenda in an attempt to take on the AfD. Cooperation with the latter would offer the sole escape from this trap. Part and parcel in other European countries, such an alliance is, however, out of the question in Germany due to the country's political culture. The inability and unwillingness on the part of the AfD to distance itself from extremist tendencies constitutes–as previously illustrated–a notorious problem. Some eastern German CDU state branches may be willing to look past this. The federal party, however, could and would never accept any sort of mere musings about a potential coalition with the AfD anywhere across the country.

Recent developments in east Germany in particular indicate that instead of the Scandinavian model, Germany may experience a synthesis between the Austrian and Dutch designs in future years. The CDU and SPD already failed to garner a majority of the vote in any of the six eastern German states (including Berlin) in the 2017 federal election.[30] A repeat in the 2019 state elections in Brandenburg, Saxony, and Thuringia could force the parties of the grand coalition to include the Greens or FDP as an additional partner, as has been the case in Saxony-Anhalt since 2016. Even a degree of cooperation between the CDU and Left Party no longer appears unthinkable–a rather ironic turn of events in light of the manner in which election campaigns of the past were conducted. The prospect of the fringe parties obtaining "negative" majorities, a scenario that almost materialized in Saxony-Anhalt but was only averted by the Greens barely scraping past the five-percent threshold, is reminiscent of Weimar Germany. It also illustrates the dramatic transformation that has been set into motion by the arrival of right-wing populism on the country's political stage.

Frank Decker is a professor at the Institute for Political Science and Sociology, Rheinische-Friedrich-Wilhelms Universität in Bonn, Germany. His main research interests focus on problems of institutional reforms in Western democracies, party systems, and right-wing populism. Recent publications include *Handbuch der deutschen Parteien*, co-edited with Viola Neu (Wiesbaden, 2018), *Europas Ende, Europas Anfang*, co-edited with Jürgen Rüttgers (Frankfurt, 2017) and *Der Irrweg der Volksgesetzgebung* (Bonn, 2016). E-mail: frank.decker@uni-bonn.de

Philipp Adorf is a research assistant at the University of Bonn. His past research has focused on the transformation of the Republican Party since the 1960s, published as *How the South was won and the nation lost* (Bonn, 2016). More recently, his scholarly attention has turned to the success of right-wing populist actors among blue-collar voters that had previously supported center-left parties. E-mail: padorf@uni-bonn.de

Notes

1. The Free Democrats' request to be seated in the center (between the Greens and Christian Democrats) rather than between the CDU/CSU and AfD did not receive the support of the Bundestag's council of elders.
2. See Frank Decker, Bernd Henningsen, and Kjetil Jakobsen, ed., *Rechtspopulismus und Rechtsextremismus in Europa: Die Herausforderung der Zivilgesellschaft durch alte Ideologien und neue Medien* (Baden-Baden, 2015); Tjitske Akkerman, Sarah L. de Lange, and Matthijs Rooduijn, ed., *Radical right-wing populist parties in western Europe: Into the mainstream?* (Abingdon, 2016).
3. See Frank Decker, "The failure of right-wing populism in Germany" in *The changing faces of populism: Systemic challengers in Europe and the U.S.*, ed. Hedwig Giusto, David Kitching, and Stefano Rizzo (Brussels, 2013), 87–106; Frank Decker, "Germany: Right-wing Populist Failures and Left-wing Successes" in *Twenty-First Century Populism: The Spectre of Western European Democracy*, ed. Daniele Albertazzi and Duncan McDonnell (Basingstoke, 2008), 119–134.
4. See Dan Hough and Michael Koß, "Populism Personified or Reinvigorated Reformers? The German Left Party in 2009 and Beyond," *German Politics and Society* 27, no. 2 (2009): 76–91, doi: 10.3167/gps.2009.270206.
5. Before the nomination of Martin Schulz, the AfD was polling at around 13 to 14 percent. By mid summer of 2017, it had dropped to below 8 percent.
6. See Decker, "The failure of right-wing populism" (see note 3).
7. See Jörg Michael Dostal, "The Pegida Movement and German Political Culture: Is Right-Wing Populism Here to Stay?" *The Political Quarterly* 86, no. 4 (2015): 523–531, doi: 10.1111/1467-923X.12204; Hans Vorländer, Maik Herold, and Steven Schäller, *PEGIDA and new right-wing populism in Germany* (Cham, 2018).
8. See Frank Decker, "The 'Alternative for Germany:' Factors Behind its Emergence and Profile of a New Right-Wing Populist Party," *German Politics and Society* 34, no. 2 (2016): 1–35, doi: 10.3167/gps.2016.340201.
9. See Daniel Oesch, "Explaining Workers' Support for Right-Wing Populist Parties in Western Europe: Evidence from Austria, Belgium, France, Norway, and Switzerland," *International Political Science Review* 29, no. 3 (2008): 349–373, here 370, doi: 10.1177/0192512107088390; Cas Mudde, *Populist Radical Right Parties in Europe* (Cambridge, 2007), 119–137; Jens Rydgren, ed., *Class Politics and the Radical Right* (Abingdon, 2013).
10. See Dani Rodrik, "Populism and the Economics of Globalization," CEPR discussion paper, Washington, 2017.
11. See Duane Swank and Hans-Georg Betz, "Globalization, the welfare state and right-wing populism in Western Europe," *Socio-Economic Review* 1, no. 2 (2003): 215–245.
12. See Frank Decker and Florian Hartleb, "Populism on Difficult Terrain: The Right- and Left-Wing Challenger Parties in the Federal Republic of Germany," *German Politics* 16, no. 4 (2007): 434–454, doi: 10.1080/09644000701652466; Simon Bornschier, "Why a right-wing populist party emerged in France but not in Germany: cleavages and actors in the formation of a new cultural divide," *European Political Science Review* 4, no. 1 (2012): 121–145, doi: 10.1017/S1755773911000117.
13. See Roger Karapin, "Radical-Right and Neo-Fascist Political Parties in Western Europe," *Comparative Politics* 30, no. 2 (1998): 213–234, here 225, doi: 10.2307/422288.
14. See Ronald F. Inglehart and Pippa Norris, "Trump, Brexit, and the Rise of Populism: Economic Have-Nots and Cultural Backlash," Harvard Kennedy School Working Paper, 2016.
15. See Alexander W. Schmidt-Catran and Dennis C. Spies, "Immigration and Welfare Support in Germany," *American Sociological Review* 81, no. 2 (2016): 242–261, doi: 10.1177/0003122416633140.

16. See Luca Manucci, "Populism and the Media" in *The Oxford Handbook of Populism*, ed. Cristóbal Rovira Kaltwasser, Paul Taggart, Paulina Ochoa Espejo, and Pierre Ostiguy (Oxford, 2017), 467–488.
17. This has diminished the impact media can have in potentially combatting the rise of populism through the stigmatization of its proponents. See Joost van Spanje and Rachid Azrout, "Tainted Love: How Stigmatization of a Political Party in News Media Reduces Its Electoral Support," *International Journal of Public Opinion Research* (forthcoming, 2018), doi: 10.1093/ijpor/edy009. For populism and its use of social media, see Benjamin Krämer, "Populist online practices: the function of the Internet in right-wing populism," *Information, Communication & Society* 20, no. 9 (2017): 1293–1309, doi: 10.1080/1369118X.2017.1328520.
18. See Eckhard Jesse, "Die deutsche Koalitionsdemokratie," *Bürger & Staat* 67, no. 2–3 (2017): 107–115, here 110ff.
19. Austria was governed by a grand coalition for forty years over the period of seven decades between 1949 and 2018. During the first period (from 1949 until 1966) under the leadership of the center-right ÖVP, while the center-left SPÖ was at the helm during the second and third periods (1987–2000 and 2007 until 2017).
20. While a "support" model includes official arrangements between all partners that are not dissimilar to an actual coalition agreement, toleration only extends to certain policy areas. The party that is merely tolerating the government accepts the fact though that the latter may seek support for its policies among other political players.
21. See Oskar Niedermayer, "Von der dritten Kraft zur marginalen Partei: Die FDP von 2009 bis nach der Bundestagswahl 2013" in *Die Parteien nach der Bundestagswahl 2013*, ed. Oskar Niedermayer (Wiesbaden, 2014), 103–134.
22. A day after the collapse of negotiations between the Jamaica parties, Schulz pressured the party executive to once again reiterate its refusal to join another grand coalition, a decision that proved to be a major tactical error in hindsight.
23. Three issues were specifically mentioned: the family reunification of refugees with subsidiary protection, temporary employment contracts, and an end to a "two-class system of health care."
24. Schulz had previously publicly ruled out entering Merkel's cabinet on a number of occasions.
25. After the election of then-foreign minister Frank-Walter Steinmeier as federal president, a major SPD achievement for which Gabriel could take credit, the office had become vacant.
26. Both CDU (26.8 percent) and CSU (6.2 percent) combined to win 33 percent of the vote with the respective shares constituting a ratio of around 4.3 to 1. Accordingly, the CSU should only have received two ministerial posts.
27. See Sheri Berman, "The Lost Left," *Journal of Democracy* 27, no. 4 (2016): 69–76, doi: 10.1353/jod.2016.0063.
28. This is a common problem for Europe's social democrats. See René Cuperus, "Social democracy and the populist challenge" in *Why the left loses: The decline of the centre-left in comparative perspective*, ed. Rob Manwaring and Paul Kennedy (Bristol, 2018), 185–202; Frank Decker, "The Plight of the SPD as a Reflection of the Crisis of European Social Democracy," *Journal of Social Democracy* 7, no. 2 (2018): 21-25.
29. See Kai Arzheimer, "Working Class Parties 2.0? Competition between centre-left and extreme right parties" in *Class Politics and the Radical Right*, ed. Jens Rydgren (Abingdon, 2013), 75–90; Sarah L. de Lange, "A new winning formula? The Programmatic Appeal of the Radical Right," *Party Politics* 13, no. 4 (2007): 411–435, doi: 10.1177/1354068807075943.
30. The AfD and Left Party won a combined 39.7 percent of the vote in the east, compared to a share of 18.1 percent in the west. The parties of the grand coalition won a respective 41.5 and 56.0 percent.

··· Chapter 2 ···

POINTING FINGERS AT THE MEDIA?

Coverage of the 2017 Bundestag Election

Alexander Beyer and Steven Weldon

The 2017 Bundestag election likely will long be remembered as a pivotal moment in German politics.[1] The far-right and openly anti-immigrant Alternative for Germany (Alternative für Deutschland, AfD) not only entered parliament for the first time, but its inflammatory and divisive campaign rhetoric pushed beyond the boundaries of what was long considered acceptable tenets of German political discourse. Like other far-right parties across Europe in recent years, the AfD rode a wave of anti-immigrant, anti-establishment sentiment and a growing backlash against European integration to capture nearly 13 percent of the vote. It is now the third largest party in the Bundestag and following the renewal of the grand coalition between the Christian Democrats (CDU/CSU) and Social Democrats (SPD) has an even more prominent platform as the official opposition party.

As we try to make sense of the AfD's sudden rise to prominence and the long-term implications for German and European politics, many have pointed a finger at the media, especially in the immediate aftermath of the election: "It's the journalists' fault!" declared the *Frankfurter Allgemeine Zeitung. Stern* took a more measured approach with a story about "Why the media is partly to blame for the success of the AfD," and how the media helped propel the AfD to success became a central issue for debate during the talk show *Hart aber Fair.*[2]

In many ways, this is understandable. The media does play a critical role in informing voters in election campaigns, and the German election happened amidst growing controversy and concern surrounding the media's influence on other recent high-profile elections, like the Brexit vote in the United Kingdom and Donald Trump's election in the United States. Face-

Notes for this section begin on page 74.

book, Twitter, and other social media outlets, undoubtedly played a key role in spreading "fake news" from fringe sources and inciting fears about immigrants and ethnic minorities in these elections. There is also a growing recognition, however, that more mainstream, traditional media outlets also played a role in disseminating and promoting such stories, especially in the United States presidential election. Was this also the case in the German election? That is, did social and mainstream media coverage advantage the AfD and help propel their breakthrough? That is the question we examine in this article.

To answer this question, we need to understand what media bias looks like. One commonly held belief among pundits and the public alike is that media bias means trying to persuade voters on specific issues or to support certain parties. Commentators on the right, for example, often speak of a left-wing media bias that is hostile to conservative principles and parties. Journalists also have tended to lean to the ideological left, and newspapers' op-ed pages and the tradition of official candidate endorsements does give them a forum to sway voters and in theory affect election outcomes.

Despite this common belief, there is little evidence the media actually presents biased coverage or persuades voters in this way, that is, convinces them to change policy positions or their vote choice. Instead, the principal way that media appears to be able to influence voters is through a process of what is called priming and agenda-setting. The key idea is that by choosing which stories to publish or promote, the media helps determine the issues that are freshest in voters' minds and salient for an election. Because different parties tend to be more or less associated with different issues, this can provide them with a "saliency bump" that favors them at the ballot box and ultimately helps tilt the election in their direction.

Applied to the 2017 German election and, specifically to the role of the media in the AfD's breakthrough, this would mean that the media published or promoted a disproportionate share of stories about the AfD or stories directly related to the party's defining issues: immigration and Euroskepticism. As we will demonstrate, this does indeed appear to be the case, especially in the final month of the campaign. In a significant departure from past elections, immigration and the European Union, dominated media coverage. Yet, as we also consider, it is not entirely clear the media should be blamed for this disparity in coverage or the change from past elections. Our analysis suggests that in a way the media was simply giving the voters what they wanted.

In this study, we draw on several textual data sources that we think offer unique insights into election dynamics and will be of keen interest to students of German politics. Our analysis focuses on online news. Internet usage has been steadily increasing since data became available and about 72 percent of the German population was online on a daily basis in 2017.[3] Although there are many ways to use the internet, the longer time spent surfing, the more likely people are exposed to a news item. Therefore, we collected and machine coded over 8,000 online articles from the four most frequently visited German-language news outlets: *Focus, Bild, Die Welt,* and *Der Spiegel.* These data allow us to examine the prominence of the AfD in media coverage relative to the other parties, the key issue topics, and how both of these changed over the campaign. Second, we use Google trend searches for "refugees" (*Flüchtlinge*) as an indicator of public interest in one of the AfD's defining issues. Finally, we draw on Twitter to assess the AfD's dominance of social media and nontraditional channels of information dissemination throughout the campaign. Twitter shares serve in this case as an indicator for public interest in the different German political actors during the campaign.

Before turning to an analysis of these unique data sources, we first review previous research on media bias, focusing on how issue salience and priming work to influence public opinion and possibly voter behavior and, thus, electoral outcomes. We then discuss why issues close to the AfD and other far-right parties, particularly immigration, may be even more prone to priming than conventional political issues. We argue this is because these types of "identity politics" issues map onto already salient social divisions in society and help activate in-group and out-group bias. After presenting our analyses, we conclude with a discussion about how "public demand" and "media as a business" interact to help shape media coverage and how that might be increasing with the rise of alternative media outlets.

The Media: Issue Salience and the Actor-Policy Options Frame

The media's power to set and shape the political agenda has long been recognized in communication studies.[4] Early research in this field quickly rejected the notion that the media's key power was in persuading the public and instead pointed to the role of agenda-setting and priming. Bernhard Cohen's assertion from 1963 might well be the most often cited insight on this: the press "may not be successful much of the time in telling people what to think, but it is stunningly successful in telling its readers what to think about."[5] Moreover, in the era of only a few media outlets and families gathering around the television each evening to watch the news broadcasts, their power to include or exclude specific topics and shape the public agenda seemed unquestioned.[6] Contributing to the importance of priming over persuasion was the normative expectation that traditional media's role in society was to act as an unbiased source of news that informed the public about political events, processes, issues, and the positions of political elites on these issues.[7]

While the explosion of mass communication and the rise of social media have undoubtedly changed the relationship between media and the public and how we consume information, there is little disagreement that priming and agenda-setting are still the main mechanisms through which the media might influence elections.[8] If anything, this tendency has only been reinforced and strengthened. People now have the freedom to choose from a much broader range of media outlets from across the ideological spectrum, and they often choose outlets that reflect their pre-existing political ideologies and biases.[9] This gives even less room for voters to learn about other parties' positions, let alone to actually be persuaded to change their position.

Central to the formation of mass opinion are differences in issue salience. Salient issues are those that are at the top of the mind to people and they are ripe for priming by media and other political actors. This is because such issues are more likely to be retrieved from memory when it is time to assess candidates or policies.[10] Especially for summary political evaluations, like checking a box on Election Day, a primed issue is more likely to be used as one of "the standards by which government, policies and candidates for public office are judged."[11] This has been extensively demonstrated for media impacts on the evaluation of U.S. presidents.[12] Research outside the U.S. reaches similar conclusions.[13]

The potential influence of mass communicated politics on individual behavior, however, goes beyond just driving issue salience. This is because issues are almost always directly connected to different political actors, and media outlets play a critical role in enhancing and reinforcing these connections. The direct connection between issues and actors means that as one increases so does the other. This, in turn, works to limit and bias voters' sense of the issue-related policy options and the actors best able to solve policy problems. Moreover, in an effort to get a saliency advantage, parties play an active role in this process. To facilitate this link, parties carefully choose their issue agendas to reflect the priorities of their supporters or potential supporters.[14] They also actively project those positions through media outlets and aim to frame issues so that they limit the perceived policy options for voters.[15] With repeated media exposure of this actor-policy choice set frame, parties are able to increase their association in public discourse with issues they want to emphasize and decrease it for issues that are not close to them.

The effect of this bias depends to some degree on the issues of the day and external events. This is because after repeated associations on "their" issues, parties only have a limited ability to increase their association to new or other issues. Moreover, consistent with the logic of priming and issue salience, taking up another party's issues risks advantaging that party because of perceptions of issue ownership.[16] As such, the interdependencies between priming and agenda-bias may affect voter support in either direction: hurting support for a party whose agenda-elements are not gaining much salience, while it benefits parties where media agenda and issue agenda are in line. Evidence suggests that effects of agenda bias affect voter preferences more strongly than tonality bias, where evaluations are consistently more favorable for one party.[17] How an actor is described matters less than the context in which it is presented. As we will argue, this likely played a critical role in the AfD's success in 2017–an external event, the influx of refugees in 2015 and 2016, helped make immigration highly salient for the election, and this was an issue with which the AfD was already strongly associated.

Priming: Immigration and Euroscepticism

For the issues close to the AfD and other far-right, populist parties, issue salience and priming seem particularly powerful in shaping public opinion and voting behavior. This is because their key issues– immigration and Euroscepticism–also map onto existing social group divisions, and therefore, lend themselves more easily to processes of in-group/out-group differentiation and bias. As social psychological research has repeatedly shown, activation of group-based identity is a powerful prime and predictor of political behavior.[18]

Political scientists, too, have long recognized the power of psychological attachment to in-groups for understanding political behavior. Much of this research has focused on the power of partisan identity.[19] Nevertheless, race and ethnicity can play an even more powerful role in structuring political attitudes and vote choice.[20] Indeed, Martin Gilens finds that over time with repeated association an issue can become so affectively laden with race that it can prime voters in favor of a specific party on its own.[21] In many European countries, religious divisions have played a similar role historically in structuring political opinion and conflict.[22]

While racial divisions have been limited in Europe and religious divisions seem to have largely faded with secularization over the past century, another type of social division–between natives and migrants–has become increasingly salient across Europe, including Germany. Migration has long been a challenge for countries, but globalization processes, increased geographic mobility, and rapidly aging populations have helped accelerate its pace. This has helped put migration squarely on the political agenda and there is little doubt it is transforming politics across Europe at the national and European Union levels.[23]

In many ways, migration, especially today, has the potential to be a much more powerful social division than race or religion. This is because it often maps onto several overlapping but distinct group divisions and markers: race, religion, and citizens versus noncitizens. Much of this has to do with how migration patterns have changed, and the reality is that today many more migrants are visible minorities while the native populations are overwhelmingly white across Europe. Like racial differences in the United States, race typically provides a visual cue that serves to repeatedly prime voters on migration in their day-to-day lives. Religion too is often tied to this, especially for Muslims and others who commonly wear clothing that signals their religious identity and marks them as “outsiders” to natives. Finally, immigration also maps onto the division between citizens and noncitizens, which functions as a state sanctioning of in-groups and out-groups. This overlapping of race, religion, and citizenship status has helped the AfD and other far-right parties tie immigration to a wide range of other contemporary political issues, including terrorism and security, social welfare, and especially cultural identity.

The AfD, Immigration, and the Refugee Influx

From the moment the AfD arrived on the German political scene in 2013, its leaders sought to promote and capitalize on divisions between Germans and “outsiders.” At first, it focused on criticism of the European Union and the German political establishment, especially regarding “German bailouts” of southern European countries after the global financial crisis. Not long after, it began to develop an explicitly anti-immigrant faction. By 2015, following the ouster of Bernd Lucke as its leader, there was no longer any doubt that the party was firmly anti-immigrant, and, under the then leadership of Frauke Petry, the AfD strengthened its ties with other far-right, populist, and anti-immigrant parties across Europe.

The AfD's transformation into a full-fledged anti-immigrant party coincided with a subsequent rise in public opinion polls. These developments, however, also coincided with an external event outside of the party's control, which made migration a highly salient issue in the German electorate, namely the influx of refugees from Syria and other countries that peaked in late 2015. It is difficult to say precisely how much this played into the AfD's rise to prominence but theories of issue salience and agenda-setting suggest that it was likely critical. Regardless, in trying to determine whether the media is to blame for the AfD's success in the 2017 election, it is not only important to know whether the media's coverage favored the AfD, but also whether the media was simply responding to public demand. We now turn to examining these questions with an in-depth analysis of party coverage, topic coverage, and public issue concerns and interests over the course of the campaign.

Data and Methods

The focus of this paper is on the political coverage of the 2017 German federal election campaign. To get a sense of what was covered we require an exhaustive collection of news texts. To collect these data, we relied on services provided by the news aggregator *Factiva*, which assembles news texts from around the world and makes them available to researchers. The mainstream sources chosen–*Focus, Bild, Die Welt, and Der Spiegel*–were based on web-traffic rank orders. Rankings were acquired from *alexa.com*, a service for online analytics. We used this index to select the four most widely read German-language online sources for news and analyzed over 8,500 articles published between 1 July and 24 September 2017, the day of the election.

Our focus here is on the general topics of articles, not their tone. We are interested in the electorate's exposure to different campaign issues. Thus, we selected the most visited websites without regard for their ideological tendencies. We use machine coding and a dictionary-based approach with word counts to measure party and topic salience. We chose seven policy areas of interest in this election and developed a list of keywords whose occurrences generate the data analyzed the article. These terms are deliberately general, with, for example, terms like *Flüchtling, Einwanderung*, and *Asyl* (refugee, immigration, and asylum) clearly indicating a focus on immigration, while *Umwelt, Elektromobilität*, and *erneuerbare Energie* (environment, electromobility, and renewable energy) capture environmental concerns. This method allows us to generate reliable indexes to assess the focus of each article. We then examine the daily share of mentions of an issue vis-à-vis all other issues.[24]

To determine the degree to which the different parties received different amounts of coverage, we assembled dictionaries with the party names, party abbreviations, and names of the party leaders. In the case of Angela Merkel and Martin Schulz, both with surnames among the most common in the German language, we also combined their respective job title and aspiration with their last names: Bundeskanzlerin Merkel and Kanzlerkandidat Schulz. We generated the sums and shares of daily mentions for each party from our textual data. This works well for the four major parties, but it does have a drawback for the Greens (*Die Grünen*) and the Left party (*Die Linke*). This is because they rarely use their official party abbreviations and run under "Greens" and "The Left" respectively. Both words are attributes as well as party names, meaning they appear far too commonly in regular language usage for us to accurately estimate a specific reference to them as political objects alone. For this reason, and since our primary focus is not on these two parties, we only include names of leaders and frontrunners for die *Grünen* and *die Linke.* Nonetheless, our results are certainly limited in underestimating the mentions of these two parties in our analysis.[25]

For both issues and party mentions, we weighted the results depending on the publication they were drawn from to account for the difference in audience reach. We want our indicator to reflect the extent to which these articles reach the electorate, not simply the overall media content, something that is critical generally, given the explosion in alternative media sources. We calculated the required factors relying on page rankings sourced from alexa.com, a popular service providing website statistics and analytics, using this formula:

$$w_{pub_i} = 1 + \log \frac{\alpha_{min}}{\alpha_{pub_i}}$$

The weight *w* attributed to an appearance in publication *i* is calculated from the sum of one plus the logarithmic function of the minimum page-ranking in the category over *i*'s ranking. Values for our four outlets range from 1 to 1.56. This is the basis on which we generated the daily share of party mentions (see Figures 2.1 and 2.2) and policy topics (see Figure 2.3), where appearances in higher-ranked publications add to a slightly higher weight in the share of mentions.

Findings: The Media and its Messages

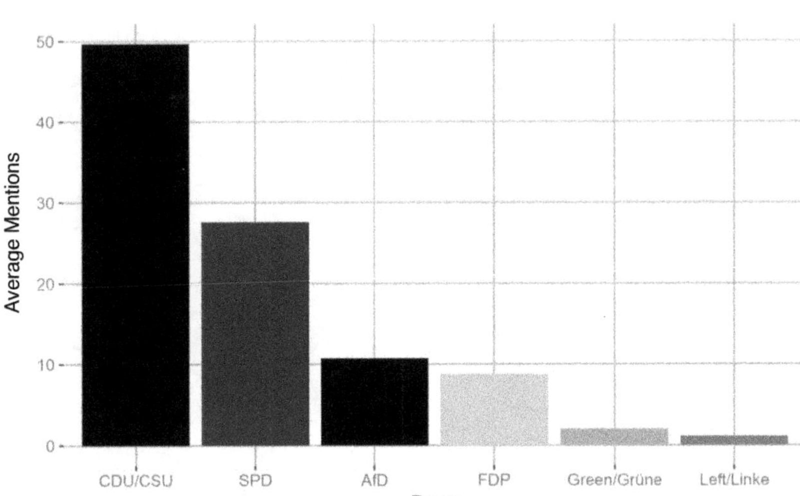

Figure 2.1: Average Share of Mentions by Party during the 2017 German Election Campaign

Source: Website articles of *Focus, Bild, Die Welt,* and *Der Spiegel* from July 1st, 2017 to September 24th, 2017.

Our analysis rests on graphical representation of the data. We start with a simple bar graph, Figure 2.1, which shows the average share of mentions by party over the whole *Wahlkampfsommer* (campaign summer). As one can see, the CDU/CSU enjoys the largest share of mentions. As we know, incumbency advantage and *Kanzlerinnenbonus* (chancellor bonus) typically lead to regular appearances in reporting, even if that is simply as a reference point for an article. References to the SPD come next, well ahead of the AfD in third with an overall-average of 10.7 percent of mentions. The Free Democrats (FDP) received enough references to put them in fourth position. Overall, the order of parties is generally in line with the official election results, and if we stopped here we would reject the notion that the AfD received a disproportional degree of exposure in the online media.

Figure 2.2, however, introduces the pattern of party mentions over time. As one can see, the lead in exposure for the Christian Democrats holds, but it decreases over time. Upon closer examination, a large part of the CDU/CSU exposure in July and early August seems to be related to the passing of the former Chancellor Helmut Kohl, who died on 16 June 2017 and who was honored with a European act of state before burial on 1 July. This initially high proportion of mentions drops off quickly, but it does recover

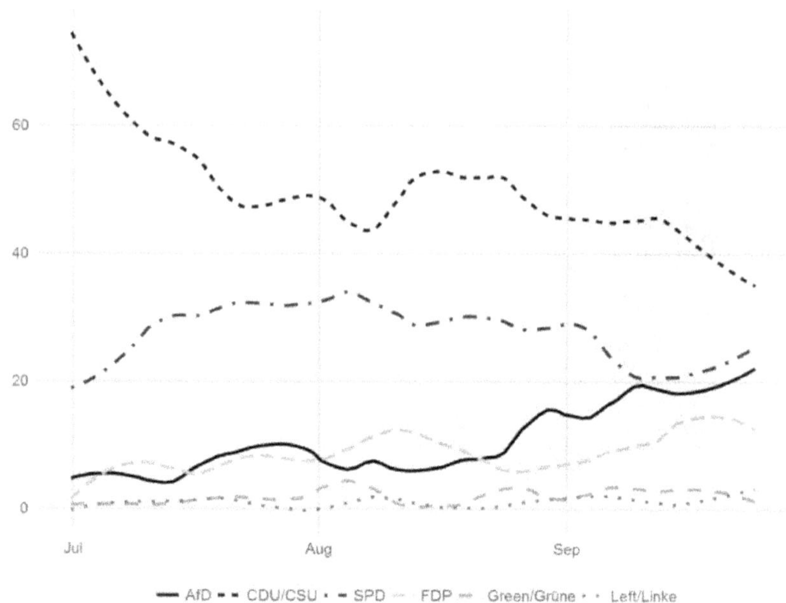

Figure 2.2: Daily Average Shares of Mentions by Parties
Source: Website articles of *Focus, Bild, Die Welt,* and *Der Spiegel* from July 1st, 2017 to September 24th, 2017.

again in mid August. This period also saw the tragic terrorist attack on Barcelona's Ramblas avenue, as well as the increasing rhetorical tension over events on the Korean peninsula, which put Merkel's role as chancellor into focus. The bump is carried further when she and her party become increasingly active as campaigners during late August, but the tendency points downwards from that point onwards.

References to the SPD do not follow either a linear upward or downward trend overall. Instead, the mentions of the Social Democrats show an increase through July and early August, during a time when Schulz and the SPD campaign made early efforts to mobilize support. This initial increase in references is only sustained until early August, after which the SPD's efforts appear to run out of steam. Relative shares drop for the SPD until the second week of September before catching a small upswing late in the campaign during the last two weeks before the election, when political reporting overall is almost entirely focused on the impeding election.

Most importantly for our purposes, we see a similar increase for the AfD around the same time. Strikingly, mentions of the anti-immigrant, far-right party get to within a few percentage points of the Social Democratic share. Data suggest an upward tendency throughout the whole summer for the

AfD, with a sharper increase starting about one month before the election. With this trajectory, the party surpassed the FDP in mentions. If we were to draw a straight line through all shares of mentions, both Free Democrats as well as the far-right party would be the only ones with a positive slope, meaning an overall increase in share of reporting. The AfD, however, gained the most exposure over the course of the campaign. It starts at about 7 percent of mentions and peaked on election day with over 21 percent of daily references–significantly more than its vote share of just under 13 percent.

The AfD's late and steady rise of mentions during the campaign is a crucial element when assessing the question of disproportionate coverage. The dynamics of political campaigns in postindustrial democracies focus increasingly on nonpartisan voters, for which priming effects are especially relevant due to the absence of well-developed partisan filters.[26] This volatile share of the electorate makes up their minds at a late stage of campaigning season. As such, the potential impact of this late reporting on the AfD is sizable. We use another approach to our data to examine hypotheses regarding why this could have happened.

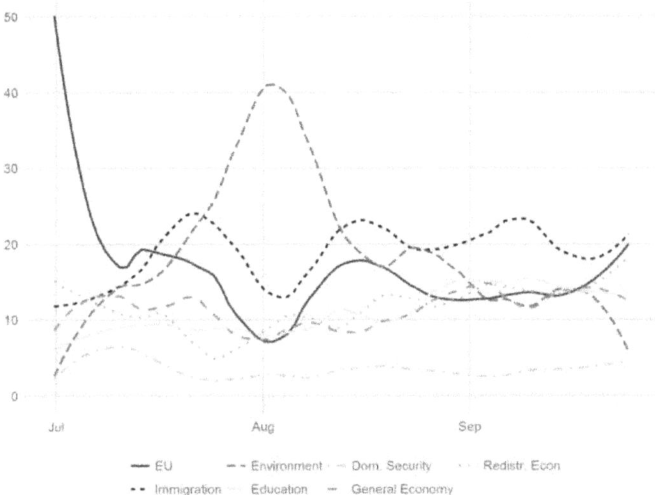

Figure 2.3: Daily Shares of Mentions by Topics
Source: Website articles of *Focus, Bild, Die Welt,* and *Der Spiegel* from July 1st, 2017 to September 24th, 2017.

The lines in figure 2.3 represent the daily share of mentions of specific issues. At first glance, no issue area appears to be stand out, and there is a great deal of variation. A closer look, along with some investigation of the collected data, reveals why: the topic areas with the largest spikes are European Union matters in early July and the environment in early August. Both of these saw events of high interest during the campaign. For EU-related matters it was the funeral and act-of-state for Kohl, one of the primary architects of the Maastricht Treaty and the Euro. Reporting included lots of words from the EU category (for example *Euro*-Parliament, European, and EU integration). As such, the late "eternal chancellor" Kohl contributed to both the strong initial standing of the CDU/CSU, as well as the early dominance of the EU topic area.

Our data include a second sizeable spike when the environment dominated the news landscape in early August. Investigating the raw data reveals that this coverage concerned an event that had the potential to change the lives of millions of German drivers. The so-called Diesel Summit (*Dieselgipfel*), a meeting of policy makers and car manufacturers on 2 August, was intended to clarify how millions of diesel engines could be retrofitted to avoid impending driving bans. The potential impact of measures translated to a high-point of over 40 percent daily topic mentions in our data.

In contrast to these two topic areas experiencing only short-term spikes in coverage, a third topic area, immigration and refugees, was a constant news item in the summer of 2017. These issues have been highly salient and on the political agenda since 2015, and there is little doubt immigration was the central focus of the media's election coverage. Indeed, this high salience

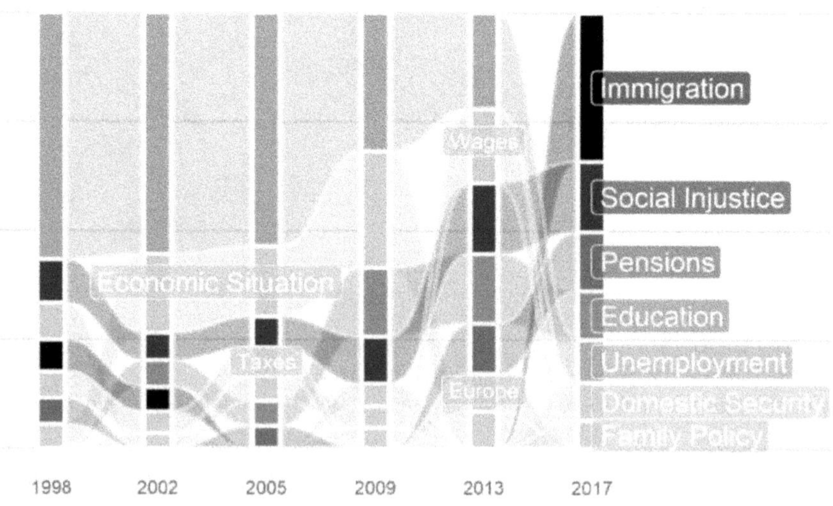

Figure 2.4: Most Important Problem during Campaign
Source: Infratest-dimap polling firm.

of refugees and immigration made the campaign of 2017 unique when compared to previous elections.

What accounts for this steady stream of coverage favorable to the AfD? As we can see in Figure 2.4, a good part of the story has to do with the public's novel amount of interest and concern over these issues. This figure represents surveys conducted over the last six elections about what the electorate saw as the "most important problem" facing Germany.[27] Unlike past elections, economic issues such as unemployment, wages, and the general state of the economy did not make it into the top four of the list. Instead, voters voiced a high amount of concern about immigration, social injustice, and the levels of pensions–three topics that clearly played into the hands of the far-right AfD. Indeed, the AfD could not have faced a more favorable electoral environment. Its issues were at the top of the mind for voters and they had clearly established their credentials on these issues. How does this connect with the media's motivators to cover certain topics more than others?

This question for the "most important problem" is a well-tested and reliable measure for a cross-sectional assessment of issue salience, but we can explore this further and get a sense of how this varied over the campaign with the biggest source of information that voters have available in the twenty-first century–the Internet. If a topic is of interest to an individual, the first instinct is often to seek more information on it and turn to Google. Because it is private, it may be an even better indicator of public attitudes than traditional surveys.[28]

To examine this dynamic over time, we focus on the daily change in searches for *Flüchtlinge* between 1 July and 24 September. To calculate this

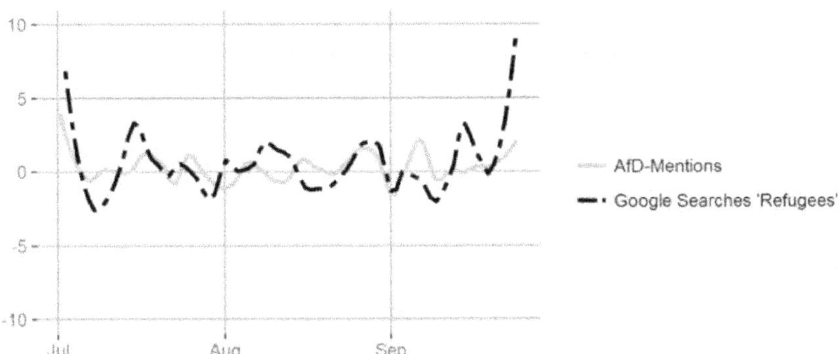

Figure 2.5: Daily Change in Share of AfD-Mentions and Google-Searches for Term "Refugees"

Source: Google-trends searches.

measure, we subtract the value of daily shares on day t from the value of daily shares on the previous day t-1. This allows us to see changes over time throughout the campaign. By overlapping it with daily mentions of the AfD on online news sites, we also can see how the two are related to one another and get a better sense of whether news coverage drove Google queries or whether Google queries drove media coverage. Figure 2.5 plots these results. At first glance, one can see that the two were indeed related to one another. On closer look and with the help of advanced time series analysis,[29] we find that for most of the surveyed timeframe, Google searches preceded the media coverage of the AfD (again, as measured by references in our data of articles from the four major news outlets). This suggests that public demand drove media coverage–at least on this issue and for this election.

Why could that be? Are media outlets, especially the for-profit ones analyzed here, somehow "aware" of Google-searches? Previous research suggests that the answer is "yes," although more research on journalists' behavior is necessary to more unequivocally resolve this issue. [30] Yet, after all, we were able to collect these data rather easily with a little bit of code, and major media outlets have far more resources than we do to track such trends and dive deeply into their intricacies. Moreover, because much of media consumption is digital today, outlets would certainly see internet searches as a better indicator of public interest than conventional tools, such as public opinion surveys. The more important question and one that goes to the heart of whether we should lay blame at the foot of the media is why they would react to this kind of information. We return to this in the summary and discussion below, but first we examine a social media source of information, Twitter, to develop a fuller picture of the media environment for the 2017 election.

We explicitly understand the Google-queries to be a proxy for the salience measure, rather than the actual mechanism connecting readers and authors. To better capture this mechanism, Figure 2.6 is a graphical representation of a different plausible link: the Twitter-landscape during the three weeks running up to the election. We collected 3.5 million German language tweets that contained one or more elements off a list of dozens of keywords[31] associated with politics in Germany. From this corpus, we then extracted all tweets that were a retweet of a different user. As such, the figure represents the degree to which specific users received attention (both accolades and criticism) from others: Each dot ("node") in our network graph represents a unique Twitter user, each connection ("edge") between users represents retweets. For simplicity, we limited our analysis to tweets that were retweeted at least ten times. We used a grouping algorithm to assign the same shades within clusters of nodes.

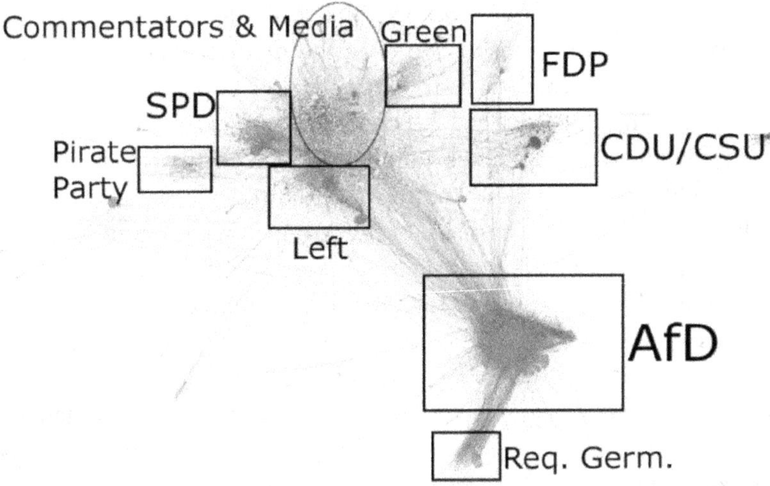

Figure 2.6: Retweet-Network of Election-related tweets during last three weeks of Campaigning
Source: Data collected via Twitter's Streaming API

The spatial distribution of nodes is purely coincidental and fully independent of any ideological leaning. The network-algorithm generates the spatial pattern in a way that best demonstrates the key patterns. The upper half of figure 2.6 represents most of the political spectrum in Germany. On the left is the Pirate Party's cluster, with all major parties fanning out to the right. Sprinkled in between are a few major media-sources and public commentators as well as a group of popular comedians–the two most retweeted being @janboehm and @heuteshow. Each of the political groups features one or two nodes, which are anchors for a semicircle of retweeters–the frontrunners and party leaders stand out by having their messages frequently amplified by other Twitter users.

Dominating the network, and hence, the Twitter landscape for the final three weeks of the campaign is the heap in the lower right of the figure, representing the network of AfD politicians and their most avid retweeters. The large number of nodes and edges indicates that this was the most active group in our data. Furthermore, their corner of the network appears to be less hierarchical: there are no nodes that stand out by being the most frequently retweeted, the cluster is the most homogenous. The part to the lower left of the AfD's group are accounts that appear to be associated with "Reconquista Germania," a digital distribution channel on the communications platform Discord that assembled a loose movement of users to boost far-right content during the run-up to the election. This group of "trolls" gained some notoriety by using sophisticated methods and appearing to be well organized.[32] In our data their Twitter outlets appear to be closely connected to the central and official AfD Twitter channels.

It is difficult to know for certain how much influence AfD and AfD friendly Twitter users had in shaping public discourse before the election. Nonetheless, the presence and size of this group adds an additional piece to an emerging picture of the connection among issue salience, the media, and the electorate. Tweets related to the AfD, often linking to media stories and sometimes fringe sources, were read, consumed, and shared at much higher rates than those related to other parties. This huge disparity fits with our contention that the media was largely reacting to at least online demand for content related to the AfD. This may have further boosted public interest in their favor and helped drive additional media coverage.

Summary and Discussion

In this study, we have sought to provide an overview of the media landscape for the 2017 German election and develop a better understanding of the extent to which the media contributed to the AfD's historic breakthrough. The results provide some evidence that the media environment was indeed friendly to the AfD–the party received a disproportionate share of media mentions. More importantly, coverage of its key issues–immigration and the European Union–were much higher than issues that traditionally resonated with German electorates. Yet, further analysis also casts doubt on the idea that the media is to blame for this. Migration was highly salient for voters in this election, far more so than past elections when bread-and-butter issues like the economy and jobs were at the top of voters' minds. Much of this seems due to events outside of the AfD's or the media's control, namely the influx of refugees into Europe and Germany throughout 2015 and into 2016. It is true that Merkel's CDU-led government welcomed a large influx of refugees into Germany, but we do not know whether that also contributed to the high salience of the migration issue. Certainly, the AfD was well placed to exploit and benefit from this issue salience.

One key question that remains unanswered is why the media would reinforce and amplify the saliency of migration, disproportionate to the AfD's actual vote share. This is especially important if we think of the media as a public good primarily meant to educate the public and even promote good citizenship.[33] We think the answer to this lies in the fact that the media outlets analyzed here are also businesses that are looking to turn a profit. We acknowledge that our sources are exclusively private enterprises. We focus on these because they are the most widely accessed websites in Germany. Shifting the focus to different media, for example the flagship newscast *Tagesschau* or the wide array of nightly talkshows on *ARD* and *ZDF* might lead to different results. With those caveats in mind, our findings add to a discussion that was largely impressionistic and lacking over-time data. We also add insight on the dynamics of dissemination through social media: The threat of alternative "shareable" outlets to traditional ones is very real, especially because people increasingly consume news online. In this study, we consciously chose online news websites to mirror the accelerated turnover of topics that is associated with shorter publication cycles. This is a context in which measures for exposure and "success" of an article are readily available for authors and editors, and through advertising revenues, they directly affect media outlets' baselines. Moreover, they increasingly do so in real time where "clicks" equate directly to profit (or loss).

Analyzing website traffic, counting page impressions, and measuring dwell time on an article are the daily business of online publications.[34] A whole branch of business is devoted to Search Engine Optimization, meant to boost exposure of pages in the listings of search engine providers. Our data suggest that these metrics have done their job. A demand for information has had an impact on the supply from the news stream. Admittedly, we analyze for-profit news outlets here. The various findings might indeed be quite different were we to include public media with their well-established norms of balance and nonpartisanship. Nevertheless, the public media are not part of the top four on-line sources of news. One other limitation is that we just looked at on-line articles and did not look at television coverage where public stations still have a larger role to play. Yet, public media also constantly monitor and are affected by on-line content and the metrics discussed above. Future research should also analyze the dynamics of television coverage.

From a normative perspective, we certainly question whether this is good for democracy. We do not think it is. But, this is a problem that all countries are grappling with and it is bigger than the media outlets that in many senses are just the messengers of a critical society-wide problem. We worry too that social media, with its "click culture" and shorter attention spans, favor affect over thoughtful reflection, and ultimately, works to the advantage of far-right parties like the AfD. That citizens are increasingly relying on on-line sources of information is thus also quite distressing. These parties prey on and fuel our basest human fears, and this undermines our collective social fabric. It seems likely that now that the AfD has broken through, it is likely here to stay, and like other European countries in recent years, the AfD is set to fundamentally reshape party competition in Germany.

Alexander Beyer is a PhD student in Political Science at Simon Fraser University. His primary research interests are in comparative political behavior and media in North America and Europe with a focus on the application of social data analytics. E-mail: abeyer@sfu.ca

Steven Weldon is Associate Professor of Political Science at Simon Fraser University. His research focuses on political representation, extremism, and elections in advanced democracies, and has been published in, among others, the *American Journal of Political Science*, the *British Journal of Political Science*, *European Journal of Political Research*, and *Party Politics*. E-mail: sweldon@sfu.ca

Notes

1. We would like to thank Denver McNeney for his assistance with the data collection, coding, and analysis, and the helpful advice at several points from Vincent Hopkins. We also appreciate feedback on the project from members of the Political Extremism Superfriends Research Group at Simon Fraser University: Federico Cerani, Andrew Fast, Vanna Lodders, Marcus Macauley, and Monica Petek. An earlier version of this paper was presented as a lecture at the 2017 Chaos Communication Congress in Leipzig, Germany.
2. Frank Lübberding, "Die Journalisten sind Schuld!" available at http://www.faz.net/aktuell/feuilleton/medien/der-afd-erfolg-sorgt-fuer-verwirrung-15220986.html, accessed 8 March 2018; Carsten Heidbrömmer, "Warum die Medien eine Mitschuld tragen am Aufstieg der AfD;" available at https://www.stern.de/kultur/tv/warum-die-medien-eine-mitschuld-tragen-am-aufstieg-der-afd-7635500.html, accessed 8 March 2018; WDR, "Hart aber Fair vom 25.09.2017–Die gerupfte Kanzlerin-wie regieren nach dem Debakel der Volksparteien?" available at http://www.ardmediathek.de/tv/Hart-aber-fair/Die-gerupfte-Kanzlerin-wie-regieren-na/Das-Erste/Video?bcastId=561146&documentId=46255678, accessed 8 March 2018.
3. ARD/ZDF Onlinestudie 2017.
4. Jennings Bryant and Dorina Miron, "Theory and Research in Mass Communication," *Journal of Communication* 54 (2004): 662–704.
5. Bernard C. Cohen, *The Press and Foreign Policy*. (Princeton, 1963), 13, emphasis in original.
6. Maxwell E. McCombs and Donald M. Shaw, "The Evolution of Agenda-Setting Research: Twenty-Five Years in the Marketplace of Ideas," *Journal of Communication* 43, no. 2 (1993): 58–67.
7. Denis McQuail, *Media accountability and freedom of publication*. (Oxford, 2003).
8. James N. Druckman, "Priming the Vote: Campaign Effects in a U.S. Senate Election," *Political Psychology* 25, no. 4 (2004): 577–594.

9. Shanto Iyengar and Kyu S. Hahn, "Red Media, Blue Media: Evidence of Ideological Selectivity in Media Use," *Journal of Communication* 59, no. 1 (2009): 19–39.
10. John R. Zaller, *The Nature and Origins of Mass Opinion.* (Cambridge, 1992).
11. Shanto Iyengar and Donald R. Kinder, *News that Matters: Television and American Opinion.* (Chicago, 1987), 63.
12. David R. Roskos-Ewoldsen, Mark R. Klinger, and Beverly Roskos-Ewoldsen, "Media Priming: A Meta-Analysis" in *Mass Media Effects Research: Advances through Meta-Analysis,* ed. Raymond W. Preiss, Barbara Mae Gayle, Nancy Burrell, Mike Allen, and Jennings Bryant (New York, 2006), 53–80.
13. Richard Johnston, André Blais, Henry E. Brady, and Jean Crête, *Letting the People Decide: Dynamics of a Canadian Election* (Montreal, 1992).
14. Stephen Ansolabehere and Shanto Iyengar, "Riding the wave and claiming ownership over issues: The joint effects of advertising and news coverage in campaigns," *Public Opinion Quarterly* 58, no. 3 (1994): 335–357.
15. John R. Petrocik, "Issue ownership and presidential elections," *American Journal of Political Science* 40, no. 3 (1996): 825–850.
16. Éric Bélanger and Bonnie M. Meguid, "Issue salience, issue ownership, and issue-based vote choice," *Electoral Studies* 27, no. 3 (2008): 477–491.
17. Jakob-Moritz Eberl, Hajo G. Boomgaarden, and Markus Wagner, "One Bias fits all? Three Types of Media Bias and their Effects on Party Preferences," *Communication Research* 44, no. 8 (2017): 1125–1148.
18. Henri Tajfel and John Turner, "An Integrative Theory of Intergroup Conflict" in *The Social Psychology of Intergroup Relations,* ed. William G. Austin and Stephen Worchel (Monterey, 1986), 33–47.
19. Angus Campbell, Philip Converse, Warren Miller, and Donald Stokes, *The American Voter* (Chicago, 1960). Gabriel Lenz, *Follow the Leader: How Voters Respond to Politicians' Policies and Performance* (Chicago, 2012).
20. Edward G. Carmines and James A. Stimson, *Issue Evolution: Race and the Transformation of American Politics* (Princeton, 2009); Donald R. Kinder and Cindy D. Kam, *Us against Them: Ethnocentric Foundations of American Opinion* (Chicago, 2009); Michael Tesler, *Post-Racial or Most-Racial? Race and Politics in the Obama Years* (Chicago, 2016).
21. Martin Gilens, *Why Americans Hate Welfare: Race, Media, and the Politics of Antipoverty Policy* (Chicago, 1999).
22. Seymour M. Lipset and Stein Rokkan, *Party Systems and Voter Alignments: Cross-national Perspectives* (Toronto, 1967).
23. Hanspeter Kriesi, Edgar Grande, Martin Dolezal, Marc Helbling, Dominic Höglinger, Swen Hutter, and Bruno Wüst, *Political Conflict in Western Europe* (Cambridge, 2012).
24. We do lose some precision for the measure by not accounting for the effects of length and placement of an article, but our focus is on broad topics rather than article-level effects.
25. This is something we hope to remedy in future studies, but it is a severe challenge, given the massive amount of data and the need to use machine coding to process it.
26. Christopher H. Achen and Larry M. Bartels, *Democracy for Realists: Why Elections Do Not Produce Responsive Government* (Princeton, 2016).
27. Data adapted from infratest dimap. Respondents were asked to name the "two most important problems" to be tackled by a future government. For 1998 through 2013 these surveys were conducted in September; for 2017 in July.
28. Seth Stephens-Davidowitz, "The cost of racial animus on a black candidate: evidence using Google search data," *Journal of Public Economics* 118, no. 1 (2014): 26–40.
29. We ran an error-correction model with a lag of one day. Model specifications are available on request.
30. Hong Tien Vu, "The online audience as gatekeeper: The influence of reader metrics on news editorial selection," *Journalism* 15, no. 8 (2014): 1094–1110.
31. This list includes all names of the six major competing parties, names and Twitter handles of their leading candidates, their associated campaigning-hashtags (for example "*#Zeit-*

fuerMartin" for the SPD, or "*#fedidwgugl*" which is short for "Für ein Deutschland in dem wir gut und gerne leben" for the CDU), as well as the general election-hashtags "*#btw*," "*#btw17*," and "*#btw2017*."

32. Julia Ebner, "How Germany's far right took over Twitter–and tilted the election;" available at https://www.theguardian.com/commentisfree/2017/sep/26/germany-far-right-election-afd-trolls, accessed 8 March 2018.
33. This role is a central legitimacy for fee-financed broadcasting, as it coexists in Germany's system of public and for-profit media. Our present research is focused on for-profit media. We intend to investigate the impact of the public system and its possible effects of opinion-leadership in a future research project.
34. Vu (see note 30).

··· Chapter 3 ···

LGBTI Rights and the 2017 German National Election

Louise K. Davidson-Schmich

In democracies such as the Federal Republic, national elections are theoretically supposed to fill core political functions: allowing citizens to articulate their interests in the run-up to campaigns, giving parties a chance to aggregate these interests into policy platforms, providing voters an opportunity to learn about and select among these competing platforms, and ultimately creating a government to then implement the citizenry's preferred policies.[1] There are, however, both theoretical and empirical reasons to expect that the electoral process will not always serve as a vehicle for transmitting the policy preferences of lesbian, gay, bisexual, transgender, and intersex (LGBTI) citizens, who have long been excluded from rights that their countrymen and women have enjoyed.[2] Sexual minorities are just that, a very small–and, at times, disliked–portion of the electorate, and parties may see little utility to courting their votes. Instead, many advances in LGBTI rights in Germany and elsewhere have been made through the judicial branch, referenda, expert commissions, or pressure from international organizations rather than as the result of electoral mandates.[3]

This article examines the 2017 German national election through the lens of LGBTI interests and examines the ways in which sexual minorities articulated their policy preferences, the degree to which these positions were taken up in party platforms and electoral campaigns, and the extent to which the resulting coalition agreement pledged to address queer citizens' concerns. I argue that this election provided sexual minorities with a high degree of responsiveness on one core issue of importance, due to the presence of what Sarah Childs and Mona Lena Krook refer to as a critical actor,

---

Notes for this section begin on page 99.

while other issues remained largely invisible during the campaign and in subsequent coalition negotiations.[4]

The discussion proceeds as follows. First, I discuss the lack of prior electoral responsiveness to many LGBTI concerns in Germany and elsewhere in order to highlight the unusual nature of the events of 2017; I also introduce the concept of a critical actor. Second, I discuss LGBTI interest articulation in the run-up to the election campaign and then turn to an assessment of the degree to which these citizens' policy concerns were taken up in political parties' election manifestos. Next, I focus on the events of the campaign itself and the resulting coalition negotiations. I conclude with a discussion of the role played by critical actors in the election. The arguments presented here are based on analysis of primary documents, including interest group statements, party platforms, opinion polls, and coalition agreements, as well as on German-language news coverage of the election campaign.

LGBTI Citizens as Strangers to the Polity

In her 2001 book, Shane Phelan characterized LGBTI citizens as "sexual strangers" to full citizenship in democracies such as those in the United States and the Federal Republic of Germany–despite decades of free and fair elections in these countries. Laws passed by the legislative branch have routinely limited the rights of sexual minorities. In Germany, Paragraph 175 of the Civil Code banning homosexual conduct impinged on gay citizens' right to privacy in their own home (Article 13 of the Basic Law). Gay men were prohibited from serving in the military, and, hence, limited in their freedom to select a profession (Article 12). Laws requiring people to undergo medically unnecessary operations and divorce their spouses before changing their sex violated the right to both bodily integrity (Article 2) and to marriage and family (Article 6). Similarly, different tax regulations for heterosexual married couples and homosexual life partners violated the equal treatment clause (Article 3).

Most of the aforementioned laws were overturned only in the twenty-first century following decisions made by the European Court of Justice and the European Court of Human Rights that then were echoed by the German Constitutional Court.[5] This pattern of judicially motivated change was repeated across Western Europe and the United States;[6] for example, the right of same-sex couples to marry in the U.S. was established by the Supreme Court's 2015 *Obergefell v. Hodges* decision. Outside of Germany, LGBTI rights also have advanced through popular referenda, such as the

2005 Swiss and 2015 Irish plebiscites opening civil unions and marriage to same-sex couples.[7] German intersex organizations pursued a "boomerang" approach to legal change, asking the United Nations (UN) to pressure the Merkel government into allowing the parents of intersex children to avoid having to select a sex for their newborn. The Christian Democratic government ultimately drafted such a law at the recommendation of Germany's nonpartisan Ethics Council, which studied the issue after the UN called on Germany to take action.[8] International pressure is in part responsible for the improvement in LGBTI rights in other European countries as well.[9] For example, a 2017 European Court of Human Rights decision led France to change its requirement that transgender people be sterilized before being allowed to change their sex on identity documents.[10] Expert commissions have also brought advances in LGBTI rights in other cases. The UK legalized homosexual intercourse at the recommendation of the Wolfenden Report, written by a nonpartisan group led by an academic; Germany's decision in early 2017 to revoke the convictions of men penalized by Paragraph 175 was spurred by research conducted by the Federal Anti-Discrimination Office.[11] In short, many of the gains in LGBTI rights made in the Federal Republic and elsewhere in recent decades have been due not to political parties implementing campaign promises made in response to voters' calls for improvements to sexual minority rights, but rather due to plebiscites, pressure from courts and international organizations, or on the basis of expert advice.

Given that LGBTI citizens make up only a minority of the electorate, it is perhaps unsurprising that parties have not often placed gay, lesbian, trans* or intersex rights at the forefront of their legislative agendas or campaign appeals.[12] Indeed, it was only in 2017 that the first large-scale pre-election opinion poll of LGBTI voters was even taken to determine the voting preferences of German sexual minorities.[13] LGBTI citizens are not only a small group, they are, even in an era of increasing acceptance, still not completely liked by the population as a whole. A 2016 study commissioned by Germany's federal Anti-Discrimination Office found almost 40 percent of Germans felt uncomfortable seeing men holding hands in public or thinking about the possibility that their child would come out as lesbian or gay. Almost 20 percent believed that homosexuality was unnatural.[14] There is thus little theoretical or empirical reason to expect political parties to pay much attention to LGBTI issues during a national election campaign such as that in the Federal Republic in 2017.

Nonetheless, there is some crossnational empirical research that indicates the presence of openly gay, lesbian, or transgender politicians can inspire legislatures to promote legal equality for LGBT citizens. In a study of ninety-six countries, Andrew Reynolds observed "the evidence suggests ... a single out LGBT [Member of Parliament] is often correlated with improved legal rights;" one mechanism through which this can occur is that such an out politician can "put issues of sexual orientation equality on the agenda."[15] Reynolds's results are consistent with arguments made by scholars of gender and politics such as Childs and Krook, who also find that single "critical actors" can go far to advance women's rights. They explain:

> we define critical actors as legislators who initiate policy proposals on their own and/or embolden others to take steps to promote policies for women... The common feature of critical actors... is their relatively low threshold for political action: they may hold attitudes similar to those of other representatives, but they are much more motivated than others to initiate women-friendly policy reforms.

In contrast to Reynolds's expectation that LGBT politicians improve sexual minority rights, Childs and Krook argued that in their view, critical actors "do not need to be women: in some situations, men may play a crucial role in advancing women's policy concerns."[16]

Thus, this scholarship suggests that one avenue through which sexual minority equality issues might actually come to command attention and action during an election campaign is at the initiative of a critical actor, possibly–but not necessarily–a lesbian, gay, transgender, or intersex politician. All of the major German political parties campaigning for the Bundestag in 2017 had openly homosexual candidates who might have served as critical actors during the campaign.[17]

The remainder of this article documents that LGBTI citizens clearly articulated policy preferences in the run-up to the national election and that these preferences were aggregated into the platforms of many German parties, especially on the left of the political spectrum. Consistent with the arguments above, however, most issues of importance to sexual minorities did not command much attention either in the election campaign itself or in resulting coalition negotiations. The one exception to this pattern–a high degree of national attention and responsiveness to the issue of marriage equality for gays and lesbians–was indeed sparked by an openly gay critical actor, long-time LGBTI rights advocate and Green party politician, Volker Beck. Before turning to the events of 2017, I provide some brief background to the issue of same-sex unions in Germany and rule out other factors that might have caused marriage rights for same-sex couples to move to the forefront of German political debate.

Background to the 2017 Election

In 2001, following over a decade of advocacy, the governing Social Democratic (SPD)-Green coalition created a legal entity known as a Registered Life Partnership, granting gays and lesbians official relationship recognition; however, this construction deliberately fell short of the rights enjoyed by heterosexual married couples.[18] In the almost two decades that followed, the Greens, Left Party, Free Democrats (FDP), and SPD all came to favor replacing life partnerships with what is known colloquially as marriage for everyone–Ehe für alle–including gays and lesbians. These parties proposed multiple bills that would either equalize life partnerships and marriage–for example by allowing life partners to adopt children–or allow same-sex couples to marry.[19] The Greens and Left Party remained outside of government and powerless to pass their proposals. Nevertheless, both the FDP and SPD did enter governing coalitions with the Christian Democrats (CDU/CSU) who opposed both adoption and marriage rights. During their coalitions with the CDU/CSU, neither the Liberals (2009–2013) nor the Social Democrats (2005–2009 and 2013–2017) pressed the Union on adoption or marriage. Both parties abandoned their earlier proposals to improve the legal status of gays and lesbians.

Despite a 2013–2017 coalition agreement pledging to "work toward" ending the discrimination of life partners vis-à-vis married couples, the CDU/CSU/SPD grand coalition acted to do so only twice. In 2014, at the insistence of the Constitutional Court, they passed a law allowing "successive adoptions" in which one life partner was permitted to adopt his or her life partner's previously adopted child; joint adoptions remained closed to life partners, however. In 2015, a Law Clarifying the Rights of Life Partners (Gesetz zur Bereinigung des Rechts der Lebenspartner) made minor adjustments to a number of employment regulations to avoid violating the EU's prohibition of employment discrimination on the basis of sexual orientation. Ignoring detailed proposals by the opposition, CDU/CSU-SPD legislation fell short of ending all the differences between married couples and life partners. Over the course of the eighteenth Bundestag, the SPD voted with the Union over twenty times in the Judiciary Committee to prevent bills allowing Ehe für alle to reach the floor of the Bundestag, despite the Social Democrats' support of these proposals.[20]

Moreover, throughout 2016 and 2017, the group "Demo für alle" vociferously opposed not only Ehe für alle but also red-green state governments' plans to include information about homosexuality and transgender people in school curricula. They organized public demonstrations against LGBTI rights in Wiesbaden and Munich, as well as petitions and postcard campaigns to legislators.[21] By May 2017, opinion polls showed strong public support for both the CDU/CSU and the even more socially conservative Alternative for Germany (AfD).[22] Half a year before the vote, then, the prospect of an election campaign focusing on LGBTI rights or the imminent legalization of same-sex marriage seemed highly unlikely. Adding to this probability was the decision by the Green Party not to place LGBTI rights activist and long-time Member of the Bundestag, Beck, on their party list following his March 2016 arrest for possession of crystal meth.[23] Beck had long been one of the few national-level politicians in Germany to actively push a legislative agenda advocating for the rights of sexual minorities.

Despite this inauspicious beginning, however, marriage equality soon became the focus of debate among the leaders of Germany's major political parties and was legalized just as election season began. What can account for the high level of responsiveness to sexual minorities in this federal election campaign? The sudden vote on Ehe für alle was not driven by a mandate from the Constitutional Court as many recent developments in German LGBTI rights have been. Nor was there any abrupt change in international pressure for marriage equality. No expert commission had weighed in on the subject since the European Parliament's 1994 Roth Report. While a decisive majority of Germans, even among the most conservative voters, favored allowing gays and lesbians to marry, this was not a recent development. The tide of public opinion in favor of marriage equality had already turned in 2015.[24] While all parties represented in the Bundestag, except the CDU/CSU, included support for marriage equality in their 2017 party platforms, they had done so in 2013 as well, the year the incumbent government had pledged to "work toward" ending discrimination of life partners vis-à-vis married spouses. The events of June 2017, I argue, were instead driven by Beck, who epitomized Childs and Krook's definition of a critical actor.[25]

LGBTI Interest Articulation in 2017

Before discussing Beck's role, I examine LGBTI interest articulation prior to the start of the campaign by documenting positions taken by the German Gay and Lesbian Association (Lesben- und Schwulenverband in Deutschland, LSVD), the country's largest LGBTI interest group. This organization has clearly expressed a large range of policy propositions designed to enhance the legal rights and well-being of sexual minorities. Moreover, opinion polling indicates a high degree of overlap between the stances of LGBTI voters and the LSVD's standpoint–over 85 percent of queer voters responding to a national survey agreed that five of the association's six issue areas depicted below were either "important" or "very important" to their community.[26]

Since 1994, the LSVD has published "Election Scorecards" (*Wahlprüfsteine)* in the run up to national votes, stating the group's policy preferences and measuring the degree to which German political parties adopt these positions in their manifestos. 2017 was no exception. In April, the group identified twenty-five key topics and asked the largest parties (CDU/CSU, SPD, Greens, Left Party, FDP, and AfD) where they stood on these issues.[27] For ease of presentation, I collapse the Association's priorities into six categories:

1. Marriage and Family Rights: The association expressed a preference for changing Paragraph 1353 of the German Civil Code to allow both same-sex and opposite-sex couples to marry. In an attempt to prevent the SPD, FDP, and Greens from ignoring this issue when negotiating a postelection coalition with the Christian Democrats, they further urged all parties to make Ehe für alle a precondition for any coalition. If marriage equality were not obtained, the LSVD urged parties to at least assist same-sex couples in exercising their right to family formation by allowing life partners to access reproductive medicine and adoption exactly as heterosexual married couples could. They also called upon parties to "modernize" family law, for example, by allowing children to have more than two legal parents. This latter issue is of importance to "rainbow families" (those headed by same-sex couples) in which there is often a biological parent who has legal ties to a child in addition to the two same-sex parents raising the child, one of whom remains a virtual legal stranger to the youth.[28]

2. Antidiscrimination Laws: The LSVD called on parties to support six different types of legislation to improve the legal status of LGBTI citizens. These included:

(a) Amending Article 3 of the Basic Law to include an explicit mention of sexual orientation and gender identity as categories protected from discrimination;

(b) Changing Germany's Antidiscrimination Law to allow class-action complaints (*Verbandsklagen)* about unequal treatment in addition to the currently permitted individual complaints. The association also called for the removal of exemptions to the Antidiscrimination Law for religious organizations;

(c) Calling on Germany to drop EU-level opposition to the inclusion of sexual orientation and gender identity as protected categories in European law, in the same way that gender and ethnicity currently are;
(d) Inserting a specific reference to homophobia and transphobia into Germany's hate crimes statute. Currently, Paragraph 46 of the Criminal Code only defines these offenses as having "racist, xenophobic, or other inhumane (*menschenverachtende*)" motivations.
(e) Allowing intersex citizens to opt for a sex other than "male" or "female" on identity documents. Since 2013, German law has allowed parents of intersex babies not to register a sex for their child at birth, but there are no provisions for intersex adults to have their identity documents changed and no permanent category on identity documents in addition to male or female;[29]
(f) Reforming Germany's Transsexual Law, which currently requires people interested in changing their sex and name on identity documents to present a medical evaluation in a court of law and receive a judge's permission before being allowed to do so. The association instead preferred sex and name changes to become simple administrative procedures that any person could initiate on their own, without having to convince a judge they are ill.

3. Health: A third set of policy preferences focused on the health needs of LGBTI citizens, favoring a vaguely-defined "diverse and equitable" (*diversitätsgerecht*) public healthcare system. In this section of the election scorecard, the LSVD also called on parties to ban non-necessary surgeries on intersex minors, to outlaw conversion therapy, and to commission a national-level study on LGBTI healthcare needs in Germany. Medical practitioners have often sought to "correct" intersex bodies to appear more typically male or female, despite there being no medical need for such interventions and these procedures often having serious side effects such as a loss of sexual functioning. Surgeries have often been performed on infants without informed consent by them or their parents.[30] Conversion therapy is a practice that seeks to "cure" homosexuality, viewing it as a disorder. There is no evidence that such therapy is effective, but it has been shown to heighten the risk of depression and suicide among young people who have experienced it. The practice has been condemned by mainstream medical practitioners including the Deutsche Gesellschaft für Psychiatrie und Psychotherapie, Psychosomatik und Nervenheilkunde, the World Psychiatric Association, and the American Medical Association.[31]

4. Refugees: The LSVD also weighed in on issues relating to immigrants, calling on parties to protect LGBTI refugees from hate crimes committed both inside shelters and in public spaces. A further demand was to ensure that LGBTI refugees would not be sent back to countries that criminalized homosexuality, such as Morocco, Algeria, and Tunisia. Currently, the Federal Republic's immigration policy considers these nations "safe countries of origin" to which gay and lesbian refugees can be deported. Finally, the Association proposed ensuring that integration courses for refugees settling in Germany contain a curriculum stressing that acceptance and nondiscrimination of LGBTI people are important democratic values.

5. Foreign Policy: A fifth set of policy preferences involved promoting human rights for gay, lesbian, intersex, and transgender people abroad. The LSVD supported training German diplomatic personnel to better advocate on behalf of these rights while serving outside the country. They also demanded that the EU and the German Foreign Office provide financial assistance to LGBTI rights groups in the global south and Eastern Europe. In addition, the Association called for financial support to the Hirschfeld Eddy Foundation, an LSVD-backed organization which assists international LGBTI rights activists through networking and informational campaigns.

6. "Everyday Acceptance" for LGBTI People of All Ages: The final sections of the election scorecard urged the parties campaigning for elective office to support a "National Action Plan Against Homophobia and Transphobia" that includes concrete targets to be implemented along a specific timeline as well as adequate funding to achieve these ends.[32] The Association stressed that these goals should include resources specifically targeted at youth (for example educational programs and counseling centers) and senior citizens (for example sensitivity training for personnel in old age homes).

In sum, Germany's lesbian, gay, bisexual, transgender, and intersex citizens clearly expressed a broad range of preferences on a wide array of issues in advance of the national election campaign.

Interest Aggregation in 2017: Parties' Stances on LGBTI Issues

The six major parties competing in the election then had an opportunity to state their stances on the above issues, both in their written responses to the LSVD and in their party programs. The LSVD then evaluated the parties on a five-point scale from "super" to "dangerous" (*gefährlich*), publishing a colorful chart with emojis illustrating parties' rankings on each issue.[33] Figure 3.1 summarizes the LSVD's assessment of party platforms. The darker the color, the closer a given party was to the gay and lesbian association's preferred positions. Clearly, the greatest convergence occurred between the LSVD and the Left Party and Greens, and the least affinity was between the LSVD and the AfD. This result is consistent with the evidence both from other research on sexuality and politics, which finds postmaterialist parties such as the Greens most likely to promote LGBT rights,[34] and from research on gender and politics, which finds that on doctrinal issues (such as marriage and family law) and class-based issues (such as funding health care for trans* people), communist and other left parties are the parties most supportive of gender equality.[35] The section below briefly summarizes the German parties' stances on the issues important to gay, lesbian, transgender, and intersex voters in 2017.

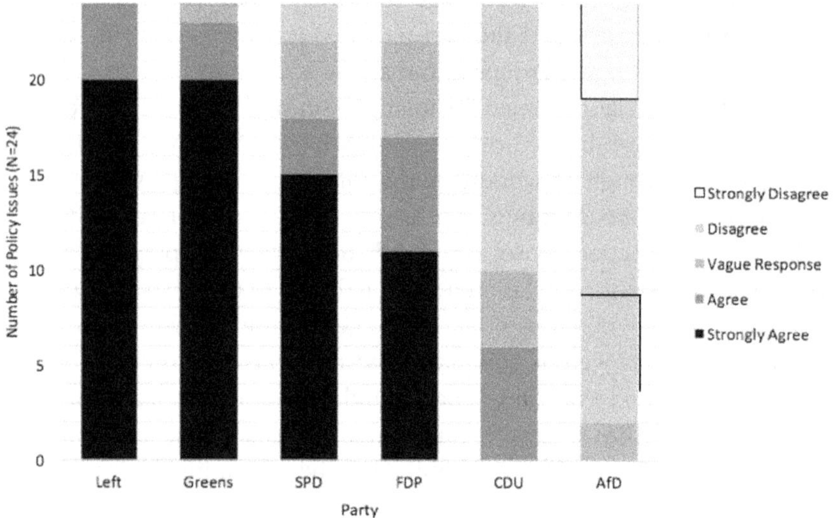

Figure 3.1: Parties' Positions on LSVD Policy Priorities
Source: Lesben- un Schwulenverband in Deutschland, "Sieben LSVD-Forderungen zur Bundestagswahl 2017."

The Left Party received the highest ranking from the LSVD on twenty-one of twenty-four points on the scorecard. The exceptions included "diverse and equitable" health care (a topic on which no party was rated "strongly agree,") promoting LGBTI rights abroad including supporting development aid for pro-gay nongovernmental organizations (NGOs) in Eastern Europe and the global south, and creating a climate of "everyday acceptance." The association rated them "agree" on these issues.

The Left's platform, entitled "Social. Just. Peace. For Everyone.," raised a number of additional issues not appearing on the LSVD's election scorecard.[36] Consistent with the party's leftist economic ideology, most of these topics were related to finances, and, in keeping with their communist roots, they supported changes to traditional, doctrinal, conceptions of family. The party argued:

> Outdated privileges for marriage should be overcome. In the future, the special protection and promotion by the state and society should benefit not married couples but those who live with children, or with people in need of care, and who need to be compensated for the disadvantages they experience as a result. ... Here it shouldn't just be monogamous two-person relationships that are allowed to care for one another, but rather any community that feels connected. That can mean a relationship encompassing more than two people. These people should enjoy unlimited rights to visitation in case of illness, the right to adopt, and the freedom to testify against one another. At the same time, special subsidies are due when a member must be cared for or where children are present.

This construction would benefit, for example, single and childless gay and lesbian senior citizens aging with friends rather than family. For rainbow families, the Left Party proposed the creation of up to four co-parents who would be able to enjoy both tax benefits and subsidies, as well as the obligation to support each other financially and share inheritances. In addition to reparations for intersex medical victims, the party also called on the federal government to investigate Nazi-era abuses of transgender citizens and to pay reparations to the victims. Finally, the Left argued that it should be a crime for media outlets to glorify anti-LGBTI violence.

The Greens issued both a platform entitled "The Future Will be Made from Courage" and a separate "Queer Electoral Program."[37] The LSVD also rated the Greens "strongly agree" on all but three issues. Moreover, the "Queer Electoral Program" went beyond some of the demands the association brought up. For example, the party advocated for the denial of visas to artists they referred to as "hate singers," such as some Jamaican reggae singers noted for their homophobic lyrics. The "Queer Electoral Program" also proposed the creation of a legal status known as co-parent (individuals with "*elterliche Mitverantwortung*,") allowing a given child two co-parents in addition to two biological parents. This construction would, for example, grant legal recognition to a gay sperm donor aiding a lesbian couple to conceive a child the three wanted to raise together. In addition, the Greens promised financial reparations for intersex citizens who have been the victims of involuntary surgeries.

In two areas, the Greens were ranked as "agreeing" (rather than "strongly agreeing") with the LSVD. Although the "Queer Electoral Platform" called on health care plans to offer free HPV vaccines and PrEP, greater access to (voluntary) HIV testing, free condoms and lubricants to people at high risk of contracting HIV, as well as hormone therapy or sex-change operations for trans* people, these healthcare-related demands did not earn the highest ranking for "diverse and equitable" health care.[38] Second, the Greens did not specifically call for additional EU or German Foreign Office funding to queer advocacy groups in developing nations, as desired by the LSVD. Finally, their support of federal funding for NGOs aiding LGBTI refugees in Germany was considered "vague;" parties making specific reference to state (as opposed to nongovernmental) actions received higher rankings on the scorecard.

The SPD's program, entitled "Time for More Justice" received a more mixed evaluation from the LSVD than did the Left's and the Greens' platforms.[39] The Socialists earned the association's highest ranking for their stances on family rights, all but one health issue,[40] and all antidiscrimination positions except hate crimes, as the party argued that the existing law's "other inhumane" motivations category was adequate to prosecute anti-LGBTI hate crimes. The Social Democrats disagreed with the LSVD's position on repatriating queer refugees to countries outlawing homosexuality. Their answers to the questions regarding integration curricula for refugees, the National Action Plan, and funding foreign LGBTI activist groups were classified as vague. While they earned an "agree" rating on all other topics, the SPD's program did not go beyond any of the issues brought up by the LSVD.

The FDP's support for libertarian policies earned them a mixed ranking from the association. On the one hand, their positions favoring pro-human rights foreign policies, deregulation for name and sex changes, and the freedom of rainbow parents to create legally binding family structures, earned them "strongly agree" marks from the LSVD in almost half of the categories on the scorecard. On the other hand, their opposition to improving antidiscrimination laws and willingness to deport LGBTI refugees to countries banning homosexuality were at odds with the organization's stances. Overall, 20 percent of the liberals' answers earned an "agree" rating and an additional twenty percent were classified as "vague."

The FDP's electoral program, entitled "Let's Rethink Things" contained several ideas not brought up by the LSVD.[41] These included support for allowing two mothers to appear on a birth certificate if the baby was conceived via sperm donation as well as creating a legal entity called a "*Verantwortungsgemeinschaft*" (communal responsibility) which would allow groups of nonmarried older people who care for each other to enjoy tax and inheritance advantages and to receive state benefits. The FDP also advocated both promoting diversity management programs that would encourage businesses to take full advantage of LGBTI workers' talents and ending the ban on gay men donating blood. Finally, they called on the federal government to pay a "victim's pension" to the men whose Paragraph 175 convictions had been reversed.

The Christian Democratic parties did not receive the LSVD's highest ranking ("strongly agree") in any of the categories examined. They did obtain "agree" scores for some of their positions on refugees and foreign policy. These included support for protecting queer refugees from violence, including LGBTI themes in integration courses, promoting LGBTI rights abroad, training diplomatic personnel to do so, and funding foreign gay rights groups. The association deemed several of the CDU/CSU's answers vague, including their positions on everyday acceptance, the Transsexual Law, and conversion therapy. Otherwise, the Union was rated as "disagreeing" with the LSVD's policy preferences in all other areas. Neither party's program explicitly mentioned LGBTI citizens at all, let alone issues of concern to them. The CSU's program merely stated in a section entitled "The State Must Justly Treat All Family Situations" that "same sex partnerships also deserve recognition. We definitively reject discriminating against these partnerships."[42] The joint CDU/CSU program simply noted: "We don't prescribe any particular family model. We respect the different forms of living together. People should decide for themselves how they want to live together and organize their daily life, for example … through registered life partnerships."[43]

While the Christian Democrats' programs by and large ignored LGBTI people, the Alternative for Germany's made some explicit references to lesbian, gay, and transgender citizens, and not in a favorable manner.[44] In one section entitled "Get Gender Ideology out of Schools and Stop the Early Sexualization [of Children]" the party complained,

> the one-sided accentuation of homo- and transsexuality in school lessons represents an unacceptable intrusion into the natural development of our children and the constitutionally protected right of parents to educate their children. Through these educational plans–often taught by people outside the school and against the will of parents–children and youth become insecure about their sexuality, overwhelmed, and filled with shame.

The party went on to oppose this type of "reeducation" in schools and called for instruction that highlighted the "proven, traditional picture of a family" instead. Another section of the program bearing the headline "End Wasting Taxpayer Money on 'Gender Research'" demanded the end of state and federal spending on professors and research studying gender issues, arguing such academic study was "not serious" and an attempt to abolish the "natural polarity between the sexes." Unsurprisingly, the LSVD did not give the AfD a single positive rating on their election scorecard. While two of their responses were categorized as vague, five were identified as being "dangerous" (strongly disagree). These were the points related to "everyday acceptance" for youth as well as the entire foreign policy portion of the scorecard. On all other points, the AfD and LSVD disagreed. The latter drafted a single-spaced, fourteen-page document entitled "The AfD: A Volatile Alternative" detailing the party's homo- and transphobic stances and warning LGBTI voters not to be taken in by the fact that one of the AfD's two lead candidates, Alice Weidel, was a lesbian.[45]

The major German political parties thus aggregated sexual minorities' political preferences to varying degrees in their party programs, with postmaterialist, leftist parties finding the most convergence and the right-leaning parties the least agreement. As discussed above, however, even postmaterialist, leftist parties faced few incentives to place these issues of interest to a minority of voters at the forefront of their political campaigns. To determine whether or not they did so, the following section traces the election campaign of 2017. This analysis is based on a Lexus-Nexis Academic search of German-language newspapers and news magazines in the six months preceding the 24 September election. The Appendix contains a list of the search keywords used. These included terms referring to the LSVD, to various sexual minorities (e.g., "bisexual,") and to the policies described above (e.g., "Antidiscrimination Law"). I find that in June and early July a surprisingly high degree of national attention was paid to one of the key issues of interest to gay and lesbian voters–marriage equality–and argue that this responsiveness was prompted by the critical actions of outgoing Green party politician Beck. Below, I detail the events that captured German public discourse in early summer and then portray the lack of attention to LGBTI issues paid in the period between mid July and the late September election.

The Election Campaign of 2017

After parties drafted their manifestos, they held conventions to ratify them. While the Left Party, the Greens, FDP, and SPD all included the LSVD's preference for marriage equality in the drafts of their electoral platforms, no party's leadership took up the Association's demand that Ehe für alle be a precondition for a coalition with the Christian Democrats. In fact, the Green's party leaders and top candidates Katrin Göring-Eckardt and Cem Özdemir strongly opposed establishing any "red lines" that the party would not cross in order to form a coalition with the CDU/CSU. They wished to appear ideologically flexible and willing to compromise, desiring a chance at governing Germany after twelve years in the opposition and failing to reach a coalition agreement with the CDU/CSU in 2013. When the Greens held their convention on 17 June, Beck–independently of the party leadership–made a motion to make Ehe für alle a precondition of a Green-CDU/CSU coalition following the election. Göring-Eckardt and Özdemir's efforts to keep this motion off of the conference agenda–correctly suspecting that it would easily obtain the support of the Green rank-and-file–failed to deter Beck who, according to *Der Spiegel*, "forced" the issue. The motion was accepted by the party rank-and-file.[46] Here Beck clearly fulfills Childs and Krook's critical actor criteria of a "lower threshold for political action" than Greens such as Göring-Eckardt and Özdemir, who shared his policy preference for marriage equality but did not prioritize the issue.

In response to the Greens, the FDP's lead candidate Christian Lindner announced a week later that the Liberals too would demand marriage equality before entering into a coalition with the Christian Democrats.[47] On 25 June, at their convention in Dortmund, the SPD decided they also would make Ehe für alle a condition of any coalition with the CDU/CSU.[48] Without the Green's impetus, it seems unlikely the FDP and SPD would have suddenly placed marriage equality at the forefront of their election promises. The FDP's campaign focused primarily on economic and educational issues and the Social Democrats had little incentive to unilaterally begin a push for marriage equality, having consistently kept Ehe für alle off the Bundestag's agenda for four years despite favoring it.

These developments–initiated by critical actor Beck–put the Union in a difficult spot. Many of their core voters opposed marriage equality, but without agreeing to it, the party would be unable to form a post election coalition with any party other than the controversial Alternative for Germany. Chancellor Angela Merkel met with the CDU leadership on the morning of 26 June and the party decided that, following the election, they would allow members of the Bundestag to make a group motion (*Gruppenantrag*) to hold a vote on opening marriage to gay and lesbian couples. This motion could then be decided by a vote of conscience, free from party discipline. Later that evening Merkel appeared at an election event sponsored by the women's magazine *Brigitte*. In the discussion with the audience, a man asked her when he would finally be able to call his partner his husband. The chancellor surprised the audience by saying she thought the discussion about Ehe für alle should go "in the direction of a conscience vote."[49]

The SPD quickly reacted to these remarks. The next morning (Tuesday, 27 June), chancellor candidate Martin Schulz said he would "take the chancellor at her word" and demand a conscience vote on marriage that week, the last week the Bundestag was in session before the election. Social Democratic Minister of Economic Affairs Sigmar Gabriel argued such a vote was consistent with the coalition agreement to "work toward" ending discrimination against life partners. Some Christian Democrats such as Volker Kauder then spoke out against the move, and charged Schulz with breaking their coalition agreement prohibiting "changing majorities," in the Bundestag. By the end of the day, however, both the CDU and CSU agreed to allow a conscience vote to take place that week.[50] Kauder changed his tune and spoke of a "breach of trust" on the part of the Social Democrats, rather than a formal breach of the coalition agreement.[51]

On Wednesday, 28 June, the Bundestag's Judiciary Committee finally voted to allow a bill regarding marriage equality on to the agenda for the last plenary session before the election. With the votes of the SPD, Greens, and Left Party, the committee sent to the plenum a 2016 Bundesrat bill changing Paragraph 1353 of the Civil Code to read "marriage is a lifelong compact between two people of the same or opposite sex."[52] After a thirty-eight-minute floor debate on Friday, 30 June, a roll call vote was taken and the law passed, 393 votes to 226. Seventy-five Christian Democrats, about a quarter of the parliamentary party group, broke ranks and voted in favor of the measure; an additional four abstained and five did not vote at all. All members of the SPD, Greens, and Left Party voted in favor.[53] On the floor of the Bundestag, Green party leader Göring-Eckardt congratulated Beck for his "unflinching" efforts to promote marriage equality, calling its ultimate achievement his "life's work."[54] It was Beck's last day as a member of the Bundestag and, amidst confetti and a wedding cake presented to him by his Green colleagues, he summarized "that was a hard fought twenty-nine years."[55] The LSVD's number one issue had been responded to in a highly visible manner at the outset of the election campaign thanks to a critical actor at the end of his political career who had nothing to lose by thwarting his party's leadership.

The issue of Ehe für alle did not disappear from the campaign immediately after the Bundestag vote. Some members of the CDU, CSU, and AfD argued the decision was unconstitutional, violating Article 6 of the Basic Law which states that "marriage and family enjoy special protection" in the Federal Republic.[56] CSU deputy and legal advisor Hans-Peter Uhl reasoned that because the two issues were linked in the constitution it meant that marriage "is set up to produce children. That only works with a man and a woman." He called for abstract judicial review of the law (*Normenkontrolle)* by the Constitutional Court. Catholic Cardinal Reinhard Marx agreed, stating he hoped "the debate isn't over yet and that the Constitutional Court can discuss it again;" conservative Catholics and Demo für alle both started petition drives encouraging party leaders to legally challenge Ehe für alle.[57] States have the option of proposing a *Normenkontrolle,* and in July the Bavarian Justice Minister announced that his CSU-governed Land was going to task two legal experts with evaluating the merits of such a procedure.[58] Such a *Normenkontrolle* would have also been possible with the support of 158 Members of the Bundestag, far fewer than had voted against the marriage bill.[59] Before agreeing to pursue such a measure, however, the CDU leadership decided to await the results of the Bavarian government's research.[60]

An opinion poll released in late June showed that a majority of Germans–even CDU/CSU and AfD voters–favored marriage equality. Nationally, 73 percent of all Germans expressed support, as did 64 percent of Christian Democratic voters and 55 percent of AfD adherents.[61] By mid July conservative party leaders appear to have ultimately determined that opposing Ehe für alle was not a winning electoral strategy after all, and the issue disappeared from the news.[62] After the election was over, and a coalition formed, the Bavarian finally government released the results of its legal evaluation, which concluded that a *Normenkontrolle* was unlikely to succeed in the Constitutional Court.[63]

LGBTI activists tried their best to keep issues beside marriage in the national spotlight following the end of the Bundestag's legislative session. When asked for commentary regarding Ehe für alle, they used interviews to stress the need to address additional issues such as discrimination and antigay violence.[64] Similarly, organizers of Christopher Street Day parades around the country underscored in the run-up to their events that marriage was not the only issue facing the queer community, raising concerns about trans* rights, education, and treatment of gay and lesbian refugees.[65] Across Germany, candidates for elective office representing all parties except the AfD made appearances at parades in their constituencies to court voters, but the concerns expressed by local parade organizers were not taken up in national discourse.[66]

Aside from Christopher Street Day, between early July and the 24 September election, most of the other issues raised by the LSVD on its scorecard, and by the various parties in their programs, did not play a major role in the campaign, which instead focused on the refugee crisis, relations with Turkey and Russia, national security, the diesel emissions scandal, and eldercare. In only three brief instances did LGBTI themes make national headlines:

(1) In June, AfD lead candidate and lesbian Weidel argued in an interview that it made "absolutely no sense" to worry about marriage equality when "millions of Muslims, for whom homosexuality is a crime, are illegally immigrating to Germany and threatening our freedom." This set off a media debate about the merits of the AfD as a pro-LGBTI party.[67]

(2) In early July, SPD Justice Minister Heiko Maas released a report by a working group tasked with reforming Germany's family law.[68] One issue not settled by the passage of Ehe für alle was what would happen if one lesbian married to another gave birth. Paragraph 1592 of the German Civil Code specifies that "the father of a child is the *man* [emphasis added] who is married to the mother at the time of birth." As a result, in contrast to married men, married lesbians still must go through the complicated legal process of adopting the child to gain parenting rights. The working group recommended allowing either a married man or a married "co-mother" (*Mit-Mutter*) to appear on a birth certificate. The release of Maas's report generated some press coverage and Catholic leaders used the occasion to speak out against assisted reproductive technologies used by same sex couples (but illegal in Germany) including surrogate mothers and egg donation.[69] No widespread commentary by political candidates followed, however.

(3) In August, the Ministry of the Interior responded to a written parliamentary question Beck had submitted during the previous legislative session, asking for a comparison of the level of violent homo- and transphobic crime committed in 2016 and in 2017. The report indicated that incidents had increased by 27 percent. Beck and Maas used the opportunity to speak out against anti-gay violence.[70]

Thus, not only did Beck serve as a critical actor in pushing for Ehe für alle as a coalition precondition, he also brought sexual minority interests into the campaign through his parliamentary question regarding hate crimes. Maas, too, played a critical role in highlighting the legal difficulties of rainbow families and echoing Beck's concerns about anti-gay violence.[71] Otherwise, as expected above, the campaign passed without any other national debate over the issues of interest to LGBTI voters.

Election Results

The election was held on 24 September, and as predicted by pollsters, Merkel's CDU/CSU emerged as the largest party. LGBTI voters' party preferences *(Zweitstimmen)* in the election were distributed quite differently however, closely paralleling the LSVD's assessment of the party manifestos–an unsurprising result, given that 95 percent of queer citizens claimed LGBTI-friendly policy stances were "very important" or "important" to their vote choice.[72] Figure 3.2 below is based on a national sample of LGBTIQ voters in Germany, conducted by collaborators at the Universities of Giessen and Vienna.

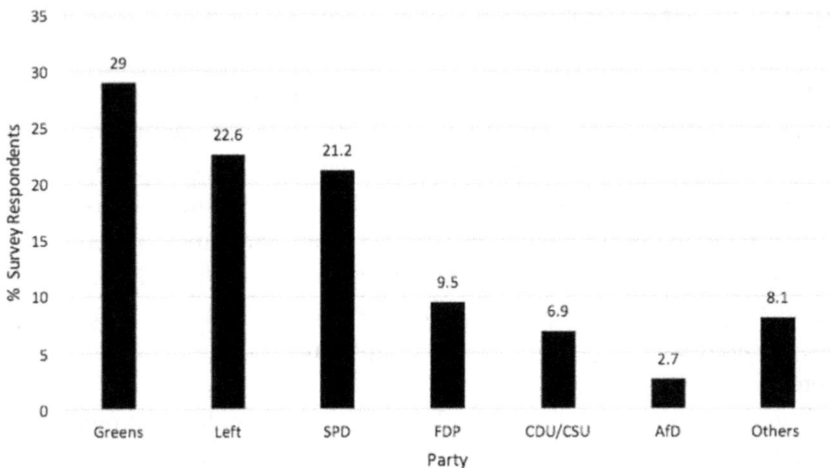

Figure 3.2: LGBTI Voters' 2017 Party Preferences

Source: Dorothée de Nève, Niklas Ferch, Tina Olteanu, and Michael Hunklinger, "Erste Ergebnisse zur Bundestagswahl in Deutschland der LGBTIQ*-Wahlstudie am 24. September 2017;" available at http://www.univie.ac.at/lgbt-wahlstudie/wp-content/uploads/2016/06/LGBTIQ-Wahlstudie-2017-Pra%CC%88sentation-Deutschland_Auswahl-PK_19.09..pdf, accessed 18 April 2018.

The Greens were far and away the most popular, gaining 29 percent of LGBTI voters' *Zweitstimmen*, 20.1 percent more than that party received in the actual 2017 election. The Left Party fared similarly well, winning 22.6 percent of the gay community's second vote, 13.4 percent more than the party received in the national election. Both the SPD and FDP experienced similar patterns within the LGBTI community and nationally, the SPD scoring 0.7 percent more among gay voters than in the national election and the

FDP 1.2 percent less.[73] Parties of the right received far less support from LGBTI voters than they did among Germans as a whole. With a mere 6.9 percent of the queer community's second vote, the CDU/CSU earned 26.1 percent less than it did in the 2017 election and the AfD's 2.7 percent support among LGBTI voters was 9.9 percent less than it enjoyed from Germans as a whole. The new Bundestag contained forty-three openly gay, lesbian, or bisexual deputies, roughly proportionate to estimates of the underlying population (6.1 percent).[74] Given the rightward swing that resulted from the election, however, these descriptive representatives did not enjoy a particularly LGBTI-friendly political setting.

LGBTI Interests and Coalition Negotiations

Just as LGBTI issues remained relatively absent from most of the campaign, sexual minorities' concerns also did not feature prominently in coalition negotiations. Immediately following the election, the CDU/CSU, Greens, and FDP sought to form a governing coalition but were ultimately unsuccessful. Part of their many difficulties in coming to an agreement stemmed from these organizations' very different stances on LGBTI-related issues. A copy of the sixty-one-page long results of the exploratory talks among the parties, released by the *Handelsblatt* newspaper, makes these conflicting views quite apparent.[75]

The Greens and the FDP agreed the "Jamaica" coalition should change the law so that a married lesbian would not have to adopt a child born to her wife–although the FDP specified this could only occur if the biological father agreed not to be the legal father. Both parties agreed that rainbow families should be able to make binding legal agreements before the birth of a child establishing who the two legal parents would be on the birth certificate. The Greens and FDP also promised to convene a commission to study whether other aspects of family law needed to be modernized. While the Greens advocated allowing lesbians and unmarried couples to access reproductive medicine, the FDP said they would agree to a conscience vote on the issue. Both parties also pledged to reform the Transsexual Law to make it easier for people to change their name and sex on identity documents and to implement a November 2017 decision of the Constitutional Court requiring a "third gender" option on such documents for intersex people. Finally, the two sides promised to develop and implement a new National Action Plan Against Homo- and Transphobia. The FDP called for this plan to include issues relating to the workplace.

In contrast, the CDU/CSU's stance overlapped with the FDP and Greens' on only a single point: agreeing to implement the Constitutional Court's ruling on intersex identity documents. In addition to language condemning "discrimination of any kind," the Christian Democrats promised to review the 2017 National Action plan's suggestions about how to combat discrimination on the basis of sexual identity and "where necessary" implement its recommendations.

The only other issue of interest to the LSVD brought up in the exploratory talks involved the question of whether Algeria, Tunisia, and Morocco should be considered safe countries of origin for immigrants. The CDU/CSU and FDP agreed they should be, while the Greens disagreed. With the collapse of the talks on 19 November, these issues became moot. Even if all parties had agreed to the LSVD's position on all the issues raised in the talks, however, the coalition agreement would have only covered five of the twenty-four issues stressed by the association.

After the failure of the "Jamaica" option, the CDU/CSU began negotiations with the SPD for a continuation of their grand coalition. The extensive and detailed agreement finally approved on 4 March 2018 contained even fewer items of interest to LGBTI Germans.[76] In a press release following its publication, the LSVD described the coalition agreement as a document "practically without lesbian, gay, trans- and intersex people: 180 disappointing pages without clear directives."[77]

While the blueprint for the nineteenth legislative period claimed, "We condemn hostility toward homosexuals and trans* people and we will work against every discrimination," the agreement contained very little by way of specifics as to how this goal would be accomplished. Instead, the coalition partners merely agreed to implement any reforms required of them by the Constitutional Court–currently this would involve allowing a "third sex" on identity documents–and pledged to "speedily align and amend" any laws that required change as a result of the already accomplished Ehe für alle. The only other domestic issue of interest to the LSVD included in the agreement was a promise to outlaw surgeries to "correct" intersex children, except in life threatening cases. The coalition did include one foreign policy goal of interest to the LGBTI community: a vow to work with the UN and EU to defend human rights abroad, including a specific mention of working to condemn violence committed against people because of their sexual orientation. The document also called for a secure funding stream for the federal Magnus Hirschfeld Foundation, a government agency devoted to "research, education, and memorializing" on LGBTI issues.[78] The LSVD, however, had instead requested funding for their own (more internationally focused)

Hirschfeld Eddy Foundation. In short, of the twenty-four points brought up on the election scorecard, only three were ultimately included in the plan for governing Germany between 2017 and 2021, and one of these was incorporated because of a Constitutional Court decision made after the election.

Conclusion

In most ways, then, the German national election of 2017 followed a predictable course. Sexual minorities clearly articulated a wide range of policy preferences and left-leaning, postmaterialist parties paid lip service to these in their party programs. When it came to stressing themes on the campaign trail (outside of localized LGBTI-events such as Christopher Street Day parades), however, politicians turned to other issues. The extensive and very detailed coalition agreements negotiated after the election included very few of the items considered "important" or "very important" to sexual minorities in Germany.

It was only due to the efforts of critical actors such as Maas and, more importantly, Beck, that LGBTI themes made their way to the forefront of national discourse in isolated incidents. It was Beck who unilaterally moved at the Greens' party conference to include language in the election program making marriage equality a precondition for a coalition and setting in motion the subsequent sequence of events described above. It was also Beck's written question about anti-LGBTI violence in Germany that spurred part of the limited additional campaign discourse regarding gay rights issues. These remarks were echoed by SPD Minister of Justice Maas, who also initiated the working group to discuss LGBT-friendly changes to family law, another one of the few times queer themes were raised in the campaign. Maas, too, may be considered a critical actor in trying to bring sexual minority issues to the fore in the 2017 German election.

Aside from the initial flurry of activity surrounding marriage equality, however, this election like many others before it, featured limited attention and responsiveness to LGBTI issues. Neither of the critical actors in the campaign retained their positions after the election. Beck left the Bundestag and Maas became Foreign Minister, in a position perhaps to promote LGBTI rights abroad, but not in domestic policy. The coalition agreement predicts very little federal action on domestic issues in the four years to come, unless the government is pressed into action by the Constitutional Court.

Louise K. Davidson-Schmich is Professor of Political Science, University of Miami, Coral Gables, Florida. Her research focuses on gender, sexuality, and politics in Germany and other long-term democracies. She is the author of *Gender Quotas and Democratic Participation: Recruiting Candidates for Elective Offices in Germany* (Ann Arbor, 2016) and editor of *Gender, Intersections, and Institutions: Intersectional Groups Building Alliances and Gaining Voice in Germany* (Ann Arbor, 2017). E-mail: davidson@miami.edu

Notes

1. Research for this article was generously subsidized by the German Academic Exchange Service (DAAD) and the International Association for the Study of German Politics (IASGP). G. Bingham Powell Jr., Russell J. Dalton, and Kaare Strom, *Comparative Politics Today*, 10th ed. (Boston, 2012), 37.
2. See for example Shane Phelan, *Sexual Strangers: Gays, Lesbians, and the Dilemmas of Citizenship* (Philadelphia, 2001). Lesbians are women sexually attracted to other women, gay men are men sexually attracted to other men, bisexuals are sexually attracted to people of both sexes, transgender people's gender identity (sense of being male or female) does not match the physical sex with which they were born, and intersex people have sexual characteristics of both sexes, for example XXY chromosomes. The terms "sexual minority" and "queer" are often used as umbrella terms to describe this group of people, although not all members are comfortable with this terminology. Moreover, some intersex advocates argue that they have a medical condition that is not appropriately grouped with sexual orientation or gender identity. Despite these problems, for ease of presentation I use the terms LGBTI, queer, and sexual minority interchangeably here. I discuss both intersex rights and LGBT rights in this article because German interest groups and parties linked the two issues throughout the campaign.
3. Lawrence R. Helfer and Erik Voeten, "International Courts as Agents of Legal Change: Evidence from LGBT Rights in Europe," *International Organization* 68, no. 1 (2014): 77–110; Yvonne Murphey, "The marriage equality referendum 2015," *Irish Political Studies* 31, no. 2 (2016): 315–330; Jonathan Symons and Dennis Altman, "International norm polarization: sexuality as a subject of human rights protection," *International Theory* 7, no. 1 (2015): 61–95.
4. Sarah Childs and Mona Lena Krook, "Analysing Women's Substantive Representation: From Critical Mass to Critical Actors," *Government and Opposition* 44, no. 2 (2009): 125–145.
5. Louise K. Davidson-Schmich, "LGBT Politics in Germany: Unification as a Catalyst for Change," *German Politics* 26, no. 4 (2017): 534–555. Paragraph 175, however, was repealed by the Bundestag in 1994.
6. See Helfer and Voeten (see note 3).
7. But see also Miriam Smith, *Political Institutions and Lesbian and Gay Rights in the United States and Canada* (New York, 2009) on how referenda can be a double-edged sword for LGBTI people.
8. Angelika von Wahl, "Throwing the Boomerang: Intersex Mobilization and Policy Change in Germany" in *Gender, Institutions, and Intersections: Intersectional Groups Building Alliances and Gaining Voice in Germany*, ed. Louise K. Davidson-Schmich (Ann Arbor, 2017).
9. Philip M. Ayoub, *When States Come Out: Europe's Sexual Minorities and the Politics of Visibility* (New York, 2016); Manuela Lavinas Picq and Markus Thiel, Editors, *Sexualities in*

World Politics: How LGBTQ *claims shape International Relations* (Philadelphia, 2015); Phillip M. Ayoub and David Paternotte, *LGBT Activism and the Making of Europe: A Rainbow Europe?* (New York, 2014); David Patternotte and Kelly Kollman, "Regulating intimate relationships in the European polity: same-sex unions and policy convergence," *Social Politics* 20, no. 4 (2013): 510–533.

10. Liam Stack, "European Court Strikes Down Required Sterilization for Transgender People," *New York Times*, 12 April 2017.
11. "Maas: Rehabilitierung Homosexueller ist überfällig," *Frankfurter Rundschau,* 22 March 2017.
12. See von Wahl (see note 8).
13. Dorothée de Nève, Niklas Ferch, Tina Olteanu, and Michael Hunklinger, "Erste Ergebnisse zur Bundestagswahl in Deutschland der LGBTIQ*-Wahlstudie am 24. September 2017;" available at http://www.univie.ac.at/lgbt-wahlstudie/wp-content/uploads/2016/06/LGBTIQ-Wahlstudie-2017-Pra%CC%88sentation-Deutschland_Auswahl-PK_19.09..pdf, accessed 18 April 2018. Notably, this poll was not financed by party think tanks or professional opinion polling firms, but instead was an academic research project.
14. "Studie zu Einstellungen gegenüber Lesben, Schwulen und Bisexuellen," Antidiskriminierungsstelle des Bundes, Berlin, 12 January 2017; available at http://www.antidiskriminierungsstelle.de/SharedDocs/Aktuelles/DE/2017/20170112_Umfrage_LSB.html, accessed 18 April 2018.
15. Andrew Reynolds, "Representation and Rights: The Impact of LGBT Legislators in Comparative Perspective," *American Political Science Review* 107, no. 2 (2013): 259–274, here 271.
16. See Childs and Krook (see note 4), 138.
17. Kriss Rudolph, "Zahlreiche schwule Abgeordnete im neuen Bundestag," *Mannschaft Magazin*, 25 September 2017; available at http://www.mannschaft.com/2017/09/zahlreiche-schwule-abgeordnete-im-neuen-bundestag/, accessed 18 April 2018.
18. Louise K. Davidson-Schmich, *Becoming Party Politicians: Eastern German State Legislators in the Decade Following Democratization* (Notre Dame, 2006).
19. Louise K. Davidson-Schmich, "Amending Germany's Life Partnership Law: Emerging attention to Lesbians' Concerns" in Davidson-Schmich (see note 8), 203–236.
20. The Greens were so frustrated by this behavior that they took the case to the Constitutional Court, demanding the court require the bill to be released for a floor vote by the end of the legislative session. The court, however, saw no reason to do so. Christian Rath, "Keine Abstimmung über die Ehe" *taz*, 21 June 2017.
21. "Aktionen" Demo für alle; available at https://demofueralle.wordpress.com/service/, accessed 15 March 2018.
22. Infratest dimap polls in May 2017 showed 47 percent of voters in favor of either the CDU/CSU or AfD.
23. "Abgestraft für den Drogenskandal," *Zeit Online*, 3 December 2016; available at http://www.zeit.de/politik/deutschland/2016-12/volker-beck-bundestag, accessed 18 April 2018.
24. Thomas Petersen, "Schneller akzeptiert als gedacht," *Frankfurter Allgemeine Zeitung*, 16 July 2015. This support, even among some Christian Democrats, did manifest itself in a few occasions in early 2017, however. Comedian and Christian writer, Hape Kerkeling, who represented the CDU in the Bundesversammlung to elect Federal President Frank-Walter Steinmeier, spoke out publicly in favor of Ehe für alle in April 2017. In May, the annual Protestant Kirchentag in Berlin featured a high-profile blessing of a union between two lesbians dressed in wedding gowns. In June, the new government of Schleswig-Holstein, led by Christian Democratic Minister-President Daniel Gunther, pledged the support of his "Jamaica" (CDU-FDP-Green) coalition for any Bundesrat initiative on marriage equality. "Frau Merkel, ran an die Buletten," *Spiegel online*, 1 April 2017; Annette Langer, "Endlich richtig heiraten!" *Spiegel online*, 27 May 2017; "Mehrheit im Norden sagt 'Ja' zu Ehe für alle," NDR, 30. June 2017; "Günther will 'Ja' zur Homo-Ehe erkämpfen," *Handelsblatt*, 16. May 2017.

25. The events of 2017 demonstrate that openly LGBTI candidates are not a sufficient condition for queer-friendly policy change. Lesbian Alice Weidel led the homophobic AfD's party list and other leading gay politicians, such as the CDU's choice of Health Minister Jens Spahn and the SPD's youth-wing leader Kevin Kühnert, did not highlight queer themes during the campaign.
26. de Nève et al. (see note 13). The one issue area of importance to the LSVD not mentioned by survey respondents was foreign policy. Instead, voters prioritized environmental protection and good wages, issues not taken up by the association.
27. The questions the LSVD asked and the answers of the parties are available at "Blockaden brechen–Respekt wählen! Gemeinsam für Freiheit und gleiche Rechte;" available at https://www.lsvd.de/politik/bundestagswahl-2017/wahlpruefsteine-uebersicht.html, accessed 18 April 2018. Figure 1 below only discusses twenty-four of these issues because by the time the LSVD published their scorecard, Ehe für alle had been achieved and this issue was dropped from their analysis.
28. See Davidson-Schmich (see note 19) for more details.
29. von Wahl (see note 8). In November 2017, two months after the election, the German Constitutional Court ruled on the grounds of the right to self-determination that the law must recognize a nonbinary sex. Carolin Henkenberens, "Wir raten, erstmal kein Geschlecht einzutragen," *Frankfurter Rundschau*, 20 November 2017, 5.
30. See Georgiann Davis, *Contesting Intersex: The Dubious Diagnosis* (New York, 2015) for more details.
31. For more information see https://www.hrc.org/resources/policy-and-position-statements-on-conversion-therapy, accessed 18 April 2018.
32. At the time the LSVD asked parties for a response, there had never been a National Action Plan on LGBTI issues. In June 2017, the grand coalition released a "Nationaler Aktionsplan gegen Rassismus" that included discussion of homophobia and transphobia, but it did not meet the criteria supported by the LSVD. For a summary of their critique, see "Scharfe Kritik am Nationalen Aktionsplan gegen Homo- und Transphobie," *queer.de*, 17 June 2017; available at http://www.queer.de/detail.php?article_id=29046, accessed 18 April 2018.
33. See note 27. In Figure 1, responses the LSVD calls "super" are coded "strongly agree," "ja" corresponds to "agree", "nein" is coded "disagree" and "gefährlich" is labelled "strongly disagree." The term "vague" is used in both the scorecard and Figure 1. On past years' election scorecards, the group only utilized a three-point scale, but with the increasing strength of the AfD, they expanded their classification to a five-point scale including the "dangerous" category.
34. Scott Siegel and Yiqian Alice Wang, "Broken Rainbows: The Partisan Politics of Marriage Equality in Europe," *European Politics and Society,* https://doi.org/10.1080/23745118.2018.1429195 and Dorothée de Nève and Niklas Ferch, "LGBTIQ* Voters in Austria and Germany: Political Preferences, Party Competition and Electoral Resonance," paper presented at the Twenty-Fifth International Conference of Europeanists "Europe and the World: Mobilities, Values and Citizenship", 28-30 March 2018, Chicago.
35. Mala Htun and S. Laurel Weldon, *The Logics of Gender Justice* (Cambridge, 2018); and Merike Blofield, *Care Work and Class: Domestic Workers' Struggle for Equal Rights in Latin America* (University Park, 2012).
36. "Sozial. Gerecht. Frieden. Für Alle," The Left Party, Hanover 9-11 June 2017); available at https://www.die-linke.de/fileadmin/download/wahlen2017/wahlprogramm2017/die_linke_wahlprogramm_2017.pdf, accessed 18 April 2018.
37. The main platform is available at https://www.gruene.de/fileadmin/user_upload/Dokumente/BUENDNIS_90_DIE_GRUENEN_Bundestagswahlprogramm_2017_barrierefrei.pdf, accessed 18 April 2018; and the Queer Electoral Program is available at https://queergruen.info/userspace/BE/bag_schwulenpolitik/Dokumente/BTW2017_Queeres_Wahlprogramm_WEB-150dpi-Einzelseiten.pdf, accessed 18 April 2018.
38. No party received the "strongly agree" rating in this category. HPV is the human papillomavirus that can cause cancer to the reproductive organs; PrEP means Pre-Exposure Pro-

phylaxis, and involves the use of anti-HIV medications to keep HIV negative people from becoming infected; HIV is the human immunodeficiency virus that, over time, can cause Acquired Immunodeficiency Syndrome (AIDS). This virus can be transmitted via anal intercourse, putting gay men at risk.

39. "Zeit für mehr Gerechtigkeit: Unser Regierungsprogramm für Deutschland," Social Democratic Party of Germany, Dortmund, 25 June 2017; available at https://www.spd.de/fileadmin/Dokumente/Bundesparteitag_2017/Es_ist_Zeit_fuer_mehr_Gerechtigkeit-Unser_Regierungsprogramm.pdf, accessed 18 April 2018.
40. No party earned the highest ranking in this category.
41. "Denken wir neu" Freie Demokraten; available at https://www.fdp.de/sites/default/files/uploads/2017/08/07/20170807-wahlprogramm-wp-2017-v16.pdf, accessed 18 April 2018.
42. "Der Bayernplan: Klar für unser Land" Christian Social Union, 2017; available at http://www.csu.de/programm/bayernplan/, accessed 18 April 2018.
43. "Für ein Deutschland in dem wir gut und gerne leben" CDU/CSU, Berlin, 3 July 2017; available at https://www.cdu.de/regierungsprogramm, accessed 18 April 2018.
44. "Programm für Deutschland," Alternative für Deutschland, Cologne 22-23 April 2017; available at https://www.afd.de/wp-content/uploads/sites/111/2017/06/2017-06-01_AfD-Bundestagswahlprogramm_Onlinefassung.pdf, accessed 18 April 2018.
45. "AfD–eine unberechenbare Alternative," LSVD; available at https://www.lsvd.de/politik/afd-eine-unberechenbare-alternative.html, accessed 18 April 2018.
46. Annett Meiritz and Ann-Katrin Müller, "Parteitag der Grünen: Ehe für alle–darunter geht nichts," *Spiegel online*, 17 June 2017.
47. Ansgar Siemens, "Ohne Ehe für alle keine Koalition," *Spiegel online,* 24 June 2017.
48. "Parteien begrüßen Merkels Kursschwenk," *Frankfurter Allgemeine Zeitung*, 27 June 2017.
49. "Merkel offen für 'Ehe für alle," *Frankfurter Allgemeine Zeitung*, 26 June 2017.
50. Günter Bannas and Majid Sattar, "Große Politik im Talkshowsessel," *Frankfurter Allgemeine Zeitung*, 27 June 2017.
51. "Merkel gibt Abstimmung über Ehe für alle in Unionsfraktion frei" *Frankfurter Allgemeine Zeitung,* 27 June 2017.
52. "Was bedeutet die 'Ehe für alle'?" *Frankfurter Allgemeine Zeitung*, 28 June 2017"; Christian Rath, "Die Ehe für alle ist wohl kein Fall für das Verfassungsgericht," *taz*, 29 June 2017.
53. "Abstimmung: Ehe für alle," *Frankfurter allegemeine Zeitung*, 30 June 2017. One deputy from the SPD and one from the Left were absent. Merkel was one of the CDU members voting against the measure, arguing afterwards on her Facebook page: "For me, the marriage mentioned in the Basic Law is the marriage of a man and a woman." Later in the summer, the bill was also approved by the Bundesrat and Federal President Steinmeier and went into effect in October 2017.
54. "Bundestag beschließt 'Ehe für alle'" *Frankfurter Allgemeine Zeitung*, 30 June 2017.
55. Robert Birnbaum, "Szenen einer Ehe," *Der Tagesspiegel*, 1 July 2017.
56. "AfD will gegen 'Ehe für alle' klagen," *Frankfurter Allgemeine Zeitung*, 6 July 2017.
57. Matthias Drobinski, "Bundesrat stimmt über Ehe für alle ab" *Süddeutsche.de*, 6 July 2017. See also Demo für alle (see note 21).
58. Reinhard Müller, "Ehe für alle ist eine Mogelpackung" *Frankfurter Allgemeine Zeitung*, 6 July 2017.
59. "Seehofer gegen 'Ehe für alle,' aber für Adoptionsrecht," *Frankfurter Allgemeine Zeitung*, 30 June 2017.
60. "Verfassungsklage hängt an Bayern," *taz*, 10 July 2017.
61. "Politbarometer: Deutliche Mehrheit für die Homo-Ehe," ZDF: *Heute in Deutschland*, 23 June 2017.
62. Jan Feddersen, "Auf dem Wege zur vollen Verbürgerlichung," *taz*, 8 July 2018.
63. "Bayerns Klage in Karlsruhe wohl aussichtslos," *Frankfurter Allgemeine Zeitung*, 6 March 2018.
64. See for example: Andreas Hergeth, "Jetzt geht die Gleichstellung los," *taz*, 29 July 2017 and Anja Kühne, "Schön wär's" *Der Tagesspiegel*, 2 July 2017.

65. Christopher Street was the location of the Stonewall Inn in New York City where the modern LGBTI rights movement was born; Christopher Street Day (CSD) events are held to commemorate the Stonewall Uprising and to increase the visibility of the queer community. For an example of such pre-CSD commentary see "Wir sind keine Igitt-Randgruppe," *Frankfurter Rundschau*, 14 July 2017.
66. Dirk Ludigs, "Wem gehört der CSD?" *taz*, 22 July 2017; Denis Hubert, "Ehe für alle kann nur der Anfang sein," *Frankfurter Rundschau*, 17 July 2017; Jan Zier, "Der CSD ist zurück," *taz*, 22 August 2017.
67. Justus Bender, "Der Alice-Weidel-Effekt," *Frankfurter Allgemeine Zeitung*, 28 June 2017.
68. Jost Müller-Neuhof, "Familie ist, wo Eier sind," *Der Tagesspiegel*, 16 July 2017.
69. Christoph Scholz, "Kirche fordert Respekt und Wahrhaftigkeit," *Berliner Zeitung*, 9 August 2017.
70. "Starker Anstieg homophober Übergriffe," *taz*, 10 August 2017.
71. Earlier in the year, Maas also initiated the law initiating rehabilitation for Paragraph 175 victims in response to a recommendation of the federal Anti-Discrimniation Office (see note 11). Consistent with Childs and Krook's observation that critical actors for gender equality are not always women, Maas is heterosexual, the partner of actress Natalia Wörner. "Heiko Maas: Who is Germany's new foreign minister?" *Deutsche Welle*, 9 March 2018.
72. de Nève et al. (see note 13.) This is also the source for Figure 2. Because there is no reliable information about the underlying population of LGBTI voters in Germany, it is not possible to assess the degree of representativeness of the survey results.
73. There was a difference in the voting patterns of gay men and lesbians in terms of the FDP, however. Gay men were more likely to support the FDP than the general population and lesbians less likely. Such sex differences were not present with the other parties.
74. "Volk und Vertreter," *Süddeutsche Zeitung*, 27 February 2018.
75. "Ergebnis der Sondierungsgespräche zwischen CDU/CSU, FDP und Bündnis 90/ Die Grünen," 15 November 2017; available at https://www.handelsblatt.com/downloads/20596948/2/jamaika-sondierungspapier.pdf, accessed 18 April 2018.
76. "Ein neuer Aufbruch für Europa. Eine neue Dynamik für Deutschland. Ein neuer Zusammenhalt für unser Land," Koalitionsvertrag zwischen CDU, CSU und SPD; available at https://www.cdu.de/system/tdf/media/dokumente/koalitionsvertrag_2018.pdf?file=1, accessed 18 April 2018.
77. Axel Hochrein, "Koalitionsvertrag praktisch ohne Lesben, Schwule, bisexuelle, trans- und intergeschlechtliche Menschen," *LSVD*, 7 February 2018; available at https://www.lsvd.de/newsletters/newsletter-2018/koalitionsvertrag-praktisch-ohne-lesben-schwule-bisexuelle-trans-und-intergeschlechtliche-menschen.html, accessed 18 April 2018.
78. "Über die Stiftung," Bundesstiftung Magnus Hirschfeld, n.d.; available at http://mh-stiftung.de/ueber-die-stiftung/, accessed 18 April 2018.

Appendix

German keywords used in the Lexis-Nexis search:

Artikel 3	*Konversionstherapie*
bisexuell	*lesb**
Diskriminierung	LSBTI
Ehe für alle	LSVD
Hassgewalt/Hasskriminalität	queer
Hirschfeld Eddy	Regenbogen Familie
homo	schwul*
intersex	transgender

··· Chapter 4 ···

KAN-DI(E)-DAT?

Unpacking Gender Images across Angela Merkel's Four Campaigns for the Chancellorship, 2005-2017

Joyce Marie Mushaben

When veteran U.S. legislator Pat Schroeder set out in pursuit of the Democratic presidential nomination in 1987, she was scrutinized from head to toe by male reporters.[1] One journalist addressed her suitability for office with the point-blank question: "Are you running as a woman?" Quick-witted Schroeder responded: "Do I have a choice?"[2]

Countless cross-national "inventories" confirm that gender stereotypes attributed to male and female candidates during major election campaigns transcend national and regional boundaries.[3] Irrespective of their backgrounds, motives, or individual paths to power, women tend to be characterized as attractive, community-minded, cooperative, demur, emotional, gentle, helpful, kind, nurturing, participatory, quiet, relationship-oriented, risk-averse, sensitive, subordinate, supportive, sympathetic, and warm, although few if any of these terms applied to the first "Iron Lady," Margaret Thatcher. Men, by comparison, are routinely described as ambitious, aggressive, assertive, competitive, controlling, daring, dominant, forceful, independent, loud, rational, rule-oriented and self-confident, traits that did largely apply to Chancellor Gerhard Schröder, even after he failed to secure a new Social Democratic Party (SPD) majority in 2005.

Fitting or not, historically rooted gender stereotypes still shape the ways in which voters and pundits perceive individual women bold enough to pursue power at the highest levels of government. As a result, female leaders often find themselves wedged between the proverbial rock and hard place. Through the 1970s and 1980s, women who conformed to ascribed gender profiles, or even "looked feminine," were judged incapable of meeting the rigors and requirements associated with a particular office: how

Notes for this section begin on page 122.

could a caring mother with young children at home participate in parliamentary debates lasting until 2:00 A.M., or fly off to a three-day global summit, for example? The Green *Feminat* of the 1980s proved that an all-woman executive could, in fact, accomplish all of its tasks during normal working hours. Given the late-night sessions often associated with political life, one could ask: why do men need so much longer to accomplish the same things?

Alternatively, if women engaged in male-normed behaviors by acting in strong, assertive, and decisive ways, it was construed as proof that they were neglecting or violating their natural, "God-given" roles for which they would also be negatively sanctioned. The seventeen men from Bavaria who showed up in "greasy" Lederhosen in 1949 to take their seats in the new Bundestag did not make the headlines, although male parliamentarians were eventually required to replace their suspenders with belts in the 1950s. By contrast, the first time Lenelotte von Bothmer addressed her fellow Bundestag members wearing a pants-suit on 14 October 1970, the *Bild Zeitung* featured her on page one with the headline: "So nicht, Frau Abgeordnete!" (Not Like That, Mrs. Deputy). The *Hannoversche Allgemeine* excoriated the Social Democratic mother of six with the headline: "Sie sind ein würdeloses Weib" (you are a dishonorable dame).[4] Angela Merkel experienced her first culture shock after the Wall fell when she was indirectly advised by interim GDR premier Lothar de Maizière to get rid of her long hippie-skirts, baggy hand-knit sweaters and "Jesus sandals" before traveling to Moscow for the Two-plus-Four Treaty negotiations.[5] Mocking her hair was the next tactic critics used to undermine her authority; those attacks finally ceased after she submitted to a "feminine make-over" in 2005.

Stereotyping can and does produce its own institutional, social, and economic realities.[6] Ironically, women can also benefit from such stereotypes: sometimes they may be perceived as more effective, either because their evaluators did not expect much from them, or because they had to meet higher standards to secure their positions in the first place. They then have to outperform others on a daily basis in order to prove that they possess the "same or equal" skills.[7]

Merkel's four national election campaigns offer a unique trajectory with regard to the salience of gender in defining "competent leadership" in unified Germany. Gender factors loomed large but were deliberately avoided by both the candidate and her party during her first national campaign in 2005. Although the incumbent Chancellor continued to eschew "women-friendly" themes during her second campaign in 2009, gender emerged as a positive asset, in my judgment, due largely to her effective management of a grand coalition (GroKo), reinforced by the presence of other strong women in her cabinet. I argue further that gender became an irrelevant variable in Merkel's third attempt to secure a conservative majority, although that campaign saw a deliberate effort to "soften" her image. Gender assumed new salience during the 2017 campaign, albeit with a different twist. While she could have stressed the women and family-friendly impact of policy reforms introduced earlier (with the help of Ursula von der Leyen), the electoral dilemma Merkel faced in 2017 had nothing to do with her own capabilities as a female chancellor. Instead, it was rooted in the need to win back alienated, if apolitical conservative men, attracted to an increasingly misogynistic and xenophobic Alternative for Germany (AfD).

The study begins with a brief assessment of the changing nature of German election campaigns, heavily influenced by the post-unification shift to a multiparty system. Next, I review major themes and images presented during the 2005, 2009, 2013, and 2017 election campaigns, respectively. I conclude with reflections on Merkel's unsung contributions to descriptive and substantive "representation" since 2005 as Germany's first eastern, female chancellor.

"Creeping Americanization" and the Changing Nature of the Party Landscape

Scholars specializing in survey research and media portrayals of candidates in national campaigns dating back to 1990 attest to the creeping "Americanization" of German electoral processes. FRG politicians are admittedly still a long way off from embracing the permanent campaign mode witnessed across the Atlantic, and have thus far avoided the steady diet of partisan vitriol, personalized attack ads, money-grubbing, and the highly scripted debates fed to U.S. voters for over a year prior to presidential elections. Since 2005, however, one does find increasing evidence of personalized candidate branding, mixed with more strategic campaign planning, reliance on external consultants, micro-targeting, and "event management."[8]

Historical factors account for an ongoing German aversion to attack ads. According to Left Party parliamentarian Stefan Liebich, "between the kaisers, the Nazis, and the Communists, the country has seen its fair share of rancor, and for the past few decades they've been relieved just to have a little peace, love, and civil campaigning."[9] German electoral contests are still, for the most part, publically funded, although corporate and interest-group spending is on the rise, notwithstanding the campaign finance scandal of the

Kohl era.[10] Parties are ensured television time proportionate to the share of votes they accrued during the previous election. Each party is entitled to a ninety-second ad for the duration of the campaign, roughly six weeks total.[11] While talk-show appearances and door-to-door campaigning are becoming more frequent, most local and state politicians continue to rely on information stands at weekly, open-air market places. Polling experts hold that Internet sources and social media continue to play a limited role.[12]

The primary function of the *Spitzenkandidat* (top candidate) is to serve as the party's standard-bearer-in-chief. Clearly defined party programs traditionally outweighed media-driven efforts to personalize the race to power through the 1990s. The chancellor, as well as opposing party leaders, are chiefly responsible for "rendering complex issue questions understandable to a broad public while making the case in a pointed fashion."[13] The more competent and trustworthy the candidate her/himself appears to be, the more likely voters are to deem her/his campaign promises credible. Increasing reliance on visual media virtually forces campaign strategists to incorporate personal qualities of their respective top candidates into their broader electoral calculations: "the personal has become the political," insofar as a candidate's character, style, and rhetoric occupy a central position in both party communications and official campaign reporting.

The first television debate featuring chancellor candidates Schröder and Edmund Stoiber took place in 2002. Though they remain "unscripted," they no longer play to party loyalists but rather to growing numbers of independents and undecided voters. Dieter Ohr, Markus Klein, and Ulrich Rosar suggest that television debates are more likely to influence voters who normally display little interest in politics. Their lack of detailed knowledge regarding public policies contributes to a higher probability that they will make their decisions based on "personality factors" derived from these face-to-face debates.[14] Aside from their ideological preferences, German voters have few grounds to question the general competence of their leading candidates, insofar as most are the products of the proverbial political *Ochsentour* (ox tour) involving years of service as local organizers, state politicians, federal ministers, or opposition leaders. In 2005, Merkel was still perceived as an exception to the rule, although by then she had accumulated eight years of Cabinet experience, had climbed the Christian Democratic Union (CDU) executive ladder at warp speed and had headed the conservative opposition for nearly four years.[15]

Two more factors affecting the nature of German election campaigns are of relevance here. The first pertains to the fracturing of the party system, especially since 1990. The arrival of the Greens on the national political stage in the early 1980s ended Germany's thirty-year characterization as a "two-and-a-half" party system, consisting of the CDU/CSU, SPD, and the Free Democratic Party (FDP). Unification saw the addition of the Party for Democratic Socialism (PDS), which later merged with western leftists, now known collectively as the Left Party (die Linke). Right-wing fringe parties of the 1980s and 1990s, such as the Republikaner, the German People's Union (Deutsche Volksunion), and the Schill Party, secured seats in local and state elections, but the Alternative for Germany was the first such entity, beyond the short-lived (heavily male) Pirate Party, to cross the 5 percent threshold, allowing it to enter the Bundestag in 2017. While partisan de-alignment was already evident prior to unification, the comings and goings of new protest parties have undermined the ability of either one of the traditional *Volksparteien* (catch-all parties) to secure a parliamentary majority in concert with a junior partner.[16] A further problem is the blurring of ideological lines, which can make for more compromise-oriented policies by way of grand coalitions but which also encourages radicalization at the far ends of the political spectrum.[17]

A final factor of relevance here is the so-called gender gap. From 1949 until the late 1960s, women disproportionately favored conservative parties. By the late 1960s, the coming of age of the baby boomers, a radicalized student movement and Willy Brandt's promise to "dare more democracy" precipitated a shift to the left among younger women, in particular. Viewed as the sociopolitical avant garde in the 1970s, the SPD lost significant feminist ground to the Greens across the 1980s and 1990s, a party that explicitly included gender equality among its four programmatic pillars. While Brandt and Schröder both benefited from strong female voting blocs, the SPD has subsequently acquired the aura of a rather stodgy, male-dominated bunch. Prior to the 2017 election, two reporters writing for *Die Zeit* explained its declining voter share in three simple words: "It's gender, stupid."[18]

Since 1990, the SPD seems to have embraced two core requirements for attaining the rank of chancellor candidate: maleness, and a last name beginning with S, as in Scharping, Schröder, Steinmeier, Steinbrück, and Schulz (unfortunately for Gabriel, having Sigmar as a first name did not suffice). The diverse policy interests of new generations of career women, working mothers, pensioners, single parents and LGBT** voters have undermined monolithic or *Kinder-Kirche-Küche* (children, church, kitchen) appeals to these groups, but appeal the parties must: by 2002, eligible female voters outnumbered their male counterparts, 31.9 million to 29.3 million.[19] By the onset of her third campaign, the female eastern chancellor had managed to turn the Union back into "the leading women's party" in Germany. By contrast, 2017 could well be described as the "Year of Angry White Male Backlash" reminiscent of the 1994 elections in the United States.[20]

"To Play or Not to Play:" The Gender Card in 2005

Once it became clear that Merkel would serve as the 2005 CDU chancellor candidate, she was immediately subjected to a physical make-over, having been mocked for years regarding her appearance (despite changes photo-documented by Herlinde Koelbl).[21] She had already declared during her years as Kohl's Women's Minister (1991-1994) that she did not identify with "feminism" or even favor a gender "quota" for her own party, though she would change her mind regarding the latter by 1995. It was therefore not surprising that she assiduously avoided discussions of so-called women's issues during her first campaign. Ironically, it was Merkel's male CDU handlers who subjected her to an extreme make-over in time for her first race. They changed her hair, added make-up, and incorporated pastels into her wardrobe for a "softer, more sophisticated look."

Although the candidate herself refused to "run as a woman," CDU gatekeepers were not oblivious to her gender appeal. Prior to campaigning, she had asked Swabian hardliner Georg Brunnhuber: "Am I conservative enough for all of you in the South?" He responded: "Forget that. We are already conservative enough on our own. You should see to it that our daughters stick with us."[22] That was the deal. The main campaign theme, following seven years of Red-Green rule, was "a new beginning." One of the first Internet videos aired during the campaign labeled Merkel "*Die Kandidatin*" (the candidate), followed by the question: "*Kann die dat?*" (can she do it?). Schröder appeared under the rubric, "*Der Kanzler*" (the chancellor), followed by another play on words: "*Der Kanz!*" (he can!)[23]

Post-election studies indicate that Merkel was not particularly disadvantaged by the media: in fact, she faced less direct criticism from the *Bild Zeitung* than did Schröder and his SPD-Green government.[24] Voters responded positively to her television debate performance, less concerned about her sex than about Schröder's privatized pension scheme (*Riester Rente*) and tough labor market reforms (Hartz IV) that challenged job security and introduced low-wage jobs. Male CDU rivals recognized the need for some, if not all of the reforms their female candidate was advocating, but they viewed her as a placeholder until one of their own could position himself for higher office.[25]

Merkel's status as the country's first top woman candidate in 2005 posed a real dilemma for gender equality activists and feminist scholars longing for the day when one of their own might finally assume the reins of power. One surprising endorsement came from western Über-feminist, Alice Schwarzer. Doris Schröder-Köpf, by contrast, declared that as a childless female leader, Merkel would be incapable of producing good family policies. Never mind the fact that her status as Schröder's fourth wife suggested that he knew even less about stable family relations–they divorced after 2016 when Doris learned through the media about his affair with an even younger Korean businesswoman. Subsequent analyses found little evidence of gendered voting, giving Merkel only a 0.6 percent advantage.

The vote tallies reported at 6:00 PM on 18 September 2005 were so close that the next morning the *Bild Zeitung* featured half-page, upside-down images of each candidate as the "winner" on page one. Visibly inebriated, Schröder's aggressive, alpha-male television performance during the so-called Elephant Round that evening united CDU/CSU stalwarts behind Merkel.[26] Within days, *Die Zeit* featured a front-page photo of a serious-looking leader crossing a big stage, wearing a black pantsuit: gone was the smiling, blond hair, blue-eyed, pastel image. My first reaction was that Union elites had decided to present their new chief executive as an honorary man. Stoiber immediately announced that her powers would be limited, however, once the CDU and SPD agreed on terms for a grand coalition. The lady-in-waiting replied: "The constitutional guideline powers [Art. 65 GG] also apply to a female chancellor." Her circle of close advisors was promptly dubbed "Girls' Camp."

CSU cabinet member Michael Gloss was the first to label Germany's first female Chancellor "Mutti" (Mommy) in 2005, hoping to discredit her as a frumpy, overly solicitous GDR figure. His characterization belied the reality: working mothers in the East not only enjoyed greater economic independence than their stay-at-home western counterparts; they also out-reproduced them in terms of average birthrates. Corresponding media images bordered on the obscene, featuring Merkel breast-feeding querulous politicians like the Kaczyński brothers in Poland, for example. While other gendered monikers lost salience over time, the *Mutti Merkel* theme persisted, although its meaning shifted dramatically over time, ironically linked to developments in the male-dominated soccer domain. Beginning in 2006, the public encountered regular photos of "the world's most powerful woman" in the middle of a smelly locker-room, standing cheek to check with national-team members like Steinschweiger, Khedira, Boateng, Neuer, Podolski, Klose, Özil, and Götze. By the time of the 2014 World Cup soccer games in Rio, it had taken on positive "mother of the nation" connotations (*Muttivierung der Mannschaft*). At the peak of the 2015 refugee crisis, Merkel was featured as a political Mother Theresa on the cover of *Der Spiegel* (September 18, 2015). She learned to grin and bear it.[27]

Election Campaign 2009: Winning with "More Merkel"

Reviewing her first four years in power, Axel Murswieck declared: "Merkel has the strength of will and the ambition but no vision and therefore no charisma; she cannot be characterized as the great leader of change."[28] Definitions of charisma and vision are themselves rooted in gendered expectations, indicating that the criteria used to assess a female chancellor have "been all too heavily imprinted with the image of deep male voices and muscle-flexing staging."[29] Murswieck was right in one respect, however: in 2009, "Experiment Merkel" came to an end, subjecting "Merkel the Incumbent" to new challenges involving crises of global proportions, starting with the 2008/2009 financial meltdown.[30] Her second campaign also lent credence to the hypothesis that the greater the chances of winning, the more personalized a candidate's campaign becomes. The same holds true for direct candidates versus candidates relegated to second-ballot party lists.[31] By 2009, *Forbes* had named Merkel the "World's Most Powerful Woman" three years in a row. It is hard to explain how someone lacking charisma could have chalked up such unprecedented popularity ratings throughout her first term, much less induced the CDU to concentrate most of its next campaign on promising voters "more Merkel."

Merkel's sex proved an indirect asset in the lackluster 2009 campaign against former grand coalition partner, Frank Walter Steinmeier, which Stephanie Geise described as an "election campaign designed to avoid election campaigning" (*Wahlkampfvermeidungswahlkampf*).[32] Personally inclined to avoid aggressive and ideological stances, the chancellor valued her opponent as a "good, competent man," based on their four years of GroKo cooperation; their mutual respect rendered their television debate "more of a duet than a duel." *Der Spiegel* featured a special-effects cover page that rotated between Merkel and Steinmeier, taking turns sitting on each other's lap. Although the CDU is known as the "black" party, Merkel's managers switched to orange to market their candidate.[33] Her spin team labeled her "Angie," at least until the Rolling Stones threatened to sue over use of their same-name song in campaign ads.[34] Having consciously refused to play the gender card the first time around, it was natural that Merkel's second campaign was also devoid of specific references to "women's" issues.

Her most effective election poster in 2009 nonetheless consisted of a larger-than-life image of the smiling chancellor, underscored with the motto, "*Wir haben die Kraft*" (we have the strength). One could read the "we" to include other strong CDU women comprising her inner circle at the time: Ursula von der Leyen, Annette Schavan, Beate Baumann, Maria Böhmer, and prominent female media moguls like Frieda Springer and Liz Mohn (Bertelsmann). The CDU affixed a 28-meter high billboard with the same slogan to the Charlottenburg city gate, consisting of 1,800 supporters' photos–albeit without the chancellor's visage. Municipal authorities claimed that the conservatives' use of the public structure violated "the neutrality of the state."[35] Even more unfortunate was a poster introduced by former GDR dissident, Vera Lengsfeld, featuring the two well-endowed CDU women in low-cut evening gowns with the slogan, "*Wir haben mehr zu bieten*" (we have more to offer)."[36] This was countered by another photo showing the chancellor cheering wildly at a soccer game, interpreted by Susanne Merkle as proof of her "mastery of a stadium visit traditionally used by male politicians" to win over the public.[37]

With other crises dominating the headlines and more voters turning to the Internet, print coverage of this campagn declined noticeably, based on a review of articles and candidate references found in the *Frankfurter Allgemeine*, the *Süddeutsche Zeitung*, the *Frankfurter Rundschau*, and *Die Welt*. The shrinking size of newspapers, and the growing role of print advertisements, in general, offer only a partial explanation.[38] The lack of intense controversy defining the campaign itself may have simply been deemed less "newsworthy." Green candidate Jürgen Trittin, facing "shame and blame" for his earlier stance on pedophilia, accused Merkel of wanting to ride "the sleeping car to power." A similar sentiment was expressed by CDU "party friend" Günter Oettinger, about to abandon his post as Minister President of Baden-Württemburg.[39] Enjoying an obvious chancellor bonus, Merkel faced more drubbing from *Die Welt* this time around–but less from the *Frankfurter Rundschau*–perhaps due to her proximity to the SPD on many issues.[40] The *Bild Zeitung* headlined the television debate results as "Yes, we gähn," playing on Barack Obama's campaign slogan "yes, we can," and the German word for yawn.[41]

More politicians adopted micro-blogging via Twitter, but younger cohorts tended to rate the "social media break-through" negatively, complaining that most partisan websites were not open to real dialogue.[42] A majority of voters continued to rely on standard communication channels. Posters featured simple photos with strong, short scripts, calling for good education, strong families, "*Ein neues Miteinander*" (new togetherness), and "*Zuversicht, Kanzlerin*" (confidence, chancellor).[43] Merkel outscored her SPD opponent in all categories reflecting personal traits, e.g., competence, likeability, trustworthiness, and the ability to get things done. Some 90 percent of the voters surveyed found the campaign posters "superfluous and devoid of content." Electoral turnout fell to record low of 70.8 percent; non-voters ranked as the "third largest party" in the eastern states.[44]

Merkel took charge of a new conservative–liberal coalition filled with petulant men who continued to engage in gender-baiting from within.[45] Even her much younger FDP Health Minister (born in 1973) engaged in sex-stereotyping at Merkel's expense: Taking the stage at the Gillamoos Volksfest in the Bavarian town of Abensberg, Philipp Rösler (adopted from Vietnam) joked in 2010: "Angela Merkel is also now available as a Barbie Doll ... It costs 300 euros. That is, the doll only costs 20 euros. But, the 40 pant-suits are really expensive."[46] "*Die Macht der Hosenanzüge*" (the power of pant-suits) as *Der Spiegel* put it, would acquire new political weight over the next seven years. While her make-up and hair-do now escape scrutiny, the chancellor is currently beleaguered by running commentaries on her modestly priced but very colorful blazer collection.[47]

Election Campaign 2013: Softening the Image

By the time the 2013 campaign rolled around, the "World's Most Powerful Woman," nine times over, needed no further introduction. The core poster once more featured Angela Merkel as *the* CDU platform, in what was described as another boring, "visionless" campaign against SPD candidate Peer Steinbrück. Now enjoying an export boom, low unemployment and tax surpluses, Germany had become a defining power in response to the Euro crisis and was leading the way to a renewable energy turnaround. Merkel had contained a military clash between Russia and Georgia and–to a degree not yet registered among "the losers of globalization"–had adopted a proactive approach to migrant and refugee integration.[48]

Tired of critiquing her hair and attire, pundits had taken to mocking the chancellor's habit of positioning her hands in a diamond-shape, her fingertips touching as if she were about to pray. By 2013, CDU strategists did not even need to show Merkel's face: the most sensational poster of the campaign was a 70 by 20 meter poster depicting Merkel's hands (labeled *die Raute*), next to the Berlin central railway station (Hauptbahnhof). The picture consisted of 2,150 individual hand images submitted by her supporters, "all of which were active and led by Ms. Merkel." The text declared, "Germany's future is in good hands."[49]

There were a number of different gender twists to this campaign, however. The SPD sought to counter Merkel's image as a popular, calm, competent, steady, and pragmatic-rational leader by personalizing its own top candidate. Steinbrück insisted on shaping his own "appeal" with disastrous consequences. Still burdened by Hartz IV, the SPD clearly chose the wrong man—a former finance minister—to address social justice issues. Claiming he wanted to "speak clearly," Steinbrück emphasized his big honoraria for speeches and his taste for high-priced Pinot Grigio wine, while deriding the chancellor's "low salary" and bragging about his online consultant with hedge fund ties. He allowed himself to be photographed "giving the middle figure" in response to questions about his characterization as *Pannen-Peer* (Problem Peer) and *Peerlusconi.*[50] His "confrontationally male style," reminiscent of Schröder's dismissive treatment of Merkel, led female voters, especially, to view him as cross between a *Panzerkandidat* (tank candidate) and a clown who merely wanted to "rock the boat."[51]

The main buzz regarding the 2013 television debate derived from the fact that Stefan Raab, from "the entertainment sector," served as one of four moderators, two of whom were women (Anne Will, Maybrit Illner). Merkel provided longer answers (more talk means fewer questions), and was less frequently interrupted than Steinbrück—whom Raab occasionally "debated" himself.[52] This time, no real exchanges between the candidates took place—Steinbruck often reacted "aggressively" to moderator interruptions.[53] Merkel's electoral strategy in relation to her opponent "was to ignore him as much as possible."[54] Her main message read: "Germany is doing well today. A strong economy, more people in employment than ever before. That cannot be taken for granted. That is what we have accomplished together."[55]

The other ironic development was a deliberate effort to play up Merkel's softer, pragmatic, warm-hearted side, perhaps to highlight Steinbrück's macho mannerisms. As noted earlier, by 2013, Merkel had re-established the CDU as a party capable of regaining a substantial share of the women's vote, exceeding eligible males by two million. In 2009, almost twice as many women aged twenty-nine to thirty-four had chosen the Union over the SPD.[56] Von der Leyen's performance as a strong labor minister in an otherwise blustering-male, conservative-liberal coalition helped to shore up Merkel's popularity, for example, with the introduction of new child-care guarantees and other reforms "modernizing" the CDU. After replacing the younger Rösler at the head of the FDP, *Spitzenkandidat* Rainer Brüderle fell on his own sword, based on allegations of sexual harassment.

Merkel pursued an unusual degree of "outreach" to women in 2013, appearing at three headliner events in six days. They included a formal

Brigitte Live interview on 2 May at the Maxim Gorki Theater under the rubric "Women vote!"–something that would have been "unthinkable" in 2005. She reportedly teared up a bit discussing her favorite film (DEFA's "Legend of Paul and Paula"), and talked about men, cooking, and church. Shortly thereafter, the CDU included her admission that she did not put enough crumbles on cakes at home to suit her husband's taste (the son of a baker) in a flyer for journalists.[57] The idea was not only to "personalize" the chancellor, e.g., as fair, honest, competent, and humorous, but also to "privatize" her. She reiterated the line, "I am not a feminist," but admitted "that as a possible role model for women, I am an interesting case."[58] Next, she appeared before the Berlin Women's Network, for a session called "meet me in the middle." She then convened a conference of 100 "leading women" in the Chancellor's Office.[59]

While she had not supported a female quota either as women's minister or as opposition leader, the chancellor eventually followed von der Leyen's (EU-inspired) lead in accepting a 30 percent corporate board quota during her third term (taking effect in 2016). Her second, very unpopular women's minister, Kristina Schröder, had supported caretaker payments demanded by the CSU for stay-at-home moms–an option she did not choose for herself after giving birth.[60] She also rejected an official minimum wage for underpaid, "pink-collar" occupations. The chancellor had gradually begun to move on these issues during her second term. Birgit Meyer noted that given anyone's inability to challenge her "most powerful woman" status and crisis management skills, Merkel could finally afford to play the gender card in 2013.[61] I argue that while her attendance at such events may have offered a partial "image correction," by then, the chancellor's actual policy reforms had already established her as more gender-friendly than many people imagined, based in part on her east German socialization.[62] This time, an empirical analysis of 480 Merkel-related articles in the *Frankfurter Allgemeine*, the *Süddeutsche*, and *Bild* from 30 August to 28 September did not detect a single reference to the chancellor's hair.[63]

For the first time since 1994, the CDU secured 41.5 percent of the vote, returning to a grand coalition, albeit with a visibly weakened SPD as its junior partner (16 percentage points behind). Matthias Jung, Yvonne Schroth, and Andrea Wolf contend that it was "actually an accomplishment of the Chancellor, that allowed her [FDP] coalition partner so unloved by the population to disappear from memory."[64] Returning to government after an eight-year hiatus in 2009, the Liberals had little more to offer in 2013 than a demand for tax cuts at a time when the public cared more about remedies to the financial crisis. The FDP is one of two parties that still rejects formal mechanisms for advancing female candidates.[65] Merkel had refused to campaign for the FDP (second ballot) vote during 2013.[66]

Women's support for the Union surpassed that of men, 44 percent to 39 percent. The CDU's best results rested with older females with 49 percent among those over sixty (women tend to outlive men). More surprisingly, the party also captured 34 percent of eighteen to twenty-nine year-old vote. The Greens lost 5 percent of their "usual" under-thirty female share, although women still outnumbered men among their constituents (10 percent to 7 percent). The SPD lost big among citizens under thirty, garnering less than an average share of female votes (24 percent).[67] These figures attest to a bona fide "Merkel effect" among many women who would have normally been averse to voting for conservatives.

Originally presenting itself as an anti-Euro party, the Alternative for Germany (AfD) arrived on the scene just in time to render the party system more chaotic. It would gain momentum a year later in conjunction with the 2014 European Parliament elections, after which it also redefined itself as an anti-migration and anti-Muslim party. While it managed to channel some protest and discontent, especially in the eastern Länder, it offered no full-fledged political platform. Both the FDP and AfD failed to cross the 5 percent threshold. In fact, nearly 16 percent of votes went to parties that did not secure seats in the Bundestag.[68]

Backlash: Election Campaign 2017

The need to manage two grand coalitions within the space of twelve years has not only affected Angela Merkel's leadership style, but also the kind of election campaign she can pursue without discrediting her own achievements. The positive effects of the chancellor bonus have yielded to a long paper trail of statements, decisions and policy promises than can be turned into negatives by pundits or voters expecting quick fixes. In fact, it could be argued that Merkel's need to exercise rhetorical restraint vis-à-vis her SPD coalition partner-turned-rival has inadvertently contributed to the vehement rhetoric of opposition groups, frustrated by the unwillingness of the larger system parties to "speak truth to power"–given that they have shared that power for two out of the past three terms. Despite a formidable list of reforms undertaken by Merkel's three governments, the presence of five or more parties in parliament renders electoral outcomes quite vulnerable to a growing share of undecided voters with little interest in, much less detailed knowledge of complex legislative processes.

These developments have been fueled by the unfettered nature of Internet exchanges across many democratic states. Europe, in general, has not only witnessed dramatic changes in the larger media and communications environment due to the proliferation of social media outlets; it has also seen a very negative shift in electoral campaign culture per se. Jürgen Wilke and Melaine Liedecker pinpoint a number of unsettling trends that are likely to render formal political campaigns ever more irrelevant in the years ahead. They note that objective, news-oriented reporting is being replaced by subjective elements like commentaries, feature articles, and "readers' fora." Journalists themselves are making less use of material from established news agencies, subject to various forms of corroboration. A reliance on visual images, talk-show exchanges, and candidate sound-bites has replaced substantive interviews. Even mainstream print media offer fewer articles with less space for direct quotations.[69]

The 2017 election saw a further push towards the "marketization" of candidates, as demonstrated by the CDU's decision to hire a foreigner more familiar with advertising luxury vehicles than political platforms–though some stalwarts were opposed. Swiss ad-man Jean-Remy von Matt had avoided a campaign consultant role for years, claiming it was "too risky, not creative and doesn't pay much." Selling the World's Most Powerful Woman (now ten times over) seemed easy: "During the course of my career I have advertised the best beer brands and the fastest sports cars, but never a product as competitively superior as Ms. Merkel."[70] His allegedly higher purpose was to combat the dangers of right-wing populism by building a "stable middle." The two were not a good match, pitting Merkel's brand of sober, rational politics and her "somnambulist tendency to avoid tough debates" against von Matt's motto, "everything I do is a statement against boredom."

The chancellor sought to avoid a "feminine font" and sweeping campaign promises ("expectations management"), while relying on "pleasing colors." The resulting posters were patriotic in tone: black, red and gold, suggesting security and order. More importantly, Merkel wanted to counter the negative emotionalism invoked by the AfD, while nonetheless reaching out to the countless volunteers who back her migration/asylum policies. She was presented as "clever, level-headed, decisive, sure to keep Germany on its path to success." The official CDU slogan, "*Ein Deutschland in dem wir gut und gerne leben*" (a Germany in which we live well and happily") was no match for the frontal attacks featured in AfD posters, nor for the extraordinary amount of time that mainstream media had provocatively devoted to the AfD, as other participants vehemently complained during the postelection Elephant Round. Statements by AfD candidates were often unabashedly xenophobic, and its poster images were often sexist in nature.

Party-internal discontent with her four-year GroKo partner Sigmar Gabriel led the SPD to pull veteran European parliamentarian Martin Schulz out of its otherwise empty candidate-options hat, who soon accused her of an "asymmetrical demobilization" of political debate. Yet, the only real point of contention between the two top candidates during the television debate was whether or not to declare Turkey's application for EU membership officially dead. Otherwise, they agreed on the basics regarding what had always been hotly contested issues between the Union and the SPD prior to 2005: migration, asylum, energy issues, Europe, and potential military engagement. While there is some truth to Schulz's complaint that Merkel has "depoliticized" many policy debates over the last decade, one could argue that this has occurred, in part, as the result of her "data-driven" decision-making and reliance on expert task-forces–good for policy, but problematic for citizen engagement. Schulz's effort to enhance his own image as a fierce defender of *streitbare Demokratie* (contentious democracy) overlooked the ways in which SPD participation in two grand coalitions has also contributed to the demise of "fundamental opposition" since 2005.[71]

Female voters' strong preference for Merkel was countered by the fact that nearly twice as many men voted for the AfD (16 percent vs. 9 percent), particularly between the ages of thirty and fifty-nine. Blaming the Union's "spectacular" 8.6 percent loss on Merkel ignores the fact that her personal popularity is what actually produced the new high of 41.5 percent in 2013. Appealing to the far right, the male-dominated CSU lost 10 percent of its 2013 share in Bavaria, so Merkel's refusal to place a cap on asylum-seekers was not the only factor undermining a Union victory.[72] Stronger eastern support for the AfD (29 percent of male voters, 17 percent of female voters) is hard to explain, objectively speaking, insofar as those constituents now enjoy a cleaner environment, better job prospects, higher pensions, more health care options, and significantly more freedom of expression than was ever the case under traditional male rule, east or west.[73]

Equally significant for this analysis is the poor job the SPD has done, despite its early advocacy of quotas, in finding top candidates who will not ignore (or, at worst, repel) female voters. As of 2018, the federal president was an SPD man, its two Groko vice-chancellors were male, and its male-dominated executive "chose" the five women (out of seven SPD ministers) in the last Cabinet.[74] Given a rare opportunity to address a *Brigitte* audience, Schulz began by thanking his supportive engineer-wife, who had been forced to take a back seat during the child-rearing years, which he blamed on the *Scheisspolitik* of previous governments. He referenced "women's problems in society" as if women, not society, were the problem. He said nothing about the macho men of the Red-Green coalition who deliberately undercut female ministers' efforts to push work-family reconciliation policies and antidiscrimination measures. According to Tine H. Hildebrandt and Bernd U. Ulrich, Schulz and his partisan comrades are likewise subject to the male disease of *Kränkung*–feeling aggrieved that they are not being taken seriously, even when they take time out to "talk tenderly about their children." While SPD men have not deliberately engaged in backlash against women and minorities to the extent witnessed among AfD sympathizers, they have ostensibly devoted more energy to feeling cheated by Merkel's ability to secure the enactment of "their" progressive policies than to proactively meliorating "the rubbing of tectonic plates between two continents of masculinity."[75]

Conclusion: Gender Still Matters, but How?

Angela Merkel's diverging roles as a challenger, an incumbent, an effective crisis manger and, finally, as "the only real alternative" on a dramatically transformed political stage provide us with a unique opportunity to assess the changing impact of gender variables on election campaigns in Germany. While many scholars concentrate on descriptive representation (DR), that is, women's physical presence in government, measured largely in numerical terms, it is much harder to trace the transformation of gender factors over time, particularly when dealing with a sample of one. A second problem with studies confined to legislative bodies is that DR data tell us little about the women behind the scenes.[76] Women now comprise nearly 50 percent of the Federal Chancellor's Office (FCO) staff, half of whom were under forty in 2008, leading to one fun fact: among the nineteen (of 450) FCO aides who gave birth during Schröder's last thirty-five months in office, few returned to work. There were forty-nine FCO births during Merkel's first thirty-two months, most of whom resumed their posts under improved family leave options enacted in 2007–by a childless CDU chief. The pool of eligibles for high administrative office has expanded accordingly. Merkel has even introduced a "Girls' Day," meeting with young women at the Chancellery. Her staying power across fourteen years (thus far) has indeed chipped away at gender stereotypes at the highest levels of government.

Increasing women's numerical strength is ultimately a function of "all things being equal," which they usually are not, obliging us to consider other gender-relevant reforms that have helped to level the political playing field. Substantive representation pertains to a leader's ability to reshape policies in ways that promote greater equality. While Merkel deliberately avoided "women's issues" during her first two campaigns, she allowed Ursula von der Leyen to lead the rhetorical charge across two terms, as her Family and Labor minister, respectively. Drawing on her GDR socialization and leveraging EU mandates, Merkel has gradually impelled lawmakers to guarantee both infant/childcare facilities and paternal leave, to adopt corporate quotas, and to fund special programs for women in the MINT/STEM fields. In September 2017, Berlin's health minister, Dilek Kolat, had to convene a crisis summit to address a shortage of midwives, as birthrates reached their highest levels in thirty years.[77] Easterners are now complaining about insufficient numbers of pediatricians as well.

Finally, I turn to transformative representation, assessing the extent to which this chancellor has succeeded in fostering a new gender regime across the political spectrum. First and foremost, she has pulled off an astonishing modernization of the CDU itself, a party steeped for decades in a *Kinder-Küche-Kirche* mentality. Secondly, beyond serving as a role model for young women attracted to politics, Merkel's "intercultural opening" policies have created new windows of opportunity for would-be politicos of migrant descent. Thirdly, her reluctance to label herself a feminist has not stopped her from pursing a holistic approach to a host of employment, science/technology, demographic, and migration-related issues, amounting to her own (albeit very limited) version of "gender mainstreaming."[78]

While four election campaign cycles have downplayed the gender dimensions of her leadership, Merkel has done more to advance opportunities for the equal participation of women and men in German society than all of her predecessors combined. Her motives have been mixed, but as Deng Xiao-ping famously opined, "it doesn't matter if the cat is black or white, as long as it catches mice." A more serious problem for Merkel is not that she lacks vision, passion or the will to lead but rather that male hardliners and malcontents oppose the direction in which she is taking them, fearing that they will lose their privileged positions. No matter what happens throughout the course of her third grand coalition, Germany's first female eastern chancellor will be a very tough act to follow.

Joyce Marie Mushaben is a Curators' Distinguished Professor of Comparative Politics and former Director of the Institute for Women's & Gender Studies at the University of Missouri-St. Louis. Her research covers social movements, German unification and identities, women's leadership, gender, ethnicity and welfare issues, EU migration and asylum policies. Recent books include *The Changing Faces of Citizenship: Integration and Mobilization among Ethnic Minorities in Germany* (New York, 2008); *Gendering the European Union: New Responses to Old Democratic Deficits,* co-edited with Gabriele Abels (Basingstoke, 2012); and *Becoming Madam Chancellor: Angela Merkel and the Berlin Republic* (Cambridge, 2017). Honored with the Chancellor's Award for Excellence in Research Creativity (2007) and the Missouri Governor's Award for Teaching Excellence (2012), Mushaben is a three-time Alexander von Humboldt Fellow, a former Ford Foundation Fellow, German Marshall Fund grantee and DAAD recipient. E-mail: mushaben@umsl.edu

Notes

1. The author gratefully recognizes the financial support extended by the German Marshall Fund, the German Academic Exchange Service and the International Association for the Study of German Politics that made it possible for her to "observe" the final week of all Bundestag elections on site, dating back to 1990.
2. "And please call me Ms. President," *New York Times*, 22 February 1999.
3. Examples include the Multifactor Leadership Questionnaire, the Leadership Behavior Inventory, the Global Transformational Leadership Scale, the Positive Organizational Behavior Model and the Ethical Leadership Scale. For mega-study evidence, see Alice H. Eagly and Linda L. Carli, "The female advantage: An evaluation of the evidence," *The Leadership Quarterly* 14 (2003): 807-834; and P.L. Koopman, D.N. Den Hartog, and E. Konrad, "National culture and leadership profiles in Europe: Some Results from the GLOBE Study," *European Journal of Work and Organizational Psychology* 8, no. 4 (1999): 503-520.
4. "Sie sind ein würdeloses Weib," *Hannoversche Allgemeine*, 15 October 1970.
5. Joyce Marie Mushaben, *Becoming Madam Chancellor: Angela Merkel and the Berlin Republic* (Cambridge, 2017), especially chapter 1; Bernd Ulrich, "Die Verwandlung," *Die Zeit*, 2 June 2005.
6. Eagly and Carli (see note 3), 821.
7. Men may be judged effective even when they perform poorly: Wall Street firms continued to pay out multi-million dollar bonuses after the 2008 melt-down, "to keep the best people"–the same men who brought down the system in the first place!
8. Frank Brettschneider, Oskar Niedermayer, and Bernhard Weßels, "Die Bundestangswahl 2005: Analysen des Wahlkampfes und der Wahlergebnisse" in *Die Bundestagswahl 2005. Analysen des Wahlkampfes und der Wahlergebnisse*, ed. Frank Brettschneider, Oskar Niedermayer and Bernhard Weßels (Wiesbaden, 2007), 11.
9. Olga Khazan, "Why Germany's Politics Are Much Saner, Cheaper, and Nicer Than Ours," *The Atlantic*, 30 September 2013. The CDU and SPD each spent roughly € 20 to 30 million in 2013, compared to the over $400 million per candidate that Barack Obama and Mitt Romney spent on television ads; Obama's reelection campaign (excluding PAC money) burned through $700 million.
10. "Bundestagwahl 2013: CDU kassiert die meisten Großspenden," *Der Spiegel*, 10 August 2013.
11. Silvano Moeckli, *So funktioniert Wahlkampf* (Stuttgart, 2017).
12. This was the response to my question at the debriefing session held at the German Press and Information Center in Berlin on 25 September 2017.

13. Dieter Ohr, Markus Klein, and Ulrich Rosar, "Bewertungen der Kanzlerkandidaten und Wahlentscheidung bei der Bundestagswahl 2009" in *Wahlen und Wähler*, ed. Bernhard Weßels et al. (Wiesbaden, 2013), 208.
14. Ibid., 209.
15. Nina Grunenberg, "Kerle, wollt ihr ewig kungeln?" *Die Zeit*, 24 January 2002.
16. Amir Abedi, "We Are Not in Bonn Anymore: The Impact of German Unification on Party Systems at the Federal and Land Levels," *German Politics* 26, no. 4 (2017): 457-479.
17. David F. Patton, "Monday, Monday: Eastern Protest Movements and German Party Politics since 1989," *German Politics* 26, no. 4 (2017): 480-497.
18. Tine Hildebrandt and Bernd Ulrich, "It's gender, stupid! Die SPD ist immer noch ein Männerverein. So kann sie die Kanzlerin nicht besiegen," *Die Zeit*, 21 June 2017.
19. Liane von Billerbeck, "Die Mitte ist weiblich," *Die Zeit*, 21 February 2002; Christiane Hoffmann, "Damenwahl," *Der Spiegel*, 18 May 2013, 16-19.
20. Hoffmann (see note 19). See also William E. Gibson, "South's 'Angry White Men' Feel Betrayed by Clinton," *Sun Sentinel*, 20 October 1996.
21. Herlinde Koelbl, *Spuren der Macht. Die Verwandlung des Menschen durch das Amt* (Munich, 1999).
22. Mariam Lau, *Die letzte Volkspartei. Angela Merkel und die Modernisierung der CDU* (Munich, 2009), 9.
23. See also "Was will (kann) Angela Merkel?" *Der Spiegel*, 11 July 2005.
24. Astrid Jansen, Gary Bente, and Nicole C. Krämer, "Wahlkampf 2005: Eine inhaltsanalytische Untersuchung der Inszenierung von Angela Merkel und Gerhard Schöder in den Fernsehnachrichten unter Berücksichtigung des Geschlechterstereotyps" in *Information, Warhnehmung, Emotion. Politische Psychologie in der Wahl- und Einstellungsforschung*, ed. Thorsten Faas, Kai Arzheimer, and Sigrid Roßteuscher (Wiesbaden, 2010), 33-50. Assessing media coverage from 20 August through 17 September, Jansen et al. found some evidence of a "chancellor bonus" regarding *Tagesschau* and *RTL aktuell* coverage, but the differences were not statistically significant.
25. Imbibing a lot of Chivas Regal, a group of young, ambitious CDU males calling themselves the "Andes Pact" had agreed on a flight en route to Santiago, Chile never to rival each other for key party positions. The same up-and-coming conservatives, e.g., Christian Wulff, Friedbert Pflüger, Jürgen Rüttgers, and Roland Koch, conspired to block her candidacy in 2002. Merkel outwitted them by undertaking a secret trip to Stoiber's home in Bavaria for Sunday breakfast to "approve" his candidacy in exchange for leadership concessions.
26. Matthias Geis, "Angezählt, aber noch nicht ausgezählt," *Die Zeit*, 22 September 2005.
27. Norbert Wallet, "Mutti lädt zum Essen ein," *Stuttgarter Nachrichten*, November 20, 2013; see the Polish title page, "Machoca Europy," *Wprost*, June 28, 2007. Italian Northern League publications also used degradingly sexist portrayals.
28. Axel Murswieck, "Angela Merkel als Regierungschefin und als Kanzler-Kandidatin," *Aus Politik und Zeitgeschichte* 51 (2009): 29.
29. Katje Glaesner, "Angela Merkel–mit 'Soft Skills' zum Erfolg?," *Aus Politik und Zeitgeschichte,* 50 (2009): 21.
30. Murswieck (see note 27), 32.
31. Brettschneider et al. (see note 8), 12.
32. Stephanie Geise, "'Unser Land kann mehr…': Visuelle Wahlkampfstrategien in der Plakatkommunikation zur Bundestagswahl 2009," *Zeitschrift für Politikberatung* 3/2 (2010): 153.
33. I pointed out during the IASGP discussion at the CDU headquarters that orange was a politically loaded color, suggesting the problematic Ukrainian revolution, unrequited soccer love in the Netherlands, "the Troubles" in Northern Ireland, and a high state of alarm at the Department of Homeland Security, but our speaker was too young to see the connections.

34. Campaign crowds sang "Angie, Angie," oblivious to the lugubrious lyrics of the Rolling Stones song they were pirating: "with no loving in our souls and no money in our coats, you can't say we're satisfied ..."
35. Helga Hochwind, "Missglückte CDU Wahlwerbung: Pleiten, Pech, Plakate," *Der Spiegel*, 3 September 2009.
36. "CDU Abgeordnete macht Wahlkampf mit Merkel Dekollette," *Der Spiegel*, 10. August 2009.
37. Susanne Merkle, "Personalisierung und genderspezifische Berichterstattung im Bundestagswahlkampf 2013–'Ausnahmefall' Angela Merkel oder typisch Frau" in *Die Massenmedia im Wahlkampf: Die Bundestagswahl 2013*, ed. Christina Holtz-Bacha (Wiesbaden, 2015), 218.
38. Jürgen Wilke and Melanie Liedecker, "Eine Wahlkampf, der keiner war? Die Presseberichterstattung zur Bundestagswahl 2009 im Langzeitvergleich" in Holtz-Bacha (see note 36), 344. *Frankfurter Rundschau* articles declined from 300 (2005) to 120 (2009); reports in the *Süddeutsche* fell from 280 to 160, from 210 to 150 in the *Frankfurter Allgemeine* and from 340 down to 175 in *Die Welt*, respectively.
39. Ibid., 343.
40. Ibid., 364.
41. Ibid., 368.
42. Reimar Zeh, "Wie viele Fans hat Angela Merkel? Wahlkampf in Social Network Sites" in *Die Massenmedien im Wahlkampf. Das Wahljahr 2009*, ed. Christina Holtz-Bacha (Wiesbaden, 2010), 255. IASGP election observers sat through one session packed with young "social media experts" who spent more time texting with outsiders than listening to questions from the audience. Most of us "escaped" by sliding down a loading-dock ramp near a side exit.
43. One study reviewed 33,048 Twitter uses from 18 June through 30 September 2009, encompassing 10 million news items. See Pascal Jürgens and Andreas Jungherr, "Wahlkampf vom Sofa aus: Twitter im Bundestagswahlkampf 2009" in *Das Internet im Wahlkampf: Analysen zur Bundestagswahl 2009*, ed. Johanna Schweitzer and Steffen Albrecht (Wiesbaden, 2011).
44. Wissenschaftliche Dienste, *Sinkende Wahlbeteiligung in Deutschland: Ursachen und Lösungsvorschläge,* Deutscher Bundestag WD 1-3000-008/15 (Berlin, 2016).
45. For a long list of gendered nick-names used by pundits and hardliners, see Mushaben (see note 5), 23-24.
46. "Gillamoos-Volksfest in Abensberg: Die Koalition: 'eine schlagende Verbindung'," *Süddeutsche Zeitung,* 6 September 2010.
47. See Julia Schramm, *Fifty Shades of Merkel* (Hamburg, 2016).
48. Mushaben (see note 5).
49. Philipp Wittrock, "Riesenplakat der CDU: Maxima Merkel," *Der Spiegel*, 2 September 2013.
50. Christina Holtz-Bacha, "Bundestagswahlkampf 2013: Der Kandidat, der nicht inszenieren lassen wollte" in Holtz-Bacha (see note 36), 1-12; "SPD verteidigt Steinbrücks Stinkefinger-Pose," *Der Spiegel*, 12 September 2013.
51. Dana Dülcke and Sascha K. Futh, "Die 'Mutter der Nation' gegen den 'Panzerkandidaten'–Gechlechterbilder in der Berichterstattung der Printmedien zum Bundestagswahlkampf 2013" in Holtz-Bacha (see note 36), 249-273.
52. Christoph Tapper and Thorsten Quandt, "Frau Bundeskanzlerin, der Herausforder ist in einer gewissen Dysbalance... ": Eine dialoganalytische Untersuchung des TV-Duells im Bundestagswahlkampf 2013" in Holz-Bacha (see note 36), 128.
53. Ibid., 138.
54. Ibid., 142.
55. Christina Holz-Bacha and Eva-Maria Lessinger, "Die Königen, der Rausschmeißer und die Gemeine Filzlaus: Die Wahlspots der Parteien im Bundestagswahlkampf 2013" in Holz-Bacha (see note 36), 82.

56. Hoffmann (see note 19), 18.
57. Merkle (see note 36), 217.
58. Hoffmann (see note 19), 18.
59. Ibid., 17.
60. Annette Henninger and Angelika von Wahl, "Das Umspielen von Veto-Spielern. Wie eine konservative Familienministerin den Familialismus des deutschen Wohlfahrtsstaates unterminiert" in *Die zweite Große Koalition: Eine Bilanz der Regierung Merkel, 2005–2009*, ed. Christoph Egle and Reimut Zohlnhöfer (Wiesbaden, 2010), 361-379.
61. Birgit Meier, cited in Hoffmann (see note 19), 17.
62. Sabine Lang, "Gender Equality in Post-Unification Germany: Between GDR Legacies and EU-Level Pressures," *German Politics* 26, no. 4 (2017): 556-573; and Mushaben (see note 5), especially Chapter 8.
63. Merkle (see note 36), 241.
64. Matthias Jung, Yvonne Schroth, and Andrea Wolf, "Wählerverhalten und Wahlergebnis: Angela Merkel's Sieg in der Mitte" in *Die Bundestagswahl 2013*, ed. Karl-Rudolf Korte (Wiesbaden, 2015), 37-38.
65. Louise Davidson-Schmich, *Gender Quotas and Democratic Participation: Recruiting Candidates for Elective Offices in Germany* (Ann Arbor, 2016).
66. Jung, Schroth, and Wolf (see note 63), 38.
67. Ibid., 44-48
68. Ibid., 42.
69. Wilke and Liedecke (see note 37), 366.
70. Von Matt had lost his most significant client, Mercedes, three years earlier. See Stefan Schirmer, "Jetzt mal mit Gefühl," *Die Zeit*, 29 June 2017.
71. Sebastian Fischer, "Kanzlerin Merkel im Wahlkampf: Nicht zu fassen," *Der Spiegel*, 22 June 2017.
72. See https://www.bundeswahlleiter.de/bundestagswahlen/2017/ergebnisse/bund-99/land-9.html, accessed 7 March 2018.
73. For a theoretical discussion on potential short- and long-term influences shaping partisan orientations in the Eastern states, see Jonathan Grix, "East German Political Attitudes: Socialist Legacies v. Situational Factors–A False Antithesis," *German Politics* 9, no, 2 (2000): 109-124.
74. Hildebrandt and Ulrich (see note 18).
75. Ibid.
76. Women's share of Bundestag seats rose from 31.8 percent in 2005 to 33.4 percent in 2009, peaking at 37 percent in 2013. It dropped to 31 percent, the lowest figure in nineteen years, following the 2017 elections. Gains by the male dominated AfD and FDP, coupled with big SPD losses, account for most of the decline.
77. Stefanie Hildebrandt, "Berlin im Baby-Boom–Kolat lädt zum Krisengipfel," *Berliner Zeitung*, 15 September 2017.
78. Joyce Marie Mushaben, "The Reluctant Feminist: Angela Merkel and the Modernization of Gender Politics in Germany," *Femina Politica* 27, No. 2 (2018): 83-94.

··· Chapter 5 ···

THE LEFT PARTY AND THE AfD

Populist Competitors in Eastern Germany

Jonathan Olsen

As is evident in the articles in this special issue, several main narratives developed following the 2017 German national election. The main headline, of course, was the Alternative for Germany's (AfD) precedent-shattering election performance. Not only did a populist radical right party gained representation in the Bundestag for the first time in Germany's postwar history, the AfD's 12.6 percent of the vote placed it as the third largest party in parliament and–given the Social Democratic Party's (SPD) decision to enter another grand coalition with Chancellor Angela Merkel's Christian Democratic Union (CDU)–the largest opposition party. Another central narrative was the fall in fortunes of the CDU and Merkel. Despite retaining its status as the largest parliamentary group with Merkel returning as chancellor, the Union plummeted to 33 percent of the vote, down 8.5 percent from its 2013 total. A third headline was the disastrous result of the SPD. The party's 20.5 percent was an historical low, and the SPD immediately announced it would go into the opposition to lick its wounds–reversing this decision a few months later and endorsing a new coalition with Merkel in March 2018. Finally, the reemergence of the FDP was another, if more muted, narrative of the 2017 election. With 10.7 percent, the Liberals rebounded strongly from their terrible election performance of 2013, consequently displaying a newfound assertiveness in coalition negotiations with the Union, even going so far as to withdraw from exploratory talks with the Greens and CDU in November 2017.

Barely registering on the postelection radar screen was the result for the Left Party (LP). Some of this undoubtedly had to do with the seeming ambiguity of its election result. Seen from one perspective, the LP was a winner

Notes for this section begin on page 138.

in the election as it increased its overall vote percentage from 8.6 percent in 2013 to 9.2 percent in 2017, a rise of 0.6 percent. Indeed, the LP even won some 500,000 more votes in 2017 than it did in 2013 and saw its voter share rise in the western states by almost 2.5 percent. It netted an additional five members of parliament (MdBs) as a result of the election and won five direct mandates (four in Berlin, one in Leipzig). Seen from another perspective, however, the Left Party was a clear loser of the election inasmuch as even though the party's election result was marginally better than the Greens, it was bested by the FDP and was thoroughly outperformed by the AfD. Moreover, the LP suffered grievously in its home base in eastern Germany where it suffered an across the board decline in vote shares. Even more significantly, this hemorrhage of voters in the east was largely attributable to the AfD: proportionally, the LP lost more votes to the AfD than any other party.

On its face, the desertion of LP voters to the AfD seems quite curious. The parties are apparent polar opposites in terms of ideology and policy prescriptions, and each made their distaste clear for the other throughout the election campaign. So why did so many former voters for the Left Party opt for the AfD in this election? This article argues that despite numerous ideological and policy differences, some of the LP's political positioning has always clearly reflected a populist style very much in synch with the populist core of the AfD and a large pool of eastern protest voters that the LP until recently attracted. Specifically, the LP and AfD share a criticism of established political elites and the state of democracy in Germany. Furthermore, some of the LP's policy positions and public statements by its leadership–its skeptical if not hostile attitude towards globalization, the EU, and free trade agreements; its friendly position towards Russia; its pessimism about the state of democracy in Germany and advocacy for the use of referenda as a way to exercise control over political elites and return power to the "people"–are almost identical to those of the AfD. In short, despite numerous policy differences voters who once voted for the LP for its anti-establishment credentials as well as a few select policy issues (Russia, free trade, and distrust of democratic institutions) may now be turning to the AfD for exactly those same reasons.

The first section of the article provides a detailed overview of election results, with particular attention paid to regions and constituencies where the LP lost votes to the AfD. Included here as well is the demographic makeup of LP and AfD voters as well as attitudinal indicators among AfD and LP voters. The next section then compares and contrasts the election manifestos of the LP and AfD before turning to a discussion of populism–

how it can be understood and how populism manifests itself in both parties. Finally, the article speculates on ways in which the AfD was able to successfully present itself as the more "authentic" and new populist representative for protest voters in contrast to the Left Party.

The 2017 Election Results for the Left Party and AfD Compared

Both the AfD and the Left Party can be said to be, with some qualifications, parties of eastern Germany. This has obviously been true from the beginning for the LP, as the origins of the party lie in the old East German Socialist Unity Party (SED). After unification, it got a second life as the Party of Democratic Socialism (PDS). The merger of the PDS with the Electoral Alternative for Labor and Social Justice (WASG) in 2005 altered the profile of the party from a left-wing representative of eastern interests to, at least nominally, an all-German party of the radical left.[1] In terms of its voters, however, the party stayed largely an eastern party until very recently. Not only was its percentage of the vote four to five times higher in eastern Germany in national elections, it routinely received between 20 and 30 percent of the vote in Land elections, serving as a coalition partner for the SPD in several state governments. Since 2011, it has been the junior partner to the SPD in Brandenburg, and, in 2014, the LP made history in Thuringia through the selection of Bodo Ramelow as minister president, the first time the party had placed one of its own at the top of government. Yet, while the 2017 Bundestag election did not completely alter the fundamental fact of the lingering "easterness" of the LP, its electoral fortunes in the two halves of Germany underscored the transition of the party away from its roots as an eastern German regional party. In eastern Germany, the LP received 17.1 percent of the vote, down about 5 percent from its 2013 election result. In other words, it lost about 20 percent of its voters in eastern Germany. In fact, in every state in eastern Germany the LP saw steep declines: down 5.3 percent in Brandenburg, 3.7 percent in Mecklenburg-West Pomerania, 3.9 percent in Saxony, 6.2 percent in Saxony-Anhalt, and 6.6 percent in Thuringia.[2] To keep these loses in perspective, it should be remembered that in the 2009 national election the party scored 32.4 percent of the vote in Saxony-Anhalt while in Brandenburg it received 28.5 percent. By contrast, in 2013 these totals were 24 percent and 22.5 percent respectively (see Table 5.1). Thus, the LP has seen its share of the vote in these two states decline by about a fourth over the course of eight years.

Table 5.1: Election Results in 2017 for the Left Party in Eastern German States

State	2017 Election Result	+/- 2013
Berlin (east)	26.1	-3.4
Brandenburg	17.2	-5.3
Mecklenburg-West Pomerania	17.8	-3.7
Saxony	16.1	-3.9
Saxony-Anhalt	17.8	-6.2
Thuringia	16.9	-6.6

Source: Bundeswahlleiter

Even in East Berlin, the Left Party saw its share of the vote erode in 2017. Although it still had some of its best overall results in eastern districts (e.g., Berlin-Lichtenberg with 29.3 percent, albeit down 5.2 percent from 2013), overall, it lost 3.4 percent against its 2013 result in eastern districts of Berlin. Meanwhile, the LP won about 2.5 percent more of the vote in western Germany in 2017 than it had in 2013, with a final result in Western Germany of 7.2 percent. It increased its share of the vote in every western German state ranging from marginal gains (plus 1.5 percent in Baden-Württemberg) to significant ones (12.2 percent in Hamburg, up 3.4 percent compared to 2013).[3] It also increased its share of the vote in every western constituency, doing notably better in key urban areas there–the aforementioned Hamburg, but also Cologne, Hannover, Bremen, Munich, and Frankfurt/Main. Moreover, in West Berlin the party gained significantly more votes, finishing with 13.8 percent, an improvement of 3 percent compared to 2013, especially in Neuköln (up 4.7 percent), Charlottenburg-Wilmersdorf (up 3.3 percent), and Tempelhof-Schöneberg (up 3.5 percent).[4] In short, in 2017, the party became much more of a national party of the radical left than any time in its history, a development which appears to have come at the expense of the LP's profile as a party of eastern interests.[5] Indeed, today the LP has as many party members in western Germany as in eastern Germany–the exact opposite of the AfD.[6]

Where did the LP's former voters in eastern Germany go? Similar to state elections in 2016 and 2017 in Mecklenburg-West Pomerania, Saxony, and Berlin, these voters went largely to the AfD.[7] Some 430,000 voters changed from the LP to the AfD in the 2017 election, the largest share of voters lost to another party by the LP (the FDP was a distant second at 60,000). Although the LP gained 430,000 former SPD voters and another 170,000 from former Green voters, these votes came overwhelmingly from western Germany.[8] Demographically, the LP lost votes among blue-collar workers and the unemployed, although these groups still represent a significant share of LP voters.[9] It gained votes from young people in western Germany but its voter base in eastern Germany continued to age and it did rather poorly with middle-aged voters. In terms of education levels, the LP did much better among those with college degrees than it did with those with lower levels of education.

Meanwhile, the AfD presented an almost mirror-image of the LP in its election result: although it hardly did poorly in western Germany (its best result being in Bavaria at 12.4 percent), it performed significantly better in eastern Germany. While in western Germany the AfD received 10.7 percent of the second vote, in eastern Germany its result was a shocking 20.5 percent. Overall, the party more than doubled its share of the vote in western Germany compared to 2013 (Hamburg excepted)–whereas in eastern Germany it almost quadrupled its vote share. At the state level, the AfD's best result was in Saxony, where it won 27 percent and was the largest party, edging out the CDU at 26.9 percent. The AfD won three direct mandates in the 2017 election, all of them districts in Saxonian Switzerland (Sächsiche Schweiz) east and south of the state capital, Dresden. Its best first vote result was 35.5 percent in the district of Sächsische Schweiz-Osterzgebirge. Overall, the AfD was up 14.2 percent compared to 2013 in Brandenburg, 13 percent in Mecklenburg-West Pomerania, 20.3 percent in Saxony, 15.4 percent in Saxony-Anhalt, and 16.5 percent in Thuringia. In Berlin, the AfD increased its share of the vote to 13.2 percent, with larger gains in East Berlin (up 11.5 percent) than in West Berlin (up 5.9 percent). Its best result in western Berlin districts was in Spandau-Charlottenburg-Nord with 14.3 percent of the vote; its best result in eastern districts was in Marzahn-Hellersdorf with 22.8 percent. The AfD took votes away from all parties as well as drawing on voters who stayed home in 2013 (some 1,200,000). From the CDU/CSU 980,000 voters went to the AfD; 470,000 former SPD voters chose the AfD in 2017; another 690,000 voters came from "other parties" (among them, the extreme right NPD). Only the Greens and FDP were relative immune.

Demographically, AfD voters have been largely middle-aged with low-to-medium levels of education. The party has won proportionally more voters among blue-collar workers and the unemployed. Its voter base has been largely male.[10] Attitudinally, AfD voters express deep fears of social and economic changes in Germany. They perceive a climate of growing lawlessness and criminality in Germany (71 percent of AfD supporters versus 39 percent of all respondents). They feel disadvantaged vis-à-vis refugees (39 percent AfD; 12 percent all respondents). 68 percent think that Germany is going in the wrong direction (68 percent versus 38 percent of all respondents) and feel personally ignored and disadvantaged (42 percent; 16 percent all respondents). Not surprisingly AfD supporters want stronger border security (85 percent versus 27 percent of all respondents) and think that the influence of Islam is too great in Germany and that German culture and language is being lost (90 percent for both questions). Finally, an overwhelming majority of AfD supporters are dissatisfied with democracy (some 80 percent; 30 percent of all respondents).[11] Viola Neu of the Konrad Adenauer Foundation summarizes AfD supporters' attitudes this way: "Among the respondents [AfD supporters], fear (including excessive foreignization), insecurity, and loss of control is coupled with the feeling that 'everything is getting worse.'"[12] Finally, and perhaps most significantly, some 60 percent of AfD voters said that they had voted for the AfD not out of conviction but rather because they were dissatisfied with all other parties.[13] This figure was significantly higher than the next group of voters (the LP at 30 percent) and more than four times as high as CDU/CSU voters (14 percent). Neu suggests that AfD voters support the party in the hope that other parties will react and then take their concerns seriously.

Recent scholarship on the 2017 election suggests that the dominant factor by far impacting vote choice for the AfD in 2017 was anti-immigrant sentiment. Michael Hansen and Jonathan Olsen, using the postelection German Longitudinal Election Study (GLES), found that this factor had the largest substantive effect on the probability of voting for the AfD, about twice the impact of another variable, political ideology.[14] Furthermore, the AfD drew voters from across demographic groups regardless of gender, education, employment status, and union membership. In addition, AfD voters in 2017 did not differ from other parties' voters in terms of their political attitudes (immigration excepted), including anxieties about globalization and their own financial situation–these voters were therefore not a unique group of "losers" of globalization. AfD and Left Party voters in 2017 were, however, statistically similar in their (dis)satisfaction with democracy and with the political establishment in Germany, unlike voters for all other parties. Why this might be the case is explored in the following sections.

On Policies and Populism: The Left Party and AfD Compared

An examination of the Left Party's and AfD's party programs for the 2017 election reveal many fundamental and profound policy differences. This is most obviously the case in regards to refugee policy, multiculturalism, and

Islam. Thus, the AfD argues that Germany's borders should be closed, rejects any accompanying family immigration for refugees, states that multiculturalism endangers German cultural achievements, and that "Islam doesn't belong in Germany." In contrast, the LP states that "we shouldn't fight against refugees but rather what causes them to flee," demands equal treatment for all cultural communities, and argues for equal rights for migrants and minority groups, including Muslims, in Germany.[15] But, policy differences between the LP and AfD are not limited to refugees and immigration. They also differ over rights for the LGBTQ community–the LP is a strong supporter, while the AfD completely rejects same-sex unions and transgender rights–the traditional family–the LP demands equal treatment, including state subsidies, for alternatives to the traditional family; the AfD only recognizes the traditional family with "one father and one mother"–abortion rights–the LP is strongly supportive; the AfD is strongly anti-abortion–and feminism–the LP makes feminism and female empowerment a central part of its program and political identity; while the AfD rejects "gender ideology" as "unconstitutional." Indeed, a comparison of almost all areas of the two party programs demonstrate completely different understandings of culture and politics, ranging from domestic security issues to economic policy to climate change and education policy.

Nevertheless, the two parties are in agreement in a few areas which resonate for some eastern German voters. For example, both the LP and AfD both have deep suspicions if not hostility towards globalization, rejecting free trade agreements such as the Transatlantic Trade and Investment Partnership (TTIP), a free trade agreement with the U.S., CETA, a trade agreement between the European Union and Canada, and the Trade in Services agreement (TiSA) involving members of the World Trade Organization (WTO).[16] This colors both parties' approach to the European Union as well, although in fairness the LP is much more sympathetic to the EU project while the AfD rejects the EU on grounds of national sovereignty. And to be sure, the two parties reject trade agreements for slightly different reasons–the AfD because it maintains that the agreements do not put German interests first, the LP because the agreements purportedly only benefit big business. Still, voters may understand little beyond the fact that the two parties are against them and that globalization (and the EU) represents an existential threat.

In addition, both the LP and AfD take a very sympathetic position towards Russia. Both reject sanctions against that country and argue for a "common security structure" which would include Russia. Indeed, pro-Russian attitudes are prevalent within both parties including statements of support for Russian President Vladimir Putin.[17] For both AfD and LP voters–or at least a significant portion of the latter–Russia is seen not as a major geopolitical threat nor a dangerous authoritarian state, but rather as a victim of unfair demonization by the political establishment, an attitude in part bequeathed by the old German Democratic Republic.

Finally, both the LP and AfD are sharply critical of existing democratic institutional arrangements and advocate the further use of referenda as a check on the political power of elites. In its election program, the AfD argues that the "political class" uses democratic institutions to shut out the concerns of the people. In response, the AfD demands that Germany incorporate regular referenda on political questions into law-making along the lines of Switzerland.[18] Not dissimilarly, the LP suggests that German politicians and institutions are in sway to the market and capitalism and that therefore Germany needs a "democratization of democracy," which would include a greater use of referenda so as to allow "greater influence of citizens on political decisions."[19]

Having noted these areas of policy overlap, it should be reiterated that many AfD voters do not appear to be in agreement with most of the AfD's policy positions and do not particularly like the party's leaders. As noted earlier, they voted for the party not out of conviction but for its anti-establishment credentials and their dissatisfaction with established parties and the state of democracy in Germany. Therefore, comparison of the two party programs may not tell us as much about why former LP voters would desert to the AfD than would an examination of the political style of the LP and AfD. In other words, an exploration of populism and the protest vote within both parties may hold greater explanatory power for explaining the LP's vote losses to the AfD.

Populism has been defined in different ways by various scholars, but there is nevertheless a red thread running through all of them. Cas Mudde, in his 2007 study of right-wing populism, defines populism as a "thin-centered ideology," which "considers society to be ultimately separated into two homogenous and antagonistic groups, the 'pure people' versus the 'corrupt elite.'" [20] Luke March, in a 2008 study of the far left in Europe, classified "social populist parties" as parties which fuse left-wing and right-wing themes "behind an anti-establishment appeal."[21] Perhaps the clearest definitions of populism is provided by Daniele Albertazzi and Duncan McDonnel who write that populism sets up a confrontation between "a virtuous and homogenous people against a set of elites and dangerous 'others' who are together depicted as depriving (or attempting to deprive) the sovereign people of their rights, values, prosperity, identity, and voice."[22] What unites various understandings of populism is: 1) its appeal to the "common man" throughout society but sometimes within a specific region, which it suggests is in conflict with corrupt elites–both economic and political; and 2) its anti-establishment emphasis, arguing that it, the populist party, is a fundamental alternative to all other (establishment) parties.

The AfD has transformed itself from being an anti-EU party with fairly conventional policy stances on other issues (including immigration) in 2013 to, beginning around 2015, a populist radical right party as defined by Mudde. For Mudde, the key concept of the populist radical right is nativism, the belief that "a state should comprise 'natives' and that 'nonnatives' are to be treated with hostility."[23] Furthermore, Mudde argues that the populist radical right holds a Manichaean worldview in which politics is defined by a sharp friend-foe distinction whereby the "Other" is demonized. Mudde constructs a typology of the other or enemies for the populist radical right which comprises both enemies within and outside the nation and within and outside the state. Immigrants–or least those "established" immigrants who already have residence in the state–are the most prominent group that falls into the category of an enemy within the state but outside the nation, i.e., even though immigrants are *de facto* residents of the state, the populist radical right sees them as not belonging to the nation. They are therefore an alien presence that must be expelled. In contrast, the political establishment or elite is an enemy "within the state, within the nation." Although not "alien" per se, the elite is an enemy inasmuch as it is seen as a traitor to the nation and a corrupter of the pure people.

The nativist and populist ideology of the AfD is clear. It rejects immigrants as an alien presence in the German social/cultural body, with most of the AfD's animus aimed at refugees and immigrants who are Muslim. Not only does the AfD state that "Islam does not belong to Germany," it conceptualizes immigrants overwhelmingly as drug addicts, criminals, or terrorists.[24] Throughout the party's election manifesto, immigrants and refugees are seen as a presence that threatens to corrupt German society. Similarly, multiculturalism is seen as a dangerous ideology threatening to eliminate true German culture. Not surprisingly, the party calls for a return to *deutschen Leitkultur* (dominant German culture), which is said to rest on Christianity, antiquity, Humanism, and the Enlightenment, while rejecting any attempt at fostering a pluralistic multicultural society. Consistent with this ethnic understanding of German society, the AfD calls for a return to a notion of citizenship based on ethnic origins or "blood" (*jus sanguinus*) instead of citizenship based on birth (*jus solis*) which Germany in part adopted in 2008.[25]

Similarly, the AfD exhibits extreme hostility to the political establishment in Germany. The AfD repeatedly refers to "the political class," "career politicians," or even "oligarchy" that thwarts the people's will. For example, in an opening section on democracy in its election program the AfD speaks of a "political class whose overriding interest is only its own power, status, and material benefit" while in another section on reforming the electoral system the AfD argues that "the political class in Germany has used the existing voting laws and voting behavior to minimize the influence of the people." [26] The party presents itself in contrast to the political establishment as a defender of democracy and a champion of the people, enthusiastically embracing the word *Volk*–a word with obvious historically problematic undertones–throughout its self-presentation.

In contrast to the AfD, the LP's (left-wing) populism is more muted. Indeed, scholars have been divided on whether the LP can even be considered properly populist. Eckhard Jesse suggests that the AfD and LP are essentially populist twins, one representing right-wing populism and the other left-wing populism.[27] March has wavered on whether to use the populist label for the LP, categorizing the party as "populist socialist," while expressing doubts about the suitability of the populist label a few years later.[28] The most sustained examination of populism in the LP, however, has been provided by Dan Hough and Michael Koβ and Hough and Dan Keith. In "Populism Personified or Reinvigorated Reformer?," Hough and Koβ found that although the LP was not as purely populist as some other political parties across Europe, it did have three elements of a populist core: 1) a disdain for the process of normal democratic institutions in favor of elements of direct democracy; 2) the identification of sets of elites (political, economic) who thwart the people's will; and 3) the need to overcome capitalism. Consistent with Albertazzi and McDonnel's understanding of populism as aimed at "elites and dangerous others" and Mudde's notion of a sharp friend/foe and internal enemy distinction, Hough and Koβ write that the LP "regularly talks in the language of elites betraying the population at large and it is frequently disdainful of the wider political process."[29] Furthermore, they found that key to the LP's self-understanding was a "very clear denunciation of 'bad guys' (namely managers, economic elites, big businessmen) and 'good guys' (the laboring classes in Germany, the poor and downtrodden in the Third World, and leftwing movements everywhere").[30]

Hough and Keith argue that in the last eight years the LP's populism has "mutated" even while its core anti-establishment message is present and continues to be activated in key areas.[31] As the PDS evolved in the 1990s to a regionalist party claiming to represent eastern German interests, the clear foe was western German political and economic elites who were said to stand in the way of the (eastern German) people's will, abusing Germany's democratic institutions in serving their own interests. As the LP has transformed itself into an all-German party of the radical left, its role as tribune of eastern Germany has diminished considerably. Yet, according to Hough and Keith, "the LP has continued to use populist rhetoric in terms of presenting a struggle between the people and elites."[32] To be sure, the LP eschews the word *Volk* when referring to the "people," instead opting for *Menschen*. Yet, the party continues to have a list of enemies who stand in the way of *Menschen*/the people and includes corporations and corporate leaders, managers of big banks, global financial institutions (the Troika, European Central Bank, etc.), and political elites of the major parties (i.e., Merkel)–all under the label of "global ruling elites." Moreover, the LP couples populism with a deep dissatisfaction with democracy, arguing that "many doubt whether elections change anything. If budget cuts and automatic debt brakes are presented as being the only options, without alternatives, then trust in democracy evaporates: what is there to still be politically decided?"[33]

The AfD: A New Populist Tribune for Eastern Germans?

Despite the ways in which the LP has from its very beginning sought to position itself as a populist, anti-establishment party–and the language it continues to use to present itself as the champion of the ordinary people against out-of-touch (and often undemocratic) elites-the Left Party has found it more difficult over the last decade to sell that image to eastern German voters. While in 2004 it positioned itself as a leader in the backlash against the Hartz IV labor market reforms, since that time it has become more firmly entrenched in the halls of power throughout eastern Germany. The LP has never participated in coalition government at the national level and is still considered something of a pariah (chiefly, although not exclusively, for its foreign policy positions). Still, over the last twenty years the party has been in power in four of six eastern German states (including Berlin). As the PDS, it served as a coalition partner for the SPD as early as 1998 (in Mecklenburg-West Pomerania[34]) and, as noted above, was able to place Ramelow as minister president in Thuringia in 2013. Along with the SPD and CDU, the LP is therefore firmly established as part of a three-party regional party system in eastern Germany. In the six eastern states (with a few exceptions), it is also largely regarded as a pragmatic political partner that attempts to achieve small policy achievements for its voters. In contrast, in western Germany the LP still has the reputation of being something of a political outsider and is more ideological. The LP's political position in eastern Germany makes it hard to reconcile with the image of an anti-establishment outsider and the policy it has helped to craft as a coalition partner are not the stuff of a political outsider breaking up the old entrenched system.

The AfD on the other hand, has solid credentials as an eastern German anti-establishment protest party. As David Patton has shown, the AfD's transformation in 2015 to a party largely articulating anti-immigrant themes rather than an anti-EU party owes much of this to its tapping into the populist, anti-establishment street protests of the Pegida movement.[35] Originating in 2014, Pegida (Patriotic Europeans against the Islamization of the Occident) rallies began to attract huge crowd throughout 2014 and 2015. It never managed a substantial number of demonstrators in western Germany, but in eastern Germany–especially in Dresden, Leipzig, and other urban areas of Saxony (the state where the AfD in 2017 had its best election result by far)–the number of protestors was significant, with some 25,000 participants in January 2015. Research on Pegida supporters indicated, along with hostility towards immigrants and Muslims and Islam generally, a high level of dissatisfaction with the political establishment. Pegida quickly became, in the words of political scientist Werner Patzelt, "the dispersion of right-wing populism in Germany," the "street arm" of the AfD.[36] Although never coordinating explicitly with Pegida, leading figures from the AfD began discussions with the leadership of Pegida and spoke at various Pegida events. Moreover, in the wake of Pegida, the AfD moved to adopt anti-immigrant and anti-Muslim positions at its national party congress in 2016. Although only about a third of Pegida participants voted for the AfD in 2013, shortly before the 2017 election, about 80 percent indicated they would vote AfD.

To summarize, although the LP has never been a pure protest party, it has long depended on an image of the anti-establishment outsider, challenging the existing parties. For many years the LP also fused left-wing populist elements to a defense of eastern German interests, suggesting that corrupt (western) elites were thwarting the will of the pure (eastern German) people. The LP could still credibly make this kind of case until a few years ago, reaching something of a high point in the Hartz IV protests of 2004. However, the party is now without a doubt a party of the political establishment in eastern Germany and a pure populist message finds a more believable representative in the AfD. Moreover, the LP appeared to have misjudged the particular populist zeitgeist on the question of immigration and refugee policy. The LP's campaign platform, which eschewed limits on refugees and took something of an "open-arms" stance towards asylum seekers and immigrants, did not sit well with many of its voters in eastern Germany. Meanwhile, its other policy positions–its critique of German democracy and democratic institutions, its Russia-friendly policy, its skepticism on globalization, the EU, and free-trade agreements–find equal expression within the AfD and resonance with a potential pool of eastern anti-establishment protest voters. The Left Party finds itself in danger of completely losing its position to the AfD as a populist tribune for eastern Germans.

Jonathan Olsen is Professor and Chair of the Department of History and Government at Texas Woman's University. He is the co-author (with Dan Hough and Michael Koβ) of two books on the LP, *The Left Party in Contemporary German Politics* (Basingstoke, 2007) and *Left Parties in National Governments* (Basingstoke, 2010), two other books on the far right in German and EU politics, and numerous articles in this and other journals including *German Politics* and *Problems of Post-Communism.* He was until recently the North American Secretary for the International Association for the Study of German Politics and has received grants from the Fulbright Program and the German Academic Exchange Service. E-mail: JOlsen1@twu.edu

Notes

1. On the merger of the PDS with the WASG, see Jonathan Olsen, "The Merger of the PDS and WASG: From Eastern German Regional Party to National Radical Left Party?" *German Politics* 16, no. 2 (2007): 205–221; David Patton, "The Left Party at Six: The PDS-WASG in Comparative Perspective," *German Politics* 22/23 (2013): 219–234.
2. All figures are from the Bundeswahlleiter; available at https://www.bundeswahlleiter.de/dam/jcr/8eb5b630-4270-43ba-8637-7e7b7642f2ca/btw17_arbtab2.pdf, accessed 1 November 2017.
3. Ibid.
4. Ibid.
5. See Jonathan Olsen, "Germany" in *Handbook of Radical Left Parties in Europe*, ed. Luke March, Fabien Escalona, and Daniel Keith (London 2018): "Its [the LP's] all-German radical left profile means that its special affinity to eastern voters could be in danger of eroding."
6. Oskar Niedermayer, "Parteimitglieder in Deutschland," *Arbeitshefte aus dem Otto-Stammer-Zentrum* (2015).
7. Benjamin-Immanuel Hoff, "Die Ergebnisse der Landtagswahlen am 13. März 2016–Wahlnachtbericht und erste Analyse," Rosa Luxemburg Stiftung (2016); available at https://www.rosalux.de/fileadmin/rls_uploads/pdfs/sonst_publikationen/2016-03-14_BW_RP_ST_WNB.pdf, accessed 15 September 2016.
8. Viola Neu and Sabine Pokorny, "Bundestagswahl in Deutschland am 24. September 2017 Wahlanalyse. Vorläufiges Ergebnis," Konrad Adenauer Stiftung (September 2017).
9. Ibid.
10. Hoff (see note 7).
11. Data from Infratest dimap and Forschungsgruppe Wahlen, cited in Neu and Pokorny (see note 8), 9–10.
12. "Bei den hier Befragten [AfD Supporters] wird Angst (auch vor Überfremdung), Verunsicherung, Kontrollverlust mit dem Gefühl gekoppelt 'alles wird Schlechter.'" Ibid., 14–15.

13. Ibid., 12.
14. Michael Hansen and Jonathan Olsen, "Flesh of the same Flesh: A Study of Voters for the Alternative for Germany in the 2017 German Federal Election," *German Politics 28*, no. 1 (2019): 1-19.
15. All citations are from the AfD Wahlprogramm, *Programm für Deutschland. Wahlprogramm der Alternative für Deutshcland für die Wahl zum Deutschen Bundestag am 24.* September 2017; and from the Left Party Wahlprogramm, *Sozial.Gerecht. Frieden. Für Alle. Die Zukunft, für die wir kämpfen! Langfassung des Wahlprogramms zur Bundestagswahl 2017.*
16. For the AfD, see https://www.afd.de/gauland-ttip-ist-von-anfang-an-falsch-angegangen-worden/, accessed 8 March 2018; on the LP, see LP Wahlprogramm (see note 14), 98.
17. See for example Justus Bender, "Alternatiwa dlja Germanii", *Frankfurter Allgemeine Zeitung*; available at http://www.faz.net/aktuell/politik/inland/afd-verteidigt-putin-auf-ihrem-russlandkongress-15149657.html, accessed 14 January 2018; Christian Fuchs, Paul Middelhoff, and Fritz Zimmermann, "Putins Afd-Truppe", *Die Zeit*; available at http://www.zeit.de/2017/34/osteuropa-wahlbeobachtung-afd-wladimir-putin, accessed 14 January 2018; Mely Kiyak, "Nachdenken über Sahra W. und den anderen," *Die Zeit*; available at http://www.zeit.de/kultur/2017-07/sahra-wagenknecht-die-linke-deutschstunde/seite-2, accessed 14 January 2018.
18. AfD Wahlprogramm (see note 14), 8
19. LP Wahlprogramm (see note 14, 108.
20. Cas Mudde, *Populist Radical Right Parties in Europe* (Cambridge, 2007), 23.
21. Luke March, "Parteien links der Sozialdemokaratie in Europa. Vom Marxismus zum Mainstream?" Friedrich Ebert Stiftung (November 2008).
22. Daniele Albertazzi and Duncan McDonnel, *Twenty-First Century Populism: The Spectre of Western European Democracy* (London, 2007), 3.
23. Mudde (see note 19), 138.
24. AfD Wahlprogramm (see note 14), 23.
25. Ibid., 32.
26. Ibid., 10.
27. Eckhard Jesse, "AfD und die Linke–Wieviel Populism Steckt in Ihnen?," *Politische Studien* 476 (2017): 41–51.
28. Luke March, *Radical Left Parties in Europe* (London, 2011).
29. Dan Hough and Michael Koß, "Populism Personified or Reinvigorated Reformers," *German Politics and Society* 27, no. 2 (2009), 78.
30. Ibid., 82.
31. Dan Hough and Dan Keith, "The German Left Party: A Case of Pragmatic Populism" in *The Populist Radical Left in Europe*, ed. G. Katsambekis and A. Kioupkiolis (London, 2018).
32. Ibid., 8.
33. LP Wahlprogram (see note 14), 108.
34. On the coalition in Mecklenburg-West Pomerania, see Jonathan Olsen, "Seeing Red: The SPD-PDS Coalition Government in Mecklenburg-West Pomerania," *German Studies Review* 23, no. 3 (2000): 557-580; Dan Hough, Michael Koß, and Jonathan Olsen, *The Left Party in Contemporary German Politics* (London, 2007).
35. David Patton, "Monday, Monday: Eastern Protest Movements and German Party Politics since 1989," *German Politics* 25, no. 4 (2017): 480–497.
36. Cited in ibid., 490.

··· Chapter 6 ···

THE CDU/CSU's AMBIVALENT 2017 CAMPAIGN

Clay Clemens

For all the upheaval in German politics during 2017, that year's election also had familiar elements–a broad catch-all party struggling to reconcile new voter groups with its traditional base, a long-popular leader not only over-reading her past mandate but clinging on too long, and a complacent campaign relying on proven formulas despite resistance in the ranks amid ominous warning signs. These challenges and misjudgments did not deny Angela Merkel's Christian Democratic Union/Christian Social Union (CDU/CSU) a mathematical victory, but finishing first was slim consolation given its record losses, historically low vote, and, thus, beneath a veneer of unity, bitter recriminations. Moreover, "winning" would compound these problems by obliging a Union already in disarray to forge Germany's next government despite unprecedented party system fragmentation and societal polarization, all fueled by rising far right populism. Therefore, both the election and its aftermath ensured even deeper divisions within the CDU/CSU over identity, strategy, and personnel as the post Merkel era approached.

This article sees the Union's shaky performance as resulting from four factors–each a subset of the other–like a set of concentric circles. First, the underlying, longer term cause behind the parties' fortunes was Merkel's leadership and her effort to modernize the CDU, which enjoyed broad but brittle support. Second, that consensus wavered after her controversial 2015 decision to admit over a million non-European refugees. Third, by paying too little heed to this growing ambivalence, her party's official 2017 campaign strategy bred complacency among her supporters and mobilized opposition among skeptics. Fourth, those problems were then compounded by tactical responses or non-responses to events during the campaign cycle itself.

Notes for this section can be found on page 160.

Merkel's Modernization of the CDU

The CDU/CSU's challenge in fashioning an electoral strategy is familiar among major mainstream European parties. Synthesizing cultural and national conservatism, Catholic social welfarism, and pro-business market liberalism, it had consistently earned in the mid 40 percent range at Bundestag elections, and, thus, often led national governing coalitions (1949-1969, 1982-1998, 2005-present). Competing just in conservative Bavaria, the CSU won absolute majorities in that state for five decades in federal and regional elections. Euphoria over longtime CDU leader Helmut Kohl's reunification of Germany sustained broad support, but from the late 1990s onwards, the Union sisters' national vote share slid into the mid 30 percent range. Results in regional bastions varied, but also fell overall–in 2008 even the CSU lost its absolute majority in the Bavarian Landtag. In an ever more secular society with a growing service sector, the relative size of traditional Union voter blocs was dwindling, and similar trends were eroding even their partisan loyalties, except among older, churchgoing Catholics. In ex-Communist eastern Germany, such party affiliations had never been deep, making for an even more fickle CDU constituency. At the federal and Land levels, the CDU could no longer count on majorities with just the smaller center-right, free market-oriented Free Democratic Party (FDP) or Liberals; broader, multiparty deals or oversized grand coalitions with its Social Democratic (SPD) adversary grew more unavoidable.

Rattled by these trends, and a major finance scandal, the post Kohl CDU opted for new leadership and a new direction after 2000. As a newcomer to politics raised in the Communist east, a secularized Protestant and a woman, it was unsurprising that Angela Merkel would espouse CDU "modernization," though given that same biography–along with her early lack of a strong intraparty power base, modest charisma, and an often reactive, dilatory decision-making style–she was not expected to succeed. But, as its federal chair from 2000 onward, she sided with those urging the Union to appeal beyond its mainly older, suburban-rural, churchgoing, traditional middle-class base by wooing the ever-larger share of more secular, industrial, or service sector urbanites, including younger Germans and women–especially those with weak partisan affiliations. That would mean abandoning familiar positions, and adopting policies better suited to an era of postindustrialism, globalization, digitalization, multiculturalism, climate change, and new family structures–even at the risk of alienating some loyal supporters. Merkel prodded her party toward more progressive stances on women, families, homosexuality, and immigration. But, after a brief push for neoliberal welfare reform proved contentious, she quickly backtracked.

Indeed, as chancellor atop a coalition with the SPD from 2005 to 2009, she persuaded her Union to adopt social policy measures closer to those of her governing partner, and even outflanking the Social Democrats from the left on labor market measures, while taking a lead on global climate diplomacy. During the 2009 to 2013 coalition with the Liberals, she pressed the Union to drop support for both conscription, and, after Japan's Fukushima disaster fueled panic, nuclear power. Back in coalition with the SPD after 2013, Merkel's Union accommodated its partner's minimum wage and rent control plans. She also played a lead role in the European Union and helped bailout indebted Eurozone states (albeit in exchange for austerity). Such consensual centrism, by narrowing differences with the SPD and Greens, aimed partly to woo their voters, a tactic unanimously endorsed by Merkel's CDU executive in its 2010 Berlin Declaration.[1] Moderating partisan differences also made it harder for center-left rivals to rally their supporters, what some called "asymmetric demobilization."

Unhappy with much of Merkel's agenda, CDU conservatives and market liberals, along with the CSU, grumbled that their Union's identity was becoming blurred, alienating longtime loyalists. Indeed, membership fell from a postunification high of around 790,000 in 1990 to 505,000 in 2010. In 2009's election, the Union vote share sunk to its lowest level since 1949, just 33.8 percent, as many market-oriented voters flocked to the FDP. Yet, Merkel could claim credit for keeping her Union in power, with the Liberals then and the Social Democrats after 2013. Her unassuming, authentic manner and calm, consensus-oriented stewardship of domestic as well as foreign policy proved broadly popular, including with voters on the left. She led her Social Democratic rivals for chancellor by double digits in both re-election campaigns, making her an electoral asset to the Union. Thanks to CDU modernization and her appeal, despite net losses, in 2009 the Union won over a million former SPD voters; in 2013 it drew some two million ex-FDP supporters and another half million from the center left (easily offsetting small losses to the new right-wing, anti-Euro Alternative for Germany or AfD). Her Union's 41.5 percent–its highest vote share since 1990–seemed to vindicate modernization and asymmetric demobilization.

As of 2015, Merkel had been chancellor for ten years and party chair for fifteen. By then, the CDU's cabinet ministers as well as most of its federal executive board, Bundestag caucus leadership, and Land-level officials were loyal "Merkelianer." Critics of modernization were hard put to resist. Their priorities often clashed: pro-business CDU market liberals were more uneasy with her welfare measures, while conservatives worried mainly a "leftward drift" away from traditional family and national values.[2] Even where they did agree, it was difficult to challenge a proven election winner's consensus policies. Internal critics also complained that CDU officeholders indebted to Merkel voted in lockstep, ignoring grassroots uneasiness about her changes, and rooted out dissenters. Thus, the market wing hunkered down within CDU small-business (MIT) and corporate (Wirtschaftsrat) affiliated groups. Dissident cultural conservatives hived off in powerless informal factions, like the Berlin Circle. Other unhappy activists and functionaries focused more on local matters. Though freer to defy the chancellor, the autonomous CSU did so only on select issues, and mainly settled for burnishing its conservative credentials at home in Bavaria.

Merkel's uncharacteristically abrupt, personal decision in summer 2015 to open German borders, allowing an influx of refugees from war-torn Syria, set off events that would test her "reinvention" of the CDU. To be sure, at first the Union, its coalition partners, and public opinion endorsed her insistence that the move was "morally required" and her confidence that "we can handle" it. But, fears soon mounted over logistical burdens, financial costs, crime, and terrorism, as did qualms about integrating a million heavily male Muslim newcomers–especially with Berlin struggling to win help from EU partners. By November, Merkel's approval ratings had plunged from 70 percent to below 50 percent and Union support from above 40 percent to the mid 30 percent range. The far right surged, especially in eastern Germany, which had little history of immigration. Street protests against "Islamization" swelled. Attacking Merkel's policy helped the AfD double its support to 10 percent, with even higher levels in the east and Bavaria, where most refugees first arrived. Under pressure by harried local and Land officials, CSU chief Horst Seehofer castigated Merkel, demanding action. Her longtime CDU critics agreed and even allies, rattled by rising grassroots anger with key Landtag elections looming, urged tighter limits. Still, at December's CDU congress, ministers, deputies, and delegates defended her from the CSU's attack; she justified her decision as consistent with Christian Democratic values, while agreeing that a slower influx lay in "everyone's interest."

Nevertheless, her approval ratings and the Union's fell further after migrants sexually assaulted numerous women in Cologne on New Year's Eve refueled fears. Even as new limits including a controversial deal with Turkey's increasingly autocratic regime began curbing migration, her approval slid. At March 2016 Land elections, the CDU lost 12 percent in one former bastion, Baden-Württemberg, and 3.4 percent in another, Rheinland-

Palatinate. The AfD shot up to 15.1 percent and 12.6 percent, respectively. In the eastern Land of Saxony-Anhalt, it drew a stunning 24.3 percent. Claiming vindication, Seehofer and CDU conservatives reiterated calls for a refugee cap. Merkel still objected that an arbitrary limit would erode the individual right to asylum, and, despite accepting some new restrictions, she still defended opening the borders. At September's Land election in her own home region of Mecklenburg-West Pomerania, the AfD won 20.8 percent, edging out the CDU (its activist base was also growing, drawing some of the 13,000 ex-Union members who had defected since 2015).

For months, Merkel was silent about standing again for chancellor, fueling doubts about her zeal and confidence. Polls showed that most Germans did not want her to seek re-election. Still, her party support remained sufficient to nix an internal challenge. Social Democratic and Green backing for her refugee policy gave her some immunity from attack. Meanwhile, broad antipathy for Donald Trump underscored her global stature, and she continued outpolling any likely SPD rival. With support for the Union stabilizing in surveys, in November 2016 she announced her plans to run in 2017, implicitly for the last time. But, more so than in both previous re-election races, her party would struggle to find a winning formula.

The CDU/CSU's 2017 Campaign Strategies

Union squabbles over campaign strategy were hardly new. The 2017 race, however, would not merely see friction between the two sisters or among CDU elites, but also pushback from many functionaries and activists. Moreover, facing both center-left rivals and–for the first time–a viable right-wing threat, the Union's debate over how to win also reflected differences over its core identity.

On one side was Merkel's CDU leadership, which had been reshaped in her image: federal ministers Peter Altmaier, Thomas de Maizière (Interior), and Ursula von der Leyen (Defense); Union Bundestag chair Volker Kauder; and most CDU western Land chairs, like Saarland's popular Annegret Kramp-Karrenbauer, Armin Laschet of North Rhine-Westphalia, Julia Klöckner of Rhineland-Pfalz, and Thomas Strobl of Baden-Württemberg. Managing the campaign from CDU federal headquarters would be General-Secretary Peter Tauber, a young loyalist she had picked to expand digital outreach. "Merkelianer" saw their CDU's programmatic modernization both as right on principle and also a vote winner. That point was vital to reassure uneasy chairs in the conservative south–Klöckner and Strobl–as well as more autonomous figures like Hesse's Volker Bouffier and Land leaders in the East (outside Berlin), where anti-refugee sentiment was highest. It was also vital to keeping finance minister Wolfgang Schäuble on side. Decades of loyal service to the party had earned this pragmatic conservative broad respect and a rare degree of independence from Merkel–his support, or doubts, would carry great weight.

Past success undergirded the political case for an election strategy still based on Merkel's reinvention of the CDU. To be sure, Tauber no longer spoke of the Union again exceeding 40 percent, settling instead for merely coming in first, blocking an all-left coalition, and keeping Merkel in office. For CDU leaders, these more modest aims were best served by remaining a self-sufficient force at the center, not as the anchor of a right-wing bloc. Backed by Forschungsgruppe Wahlen pollster Matthias Jung, Tauber insisted that the Union was still competing primarily for mainstream, especially younger, urban Germans, including women. "We can't reach all voters to the same degree but must choose," he declared, focusing on "achievers." Laschet emphasized that "the Union only wins elections when it recognizes the concerns of the middle, solves problems and holds to its 'C' brand."[3] Such a strategy, he argued, was essential, first, to retain the party's current voters. Most were still older, rural or suburban, better educated and well-off, generally patriotic and religious, if also open to Europe and globalization. After a decade of "modernization" and infusions of new voters, however, CDU supporters were less committed to pure capitalism and more supportive of the welfare state, as well as increasingly open to different ideas of the family and gender roles. The party's electorate thus "clearly [stemmed] from the center of society." Since two of three Germans did as well, targeting the middle could also cut further into SPD support.

Merkel's team dismissed concerns that this strategy would fuel the AfD. They noted that the latter's Land election gains had come mainly from former nonvoters or from other parties' supporters; CDU defectors composed less than a third of its support. They also insisted that any losses could best be recouped by exposing right-wing populism's lack of serious policies, not by recasting the CDU as the dominant force in a right-wing bloc: a *Lagerwahlkampf* would only fuel polarization and alienate centrists. In Baden-Württemberg's 2016 Landtag election, for example, downplaying Merkel's refugee policies had not helped her CDU stem losses to the AfD and may have driven another 100,000 of its voters to the Greens. Merkel herself depicted the party as holding the middle, noting it would face "challenges from all sides." As she put it: "From the right like never before [with] the deep polarization of our society [and] from the left with the prospect of a red-red-green federal government." Tauber added that this election was not about the AfD, but "as always" over whether his CDU or its SPD rival would hold the chancellery.[4]

CDU leaders planned to focus their campaign on Merkel. Rather than trying to craft a new image for a three-term chancellor, they planned to double down on her experience, global stature, and credibility. This approach would echo the CDU's pitch in 2013 when it had played up Merkel's image as a national mother-figure and she had closed the televised debate by reminding viewers "you know me." Despite the turmoil of 2015, party strategists counted on her still outpolling any SPD challenger. Acknowledging that some voters might resent Merkel seeking a fourth term, she made clear her plans to step down in 2021. Although her ardor for campaigning seemed less than ever, they planned a large number of rallies. While opting for this personal campaign over a team approach, the party would also play up key ministers who embodied its policies, especially Schäuble for the economy and de Maizière for law and order. Substantively, the campaign would emphasize three dimensions of security–a strong economy, social protections, and law enforcement. Selling points would include Germany's solid growth, low unemployment, and sound finances. The party would offer modest tax relief but vague proposals on pension funding, energy prices, and infrastructure. It would defend Merkel's refugee decision and reject a cap on numbers, but also stress efforts to limit the influx, require newcomers to integrate and–especially after a December 2016 attack on Berlin Christmas market–combat Islamic terrorism. To craft its message and sell its candidate, the party signed a euro 20 million contract with ad agency Jung von Matt, inexperienced in politics but known for clever, heart-warming commercials.

Skeptics of the CDU leadership's 2017 campaign included dissident conservative Wolfgang Bosbach's Berlin Circle, market wing spokesmen Carsten Linnemann, and Young Union chair Paul Ziemiak. The few maverick Bundestag deputies who had openly opposed Merkel even before 2015, generally with secure seats thanks to nomination by their local party branch (not high ranking on an approved list), now found support from others rattled by grassroots backlash over the refugee issue.[5] Eastern Land-level leaders and many local CDU officials also questioned the centrist strategy. Most articulate among the critics was Jens Spahn: the thirty-something Catholic, openly gay deputy voiced conservative and market liberal views, and had tacit backing from Schäuble, who had aided his bid to replace a Merkel loyalist on the CDU presidium and appointed him junior finance minister.

Some critics resisted Merkel's entire modernization agenda, while others felt trying to reverse it was unrealistic, even undesirable. But, all worried that their CDU had lost touch with key parts of its base–market liberals and cultural conservatives, as well as ordinary local activists. Even those like Spahn who favored the party shedding its image as one run by "old white men" (and who endorsed gay marriage) argued that recent changes were undercutting its association with capitalism and patriotism. As he noted, "the middle of society now lies to the right of the CDU."[6] For them, the wrong campaign risked shrinking their party's scope further–something they warned would also help two rivals. Although the Liberals were barely above the 5 percent electoral threshold in polls by late 2016, they had gained in most Land elections by drawing Union voters disenchanted with grand coalition policies like the minimum wage. FDP chief Christian Lindner was also capitalizing on uneasiness over refugees, faulting the chancellor for allowing chaos. By late 2016, Merkel was less popular among Liberal voters than among SPD and Green supporters. Losing voters to the FDP, however, was not new. Merkel's critics worried more about a centrist strategy driving longtime supporters uneasy with the EU, new family structures, immigration, and political correctness to the AfD. In 2016, it had lured more voters from the CDU than any other party–and 75 percent of defectors cited the refugee crisis as the decisive reason.[7] Even a third of CDU voters saw the refugee policy as mistaken.

For Merkel critics, a *Lagerwahlkampf* was thus vital to retain core supporters and regain many who had flirted with the FDP or AfD. "It's no longer about asymmetric demobilization," Spahn insisted, "but asymmetric mobilization."[8] This meant pushing bold welfare state measures like delaying the pension eligibility age and cutting burdensome energy prices for business. Above all, critics wanted the Union platform to back a ban on entry for the family members of refugees already in the EU; measures for addressing "cultural insecurity" caused by criminal, misogynistic, or homophobic conduct among migrants; stricter rules for integration into a *Leitkultur* (dominant culture), and a law governing Islamic practices in Germany. Although by late 2016 even these skeptics endorsed Merkel as lead candidate, they warned that the chancellor, a bland campaigner in the best of times, could not now be the party's main selling point. Moreover, in seeking a fourth term Merkel would also face the very charge of clinging on too long that she had leveled against Kohl decades earlier. Conservatives and market liberals thus preferred a team approach highlighting others, especially Schäuble, but also a younger generation–above all Spahn.

Even before the campaign began, these divisions deepened. Prior to the CDU's annual congress in Essen in December 2016, the executive committee endorsed a resolution entitled "Orientation in Difficult Times." It labeled the Merkel era "good years for our country" and called for continuity in Europe. As concessions, it pledged to avoid repeating the chaos of 2015, expedite deportations, support a conditional burka ban, and delay tax hikes. Otherwise, party leaders planned a coronation. Merkel spoke in unusually personal terms of becoming chair in 2000 and her struggle over whether to run again. Underscoring her image as an anchor of global stability, she called for a strong EU. Delegates applauded warmly if not euphorically and some insisted that she had allayed their concerns. But, with many conservatives having already spoken of no longer feeling at home in her CDU, others complained that Merkel had only briefly alluded to regaining voters lost to the far right and set out no real strategy for doing so–unlike most speakers, she had not even mentioned the AfD by name. Though her re-election as chair was never in doubt, ninety-nine delegates voted no and the 89.5 percent she earned marked her second worst result ever–her worst being a point lower in 2004 before she was Chancellor. Moreover, the Young Union moved a resolution demanding tight limits on dual citizenship for second generation immigrants. Merkel, Tauber, and de Maizière objected that no coalition partner would go along. Conservative delegates, for whom dual citizenship symbolized the Union's leftward drift, cheered Spahn's retort that a CDU congress should set out party positions. In the end, the measure narrowly passed. Rebuffed, Merkel shrugged that a government led by her would not enact it anyway, further irking critics.

The CSU's own internal dynamics would also shape that party's campaign. When his party clawed back its absolute majority in Bavaria in 2013, Seehofer had announced this would be his last term as minister-president, if not as party chair. As rivals lined up to succeed him, however, he balked at leaving, and the refugee crisis gave him an opening. His attacks on Merkel's open-door policy bolstered his stature as the Union's dominant conservative, even fueling rumors he might become chancellor if she fell. Sensing this new stature could help ensure their sacred absolute majority in both the 2017 Bundestag race and at the all-important 2018 Landtag election, and leery of a succession fight amid both campaigns, most in the CSU were content to have Seehofer remain in his two jobs–so long as he seemed a winner.

Yet, beyond touting Bavaria's robust economy and hardline law enforcement, crafting a clear 2017 strategy would be tricky. Merkel had some allies in the CSU's Bundestag delegation, but her policies rattled its ministers in Munich, their powerful Landtag caucus, and many local officials. Especially after the refugee crisis, they worried that being yoked to a leftward-drifting CDU risked alienating enough voters in Bavaria to cost their party its absolute majority in both looming elections. For two years, Seehofer had played tough–inviting Merkel to his CSU's annual congress only to publicly accuse her of tolerating lawlessness, and even threatening to sue her federal government for not controlling German borders. He had hinted that his party should run independently of the CDU in 2017 so that "voters know they are not choosing Merkel but the CSU."[9] Some colleagues warned that the chancellor still had support in Bavaria, and that attacking her there while governing with her in Berlin sent mixed signals. The 2017 election year began with the CSU still not having formally endorsed her and demanding a cap on refugees as its price for joining any government–a gambit to secure its right flank that carried real risks.

In sum, the Union would in effect wage two parallel campaigns–the CDU leadership's official strategy based around Merkel outcompeting her SPD rivals for the center, and an only-partly overlapping counter effort, waged by some within her party and by its Bavarian sister, that aimed mainly at preventing the AfD from establishing itself on their bloc's right flank. Further fueling debate was the question of how campaign strategy might affect their party's choice of potential governing partners, especially given that the electoral math seemed sure to complicate its options. Both the Left and the AfD appeared set to win nearly 10 percent of the seats each, and, since the Union had ruled out a coalition with either, that made getting to a Bundestag majority with just one other partner trickier. Even if the FDP surpassed 5 percent and once again held seats, it seemed unlikely to win enough to ensure a majority for an alliance with Merkel's Union alone as from 2009 to 2013. A CDU/CSU-Green tandem had somewhat better odds, but that too was uncertain. The only sure legislative majorities were an unwieldly, experimental CDU/CSU-FDP-Green or "Jamaica" quartet (named for that country's black-yellow-green flag) or yet another grand coalition.

Merkel's strategy kept all options open. Competing for the center offered hopes of besting the SPD without burning all bridges to a rival with whom she still governed and might gain. Indeed, she agreed to endorse Social Democrat Frank-Walter Steinmeier for federal president in 2017. Yet, while voters gave a grand coalition high marks, it could at best be a last resort–her Union would eschew sharing power equally with its main foe again if it saw any hope of leading an alliance with smaller partners. So, Merkel's centrist strategy implicitly envisioned governing with the FDP, though she avoided calling that party her CDU's natural ally. Especially in light of Lindner's attacks on her refugee policies, she was more comfortable with the Greens: a deal with their moderate leaders, if not vetoed by the party's left, would also consolidate the CDU's modernization course. Altmaier and

Tauber favored that option; Kramp-Karrenbauer, Strobl, and Bouffier had all governed with the Greens in their Länder. While a few CDU conservatives like Spahn had also worked for such a novel alliance, their hard-right campaign strategy seemed to undercut it. Most Union market liberals and conservatives openly called the FDP their Union's natural partner, but differed on their preferred fallback: while the former strongly opposed another grand coalition, even preferring a fling with the Greens, the latter–above all Seehofer's CSU, mindful of irking its Bavarian base–rejected cozying up to the ecological party. Given the uncertain math and these internal differences, the Union entered 2017 with no formal coalition pledge.

All parts of the CDU/CSU agreed on one aim–barring an SPD-Green-Left Party alliance. Since 2013, those three parties combined had a Bundestag majority. Differences had always blocked a federal-level coalition, but they had collaborated in many eastern Länder, and some Social Democrats kept touting "red-red-green." Attacking any such prospect of the Left Party in power (albeit without resorting to past tactics of labeling it communist) would help the Union mobilize voters. But, the CDU leadership's centrist strategy also seemed likely to strengthen the hand of SPD and/or Green moderates who saw governing with Merkel's Union as less risky than red-red-green. By contrast, a polarizing *Lagerwahlkampf* risked alienating and undercutting those potential partners, driving their parties toward a deal with the Left.

Campaign Developments

Merkel's CDU leadership largely stayed on script throughout 2017, even when confronted by unexpected developments. Indeed, ultimately it found ways of interpreting or reacting to them so as to reaffirm a chancellor-based centrist election strategy–but in doing so also ignored warning signs.

Winter/Spring

The campaign's biggest surprise came early. CDU strategy rested on Merkel once again outpolling any rival, but, in late January, Social Democrat leader Sigmar Gabriel–blamed for his party's failures in Merkel's second grand coalition–made way for Martin Schulz. With a compelling narrative based on his early personal struggles, this former municipal politician who had risen to lead the EU Parliament exhorted Social Democrats to uphold their core mission of social justice, even to disavow the neoliberal welfare reforms enacted when they last led the government. The long-divided party rallied to this passionate appeal and elected him chair unanimously. Schulz's candidacy and the SPD's newfound unity triggered an overnight surge in the poll ratings of both. For the first time in years, his party pulled even with the Union in the low 30 percent range.

Merkel's team appeared to be caught off-guard. Having prepared for another "feel good" campaign against a cabinet colleague, she now faced attacks from an energetic outsider. Rather than hit back, she shrugged "competition is good," renewing concern about her zeal for battle. Moreover, the SPD's newfound unity underscored Union discord. The CSU did finally endorse her candidacy at a February retreat, but this belated, lukewarm endorsement came with poor optics–a weary, uncomfortable chancellor icily ignoring Seehofer's jokes–a shaky compromise on the refugee issue, and agreement to defer the joint election manifesto that ensured months more of wrangling. Within the CDU, conservatives warned that Schulz's surge exposed the flaws of relying on Merkel and asymmetric demobilization by showing how fickle centrist voters could be, and bolstered their case for shoring up its right wing. Officials from the market wing warned that the party needed to counter the SPD candidate's "social populism." But, rather than alter course, the CDU doubled down on Merkel's centrism. Internal wrangling was actually eroding AfD poll ratings, but with the SPD above 30 percent, a red-red-green Bundestag majority was again within reach, and that alliance seemed Schulz's only realistic route to the chancellery. To slow his momentum, CDU leaders hit hard at the risks of a shaky government beholden to the far left.

Three spring Land elections became testing grounds, the first in Saarland in March. Popular CDU Minister-President Kramp-Karrenbauer's low-key centrism mirrored Merkel's, but with the Schulz surge raising SPD hopes, some quietly warned that association with the Chancellor might prove a burden. "AKK" as she is known campaigned mainly on her own grand coalition's record and warned against replacing it with a red-red-green alliance that included Saarland's strong Left Party. While spurning calls for a refugee cap, she did take a hard line on crime (and against Turkey's regime for mobilizing its resident nationals in Germany to vote in a referendum expanding its autocratic president's power). On 26 March, Saarland's CDU exceeded forecasts by rising five points to 40.7 percent, while the SPD fell below 30 percent. Most credited Land-specific issues in this small, unique region. CDU leaders, however, also saw vindication of their national strategy: a Merkel clone had outcompeted the SPD for centrist voters by warning against an all-left government, and there had been no "Schulz effect." With the AfD having won just 5 percent there and slipping in national polls,

Tauber voiced doubt that it would now even make it into the Bundestag come fall. In any case, he insisted, his CDU was right to focus not on the far right but "important" themes: "As always, the campaign will be about whether a Christian Democrat or Social Democrat sits in the chancellery."[10]

Bigger tests were set for May. Initially red-green majorities were expected to survive in both Schleswig-Holstein and populous North Rhine-Westphalia (NRW), long an SPD bastion. Amid the Schulz surge, polls there even put it above 40 percent. The CDU's unknown young Schleswig-Holsten Chair Daniel Guenther exploited his SPD rival's complacent, gaffe-prone campaign and hit hard on domestic security. Likewise, NRW party chief Laschet–a mild Merkelianer who fully backed her refugee policy–chided the SPD Land government's laxity before the New Year's attacks in Cologne in 2016. He promised firmer law and order, suggesting the CSU as his model, and invited Seehofer to speak at CDU rallies. Laschet even made joint appearances with Merkel's chief conservative critic Bosbach, promising that–if they won– this hardline security expert would be tasked with evaluating NRW's counterterrorism preparedness.

In both contests on 14 May, the CDU won a third of the vote, edging out its SPD rival for first place; Lindner's FDP surged to low double digits; and the AfD barely topped 5 percent. The math pointed to a Jamaica coalition in Schleswig-Holstein and a CDU-FDP governing majority in NRW. Conservatives credited the hard line on security and cautioned that AfD gains even amid internal strife confirmed a voter shift to the right. Yet, Merkel's team celebrated again: outcompeting the SPD for centrist voters, not a *Lagerwahlkampf,* had burst the Schulz bubble. Reassuring national polls put her Union back in the high 30 percent range, with a double-digit lead over the SPD, the FDP safely at 8-10 percent, and more AfD slippage, vindicating their plans for a fall campaign based on Merkel and a good economy. Such trends made it easy to dismiss concerns raised by Schulz's initial success: was her popularity fragile, was her low-key style vulnerable to tough populist attacks, and was her Union unduly complacent when it came to how voters felt about the economy? And, if warning against red-red-green had helped drive SPD ratings back down, did that tactic now lose utility with polls again showing no hope of an all-left majority?

Summer/Fall

Yet as summer began, Merkel's team–leery of risking the party's fresh momentum–sought to avoid controversy or contention. A banner at major events read simply "CDU. The center." While posters unveiled in mid June did shelve the orange motif of past campaigns in favor of the German flag's black-red-gold, Tauber insisted that this symbolized "an enlightened, open, modern patriotism," not nationalism. Four posters underscored CDU themes–security, jobs, family, and Europe. Two others, one with Merkel smiling benignly, read "For a Germany in which we live well and gladly." Tauber converted that line into an unpronounceable, slightly self-mocking hashtag #fedidwgugl.[11] While the slogan associated her party with good economic times, critics derided it as vacuous and complacent, as they did a flyer depicting a woman dozing in a meadow with the tagline "Enjoy summer and vote the right way this fall." Satirical news stories reported that drug testing agencies had certified Merkel's low-key campaign as a sleep aid.

Caution also dominated CDU policy positions. One editorial noted that its competition with the SPD was not about "whether," but more about "how, how much, or how fast."[12] With all mainstream rivals making approval of gay marriage a condition for any coalition, for example, Merkel abruptly agreed to a Bundestag vote free from caucus discipline. While she joined a Union majority in voting no, other CDU deputies helped the measure pass, removing an obstacle to her coalition options and grounds for SPD attack. A frustrated Schulz charged her with dampening real debate to depress turnout, calling it an attack on democracy, but was caught between vainly competing with her for the center or shifting left.

Similar priorities shaped Merkel's negotiations over a joint Union election manifesto. Early on, she had replaced Tauber atop her select team with another loyal *bête noire* of the right, Chancellery chief Altmaier, who would carry more weight in bargaining with the CSU. They rebuffed Seehofer's demands that the program include a firm upper limit on refugee numbers, as well as calls from CDU conservatives to codify the Essen congress resolutions on dual citizenship and transit centers for migrants or a law regulating Islam in Germany. Especially after Schulz's surge, Merkel's team also shied away from planks that might be castigated as socially harsh or too pro-business, irking their own market liberals; nor, despite SPD demands, did they spell out specific plans for ensuring the long-term viability of Germany's public pension system. In early July, the two Union sisters finally signed the manifesto. Her CDU executive had one morning to approve the contents before a press conference to unveil it. The document pledged modest middle-income tax cuts, higher child subsidies for families, more defense spending, full employment with another balanced budget, new anti-crime measures, and more police funding. A brief sub-section on refugees near the end pledged to curb the influx, but without a formal cap. Conceding defeat, Seehofer insisted that restrictions he could not get Merkel's CDU to endorse now would appear in a separate CSU *Bayernplan*; differences could then be resolved after the election. Downplaying past clashes, he proclaimed "blind confidence" in her leadership. Making a virtue of necessity, he implied that campaigning with divergent positions might allow each Union sister win different types of voters, giving the CSU new clout in a post election bargain.

By mid-summer, the chancellor led Schulz by twenty points without even having campaigned. Hosting the G-7 summit in Hamburg underscored her image as a world leader; unruly protests there only reinforced her admonitions about instability. Touring north German beach resorts, she conceded that no one party would totally satisfy everyone, underscoring the CDU campaign's focus on her. With the Union near 40 percent in most polls, not just loyalists, but also Seehofer and Lindner declared it obvious that she would remain in office, atop whatever coalition. Yet, the parallel campaign also continued. The CSU sought to mobilize conservatives with its *Bayernplan*, highlighting the refugee cap, as well as a strong law and order lead candidate, Bavaria's Interior Minister Joachim Hermann. No CDU leader was asked by more Bundestag colleagues to campaign in their districts than Spahn, whose message earned lusty cheers. Contradicting Merkel, he insisted that not all new cultures benefitted Germany, warning that refugees had fostered more antisemitism, homophobia, chauvinism, and violence.

Merkel declared her own desire to regain voters lost to the far right, albeit without concessions to its views. For example, she admonished CDU colleagues in Saxony-Anhalt's Landtag for backing an AfD resolution condemning left extremism. For its final push, the party doubled down on the chancellor's global and domestic stature as a consensus builder, with new posters and a tagline, "fully mother-vated." Her first of fifty speeches pledged security in all forms and disparaged populism, without naming the AfD. Party officials lined up endorsements from entertainers and sports stars. Jung von Matt produced a television ad that featured Merkel asking "In what sort of Germany do you want to live?" Her answer cautioned against hate, while the montage of idyllic images gave no hint of the refugee crisis–or any rival party.

Despite some tiny slippage in Merkel's approval in late August, she remained far ahead of Schulz. Union support was leveling off but still in the high 30 percent range, 10–15 percent above the SPD. Respondents overwhelmingly predicted Merkel would be re-elected. The only scheduled event that gave Schulz an opening was an early September televised debate. While he attacked her vagueness on pensions and other issues, in many areas, the two seemed in accord. Merkel exuded calm, confidence and experience. Viewers and pundits labeled her the victor. Thus, while Union support remained stable, the SPD's kept sliding. She dismissed Schulz's call for more debates.

Yet, this campaign differed sharply from her 2013 re-election bid in one way. At most late summer rallies, hecklers on the fringes drowned out her speeches with boos, loud whistling and shouts like "traitor to the people," "Merkel hates Germany," or "get out." Most held AfD signs. Protesters were especially unruly in eastern venues. Yet, even in prosperous Bavaria, including towns at the center of the refugee influx, nervous supporters were encircled by mobs yelling "Merkel must go." At one rally, her campaign helpers were injured in scuffles, at others, agitators ripped CDU posters from supporters' hands as children sobbed. Merkel generally plowed through her standard forty-minute speech, barely mentioning the chaos or at most commenting mildly that hecklers had little to offer. Ultimately, she had to speak from behind barriers to deflect projectiles like produce. All of this was accompanied by a wave of online attacks vilifying her (albeit with little evidence of "fake news" or external meddling).

Televised town-hall style forums in early September were more civil, but there too Merkel faced often hostile questions from ordinary voters about schools struggling to integrate foreign students, under-resourced police, and crime by young male immigrants–as well as anxious queries about deportation and rising racism from the few non-white participants. She held her ground, expressing sympathy while still rejecting a refugee cap and cautioning against stereotypes, though some in the audiences continued to evince skepticism. Others spoke angrily of retirees barely getting by on modest pensions or without long-term care. Again, voicing concern, Merkel sought to paint a more positive picture, but one women's dismissal of her reassurances as a "joke" drew wide coverage.

What such hostility portended was unclear. Despite the Union's lead, the share of undecideds was the highest in two decades–a quarter or more. Voters ranked jobs and growth–Union strong suits–as less important than social services, crime, terror, and, especially immigration.[13] While a plurality rated the CDU/CSU as most competent on domestic security and migrants, a majority still disapproved of Merkel's refugee decision–including a third of her own party's voters, two-thirds of FDP supporters and 100 percent of AfD supporters. By contrast, 78 percent of Green backers approved it.[14] Moreover, throughout August and September, the share of AfD voters steadily climbed. Union campaigners outside Berlin grew ever more uneasy that it was eating into their base. The AfD repurposed a Kohl-era CDU placard warning against refugee abuse of German asylum laws in the 1990s. In Bavaria one posters declared "we do what the CSU promises."

Another claimed that long-time Christian Social icon Franz Josef Strauss would vote AfD were he still alive. The latter's family and Seehofer's party objected, but media stories spread the images. Reporters also quoted Bavarians lamenting that current problems would have been unimaginable under Strauss as he would have shut the borders and cracked down on refugee crime.

On balance, though, Merkel's apparent inevitability still seemingly trumped her vulnerability, and to the very end, major polls placed her Union at 35–37 percent, far ahead of the SPD. Her last east-north-south campaign swing ended in Munich, where she and Seehofer offered a show of harmony. Via Twitter the CSU declared itself "fully-mothervated." Yet tellingly, even there she was heckled and drowned out by shrill whistling. Moreover, the last survey, albeit by YouGov–whose online methodology many pollsters questioned–showed Merkel's Union falling to 34 percent and the AfD at 13 percent.

Results and Aftermath

These warning signs prepared few for election night. Merkel's Union unsurprisingly emerged as the largest party, but landed at just 32.9 percent–down over 8 percent from 2013, its biggest drop ever and its worst showing since 1949. The CDU alone garnered a mere 26.8 percent and topped 35 percent only in Rhineland-Palatinate with its largest losses in the east. Seehofer's CSU struggled to a meager 38.8 percent in Bavaria, its worst federal showing by far since 1949. That the SPD also fell to a postwar record low, 20.5 percent, was scant consolation. By contrast, Lindner's FDP surged to 10.6 percent, thanks in part to 1.3 million Union defectors. But, it was the AfD's stunning 12.6 percent that dominated headlines: the far-right populists won near or above a fifth of the vote in every eastern Land, even edging out the CDU for first place in Saxony. A third of its support came from former non-voters, but another quarter–almost a million–from Merkel's Union. Two-thirds of those who left her party said it had ignored ordinary people's concerns amid the refugee crisis.

Election night supporters at CDU headquarters applauded party leaders and chanted "Angie," all to the same music as in 2013, but their mood was far more subdued–nor did anyone on the podium dance. Merkel's team claimed success in achieving its goals–largest party, no left-wing majority, and the chancellorship. While conceding disappointment at the vote share, Tauber noted that it was comparable to Union results in 2005 and 2009, downplaying comparisons to a banner year like 2013 as unfair. CDU leaders cited high losses to the FDP by tactical voters pushing for a center-right majority, noting that "only" a third of Union defectors went to the AfD. Insisting that her strategy had been well thought-out, the next morning, Merkel denied seeing anything she should have done differently.

Conservatives, however, labeled this result a "debacle." While Spahn held back, dissident Bundestag deputies, some corporate leaders, and Land or local-level politicians especially in the east and south, squarely blamed Merkel's refugee policy. Conservative media accused her of having helped the far right establish itself. Only a few, mainly in the Berlin Circle, called on Merkel to step down, but allies paid a price: one in four Union Bundestag deputies voted against re-electing Kauder caucus chief. While conceding the party had "left its right flank open," Seehofer insisted that his mix of hardline demands and shows of solidarity with Merkel had spared the CSU an even worse result, but critics blamed this inconsistency for the debacle, and his job as minister-president was already in jeopardy.

On balance, Merkel's team could persuasively maintain the Union had more to gain, short- and long-term, by competing for the center. But, it had dropped traditional positions by arguing that the zeitgeist left no alternative and party unity permitted little internal debate, debate that might have compelled it more fully convince skeptics. The makeover of the CDU leadership had left few major figures who could still credibly pitch changes to right-wing voters. Modernization thus came to rest on broad but brittle acceptance, undergirded mainly by the electoral value of Merkel's popularity. Her compassionate refugee policy marked the apotheosis of this "revolution" and put it at risk–as public uneasiness grew, the chancellor never found words to reassure older Germans, easterners, or others that she fully grasped their concerns. That made it easier for the emerging far right to transform this most consensual politician into a polarizing figure for the first time. Yet, convinced that what mattered was the horse race with her SPD rival, CDU planners built a campaign around the chancellor and a strong economy rather than shift right or merely take on the AfD directly and seek to contain it by fronting conservatives who could more credibly sell their party as a guarantor of stability.

Campaign events compounded the problem. Schulz's brief success with the social justice theme reinforced both Merkel's wariness of pro-market reforms that could be slammed as anti-welfare state, making it harder to retain voters being wooed by the FDP, and her tendency to opt for vagueness on issues like pensions and long-term care–a weak point for the Union. Moreover, while warning that Schulz would bring the Left to power briefly mobilized her party and helped burst his bubble, that tactic lost punch once prospects of a "red-red-green" majority receded, and right-wing discontent refocused on Merkel. Likewise, the spring Land election victories gave her team undue confidence in its centrist strategy when other factors were at play. If Seehofer was to blame for his own inconsistency, by conceding no ground to him, the CDU underscored his lack of clout. The swelling summer consensus that Merkel had yet another term locked up, reinforced by her debate with Schulz and mild manner on televised forums, sowed complacency among supporters, but also mobilized right wing opponents. Nor did the CDU effectively counter AfD efforts to revive uneasiness over refugees, and however staged the far right's disruptions of her rallies, Merkel's plodding stump speeches conveyed a feeble response. Only a quarter of late-deciding voters opted for her Union, just barely more than chose the FDP.

Given where the 24 September 2017 election had left coalition politics, the Union had little time to process the result and resolve personal issues let alone strategic differences. Indeed, the task of trying to form any new government in a Bundestag with seven parties and few attractive options compounded its dilemmas: Lindner's FDP would drive a hard bargain yet by itself could not provide a majority. Any new deal with center-left rivals would further rile the Union right, while fueling the AfD. Stalemate or new elections just seemed likely to feed the populist narrative. Thus, especially for Merkel and those intent on preserving her legacy, the election's one consolation–coming in first–was a poisoned chalice.

Still, she prepared for exploratory talks and, in light of the SPD's swift rejection of a new grand coalition, aimed for Jamaica, the only other plausible majority. Merkel had long favored such a deal, and now it was also Seehofer's only shot at vindication too. Knowing the FDP would demand his post, she first eased Schäuble out of the finance ministry. Then, the Union sisters finally hammered out a joint negotiating position on refugees–an annual limit on new refugees of 200,000, which could be adjusted upward depending on the number of deportations and voluntary departures, and which excluded new immigrants admitted for economic reasons. While the Greens rejected that compromise offer, they were generally eager to bargain. Throughout October, word emerged of compromises on refugees, climate, and other major issues. Skeptics in one party or the other, however, often quickly disavowed those deals. Citing that pattern as a sign of unbridgeable mistrust, Lindner's FDP–the partner least eager for a coalition–broke off talks in November. While he drew most blame for their failure, the ongoing crisis further undermined Merkel and Seehofer, who was also resigning as Bavarian minister-president if not yet CSU chief. In the context of broad resistance to a minority government or new elections, the SPD backtracked and in early 2018 moved haltingly toward accepting another grand coalition under Merkel–but only after she granted them the finance ministry and major policy concessions that further riled her critics. Seeking to make the deal more palatable to conservatives, she named Spahn to the new cabinet.

Merkel thus began her final term as chancellor atop a government that would test even her skills at consensus building. She would face that challenge while seriously weakened in the CDU and with her long run as chair rapidly nearing an end. In a step interpreted as paving the way for an heir, she nominated Kramp-Karrenbauer as party general-secretary. Given the ambitions of others, that move by no means precluded a succession struggle amid or after this *Merkeldämmerung.* But even with a smooth transition, the CDU faced an inevitable struggle over identity and strategy. Eastern Land branches, above all Saxony's, talked openly of revolt against the federal party, even of cooperation with the AfD. More temperate conservatives cast an envious eye south at the Austrian Peoples Party's electoral success in shifting right to co-opt its own populist rival, the Freedom Party. But while such a course was possible for the post Seehofer CSU, modernizers uniformly insisted that seeking to outflank the AfD would be futile and counterproductive–and they remained well-entrenched within party ranks. Even Spahn had now been co-opted into the cabinet, while Kramp-Karrenbauer–a Merkel fan who, as a conservative Catholic, also enjoyed broad intraparty appeal–had the credentials to restrain demands for a radical swing. Yet, that left open the prospect of an internal stalemate among roughly equal camps, each citing a different electoral imperative, a plight all too-similar to the SPD: in the 1990s a popular chair and chancellor had kept it in power by persuading the party to abandon traditional positions only to see a challenger on their flank take that political space, and a decade later Germany's other catch-all party was still torn over its road to recovery. Avoiding its chief rival's fate would be the top priority of a post Merkel leadership, and–short of the AfD self-destructing–no easy scenarios present themselves.

Clay Clemens teaches Government at the College of William and Mary. His research specialization is contemporary German party politics and institutions. His recent articles on those topics have appeared in the journals *German Politics* and *German Politics and Society.* E-mail: cmclem@wm.edu

Notes

1. The author thanks the German Academic Exchange Service (DAAD) for its support of his research on the election. Christian Democratic Union, *Berliner Erklärung: Unsere Perspektiven 2010–2013*, Resolution of the CDU Federal Executive, 14–15 January 2010.
2. Berliner Kreis in der Union, *Erklärung*, 11 May 2016.
3. "CDU Vize Laschet warnt vor eine Rechtsruck," *Spiegel-online*, 9 December 2016; available at http://www.spiegel.de/politik/deutschland/armin-laschet-cdu-vize-warnt-vor-rechtsruck-a-1116780.html, accessed 16 April 2018.
4. Interview mit Peter Tauber, *Rheinische-Post-online*, 10 April 2017; available at http://www.rp-online.de/politik/deutschland/interview-mit-peter-tauber-die-spd-ist-bei-der-linkspartei-auf-einem-auge-blind-aid-1.6746494, accessed 16 April 2018.
5. Ferdinand Knauss, "Warum niemand den Aufstand gegen Merkel wagt," *Wirtschaftswoche*, 1 December 2016.
6. Marc Brost and Peter Dausend, Interview with Jens Spahn, "Die Mitte liegt rechts von der CDU," *Zeit-online*, 16 March 2017; available at http://www.zeit.de/2017/10/jens-spahn-cdu-fluechtlingspolitik-integration-interview, accessed 16 April 2018.
7. Infratest dimap, "Direkt zu den Wahlen am 13.3.2016," ARD; available at wahl.tageschau.de, accessed 16 April 2018.
8. Hauke Reimer, "CDU-Hoffnungsträger Jens Spahn fordert Lagerwahlkampf," *Wirtschaftswoche*, 25 November 2016.
9. "CSU contemplates independent campaign against Merkel's CDU in 2017 Election," *Deutsche Welle*, 7 May 2016.
10. Interview with Peter Tauber (see note 4).
11. Robert Rossman, "Politische Verpackung, *Süddeutsche Zeitung*, 22 June 2017.
12. Katharina Schuler, "Schulz fehlt die Angriffsfläche," *Zeit-online*, 20 June 2017; available at http://www.zeit.de/politik/deutschland/2017-06/bundestagswahlkampf-martin-schulz-angela-merkel-chancen, accessed 16 April 2018.
13. Infratest dimap, ARD-DeutschlandTREND September 2017 II/KW37.
14. Infratest dimap, Bundestagswahl 2017, ARD; available at wahl.tagesschau.de, accessed 16 April 2018.

··· Chapter 7 ···

YET ANOTHER GRAND COALITION

The Social Democrats at the Crossroads

Andreas M. Wüst

For the Social Democrats (SPD), the result of the Bundestag election of 24 September 2017 was a disaster. With a vote share of just 20.5 percent, the party had to face its worst result in a national election since 1949. The outgoing Grand Coalition lost 13.8 percentage points; albeit the CDU/CSU more (-8.6 points) than the SPD (-5.2 points). In light of the success of the right-wing Alternative for Germany (AfD, 12.6 percent)–now the third largest parliamentary group in the Bundestag–and the return of the Free Democratic Party (FDP, 10.7 percent), there not even is an option for the SPD to form a coalition of the political Left (*Linksbündnis*) anymore. The SPD (20.5 percent), Greens (8.9 percent) and the Left Party (9.2 percent) currently only hold a minority of seats in the Bundestag. In recent years, this has been the case only after the 2009 Bundestag election and during the long chancellorship of Helmut Kohl from 1983 to 1998.

The continuous decline of the SPD in government since Gerhard Schröder won by a landslide in 1998 (40.1 percent), may well indicate Social Democrats being on a "wrong" course. Governing the country, and especially being the junior partner in a Grand Coalition, has so far not been beneficial for the SPD. In the view of many party members, the time to leave the Grand Coalition was now. And such an exit was exactly what Martin Schulz, SPD frontrunner and chairman during the election year, declared on 24 September 2017, right after the polls had closed. Party members and supporters at the Willy Brandt Haus, the party's headquarters, applauded this announcement frenetically. In addition to worries about the SPD's future, there were at least two more reasons for justifying such an exit: the rise of the right-wing AfD, which could become the leader of the opposition, and the fact that the election results for the CDU/CSU, FDP and the Greens would allow for the forma-

Notes for this section begin on page 171.

tion of a so-called Jamaica coalition–the colors of the Jamaican flag are black (CDU/CSU), yellow (FDP) and green.[1] It seemed to be rational for the Social Democrats to not strive for another period of participation in government.

A record 171 days later, Angela Merkel was reelected chancellor of the Federal Republic of Germany as head of yet another grand coalition. Considering the long-term electoral decline of the SPD, the mood inside that party, and strategic considerations, the path for the party to form this coalition was long, hard, and costly. For all political actors, the time between the election and the formation of a new government resembles a roller coaster ride. But for the SPD, the roller coaster went on additional loops. In the end, however, joining the CDU/CSU in governing the country proved to be without any promising alternative.

This article takes a closer look at the coalition agreement that the biggest German parties have made for the current legislative term (2017–2021). It does so by starting with an overview of the political agenda supported by the German public. It proceeds with a description of the legal framework, the crucial role of the German president, and of the long path that was necessary for the Social Democrats to enter a new coalition with the CDU/CSU. The main part of the article then analyzes the core issues of the coalition agreement in light of the SPD's election program. Subsequently, the consequences of a rejection of the coalition agreement by the SPD members are outlined. Finally, the chances and risks of the formation of another Grand Coalition for Germany are discussed.

The Political Agenda

Since 2015, the most important issue in Germany has been immigration. The rise of the issue had been caused by the record-high influx of refugees into Germany, primarily in the second half of 2015.[2] Immigration-related issues have dominated the public discourse and the election campaign of most parties. It has also contributed significantly to the success of the AfD in all state elections since 2014 and in the Bundestag election of 2017. As Figure 7.1 documents, far behind immigration, pensions, social justice, and education were mentioned as important problems in Germany on the eve of the Bundestag election. If asked which party could solve the problems named, a relative majority of the voting-age population answered the CDU/CSU with the SPD ranking second. This order is only reversed pertaining to social justice, with the Left Party being mentioned by another 15 percent. Contrarily, for 12 percent of the electorate, the AfD was considered to be the most competent

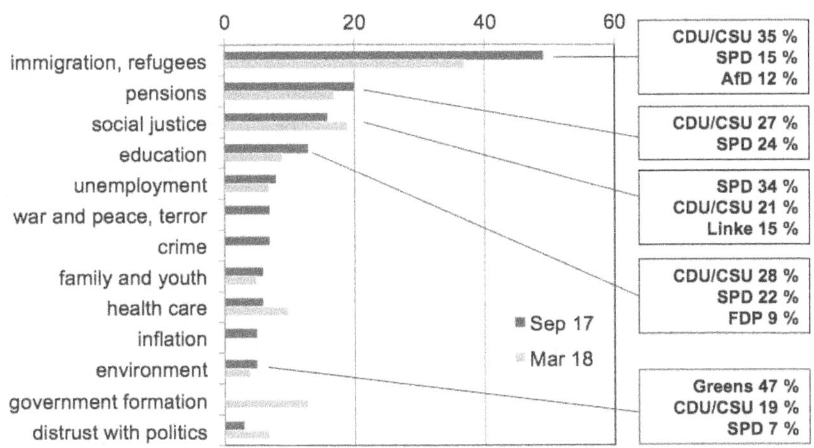

Figure 7.1: Most Important Problems in Germany in September 2017 and in March 2018 and Ascribed Competences in Solving Problems in September 2017 *

* in percent of two problems that could be named

Source: Forschungsgruppe Wahlen e.V., pre-election survey week 37/2017 and Politbarometer 11/2018.

with respect to (curbing) immigration, and 9 percent considered the FDP to be the most competent concerning education. Finally, the Greens traditionally have been considered to be the most competent concerning (the protection of) the environment. In a nutshell, the political agenda and the party competencies mirror a quite heterogeneous electorate with no decisive preference for either the left or the right before the 2017 Bundestag election.[3]

As of March 2018, immigration has lost some of its earlier importance. After the long and partially frustrating negotiations among the parties during winter (see the article of Frank Decker and Philipp Adorf in this issue), the formation of a government was of concern to some. Along those lines, distrust in politics and in politicians has increased. Finally, social justice and healthcare are now more frequently mentioned as important problems. This certainly has to do with the discussion among SPD members about the conditions under which the party might consider negotiating a new Grand Coalition.

To Eat Humble Pie or Canossa via Bellevue

In general, the German federal president does not have much power. In times of (potential) instability of the political system, however, the position of the president can be quite strong. Three times in the history of the Federal Republic, presidents had to decide on whether or not to allow the dissolution of parliament and conducting new elections. According to Article 68 of the Basic Law, this right is conditional on a negative vote of confidence initiated by a German chancellor and his or her subsequent request to dissolve parliament. In all of the three cases–Willy Brandt in 1972, Helmut Kohl in 1982, and Gerhard Schröder in 2005–German Presidents Gustav Heinemann, Karl Carstens, and Horst Köhler complied with the request.

After the 2017 Bundestag election and especially after the failure to form a Jamaica coalition was announced late on 19 November, a different article of the Basic Law put the German president in a crucial role. Article 63 gives the president the exclusive right to propose a candidate for chancellor to parliament. Nevertheless, no federal president ever came up with a name not supported by parties with a majority of seats in the Bundestag. And right after the failure of CDU/CSU, FDP and Greens to enter formal coalition talks, President Frank-Walter Steinmeier was not willing to break with that tradition. Within one week, he summoned the leaders of all parties represented in the Bundestag individually to remind them on their responsibility to their voters and for the country.

The president's action thwarted the SPD's strategy to not reenter a coalition with the CDU/CSU. In an unforced error, the SPD even reaffirmed this position on 20 November,[4] just days before Schulz was scheduled to meet the president at Schloss Bellevue–the federal president's official residence in Berlin–to talk about the responsibility of parties and *raison d'état* on 23 November. Indeed, right after Schulz's private conversation with the president, the party executive met again and suddenly signaled openness to enter talks with the Christian Democrats. When Schulz visited the national convention of the SPD's youth organization, the JUSOS, in Saarbrücken on 24 November, he was heavily attacked for this change in position. By now the slogan "No GroKo" (no to the Grand Coalition) had become popular among the party faithful. The new dilemma for the SPD crystallized in the following public response by Schulz: "When the president invites me, shall I respond 'kiss my ass' (*du kannst mich mal*)?"[5] By 24 November, it became abundantly clear that the SPD's strategy needs to be revised.

To a significant degree, the late shift by the SPD was the result of Steinmeier's belief that a failure of party elites to form a government would be the wrong signal to the public.[6] Moreover, according to article 63 of the Basic Law, the president has leeway on when to propose a candidate for chancellor to the Bundestag. There is no pressure on the president to act fast, but once the president starts the process, time runs quickly. Within a period of fourteen days of balloting, either a new chancellor (by absolute or relative majority) is elected and appointed by the president, or, after an additional seven days, the president can dissolve the Bundestag and new elections will take place. If a candidate for chancellor is elected by an absolute majority within fourteen days, the president can only appoint the person elected. If a candidate only gets a relative majority of votes in the final ballot after fourteen days of balloting, it is at the president's discretion to either appoint this candidate as chancellor or to dissolve parliament (and thereby call for a new election). All candidates for chancellor in the history of the Federal Republic have been elected in the first ballot by an absolute majority of Bundestag members. In March 2018, Angela Merkel was once again elected in the first ballot by an absolute majority of 364 (out of a potential 709) votes. In fact, 315 voted against her and there were nine abstentions and four invalid votes.

Yet, before Angela Merkel could get reelected by a majority of Bundestag members, the party executive of the SPD had to gain the support of delegates and of their party members. First, delegates had to grant permission for exploratory talks about a coalition with the CDU/CSU at a party convention on 7 December 2017. Second, on the basis of the results of this "exploration" (*Sondierung*) with the CDU/CSU, delegates had to decide on whether to start actual coalition talks at a party convention on 21 January 2018. Finally, all party members were asked whether or not to accept the coalition agreement concluded on 7 February 2018 (the voting period was 20 February until 2 March 2018). While only 56 percent of the representatives at the party convention in January voted for coalition talks, 66 percent of the SPD members eventually came out in favor of the actual coalition agreement.

As this roadmap clearly indicates, the SPD's path to their fourth GroKo in German history–and to the first ever continuation of a Grand Coalition–was a rocky one. Yet, it helped the party not only to sell the new government, but also to mitigate the frustration of many party supporters with the Social Democrats's zigzag course. If the SPD was to keep Merkel in power, it had to make core parts of its election program crucial elements of the coalition agreement. This seemed to be the new strategy of the party, and it worked.

A Social Democratic Government?

The coalition agreement between the CDU/CSU and SPD is a booklet of 175 pages–the longest coalition agreement in the history of the Federal Republic. And it can well be considered a social democratic document. Indeed, "70 percent of the text stems from the party program of the SPD," as researchers at the Karlsruhe Institute of Technology (KIT) detected through a computer-based analysis of the document.[7] Without doubt, it is an agreement that made it relatively easy for SPD members to vote for it–if they voted based solely on substantive policy issues. Referring to the political agenda of the electorate (Figure 7.1), migration-related issues, various social policy issues, education, and healthcare were considered most important. Consequently, let us look at these issue areas in the coalition agreement[8] compared to the content of the SPD's election manifesto.[9]

Migration-related Issues

This policy area was not only one of the most difficult topics to traverse during the coalition talks, but was also the most contested during the election campaign itself. Chancellor Merkel's failure to reject the mass of refugees–the position of the right-wing AfD and its supporters–made it extremely difficult for the SPD to succeed with their intention to reopen family-based immigration for "persons eligible for subsidiary protection," but who had failed to get refugee status.[10] In the end, a meagre 1,000 nuclear family members of the subsidiary protected category will be able to come to Germany per month, starting in August 2018.

Germany will also not get the "point-based immigration law" for which the SPD had campaigned. Instead, it is likely to get a leaner set of more transparent rules for economically based immigration, something the SPD had also advocated. The Social Democrats have, however, been successful in establishing independent counseling for asylum-seekers across the country. On the other side, the CDU/CSU succeeded in establishing refugee centers (so-called ANkER Einrichtungen) in which the admission, asylum certification process, distribution across the country, but also the deportation of nonrecognized asylum seekers is organized altogether. With respect to integration, the coalition agreement primarily indicates that policy should become more efficient and effective. Furthermore, it contains some improvements in healthcare for older immigrants and greater support for refugees enrolled in an apprenticeship program (two additional years of residence; the so-called "three+two rule"). All in all, migration proved not to have been a policy area in which the SPD appears to have been a successful negotiator in the coalition talks. It should also be noted that they lost the cabinet position of commissioner for integration to the CDU.

Social Policies

The policy area of social affairs can be considered the soul of the Social Democratic Party. After Chancellor Schröder had started with the Agenda

2010 reform program, the SPD had to face a new competitor in this policy area: the Left Party.[11] Largely because of these reforms from the early 2000s, a significant portion of the unemployed and blue-collar workers no longer supported the SPD, but rather switched to the Left, and, eventually, also to the CDU, CSU, and, most recently, to right-wing parties. In 2017, not only the unemployed and workers, but even a high portion of union members voted for the AfD.[12] In light of a rather liberal course in social policy in the Merkel governments, the SPD now faces competition in social policy from the left, far right, and from the moderate right. It is crucial for the SPD's success in the near future to regain issue ownership and perceived competence in social policy. Looking at the coalition agreement, this seemed exactly to have been the SPD's strategy.

In almost every subfield of social policy, the SPD produced success: euro 4 billion for the long-term unemployed, euro 3.5 billion for childcare, a monthly raise of euro 25 in child allowances, euro 2 billion for social housing, abolishment of the solidarity surcharge for the big majority of taxpayers (90 percent of them), 10 percent supplement for life-long workers with only a minimum pension, just to name the extra spending and tax cuts. While the coalition agreement provides for setting up a new commission on pensions, both the pension payments of the employed and the level of pension payouts have been fixed until 2025. Furthermore, the monthly payment of employers and employees to the unemployment insurance fund will be reduced by 0.3 percent. All in all, the SPD was able to realize virtually every single goal from its election manifesto, even if the policy instruments to achieve the policy goals were sometimes specified differently.

Another important subfield of social policy concerns work-related measures. A new goal of the government and "third-order change" in Peter Hall's terms[13] is the announcement of a policy of full employment. If achieved, this would especially lead to a higher share of the population in the social insurance system, and, thus, to decreased state expenses, especially pertaining to unemployment. A newly agreed-upon instrument is the so-called "master bonus" (*Meisterbonus*) that would at least partially refund fees to get a master's certificate for craftsmen. A very different measure is the right for employees to reduce their working time for a limited period of time, but ensuring the right to return to full-time employment eventually. According to the coalition agreement this will soon be possible if a company has more than forty-five employees. That said, the SPD could only realize in a fragmented fashion the ending of time-limited contracts without cause. Still, based on the agreement, it will soon be more difficult to contract for a rather long limited time or to renew such contracts.

Education

A change in political philosophy or of "third-order" can be found in the policy area of education. The coalition agreement strives for a change of the Basic Law to allow the national government to spend money for the (local) educational infrastructure. This was a main demand of the SPD, and, previously of the FDP in the unsuccessful Jamaica negotiations (back then vetoed by the only Green minister-president). Euro 2 billion are planned for investment into all-day schools and school pupils' care. Euro 5 billion will be invested into a "digital upgrade" (*Digitalausbau*) of schools. Moreover, support for schoolchildren from economically weak families, the so-called "school starter package" will become thicker and more widespread. Except for the digital upgrade, most of the announcements pertaining to education can be characterized as social policy.

Healthcare

Part of the Agenda 2010 reform was a break with the financing of public health insurance by employers and employees on equal terms. Just like the SPD announced in their election manifesto, the coalition agreement comprises a return to parity concerning health insurance. In addition, more time for patients at doctor's appointments and increased subsidies for dentures were agreed. It is also now more difficult for the self-employed to avoid being insured. Yet, the SPD was not successful in installing a new insurance system, the so-called *Bürgerversicherung*, which would have terminated the privileged treatment of civil servants who are privately insured, but heavily subsidized by the state.

The list of policy proposals, however, also includes measures for nursing care, especially targeted for the growing body of elderly people. An emergency plan is supposed to raise the number of caregivers by 8,000. This is a small increase, but at least it is an increase. The main challenge remains: to attract people to become professional caregivers or nurses. In the coalition agreement, it is at least documented that government would like to strive for better compensation of jobs in the care and social sector. Nevertheless, such issues are to be dealt with when pay negotiations among social partners take place, not by the government.

Beyond Franz Müntefering's "Opposition ist Mist"?

Having looked at the most important agreements made in crucial policy areas, the coalition agreement of CDU/CSU and SPD certainly has a social democratic imprint. This general conclusion does not change if all policy areas were included in the analysis. Based on this content and realizing that the SPD got a meagre 20 percent share of the votes in the 2017 Bundestag election, it would have been highly irrational for the SPD members to reject the agreement.

But, for medium- to long-term strategic reasons, however, the agreement could well have been rejected. This is exactly what the JUSOS and their chairmen, Kevin Kühnert, demanded.[14] According to them and to others from the party's left wing, another GroKo would be dangerous for the SPD and for the country, since the political alternatives between the big catch-all parties (*Volksparteien*) would–once again–become indistinguishable. They also worried that the ultimate beneficiary of a neoliberal policy could be the right-wing AfD with rising blackmail potential.[15] If the AfD gets stronger and remains in opposition, CDU/CSU and SPD might no longer have enough seats to form a GroKo. The established parties would then be forced to form new multi-party coalitions across cleavages that used to serve as political boundary lines.

Yet, what would have been the consequences if the SPD had not reentered the GroKo? Steinmeier likely would have started the voting procedure, proposing Merkel as new chancellor. It would have been Merkel and no one else receiving a relative majority of votes of Bundestag members in the last round of balloting. Presumably, neither Merkel nor Steinmeier would have had an interest in a minority cabinet–and Merkel certainly is not the type of politician for debating every issue in parliament and building ever-shifting short-term alliances. The very probable consequence of all of that would have been a new election. The result of such an election would likely have been very similar to the one in September 2017: maybe a stronger AfD, perhaps some gains for the CDU/CSU, or even better results for all smaller parties.

And the SPD in this scenario? Losses would be quite likely. Would there be enough seats to build a coalition of the leftist parties? This outcome would also be unlikely. Would there be enough seats to build another GroKo? This would also be uncertain, but, more importantly, it would be strategically almost impossible. Why? If there were a new election, voters would know that the SPD already had their chance to form a Grand Coalition with many policy issues tackled in a rather social democratic way. It would then not even be easy to reenter coalition talks with the CDU/CSU, not to mention the likelihood of a worse agreement for the Social Democrats compared to the previous one.

Consequently, a rejection of the coalition agreement would have meant taking risks well beyond the following Bundestag election. By contrast, joining the government allows the party to govern the country in a social democratic way, and to improve the life of Germany's citizens. Thus, this opportunity was without a real alternative, going well beyond Franz Müntefering's legendary *bon mot* "Opposition ist Mist" (opposition is bullshit).[16]

Discussion: The Risks of Yet Another Grand Coalition in Germany

A new Grand Coalition allows for dealing with voters' concerns from a broad electoral base. In times of increasing international instability–in light of Brexit and the foreign policies of Donald Trump, Vladimir Putin, and Recep Tayyip Erdogan–and the more generalized distrust in political elites, it is advantageous to have a veteran chancellor and experienced parties in government. An open question is whether this government will be able to adequately respond to current and rising challenges. The Green party doubts this especially with respect to climate change, both FDP and Left Party criticize various policies (taxes, social policy, education), and the AfD seems to strive primarily to "turn back the clock" to some vague golden age located somewhere between the 1950s and 1980s.

The Grand Coalition is representative of a pluralistic, European Germany with the social market economy as a central pillar–economically strong with a wide range of social benefits–but the new government only promotes incremental policy change. While such a policy might well satisfy the ("two-thirds") majority of the population, the main risk is the dependency on economic growth in various respects. Germany's social insurance state works well as long as the employment rate is high. If the economy suffers, unemployment will grow and social policy expenses will do so as well. In addition, a significant share of the expenses for social policy is already financed by the German taxpayer, accounting for about one-third of all social policy expenses.[17] If the coalition agreement is realized in practice, this share will likely continue to rise.

More than half of the expenses in the whole federal budget in 2017 was already devoted to social benefits. With the baby boom generation on the cusp of retirement–and their retirement benefits primarily payed by the currently employed–the costs for nursing care will inexorably rise. Germany is not well prepared for these challenges. Moreover, one gets the impression that the savings from the reforms that Schröder initiated and that cost him the chancellorship are currently spent by the governing parties. It is time for a new Agenda (2030?), but this probably will not happen soon enough or at all.

On the other hand, the new Grand Coalition will certainly make life easier for families and for employed people with low wages. If more unemployed people will get a job through the measurements envisaged, benefits will be manifold. If the GroKo is successful with some of its plans, including the initiation of reforms that the commissions on pensions and energy are likely to propose, this might also help to fight the main political challenge for the current legislative term: reducing the blackmail potential of the Alternative for Germany whose name is certainly misleading, since forward-looking policy initiatives of the AfD are missing.

For both the Social Democrats and for the Christian Democrats, the success of this government is essential to remaining the main political forces on the moderate left and on the moderate right. Neither is it sure that this coalition will last the whole legislative term, nor that it will be successful. Governing, however, was and is the best option for the *Volksparteien* to demonstrate their ability to work for the good of the people. Yet, for a functioning democracy and party system, the GroKo should remain a temporary alliance to be succeeded by a different coalition under new leadership in 2021.

Andreas M. Wüst received his PhD in 2002 from University of Heidelberg. He is currently External Lecturer at the University of Stuttgart and External Fellow at the Mannheim Center for European Social Research. His research focus is political sociology. Recent publications include: "Incorporation beyond Cleavages? Parties, Candidates and Germany's Immigrant-Origin Electorate," *German Politics* 25, no. 3 (2016): 414–432; "Der migrationsspezifische Einfluss auf parlamentarisches Handeln: Ein Hypothesentest auf der Grundlage von Redebeiträgen des Abgeordneten des Deutschen Bundestags 1996–2013," *Politische Vierteljahresschrift* 58, no. 2 (2017): 205–233 (with Andreas Blätte). E-mail: andreas.wuest@sowi.uni-stuttgart.de

Notes

1. These arguments were articulated by Martin Schulz in the Willy Brandt Haus and a little later also in the so-called Elefantenrunde of party leaders on television.
2. Valid numbers for refugees that have crossed the German border in 2015 are not available, particularly because registration took place with significant delays, and asylum applications have very often only been filed in 2016. It is however estimated that about 890.000 asylum-seekers entered Germany in 2015. See also https://www.welt.de/politik/

deutschland/article158465433/Deutschland-korrigiert-Fluechtlingszahl-fuer-2015.html, accessed 5 April 2018.

3. Arithmetically, the non-leftist parties CDU/CSU, FDP and AfD would have a majority of seats in parliament. However, the ideological distance between the AfD and FDP both concerning the economy and society appears to be bigger than the distance between FDP and SPD (data provided by Marc Debus, unpublished).
4. "Martin Schulz schließt große Koalition aus," *Die Zeit online*, 20 November 2017; available at http://www.zeit.de/politik/deutschland/2017-11/spd-schliesst-grosse-koalition-aus, accessed 5 April 2018.
5. "Martin Schulz bei den Jusos: 'Soll ich sagen, du kannst mich mal?'" *Der Spiegel online*, 24 November 2018; available at http://www.spiegel.de/politik/deutschland/martin-schulz-wenn-die-merkel-das-unterschreibt-haben-wir-die-groko-a-1180253.html, accessed 5 April 2018.
6. "Steinmeier lehnt Neuwahlen nach Scheitern von 'Jamaika' ab," *Reuters*, 20 November 2018; available at https://de.reuters.com/article/deutschland-koalition-idDEKBN1DK1HS, accessed 5 April 2018.
7. Marcus Jung, "GroKo-Einigung: Koalitionsvertrag zu 70 Prozent aus SPD-Feder," *Frankfurter Allgemeine Zeitung online*, 12 December 2017; available at http://www.faz.net/aktuell/wirtschaft/kuenstliche-intelligenz/koalitionsvertrag-besteht-zu-70-prozent-aus-spd-forderungen-15443775.html, accessed 5 April 2018.
8. https://www.cdu.de/system/tdf/media/dokumente/koalitionsvertrag_2018.pdf?file=1, accessed 5 April 2018.
9. https://www.spd.de/fileadmin/Dokumente/Bundesparteitag_2017/Es_ist_Zeit_fuer_mehr_Gerechtigkeit-Unser_Regierungsprogramm.pdf, accessed 5 April 2018.
10. EU directive 2011/95/EU; available at http://eur-lex.europa.eu/legal-content/EN/TXT/?uri=celex:32011L0095, accessed 19 April 2018.
11. Andreas M. Wüst and Dieter Roth, "Schröder's Last Campaign: An Analysis of the 2005 Bundestag election in context," *German Politics* 15, no. 4 (2006): 439–459.
12. Forschungsgruppe Wahlen e.V., *Bundestagswahl. Eine Analyse der Wahl vom 24. September 2017* (Mannheim, 2018), 53.
13. Peter Hall, "Policy Paradigms, Social Learning and the State. The Case of Economic Policy Making in Britain," *Comparative Politics* 25, no. 3 (1993): 275–296.
14. "Kampf gegen GroKo: Juso-Chef Kühnert startet Kampagne in Leipzig," *Leipziger Volkszeitung online*, 6 February 2018; available at http://www.lvz.de/Leipzig/Lokales/Kampf-gegen-GroKo-Juso-Chef-Kuehnert-startet-Kampagne-in-Leipzig, accessed 5 April 2018.
15. It is however more likely that a policy shift of (some) established parties will result in a decrease of support for the blackmail party, see Giovanni Sartori, *Parties and Party Systems* (Cambridge, 1976).
16. Quoted in *Süddeutsche Zeitung online*, 13 November 2009; available at http://www.sueddeutsche.de/politik/muenteferings-aphorismen-stakkato-franze-1.147401-3, accessed 5 April 2018.
17. Manfred G. Schmidt, *Das politische System Deutschlands*, 3rd edition (Munich, 2016), 353.

··· Chapter 8 ···

The Race for Third

Small Parties in the 2017 Bundestag Election

David F. Patton

Small German parties achieved unprecedented success in the 2017 Bundestag election.[1] Leading the pack, the Alternative for Germany (AfD) took 12.6 percent of the vote to finish third, marking the first time since the Federal Republic's founding that a far-right party had cleared the 5 percent hurdle nationally. The Christian Democratic Union/Christian Social Union (CDU/CSU) and Social Democratic Party (SPD), as *Volksparteien* or catch-all parties, could not build upon their mini-comeback in 2013, but rather faded to their lowest combined mark ever. Fifteen years earlier, they had won 77 percent of the vote, but now they mustered just 53.5 percent. A record seven parties won more than 5 percent, resulting in a Bundestag with six caucuses (*Fraktionen*). The small parties stood at the heart of the German party system's transformation.

This article explores the small parties' success in 2017, assessing both long-term and short-term factors. It analyzes each of the main small parties in turn, and considers their recent performances, their goals, campaign strategies, and election results. Finally, it examines why their electoral gains have not led to greater executive power.

Growing Support for the Lesser Parties: A Long Wave or Election-specific?

In the 2017 federal election, the small parties grew their combined vote share from under 33 percent in the preceding election to over 46 percent, the highest postwar share. The distance between the traditionally "big" and "small" had narrowed. In 2013, the CDU/CSU and SPD had averaged 33.6,

Notes for this section begin on page 188.

while the Left Party (die Linke), Free Democratic Party (FDP), and Greens had averaged 6.6 percent of the vote. Four years later, the catch-all parties had fallen to 26.7 percent on average, while the four smaller ones had risen to 10.4 percent on average. In 2013, nearly eighteen percentage points had separated the second place SPD from the third place Left Party; in 2017, however, the third place AfD trailed the SPD by less than eight percentage points, the smallest postwar gap between a small party and a *Volkspartei*.

Although the scholarly literature commonly distinguishes between Germany's big *Volksparteien*, the established smaller parties (*etablierte kleinere Parteien*), and the minor, non-established ones that do not make it into parliament (*Sonstige*), the closing gap between the *Volksparteien* and the established small parties calls this classification system into question.[2] And it was not just that the small parties did well as a group, there are now more of them in the Bundestag than at any time since the 1950s. In 2017, four won comfortably more than 5 percent of the vote, with results ranging from 12.6 percent for the AfD, to 10.7 percent for the FDP, to 9.2 percent for die Linke, and to 8.9 percent for the Greens. In short, 2017 was a banner year for the small German parties, as Table 8.1 shows.

Table 8.1: Small Parties' Second Ballot Vote Share in Recent Bundestag Elections (in percent)

	2005	2009	2013	2017
CDU, CSU, SPD	69.4	56.8	67.2	53.5
Small Parties	30.5	43.2	32.7	46.4
FDP	9.8	14.6	4.8	10.7
Left Party	8.7	11.9	8.6	9.2
Greens	8.1	10.7	8.4	8.9
AfD			4.7	12.6
Other	3.9	6.0	6.2	5.0

Source: Bundeswahlleiter. Due to rounding, total may not add up to a 100 percent.

Ongoing socioeconomic changes diminished the large catch-all parties and set the stage for small party gains.[3] A decline in trade union and business group associations, a growing service sector, higher levels of educational attainment, and more individualism complicated the efforts of the *Volksparteien* to bind in large sections of the increasingly diverse German population. They confronted the erosion of social milieus that had long undergirded them. The CDU/CSU draws on a smaller pool of religious, socially conservative voters; the SPD faces a declining industrial working class with a lower rate of unionization. Christian Democracy's travails and Social Democracy's woes are not limited to Germany. In Austria, Belgium, Italy, and the Netherlands, Christian Democratic parties suffered even greater losses than did the CDU/CSU in Germany.[4] Social Democratic parties, which had governed in much of western Europe in the late 1990s, are now struggling across the continent.

Rightwing and leftwing populist parties have siphoned off support from the catch-all parties, as well as from small centrist ones. Voters blamed elites for austerity and immigration and turned toward challengers pledging to oppose the political establishment. In 2009, the global financial crisis had helped lift Germany's Left Party to a record election result, while the Eurozone crisis of the early 2010s and the refugee crisis of 2015 were the external shocks that conditioned the AfD's ascent in 2013 and its triumph four years later. By 2017, both the SPD and CDU/CSU were competing with established populist parties on their wings. What the former CSU leader Franz Josef Strauss had long ago warned against had come to fruition–namely, a democratically legitimate party to the right of the CSU had taken root.

The establishment of parties on the ideological wings represented in a sense a normalization of postwar German politics. The "German trauma" of the 1930s and 1940s set the ideological parameters in the Federal Republic for decades. The legacy of National Socialism discredited the far right, while the postwar division of Germany marginalized the far left. [5] With the passing of time and the Cold War's end, longstanding taboos gradually lost salience for German voters. As a result, the Bundestag now has what many of the Federal Republic's neighbors have long had: a radical left-socialist party and a rightwing anti-immigrant party.

Yet, long-term socioeconomic and political cultural changes have not been the only reason for the small parties' success. In 2005 and 2013, the CDU/CSU and SPD formed a centrist grand coalition, thereby opening up space on the wings. In 2009, the FDP, Left Party, and Greens all finished with double-digit results. After the 2013-2017 grand coalition, the small parties did even better. In late 2017, the collapse of "Jamaica" talks between the CDU, CSU, FDP, and Greens led to yet another grand coalition and marked the first time that one had followed the other. This alignment may hinder a clear alternation of government power, promote centrifugalism, and lead to irresponsible oppositions that outbid on the flanks. In Austria, for example, the Social Democrats (SPÖ), who had governed after 1983 with the small Freedom Party of Austria (FPÖ), entered into a grand coalition with the Austrian People's Party (ÖVP) after the right-wing populist Jörg Haider became FPÖ leader and radicalized the previously liberal party. During the thirteen years of that grand coalition (1987-2000), the FPÖ vote share surged from 9.7 percent in 1986 to 26.9 percent in 1999. In West Germany, a CDU/CSU-SPD coalition in the 1960s accompanied the rise of the far-right

NPD and the far-left extra-parliamentary movement (APO). In recent grand coalitions, the catch-all-parties kept a centrist course, which played into the hands of the Left Party, the AfD, and the pro-business FDP. If history is a guide, we should expect a strong showing for the small parties in 2021 as the third grand coalition government since 2005 comes to an end.

An additional feature of the 2017 race favored the small parties. By late summer, it had become clear that Angela Merkel would stay on as chancellor. The distance between the two main parties was simply too great. Polls showed the CDU/CSU with more than a fifteen percentage point lead over the Social Democrats. When Merkel emerged largely unscathed in early September from her sole television debate with Martin Schulz, the SPD chancellor candidate, pundits and voters alike reasonably concluded that the contest for chancellor was all but over. Fueled by the media and by the small parties themselves, other questions rose to the fore: Which coalition would Merkel lead? Would it be another grand coalition? One with the FDP? One with the Greens? Or one with both the FDP and Greens? Which of the small parties would come in third and, in the event of another grand coalition, become the largest opposition party? With the four small parties essentially tied in the polls–a leading pollster had each at 8 percent in early August, the race for third was hotly fought over and politically significant.[6] This helped the small at the expense of the large. Former CDU/CSU and SPD supporters cast strategic votes for small parties in the hope of avoiding another grand coalition or of sending a message of protest. This may explain why polls had underestimated small party support prior to election day.

The Small Parties in the 2017 Bundestag Election

Let us now consider the starting positions, campaigns, and election results of the leading small parties. Whereas in 2013 the FDP, AfD, and Pirates had all fallen short of 5 percent but received at least 2 percent, in 2017 none of the non-Bundestag parties received more than one percent.

AfD

Just months after it had formed, the Alternative for Germany (AfD) won 4.7 percent of the vote in the 2013 federal election and narrowly missed entering the Bundestag. It had campaigned against the bailouts to heavily indebted Eurozone countries, rejecting Merkel's claim that such a policy was "*alternativlos.*" Led by the economics professor Bernd Lucke, the party called for an orderly dissolution of the Eurozone. With its heavy focus on monetary union, the AfD resembled a single-issue party, although its initial manifesto did also call for tax simplification, deficit reduction, a Canadian-style points-based immigration system, direct democracy, and the primacy of the heterosexual nuclear family unit. After the 2013 election, the party stood at the crossroads, faced with the choice of highlighting its neoliberal reform agenda (aspiring to be a "better FDP"), its social conservativism (aspiring to be a "better CSU"), or its rightwing populism (aspiring to be a "better Republikaner").[7]

After the party's national-conservative wing upended Bernd Lucke in an intense power struggle in mid 2015, the AfD adopted openly populist anti-immigrant, anti-Islam positions that mirrored those of rightwing populists elsewhere.[8] In its 2016 party program, it positioned itself as the party of law-and-order, called for tougher border controls, opposed large-scale immigration and a right to naturalization, and rejected multiculturalism and multilingualism. The party reaffirmed this stance in its 2017 election program. Its earlier economic liberalism receded while its opposition to immigration and Islam moved front and center. Co-chair Frauke Petry, who had led the national conservatives against Lucke in 2015, belatedly tried to steer the party in a more pragmatic direction by which it would distance itself from racism and ethnic nationalism and would follow a "realistic political strategy" in which the AfD as a "bourgeois catch-all party" might join governments and implement its policies.[9] Yet her efforts came to naught. After her setback at the 2017 party congress, Petry withdrew from the spotlight, although she remained a candidate in Saxony. Alexander Gauland and Alice Weidel led the party in the federal campaign, attacking the mainstream parties for their policy choices during and after the 2015 refugee crisis. The topics of immigration, integration, and Islam figured prominently in the party's campaign posters and television ads.

In late May, Alexander Gauland tweeted a nasty remark about Jerome Boateng, a member of the German national soccer team. In September, Alice Weidel walked off the stage of a televised talk show in response to supposedly unfair treatment. These kinds of incidents, which occurred throughout the campaign, were consistent with the recommendation of an internal strategy paper in late 2016, adopted by the federal executive, that the AfD must:

> be deliberately and quite systematically politically incorrect over and over again, seize on vivid language (*zu klarem Wort greifen*) and not shy away from carefully planned provocations. ... The more they [i.e., the 'old parties'] try to stigmatize the AfD on account of its provocative words and actions, the better it is for the profile of the AfD.[10]

This strategy of deliberate provocation animated protest voters and kept the party in the news. Behind the scenes, the AfD ran a successful social media campaign. During a ten-day period in September, the topic of the AfD and its candidates comprised a whopping 30.1 percent of all the Twitter traffic about German politics.[11]

In early 2017, it seemed that the AfD would not be able to duplicate its sensational results of 2016 when it had achieved double-digit finishes in five regional elections, including 15.1 percent in Baden-Württemberg and 24.3 percent in Saxony-Anhalt. These elections had occurred in the wake of the 2015 refugee crisis when concerns about immigration and integration dominated the political debate. By spring 2017, the AfD was back polling in single digits. In the hot phase of the campaign, however, migration-related issues again received extensive media coverage. For instance, in the widely viewed television debate between Angela Merkel and Martin Schulz, nearly forty of the ninety-seven minutes were spent on migration, refugees, and Islam. The four most discussed topics were migration and deportation; Turkey; terrorism and internal security; and Islam.[12] This framing played into the hands of the AfD whose populist demands stood out.

In the election, the AfD received 12.6 percent of the national vote, 10.7 percent in the west, and 21.9 percent in the east. In Saxony, it finished first with 27 percent and won three districts outright. Its top western results were in Bavaria (12.4 percent) and Baden-Württemberg (12.2 percent), while it was relatively weak in the northern regions of Hamburg (7.8 percent) and Schleswig-Holstein (8.2 percent). It drew the most new votes from previous nonvoters (approximately 1,200,000), but also took votes from all the other parties, especially the CDU and CSU (980,000), SPD (470,000), and the Left Party (400,000).[13] The party performed disproportionately strongly among men, among middle-aged voters, those with middle to lower levels of education, and among workers and the unemployed. Culturally pessimistic, more than 90 percent of the party's supporters expressed deep concerns about the loss of German culture, the rapid tempo of change, too great an influence of Islam, the drifting apart of society, and a massive increase in crime in the future. Nearly twice as many AfD voters (61 percent versus 31 percent) had backed the party out of disappointment with the other parties rather than out of conviction for the AfD.[14]

On election night, a triumphant Gauland promised relentless opposition: "we will hunt Frau Merkel."[15] Rather than ninety-four, the AfD settled for ninety-two members in its Bundestag caucus after Frauke Petry and another deputy left the party but kept their seats. Once the new Bundestag had convened, the AfD did not hold back on its views on refugees and immigrants, thereby drawing the ire of the other parties. Nonetheless, its three nominations to chair Bundestag committees were approved in late January 2018, even though they did face opposition, something that has been unusual in the selection of committee chairs. The party's choice for the board that oversees the secret services (PKGr) passed in a second round of voting after having been initially rejected. Despite three tries on the part of the AfD, however, its controversial candidate for the post of Bundestag vice-president was not approved. In late fall 2018, another AfD candidate for the vice-president position failed to secure sufficient Bundestag support. In early 2019, the Office of Constitutional Protection indicated that it was monitoring (*Prüffall*) whether the AfD as a whole should be placed under formal observation for possible anti-constitutional tendencies. In early February 2019, one leading poll put the AfD at 15 percent nationally, just one percentage point behind the SPD.[16]

FDP

In 2013, the FDP did not achieve representation in the Bundestag for the first time in its history. Although long a mainstay in national politics, and in government more than any other, the FDP now struggled to remain relevant.[17] It had alienated many of its past supporters following a difficult stint in power between 2009-2013 when it had failed to implement the far-reaching tax cut that it had promised, repeatedly crossed swords with its coalition partner, the CDU/CSU, and backed unpopular bailouts within the Eurozone. The party confronted an upstart anti-euro party, the AfD, that siphoned away more votes (430,000) from the FDP than from any other party in 2013.[18] The FDP had fallen out of the Bundestag and most regional parliaments and governed in only one region. It now had an overriding goal: rejoin the Bundestag in 2017.[19] Christian Lindner, who had served as FDP general secretary until late 2011, became the party leader at this time of crisis.

Rather than fundamentally overhaul its program and brand, the FDP instead broadened its message to include a greater emphasis on education, immigration policy, and digitization; changed its public logo (the color magenta was added); featured Lindner as the young, fresh face of a new leadership; and stressed that it had changed during its time in extra-parliamentary opposition. The party initially struggled in regional elections, but in 2015 had success in Hamburg and in Bremen. The next year, it built upon these victories by entering assemblies in Baden-Württemberg, Rhineland-Palatinate and Berlin. With its strong 2017 showings in Schleswig-Holstein (11.6 percent) and in populous North Rhine-Westphalia (12.6 percent), and national polling comfortably above the 5 percent mark, the party seemed all but assured of returning to the Bundestag in September.

Lindner stood out in an FDP election campaign that at times resembled a "one-man show." Showing a stubble-wearing Lindner putting on his jacket, glancing at his phone, rolling up his sleeves, or looking down, the FDP's campaign posters included such slogans as "Not doing anything is a misuse of power;" "Digital first, reservations second;" "Greatly increase spending on education," and "Impatience is also a virtue." As the party's chairman and its lead candidate, the youthful Lindner proved an energetic campaigner, effective on the trail and in talk shows, as he made the case for far-reaching reforms. Lindner, who enjoyed the second highest favorability rating among the lead candidates, led the FDP to a strong election result.[20] Indeed, 42 percent of FDP supporters indicated they would not vote for the party without Lindner, whereas 70 percent of all voters indicated that it did not stand a chance without him.[21]

In 2017, the FDP was careful not to allow itself to be defined primarily as a party of tax cuts, choosing also to emphasize education, digitization, less bureaucracy, more police, and the need for an immigration law. Although the party still stood for European integration and a tolerant society at home, critics nonetheless accused it of having positioned itself as "AfD light."[22] Its positions on immigration and the Euro had shifted rightward as a comparison of its 2013 and 2017 election manifestos showed. In regard to dual citizenship, the FDP now called for restricting the option to the children and grandchildren of those who had become German citizens through naturalization. In addition, it now favored differentiating between those who entered Germany as asylum seekers and those who came as wartime refugees; those in the latter group "should as a rule return to their home countries once the war had ended" unless qualifying for citizenship.[23] Sixty-six percent of voters who backed the FDP concurred with the statement: "I approve of the party's tougher position toward refugees."[24] Other than those supporting the AfD, FDP voters were more dissatisfied with Merkel's refugee policy than those of any other party.[25]

The party had also hardened its approach toward the Eurozone. It favored reducing and in time eliminating the European Stability Mechanism's lending facility and for new rules by which indebted states could declare bankruptcy and depart from the single currency. Both positions bore similarities to those of the AfD. In August 2017, Lindner appeared to break ranks with the mainstream parties by offering that Russia's annexation of the Crimea might need to be regarded as a "permanent interim arrangement" and by considering the relaxation of Russia sanctions.[26] The AfD was calling for an end to sanctions.

On 24 September, the FDP garnered 10.7 percent of the vote, increasing its 2013 share by a record 6 percentage points. Voters attributed to the party the most problem-solving competence in the areas of the economy (9 percent), tax policy (9 percent) and educational policy (7 percent.) The FDP performed somewhat better among the youngest voters (12 percent) than among those above sixty and did much better among the self-employed (19 percent) than among workers and the unemployed.[27] Likewise it achieved more support from men than women (12 percent versus 9 percent).[28] Its best results were in the western regions of North-Rhine Westphalia, Baden-Württemberg and Schleswig-Holstein; six of its seven weakest results were in eastern Länder (plus Saarland). Overall, the party had achieved an impressive result and seemed likely to form a government with the CDU, CSU, and Greens.

Eight weeks later, Lindner announced that the FDP had pulled out of the Jamaica coalition (named after the colors traditionally ascribed to the parties) talks. To Lindner, "it was better not to govern than to govern wrong." He reasoned that the party's voters had backed it in order to achieve real policy changes (*Trendwenden*), but a CDU/CSU-FDP-Greens government would not have been able to deliver this in the areas of education, tax relief, a more flexible society, a stronger market economy, and immigration policy.[29] That the party previously had struggled as a junior coalition partner in a Merkel-led government, contributing to its 2013 election debacle, surely colored its view of playing second or third fiddle to Merkel and the Greens.[30] Lindner may have thought to align the FDP as a rightwing national-liberal force in order to attract the AfD's more moderate voters who were likely to grow disillusioned with its radicalism. Such a strategy, as Herfried Münkler has noted, would have been much more difficult to follow had the FDP joined Merkel and the Greens.[31] Whatever its motives, the FDP was widely blamed by the other parties and the media for the impasse. If Lindner had anticipated that being in the opposition would prove a tonic for the FDP, he was likely disappointed when his party garnered a modest 5.1 percent and 7.8 percent of the vote in October 2018 regional elections in Bavaria and Hesse.

The Left Party

Although all four small parties were stronger in 2017, the two on the left recorded much smaller gains than those on the right. Whereas die Linke and the Greens had finished third and fourth in 2013, they now settled for fifth and sixth place, notwithstanding modest percentage point increases of 0.6 and 0.5, respectively. They also found themselves once more in the opposition, something the Greens at least had sought to avoid.

The Left Party had captured nearly 12 percent of the vote in 2009, but, by 2013, its share had dipped to 8.7 percent, raising the question as to whether it had already passed its peak.[32] That year, the party had achieved a small consolation prize: it was the largest opposition party during the ensuing grand coalition. Its parliamentary party was led by Gregor Gysi (until 2015) and by Sahra Wagenknecht and Dietmar Bartsch (after 2015). In the 2017 campaign, the party had to make do with the fact that Oskar Lafontaine and Gysi, two of its best-known members, were no longer in the front row. The party chose its Bundestag caucus co-chairs, Wagenknecht and Bartsch, to lead the campaign. Bartsch represented the moderate reform wing, which was well anchored in eastern regional assemblies and generally open to governing with the SPD and Greens, while Wagenknecht, a familiar face on German talk shows, had long been a leader of the party left, which was strong in western Germany and generally very critical of the SPD. In recent years, she and her husband Lafontaine, a former party co-chair, had attracted attention for comments about refugees and deportation that were at odds with their party's positions.

The Left Party called for greater social justice during its 2017 campaign. Its election manifesto, entitled "Caring, Fair and Peace for All: The future for which we fight–Die Linke," stated that "social injustice is one of the greatest problems of our time."[33] This was a familiar and promising topic for a party that had long foregrounded its commitment to economic equality at home and abroad while attacking its competitors for their shortcomings in this regard. Although the German economy was strong and unemployment relatively low, the gap between rich and poor had increased. In July 2017 polling, Infratest dimap found that voters viewed social injustice as the second most pressing political problem (after migration) for the parties to solve.[34] Under Schulz, the SPD had pledged to put social justice at the forefront of its campaign, but failed, after a short-lived surge in early 2017, to gain much traction with this issue during the campaign.

As it had done in the past, the Left Party outbid its competitors on welfare-state expansion in part because it had no realistic chance of assuming power. It called for a minimum wage of euro 12 per hour, an end to precarious jobs that did not include benefits or job security, overturning the Hartz IV measures which had cut unemployment benefits, raising pensions, working toward free public transportation and toward reducing the work day to six hours at full pay, and for higher taxes on the wealthy. Sixteen percent of voters regarded the Left Party as the party that cares the most for social justice; 38 percent named the SPD. This twenty-two percentage point deficit was the smallest ever recorded between die Linke and SPD. 14 percent credited the Left Party with having the most policy-making competence in regard to ensuring appropriate wages, whereas 53 percent said that it stands up the most for the economically weak. 81 percent agreed that "while it does not solve any problems, it calls out things as they are."[35]

Immigration proved a challenging issue for the Left Party. In its election manifesto, it espoused a very open approach: "Die Linke demands comprehensive visa liberalization or revocation of the visa requirement. We want to overcome wars and poverty and create just living conditions and open borders for all people." Yet, most Germans opposed open borders and many had been against Merkel's decision to let in large numbers of refugees. For these voters, the Left Party became less attractive as an outlet to express protest. In various 2016 elections, the party's vote share dropped from 18.4 percent to 13.2 percent in Mecklenburg-West Pomerania and from 23.7 percent to 16.3 percent in Saxony-Anhalt. It trailed the AfD in both Länder. Given the salience of migration-related issues in the federal election campaign, the Left Party faced losing those who were against a less restrictive border regime.

The topic laid bare a division within the party between a group around Sahra Wagenknecht and Oskar Lafontaine, who saw the nation-state and its borders as central to the struggle for social justice and who saw the economically precarious as the Left Party's natural constituency, and those in the party, such as Katja Kipping, who advanced a postnational cosmopolitanism that resonated among young, urban, educated voters.[36] Although Wagenknecht had not strayed from the party line during the campaign, after the election she attributed the Left Party's less than outstanding result to its stance on migration. Kipping countered that the party had had the right answers in this area.[37]

On election day, the Left Party received 9.2 percent of the vote and won five constituencies–four in Berlin and one in Leipzig. Although on the surface this represented little change from its 2013 result, in fact, the party's electorate had shifted appreciably. In the east, the heartland of the former PDS, its vote share fell from 22.7 to 17.8 and it finished behind the CDU and the AfD. In the west, the party improved from 5.6 percent to 7.4 percent. There it did particularly well in Bremen (13.4 percent), Saarland (12.9 percent), and Hamburg (12.2 percent). In Bavaria and Baden-Württemberg, where in 2013 it had received 3.8 percent and 4.8 percent, respectively, it now finished with more than 6 percent of the vote. The Left Party's new Bundestag *Fraktion* has forty-three deputies from the western party chapters and twenty-six from the east; during the previous legislative period there had been parity (thirty-three to thirty-three). This pointed toward a hard-left orientation on the part of caucus.[38]

Although the Left Party still received disproportionate support among workers (11 percent) and the unemployed (11 percent), its standing among both groups fell, especially among the jobless, which had plummeted 12 percentage points from 23 percent in 2013.[39] For the first time, it performed better among more educated voters than among the less educated.[40] The party disproportionately attracted those under thirty-five years of age and it did much better among those who were dissatisfied with their economic situation.[41] It took net votes from all but the AfD and FDP, gathering in 430,000 former SPD voters and 170,000 from the Greens.[42] The Left Party lost ground in the three sociocultural milieus in which the AfD recorded strong gains: the precarious; the bourgeois middle; and the traditionalists.[43] Its electorate was now more like that of the Greens than had been the case in the past.

After the election, party co-chairs Kipping and Bernd Riexinger proposed that they have the right to speak first in the Bundestag and that they have an enhanced say within the party's parliamentary caucus. Wagenknecht darkly warned of internal intrigue, threatened to resign, and in the end succeeded in blocking both measures.[44] The ongoing rivalry between Wagenknecht and Kipping, fueled by personal animosity as well as policy differences, threatened the unity of the Left Party. In summer 2018, Wagenknecht founded a bipartisan, extra-parliamentary leftwing movement, "rise up" ("*Aufstehen*"), to unite the opponents of neoliberalism, even as Kipping and other party leaders, wary of the emergence of a possible rival to the Left Party, distanced themselves from the enterprise.

Alliance 90/Greens

Although the Greens had been polling in double digits, after the SPD surged in the polls in early 2017 they fell to a range between 6 and 8 percent where they generally remained during the campaign, above the 5 percent threshold, but not comfortably so. They struggled in two of the three regional elections of Spring 2017. In the Saarland, they received only 4 percent and dropped out of the regional assembly. On 14 May in North Rhine-Westphalia (sometimes dubbed a mini Federal Republic due to its size and diversity), their vote share sharply fell nearly 5 percentage points to 6.4 percent–just over half the level of support that their rival the FDP had garnered, and they left the government for the opposition. This was hardly the kind of send-off that the Greens had hoped for on eve of the hot phase of the federal election campaign.

In the Bundestag election, the Greens envisioned a strong showing that would set them up to join the next federal government. They chose Katrin Göring-Eckardt and Cem Özdemir to head the campaign. Göring-Eckardt had previously carried the banner in 2013, but Özdemir, from the Realo stronghold of Baden-Württemberg, now took the place of the leftist Jürgen Trittin who had been a lead candidate four years earlier. In their 2017 election manifesto, the Greens focused heavily on environmental issues and tacked more to the center on economic issues than had been the case in 2013. The party called for shuttering the twenty dirtiest coal-powered plants immediately and for the subsequent phasing out of coal altogether; 100 percent renewal electrical generation by 2030; the licensing of only emissions-free cars; and the ecological transformation of German agriculture, including the humane treatment of livestock.[45] The party program also featured calls for more social justice, an immigration law, automatic citizenship on the basis of birthplace (*jus soli*), protection of the right to asylum with no upper limit in the number of applications, and an EU policy based on supranational integration and solidarity rather than fiscal austerity. As its campaign posters revealed, the environment figured heavily in the Greens' campaign. They conveyed such messages as: "The environment is not everything but without the environment there is nothing," "Either the end of coal or the end of the climate," "No one has more from less Europe," "One must carry out integration not sit it out," "Child poverty can be played down or fought hard," "Only when one gets chances can one use chances;" "If one accomplishes the same, then a woman should receive the same," "Our climate goal: to finally act–Katrin Göring-Eckardt," and "There is no 'or' between environment and economy–Cem Özdemir."

The emphasis on the environment made sense for two reasons. More than any other issue, the environment embodied the brand and identity of the Greens. The Greens were well known and widely respected for their competence in the area of environmental policy-making. Indeed, 56 percent attributed to the party highest policy-making competency in this area. Its next highest values were 7 percent in the policy domains of family, education, and refugees.[46] The party's emphasis on the environment made further sense in light of its coalition options. A prominent leftwing economic platform would have left less of a basis for a CDU/CSU-Greens coalition. To ensure that "Black-Green" remained plausible, the Greens highlighted their environmental over their left-libertarian positions.[47] Moreover, had it opted for a heavier focus on economic redistribution, the party would have had to compete in the crowded policy domain of social justice with the SPD and Linke, both of which enjoyed strong reputations in this area.[48]

The Greens started the campaign with a realistic chance to enter a Black-Green coalition or a Jamaica coalition following the election. The former constellation had arisen first in Hamburg and then in Hesse and Baden-

Württemberg. The latter was tried in Saarland in 2009 and in Schleswig-Holstein in 2017. Like the Greens, the CDU under Merkel had moved to the center. The chancellor's decision to open Germany's borders to refugees in 2015 enjoyed especially strong support among the Greens. Whereas only 43 percent of Green voters had been satisfied with Merkel's job performance in 2013, well below the national average of 71 percent, now three-quarters of the Green voters approved of Merkel's work–well above her average of 64 percent.[49]

On 24 September, the Greens won 8.9 percent–a small success for a party that had been polling at less than that. They had netted 430,000 former SPD votes, but lost votes to the Left Party (170,000) and FDP (60,000). As in the past, it did much better in western Germany than in the ex-GDR. It performed disproportionately well among the young, those with higher levels of education, among civil servants, and women, while it underperformed among workers, those with little formal education, and those over sixty years old.[50] About a quarter of its voters cited coalitional-tactical reasons rather than conviction. 71 percent had backed the party for its program rather than for longstanding party ties or for its candidates. That said, Özdemir enjoyed a high approval rating of 55 percent among voters.[51]

After Martin Schulz declared on election night that the SPD would not be joining a government, the Greens, FDP, the CDU, and CSU were left with the daunting task of making "Jamaica" work. In 2013, the Greens had ended preliminary Black-Green talks. This time around, the parties seemed far apart on the issues of Europe, immigration and refugees, and taxes. The FDP ended the talks and the Greens returned to the opposition, sparing their members a decision about whether to support a coalition agreement with the center-right Christian Democrats and Liberals. At their party congress in January 2018, the Greens picked two centrist co-leaders, not adhering to their tradition of choosing one each from the Realo wing and the left wing. This portended further centrism on the part of the Greens. In October 2018, the Greens won an impressive 17.6 percent and 19.8 percent of the vote, respectively, in regional elections in Bavaria and Hesse. In early 2019, the party was consistently polling ahead of the SPD nationally.

Conclusion

The race for third was hotly contested and the stakes were high. If another grand coalition formed, then the third biggest party would enjoy the prestige of being the largest opposition in the Bundestag. If a small party finished strongly, it could lay claim to inclusion in a government or to more attractive ministerial posts within that government. Although the four main small parties competed intensely with one another, they largely did so on their own terms. The Greens focused on the environment; the Left Party on social justice; the AfD on immigration; and the FDP on education, digitization, deregulation, and taxes.

In 2017, the increased vote share for the small parties did not translate into a greater share of cabinet seats. Quite the opposite. Notwithstanding their collective and individual strength, the small parties did not take part in the next government. There were two primary reasons for this. The first concerned the number and overall size of the small Bundestag parties; their relative weight vis-à-vis one another; and the number deemed unfit for government. In 2017, four small parties had entered the Bundestag and filled 310 of the 709 Bundestag seats, or 43.7 percent. The gap between the largest (AfD at 12.6 percent) and the smallest (the Greens at 8.9 percent) was less than four percentage points. Two of the four (the Left Party and the AfD) were not part of coalition talks. As a result of these four circumstances, the options for coalition formation had narrowed considerably in 2017.

Second, and relatedly, the small parties' inability to translate their enhanced size into cabinet seats stemmed from the fact that expectations surrounding party system formation in Germany have not adequately adjusted to the fragmented and increasingly polarized system that has emerged. In 2017, other than another grand coalition, a two-party coalition was not possible. The "natural" alliances of years' past, whether CDU/CSU-FDP or SPD-Greens, did not enjoy a Bundestag majority. Yet, the formation of a multiparty coalition, such as Jamaica, that spanned broad ideological differences would have required a greater willingness to compromise than was demonstrated by the prospective partners. If small party gains continue, Germany in the future may find itself either experimenting with complicated, heterogeneous multiparty coalitions, such as the one that formed in the Netherlands in 2017 more than 200 days after the election, or trying out less centrist alternatives, such as the government that arose in Austria in 2017 after the center-right ÖVP teamed up with the far-right FPÖ.

David F. Patton is Joanne Toor Cummings '50 Professor of Government and International Relations at Connecticut College in New London, Connecticut. He teaches classes on European politics and his research focuses on party politics and foreign policy in the Federal Republic of Germany. E-mail: dfpat@conncoll.edu

Notes

1. I would like to thank the German Academic Exchange Service (DAAD) and the International Association for the Study of German Politics (IASGP) for arranging a Bundestag election trip in September 2017.
2. See David F. Patton, "Small Parties and the 2013 Bundestag Election: End of the Upward Trend?" *German Politics and Society* 32, no. 3, Special Issue (2014): 26–45, esp. 27–28
3. See Elmar Wiesendahl, *Volksparteien. Aufstieg, Krise, Zukunft* (Opladen, 2011).
4. Tim Bale and André Krouwel, "Down but Not Out: A Comparison of Germany's CDU/CSU with Christian Democratic Parties in Austria, Belgium, Italy and the Netherlands," *German Politics* 22, no. 1 (2013): 16–43.
5. Gordon Smith, "West Germany and the Politics of Centrality," *Government and Opposition*, 11, no. 4 (1976): 387-407, esp. 402–404.
6. Forschungsgruppe Wahlen, 21 July 2017, 11 August 2017; available at http://www.wahlrecht.de/umfragen/politbarometer.htm, accessed 4 February 2018.
7. Patton (see note 2), 39–40.
8. David F. Patton, "The Alternative for Germany's radicalization in historical-comparative perspective," *Journal of Contemporary Central and Eastern Europe* 25, no. 2 (2017): 163–180. For the role of the Pegida protest movement in the AfD's transformation, see David F. Patton, "Monday, Monday: Eastern Protest Movements and German Party Politics since 1989," *German Politics* 26, no. 4 (2017): 480–497.
9. Patton, "Alternative for Germany" (see note 8), 165–166.
10. Alternative für Deutschland, "AfD–Manifest 2017. Die Strategie der AfD für das Wahljahr 2017," 22 December 2016; available at http://www.talk-republik.de/Rechtspopulismus/docs/03/AfD-Strategie-2017.pdf, accessed 3 March 2018.
11. Lisa-Maria Neudert, Bence Kollanyi, and Philip N. Howard, "Junk News and Bots during the German Parliamentary Election: What are German Voters Sharing over Twitter," *COMPROP DATA MEMO*, 2017.7, 19 September 2017; available at http://comprop.oii.ox.ac.uk/wp-content/uploads/sites/93/2017/09/ComProp_GermanElections_Sep2017v5.pdf, accessed 3 March 2017.
12. Marie Segger, Christoph Sydow, and Caroline Wiemann, "Daten-Auswertung zum TV-Duell: 31 Prozent Abschiebung, 9 Prozent Diesel–0 Prozent Bildung," *Spiegel-Online*, 4 September 2017; available at http://www.spiegel.de/politik/deutschland/tv-duell-angela-merkel-vs-martin-schulz-keine-zeit-fuer-bildung-und-klima-a-1166078.html, accessed 3 March 2018.
13. Infratest dimap, "Bundestagswahl 2017: Wanderung AfD;" available at: https://wahl.tagesschau.de/wahlen/2017-09-24-BT-DE/analyse-wanderung.shtml, accessed 5 February 2017.
14. Infratest dimap, "Bundestagswahl 2017: Umfragen zur AfD;" available at: https://wahl.tagesschau.de/wahlen/2017-09-24-BT-DE/umfrage-afd.shtml, accessed 5 February 2017.
15. "Gauland über AfD Erfolg: 'Wir werden Frau Merkel jagen,'" *Spiegel-Online*, 24 September 2017; available at http://www.spiegel.de/politik/deutschland/afd-alexander-gauland-wir-werden-frau-merkel-jagen-a-1169598.html, accessed 5 February 2018.
16. Emnid, "Sonntagsfrage," 2 February 2019, available at http://www.wahlrecht.de/umfragen/emnid.htm, accessed 3 February 2019.
17. David F. Patton, "The Prospects of the FDP in Comparative Perspective: Rest in Peace or *Totgesagte leben länger?*," *German Politics* 24, no. 2 (2015): 179–194.
18. Infratest dimap, "Bundestagswahl 2013. Analysen Wählerwanderung;" available at http://wahl.tagesschau.de/wahlen/2013-09-22-BT-DE/analyse-wanderung.shtml, accessed 4 March 2018.
19. See David F. Patton, "The Free Democrats' Second Chance," *German Politics*, no. 1 (2018): 136–140, published online 22 February 2018, 1–5.

20. His favorability rating tied that of Martin Schulz and was second to Chancellor Merkel's. Forschungsgruppe Wahlen, "Wahlanalyse Bundestagswahl," 24 September 2017; available at http://www.forschungsgruppe.de/Aktuelles/Wahlanalyse_Bundestagswahl/, accessed 23 October 2017.
21. Infratest dimap, "Bundestagswahl 2017 Deutschland. Umfragen zur FDP," 24 September 2017; available at https://wahl.tagesschau.de/wahlen/2017-09-24-BT-DE/umfrage-fdp.shtml, accessed 18 February 2018.
22. Wolfgang Michal, "AfD light: Lindners neue FDP," *Blätter für deutsche und internationale Politik*, August 2017; available at https://www.blaetter.de/archiv/jahrgaenge/2017/august/afd-light-lindners-neue-fdp, accessed 25 October 2017.
23. Free Democratic Party, "Denken wir neu," 2017 federal election platform, esp. 68-69 and 123-125; available at https://www.fdp.de/sites/default/files/uploads/2017/08/07/20170807-wahlprogramm-wp-2017-v16.pdf, accessed 23 October 2017.
24. Infratest dimap (see note 14).
25. Infratest dimap, "Bundestagswahl 2017 Deutschland. Umfragen zur Flüchtlingspolitik," 24 September 2017; available at https://wahl.tagesschau.de/wahlen/2017-09-24-BT-DE/umfrage-fluechtlingspolitik.shtml, accessed 3 March 2018.
26. "FDP-Chef Lindner zur Ukraine: Russische Krim als 'dauerhaftes Provisorium' ansehen," *Spiegel-Online*, 5 August 2017; available at http://www.spiegel.de/politik/deutschland/christian-lindner-zur-ukraine-russische-krim-als-dauerhaftes-provisorium-ansehen-a-1161494.html, accessed 18 February 2018.
27. Infratest dimap (see note 14).
28. Forschungsgruppe Wahlen (see note 6).
29. "Christian Lindner: 'Es ist besser, nicht zu regieren, als schlecht zu regieren,'" *Zeit-Online*, 20 November 2017; available at: http://www.zeit.de/politik/deutschland/2017-11/christian-lindner-sondierung-jamaika-abbruch-fdp, accessed 18 February 2018.
30. Patton (see note 19), 4.
31. "Herfried Münkler zur großen Koalition," *Der Tagesspiegel*, 5 February 2018; available at http://www.tagesspiegel.de/politik/herfried-muenkler-zur-grossen-koalition-angela-merkel-kann-keinen-aufbruch/20926242.html, accessed 18 February 2018.
32. Gero Neugebauer and Richard Stöss, "Den Zenith überschritten: Die Linkspartei nach der Bundestagswahl 2013" in *Die Parteien nach der Bundestagswahl 2013*, ed. Oskar Niedermayer (Wiesbaden, 2015), 159–173.
33. "Sozial. Gerecht. Frieden. Für Alle. Die Zukunft, für die wir kämpfen," Bundestag Election Manifesto of the Left Party, approved at the Federal Party Congress, 9–11 June 2017, Hanover, 8.
34. Interview data from July 2017. André Pätzold, Julius Tröger, David Wendler, and Christopher Möller, "Bundestagswahl 2017: Das sind die 15 wichtigsten politischen Probleme in Deutschland," *Berliner Morgenpost*, 18 September 2017; available at https://interaktiv.morgenpost.de/probleme-bundestagswahl-2017/, accessed 24 February 2018.
35. Infratest dimap, "Bundestagswahl 2017 Deutschland. Umfragen zur Linkspartei," 24 September 2017; available at https://wahl.tagesschau.de/wahlen/2017-09-24-BT-DE/umfrage-linkspartei.shtml, accessed 19 February 2018.
36. See "Sahra Wagenknecht im Interview über Soziale Gerechtigkeit und die Große Koalition," *Magazine web.de*, 3 February 2018; available at https://web.de/magazine/politik/sahra-wagenknecht-interview-soziale-gerechtigkeit-grosse-koalition-32765198, accessed 3 March 2018. Rainer Balcerowiak, "Die Linke in der Krise. Schlammschlachten und Grabenkämpfe," *Cicero*, 19 October 2017; available at https://www.cicero.de/innenpolitik/die-linke-in-der-krise-grabenkaempfe-und-schlammschlachten, accessed 3 March 2018.
37. Johannes Altmeyer, "Lafontaine rechnet mit Asylpolitik der Linke-Chefs ab," *Die Welt*, 29 September 2017; available at https://www.welt.de/politik/deutschland/article169093389/Lafontaine-rechnet-mit-Asylpolitik-der-Linke-Chefs-ab.html, accessed 25 February 2018.

38. Kevin Hagen, "Linke nach der Wahl: Das Ende der Ostpartei," *Spiegel-Online*, 27 September 2017; available at http://www.spiegel.de/politik/deutschland/die-linke-nach-der-bundestagswahl-2017-das-ende-der-ost-partei-a-1170037.html, accessed 25 February 2018.
39. Wahlnachtbericht Bereich Strategie & Grundsatzfragen Die Linke, "Wahlnachtbericht zur Bundestagswahl 2017," corrected and revised version, 27 September 2017, 20.
40. Ibid.
41. Ibid., 18.
42. Infratest dimap, "Bundestagswahl 2017, Wählerwanderungen;" available at http://wahl.tagesschau.de/wahlen/2017-09-24-BT-DE/analyse-wanderung.shtml, accessed 24 February 2018.
43. Robert Vehrkamp and Klaudia Wegschaider, "Populäre Wahlen: Mobilisierung und Gegenmibilisierung der sozialen Milieus bei der Bundestagswahl 2017," Bertelsmann Stiftung, October 2017, 64; available at https://www.bertelsmann-stiftung.de/fileadmin/files/BSt/Publikationen/GrauePublikationen/ZD_Populaere_Wahlen_Bundestagswahl_2017_01.pdf, accessed 25 February 2018.
44. "Machtkampf bei Linkspartei: Wagenknecht droht mit Rücktritt," 17 October 2017; available at https://www.tagesschau.de/inland/linkspartei-153.html, accessed 25 February 2018.
45. "Bündnis 90/Die Grünen, "Zukunft wird aus Mut gemacht. Bundestagswahlprogramm 2017," passed by the 41st Federal Delegate Conference, Berlin, 16–18 June 2017.
46. Infratest dimap, "Bundestagswahl 2017 Deutschland. Umfragen zu den Grünen," 24 September 2017; available at https://wahl.tagesschau.de/wahlen/2017-09-24-BT-DE/umfrage-gruene.shtml, accessed 25 February 2018.
47. Charles Lees, "The German Greens and the 2017 Federal Election: Between Strategic Calculation and Real-World Politics," *German Politics* (2018), published online 20 February 2018, 4; "Bündnis 90/Die Grünen (see note 45).
48. Jochen Weichold, "Die Grünen zwei Monate vor der Bundestagswahl: Soziale Frage im Abseits," Publikationen der Rosa Luxemburg Stiftung, 12 July 2017, 2; available at https://www.rosalux.de/publikation/id/37592/die-gruenen-zwei-monate-vor-der-bundestagswahl-soziale-frage-im-abseits/, accessed 26 February 2018.
49. Infratest dimap (see note 46).
50. Sebastian Bukow, "Bundestagswahl 2017: Ergebnisse und Analysen, böll.brief: Demokratie & Gesellschaft, no. 5 (September 2017), esp. 16–17, 20; available at https://www.boell.de/sites/default/files/boell-brief_bundestagswahl_2017.pdf?dimension1=division_demo, accessed 26 February 2018.
51. Infratest dimap (see note 46).

··· Chapter 9 ···

Two of the Same Kind?

The Rise of the AfD and its Implications for the CDU/CSU

Matthias Dilling

To the Right of the CDU/CSU...

By more than doubling its 2013 result and winning 12.6 percent of the votes at the 2017 federal election, the Alternative for Germany (AfD) put an end to an era. For the first time since 1957, a party that had explicitly positioned itself to the right of the Christian Democratic Union (CDU) and Christian Social Union (CSU) had succeeded in entering the Bundestag. It has been a new climax in the party's development after it had already entered parliament in thirteen of Germany's sixteen states (sometimes with startling results, see Table 9.1).

The AfD's rise has occurred against the backdrop of the increasing alienation of many conservatives from the CDU leadership around Angela Merkel. While Merkel has been holding the chancellorship for the Christian Democrats since 2005, many issues important to conservatives, like support for conscription and nuclear energy, have been abandoned under her watch. She was consequently criticized for gradually eroding the CDU's ideological distinctiveness and thereby creating the demand for another conservative party option.[1] When Merkel agreed to bailout EU member states affected by the Eurozone crisis, a group of former CDU members around Bernd Lucke and Alexander Gauland ultimately formed the AfD.[2] Later, they thrived on the fierce opposition of parts of the German public against Merkel's response to the refugee crisis in 2015 and 2016.

The context of the AfD's surge lends itself to considering the party a primary threat to the Christian Democrats. This impression is reinforced by

Notes for this section begin on page 208.

the fact that the success of right-wing challengers in other European countries, like Austria, the Netherlands, and France, has put enormous pressure on their respective mainstream center-right parties.[3] It also corresponds to the intuition we may derive from spatial theories of party competition. They make us expect a right-wing party to be a more serious competitor for the electoral basis of center-right rather than center-left or left-wing parties.[4] It is also well-known, however, that the support base of right-wing challengers is often not adequately captured in spatial terms.[5] Assessing the extent to which the AfD has primarily been a threat to the CDU and CSU does not only speak to this debate. It is also particularly relevant at a time when the Christian Democrats have been debating how to respond to the AfD's success in 2017. The CSU and the CDU's Land branch in Saxony have promoted shifting the parties' appeal to the right in order to reconquer the space lost to the AfD, whereas others have warned against abandoning the moderate course adopted under Merkel's leadership.[6] Since a mainstream party's decision to absorb positions put forward by a radical challenger depends on the latter being an electoral threat,[7] assessing the extent to which the AfD has threatened the CDU/CSU is key for informing the lessons they will draw from the 2017 Bundestag election.

I argue that while CDU and CSU have suffered from the advent of the AfD, considering the latter a primary threat to the Christian Democrats ignores the complexity of the AfD's platform, electorate, and internal factionalism between 2013 and 2017. In a first step, I argue that the AfD has substantially transformed its initial party platform which made the party appeal to a heterogeneous electoral basis. Comparing the AfD's 2016 basic program and 2017 election manifesto to findings on the party's earlier programs, I show that the AfD transitioned from being a conservative challenger to the Christian Democrats toward becoming a populist radical right party. This transformation, I proceed to outline, is reflected in the AfD's vote base in the 2017 election. It represents, as survey data underlines, the coming together of strange bedfellows:[8] conservatives who voted Christian Democratic in the past and a heterogeneous group of voters who are dissatisfied with the current state of German democracy, hold nativist views, and support far-left ideas. The AfD has so far been unable to integrate such diverse groups and lost large parts of its moderate wing during the party's shift toward the far right, as I demonstrate in a final step by discussing the party's internal factionalism. I conclude that it is therefore dubious whether the AfD will succeed in remaining an option for discontented Christian Democrats. Appeals to move the CDU/CSU to the right to fight off the AfD may therefore be premature.

Table 9.1: AfD Election Results, 2013 to 2017

Year	Election	Vote share (percent)
2013	Federal	4.7
	Hesse	4.1
2014	European Parliament	7.1
	Saxony	9.7
	Brandenburg	12.2
	Thuringia	10.6
2015	Hamburg	6.1
	Bremen	5.5
2016	Baden-Württemberg	15.1
	Rhineland-Palatinate	12.6
	Saxony-Anhalt	24.3
	Mecklenburg-West Pomerania	20.8
	Berlin	14.2
2017	Saarland	5.9
	Schleswig-Holstein	6.2
	North Rhine-Westphalia	7.4
	Federal	12.6
	Lower Saxony	6.2

Source: Federal and Land returning officers

The AfD's Shift from Fiscal and Social Conservatism to the Populist Radical Right

The AfD's Entry as a Conservative Challenger to the CDU/CSU

Since Merkel became chancellor in 2005, she has been criticized for gradually eroding the CDU's ideological distinctiveness and thereby creating the demand for a new party to the right of the political center.[9] While this view finds only limited empirical support when analyzing the CDU's programs and manifestos,[10] the perceived "social democratization" of the party was stimulated by its departure from some core positions.[11] This included moving away from its support for mandatory military service, nuclear energy, a skeptical view of immigration, and a traditional family definition.[12] This development attracted substantive media attention and was seen as steps toward ideological indistinctiveness.

It was in this perceived ideological gap that the AfD entered party competition in 2013.[13] While the Merkel government's handling of the European debt crisis provided the trigger for party formation, the AfD leadership around Bernd Lucke, Konrad Adam, and Alexander Gauland aimed at occupying the space previously dominated by the Christian Democrats.[14] While campaigning for a far-reaching reorganization of the EU in 2013,[15] the AfD politicized Merkel's bailout policies as evidence that the CDU/CSU had lost their economic and fiscal competence and their identity as the defender of Germany's social market economy. On sociocultural grounds, the AfD endorsed positions of traditional morality. They promoted family-oriented welfare policies, an understanding of marriage as being exclusively between two heterosexual partners, and a more restrictive stance on immigration. Consequently, its 2013 election manifesto included many views Merkel has been criticized for having abandoned.

The AfD's Transformation into a Populist Radical Right Party

The AfD maintained some of its initial positions that resembled those of the CDU/CSU's conservative wing in its Political Guidelines from May 2014.[16] Similarly, the AfD's basic program from 2016 and its manifesto for the 2017 election still expressed support for social market economy, subsidiarity, and opposition against the Euro and the European Union in their current format.[17] They also included traditionalist views on family policies, opposition to abortion, and social policies aimed at supporting families with multiple children.[18] The AfD promoted Germany's selective secondary and higher education system, the abolishment of gender quotas, the reintroduction of conscription, the use of nuclear energy, and classic law and order positions.[19] Moreover, and most importantly, by adopting a strong anti-immigrant stance, the AfD provided an option for those dissatisfied with the CDU/CSU's policies during the European refugee crisis. Merkel's inclusive response to the arrival of over 1 million asylum seekers in Germany since 2015 had provoked major opposition from outside and inside her own party.[20] The two sister parties CDU and CSU turned "into distant relatives."[21] Merkel also faced severe opposition from CDU state leaders. Julia Klöckner (Rhineland-Palatinate), Reiner Haseloff (Saxony-Anhalt), and Guido Wolf (Baden-Württemberg) promoted a more restrictive stance on the refugee issue and openly criticized Merkel's policies in their respective election campaigns in 2016.

Fiscal and social conservatism, however, were increasingly sidelined in the AfD's platform by a populist radical right appeal based on authoritarianism, populism, and nativism.[22] The AfD has thereby markedly moved away from competing for a similar political space as the Christian Democrats. Already the campaign slogan for the 2014 European Parliament election–"Courage for Germany" (*Mut zu Deutschland*)–indicated the beginning of the party's shift toward the populist radical right.[23] The alleged threat that Islam and immigration posed to Germany's society and welfare system as well as anti-establishment rhetoric ultimately took hold in the party's platform in the run-up to the state elections in eastern Germany in late 2014.[24] The AfD also started forging ties with far-right organizations, like the anti-Islam and xenophobic Patriotic Europeans Against the Islamization of the Occident (Pegida), which Gauland characterized as the AfD's "natural ally."[25]

The AfD's 2016 program and 2017 election manifesto included a strong authoritarian element. It reflects a "belief in a strictly ordered society, in which infringements of authority are to be punished severely."[26] The AfD wants to toughen the punishment for assaults against law enforcement forces, only apply adult criminal law to any suspect of eighteen years of age or older, lower the age of criminal liability from fourteen to twelve years, put offenders suffering from a mental illness into preventive detention rather than psychiatric hospitals, and deport any foreign nationals found guilty of a criminal offense.[27] Similar positions are expressed in the 2017 manifesto.[28]

While the respect for social order and hierarchy has also been traditionally shared by many conservative Christian Democrats, the AfD and CDU/CSU differ in their degree of authoritarianism. The AfD has been located closer to the authoritarian pole of the party system than the Christian Democrats.[29]

More importantly, the AfD has given up its initial image as the CDU/CSU's "conservative conscience" by endorsing an anti-system position in relation to all parties.[30] It presented itself as the defender of an exploited and disfranchised people against a fraudulent and power-hungry political elite. This antagonism, defining populist rhetoric,[31] was the dominant theme of the party's basic program in 2016. It guides the party's remarks on a wide range of policy fields, including education, finances and taxation, immigration, inner security, energy, and European policies. The so-called "political class of career politicians," "secret sovereign," or "political cartel" is blamed for undermining the rule of law and freedom of speech and deceiving "the people" for its own material advantages.[32] While figuring less prominently, populism remained a pillar of the AfD's election manifesto in 2017.[33]

The most visible departure from the AfD's conservative beginnings, however, lies in the rise of nativism. Nativism postulates that "states should be inhabited exclusively by members of the native group ('the nation') and that non-native elements (persons and ideas) are fundamentally threatening to the homogeneous nation-state."[34] The AfD draws a picture of a German nation whose inner security, welfare system and identity are threatened by the spread of Islam and mass migration.[35] The EU's external frontiers would therefore need to be closed. Controls along Germany's borders with its European neighbors would have to be reintroduced.[36] Moreover, the AfD demands to keep asylum seekers away from German territory in so-called "protection and asylum centers" that are "regionally and culturally close" to their countries of origin.[37] Endorsing welfare chauvinism, the AfD argues that most asylum seekers and migrants would come to Germany to freeride on its welfare provisions. Their access to social support, the AfD claims, must therefore be restricted.[38] Refugees would be denied paths toward citizenship or a permanent residence permit.[39] If these measures do not reduce Germany's net migration rate to zero, the AfD demands a minimum annual deportation quota.[40] Moreover, the party wants to limit Muslims' right to practice their religion.[41]

In comparison to its 2016 program, the AfD expressed its nativist positions even more bluntly in its 2017 election manifesto. In its section on asylum policies and immigration, the party stated: "The aim is the self-preservation, not self-destruction of our state and people (*Volk*)."[42] The party "want[s] to leave our descendants a country that is still recognizable as our Germany."[43] When outlining its proposed family policies, the AfD warned against the "shrinkage of our native population" and presented itself as the political force that "braced itself against this trend toward self-abolition."[44] In fact, Germany would require a paradigm shift toward "national demographic policies," aimed at increasing the birth rate of the "native population."[45] The preservation of Germany's "constitutive people" (*Staatsvolk*) should be included in the German constitution.[46] Such nativist language has usually not been used by political parties in Germany apart from the extreme right because of its association with the country's Nazi past. The fact that the AfD openly included it in its manifesto emphasizes the transformation of the party's platform.

Hence, the AfD started off with a platform that aimed at representing positions previously abandoned or neglected by the CDU/CSU. While such positions are still visible in the AfD's programmatic platform, they have been sidelined given the party's endorsement of authoritarian, populist, and nativist positions. The AfD thereby competes for a very heterogeneous electorate that does not equal that of the Christian Democrats.

The AfD's Vote Base as a Coalition of Strange Bedfellows

Regardless of the AfD's transformed platform, a first glance at the results of the 2017 election still seems to suggest that the CDU/CSU and AfD are two sides of the same coin. Although the CDU remained the strongest party and, together with the CSU, will continue to be the largest parliamentary group in the Bundestag, the Christian Democrats suffered massive losses (-8.6 percent compared to 2013). In contrast, the AfD improved its 2013 vote share

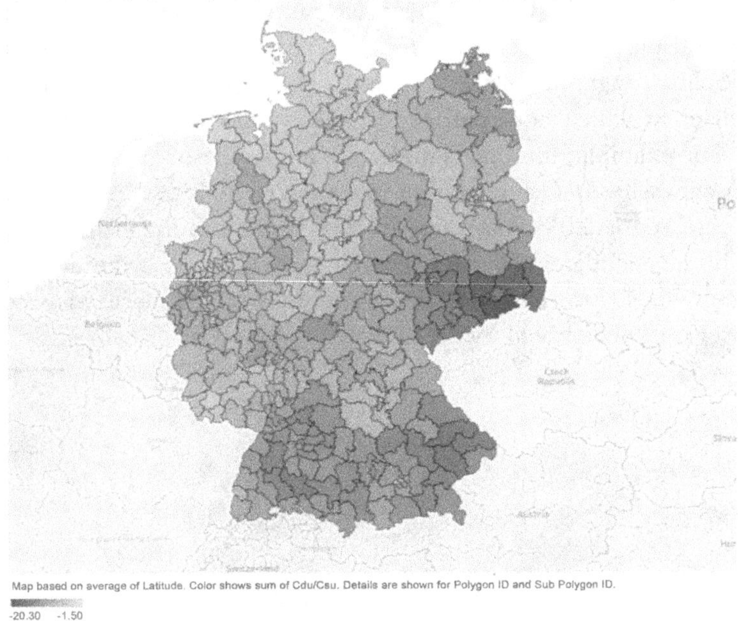

Figure 9.1.1: Change in CDU/CSU Vote Share by Constituency in 2017
Source: Second vote (*Zweitstimme*), Federal returning officer.

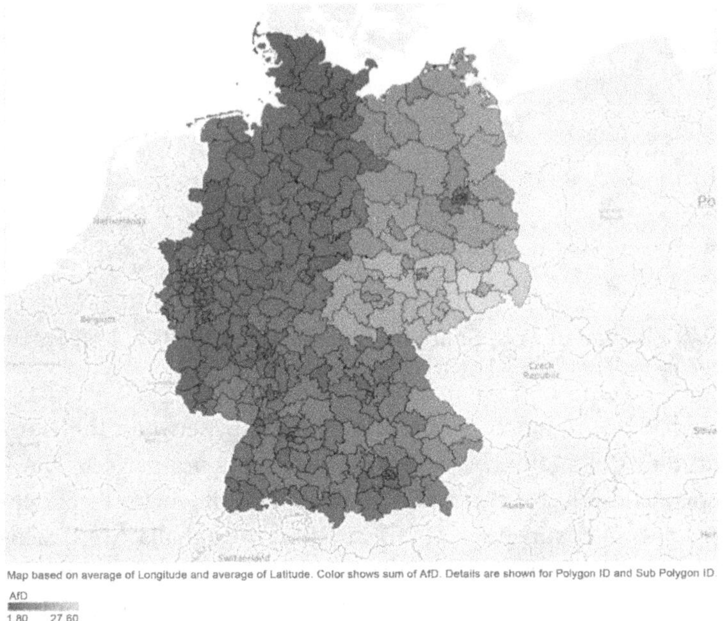

Figure 9.1.2: Change in the AfD Vote Share by Constituency in 2017
Source: Second vote (*Zweitstimme*), Federal returning officer.

by almost 8 percent. It made particular gains in Bavaria and Saxony, particularly in the southeast (light areas in Figure 9.1.2). These were not only traditional strongholds of the CSU and CDU respectively but also the constituencies in which both parties lost most votes (opaque areas in Figure 9.1.1). For example, the CDU suffered its highest losses in the constituency Sächsische Schweiz-Osterzgebirge in Saxony (-20.3 percent), whereas the AfD increased its 2013 vote share by 27.6 percent in the same district. The three direct mandates the AfD secured in Saxony by winning most constituency votes (*Erststimmen*) under Germany's mixed electoral system had also previously been held by the CDU.[47]

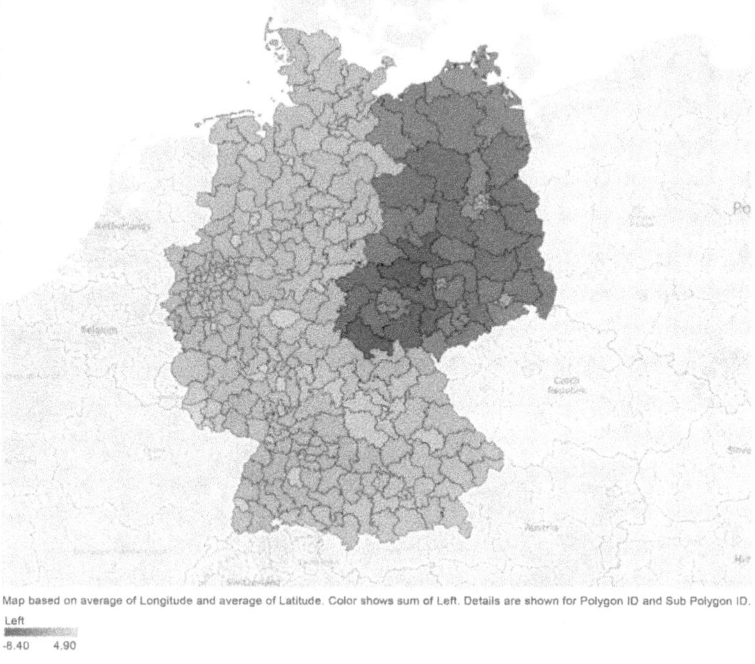

Figure 9.2: Change in Vote Share by Constituency in 2017, Left Party
Source: Second vote (*Zweitstimme*), Federal returning officer.

Although there is much geographical overlap between the CDU/CSU's losses and the AfD's gains, however, the overlap is not perfect. The Christian Democrats also lost substantially in some constituencies in Baden-Württemberg (southwest) and parts of North Rhine-Westphalia (west) where the AfD gains were relatively less striking. Moreover, the AfD's gains in eastern Germany were often much higher than the losses suffered by the CDU. Gains by the AfD in the east were, in turn, accompanied by (at times substantial) losses for the socialist Left Party (Die Linke). It declined in all eastern German constituencies outside of Berlin, while increasing its vote share in almost all of western Germany (Figure 9.2). This encourages a move from macro- to micro-level data to analyze vote shifts between parties.

Individual-level data on vote shifts, based on estimates by Infratest dimap, shows that the AfD's vote base was indeed quite diverse in 2017. While the group of former CDU/CSU voters accounts for more than a quarter of the AfD's gains, the party drew substantial support from former nonvoters, other minor parties (including right-wing extremist parties, like the NPD), the Social Democrats and the Left Party (Table 9.2).

Table 9.2: Vote Shift Toward the AfD in 2017

Absolute Numbers	Share of AfD Gains (in percent)
1,200,000 from nonvoters	31
980,000 from CDU/CSU	26
690,000 from minor parties	18
470,000 from SPD	12
400,000 from Left	11
40,000 from FDP	1
40,000 from Greens	1
Total: 3,820,000	100

Source: Infratest dimap, "Wählerwanderungen Bundestagswahl 2017", percent rounded to nearest integer.

Just because the AfD gained the largest number of voters from the Christian Democrats compared to other established parties does not mean that the AfD was primarily a threat to the CDU/CSU. To make such an assessment, we need to take a party's baseline vote share into account because a loss of 10,000 votes, for instance, is more severe for a party that had previously gained 20,000 votes than for a party of 100,000 votes. To compare which party lost most of its electorate to the AfD, I calculate the relative losses of each party to the AfD in all elections between 2013 and 2017 (Table 9.3). The table reads: In 2013, the CDU/CSU lost two percent of the voters who had voted for them in the 2009 federal election to the AfD.

Table 9.3 illustrates that, in terms of the proportion of voters lost to the AfD, the latter has not been a primary challenge to the Christian Democrats. Instead, and with the partial exception of the Greens, the AfD gained from all parties, thereby not allowing to derive a clear ideological pattern. While the CDU lost a larger proportion of its previous electorate to the AfD than the SPD, the difference between both parties has often been quite marginal. More importantly, the parties that, in relative terms, lost most voters to the AfD were minor parties, like the Pirates and the far-right NPD, and the Left Party (in bold in Table 9.3). At least temporarily, former FDP voters were also

Table 9.3: Share of Voters Lost to the AfD by Party (in percent)

Year	Territory	CDU to AfD	SPD to AfD	Green to AfD	FDP to AfD	Left to AfD	Others to AfD	Nonvoters to AfD
2013	National	-2	-2	-2	**-7**	**-7**	.	-1
	Hesse	-2	-1	-3	-5	**-6**	**-20**	.
2014	European Parliament	**-6**	-3	-1	-2	**-6**	.	.
	Saxony	-5	-4	-3	**-10**	-4	**-23**	-1
	Brandenburg	-7	-3	-1	**-17**	-5	**-27**	-2
	Thuringia	-5	-6	-2	**-14**	-6	**-24**	-1
2015	Hamburg	-1	0	0	**-2**	0	**-5**	-1
2016	Baden-Württemberg	-10	-8	-6	-7	**-16**	**-55**	-8
	Rhineland-Palatinate	-8	-6	-2	-10	**-21**	**-38**	-7
	Saxony-Anhalt	-12	-9	-4	**-16**	-12	**-48**	-10
	Mecklenburg-West Pomerania	**-14**	-6	-5	.	-13	**-23**	-8
	Berlin	-11	-6	-2	**-15**	-7	**-23**	-7
2017	Saarland	-2	-2	0	.	**-5**	**-13**	-3
	Schleswig-Holstein	**-3**	-1	-1	**-3**	.	**-19**	-1
	North Rhine-Westphalia	-2	-2	-1	-4	**-5**	**-32**	-4
	National	-5	-4	-1	-4	**-11**	**-21**	-7
	Lower Saxony	-3	-1	0	-2	**-9**	**-48**	-3
Average		-5.8	-3.8	-1.9	-7.8	**-8.3**	**-28.0**	-4.3

Source: Infratest dimap; Federal and Land returning officers. The data refers to both CDU and CSU in nationwide elections but excludes the CSU for all Land elections shown above because it only competes in Bavaria. I have used the party-list vote (*Zweitstimme*). Bremen 2015 is not included because each voter has up to five votes which makes it impossible to derive a party's number of voters. The two largest losses per election are in bold.

more receptive to vote AfD than former CDU voters. The results therefore suggest that the AfD's rise cannot be sufficiently explained by the defection of discontented Christian Democrats. This corresponds to the development of the party's platform outlined in the previous section of this article.

The heterogeneity of the AfD's electoral gains encourages some further exploration on what characterizes AfD voters in contrast to non-AfD voters. For this purpose, I use the pre-release of the GLES 2017 Postelection Cross-Section dataset.[48] Of the 2,115 people who were interviewed for this survey between 25 September and 30 November 2017 I focus on the 2,036 people who were eligible to vote in the 2017 federal election.

I use a logistic regression model. My dependent variable is "AfD vote choice" in the 2017 election. It contrasts people who said they had voted AfD in the 2017 election with those who said they had not (including those who casted an invalid ballot and those who did not turn out). The proportion of AfD voters in the sample, bearing in mind that nonvoters and casting an invalid ballot have been coded as non-AfD voters to make maximum use of the information available in the data, is 8.5 percent. While this is a relatively small share, it is still well beyond the threshold specified by Gary King and Langche Zeng who have suggested adjusting estimation techniques for binary dependent variables with a proportion of positive cases under 5 percent.[49]

The key independent variables seek to capture the ideological vote base of the AfD. Given its origins as a conservative challenger to the Christian Democrats, I include variables usually associated with the CDU/CSU's conservative wing. They include items asking respondents how religious they would consider themselves, whether they feel that Merkel represents the values and political ideas of the CDU/CSU, and whether they think same sex marriage should be legal. While the latter had been legalized just before the Bundestag went out of session in 2017, it is a good item to include given the salience of the topic in the public discourse just before the federal election. The model also includes a question on whether respondents are in favor of or against the introduction of an upper limit for the yearly intake of refugees. This has been a highly controversial topic during the refugee crisis. Many conservatives have favored an upper limit. Yet, it is also unlikely to be opposed by voters holding nativist attitudes. I also include an item that asks respondents how much they fear the refugee crisis. As an alternative measure, I include a question that investigates whether respondents perceive immigration as a threat to German culture. To measure populist attitudes, I use an item asking about the satisfaction with the way democracy has been realized in Germany. This fits what we know about populist radical right parties which, rather than opposing democracy, criticize that it has been deprived of its true meaning by the political elite.[50] I also include an item for subjective deprivation which asks whether respondents think that their own economic situation has deteriorated over the last one or two years. Finally, given the losses of the Left Party to the AfD shown above, I also include a dummy seeking to measure pro-socialist attitudes. It asks whether respondents either fully or partially agree that socialism is a good idea that has only been badly implemented. I also include controls for gender and age group.

Most attitudinal variables have been dichotomized for the purpose of this study. This strategy comes at the cost of some nuance. The theoretically most meaningful and unambiguous cut-off point, however, is between those who tend to or fully hold conservative, populist, nativist, and socialist views respectively and those who do not (including the "neither-nor"/"undecided" response category). "Refused," "no response," and "don't know" were coded as missing and excluded from the analysis.

Table 9.4 presents the respective odds ratios for different specifications of the model. My results correspond to the development of the AfD's platform over the past years and underline the party's heterogeneous basis. Despite the decreasing sample size due to listwise deletion, the results are robust across specifications without any major shifts in the size or direction of the effects.

Corresponding to previous research, I find a substantive gender gap in accounting for AfD support.[51] Men are twice as likely as women to have voted for the AfD in the 2017 election. Moreover, the odds of voting AfD are twice to three times as high for middle-aged respondents compared to eighteen to twenty-nine-year-olds. These results hold across all eight specifications.

Regarding the AfD's appeal to a traditionally conservative and Christian democratic electorate, the results show an interesting and ambiguous picture. Respondents expressing disagreement with the legalization of same sex marriage and who see Merkel as not representing the values and political positions of the CDU/CSU are significantly and substantively more likely to be AfD voters than those not holding such views. This points toward the AfD having gained traction among voters holding views that have been associated with the criticism against the alleged erosion of the Christian Democrats' political identity. At the same time, however, the odds of voting AfD decrease the more respondents identify as religious. Those stating that they are somewhat or very religious are only half and 25 percent as likely to vote AfD respectively than people saying that they are not at all religious. Again, these results hold across all eight specifications. This suggests that the AfD's support base does not equal the CDU/CSU's right wing. The latter has upheld conservative views but also been characterized by a high level of religiosity and an emphasis on the "C" in CDU/CSU.[52]

Attitudes regarding the refugee crisis and immigration are a second important set of variables. Adding them to the model almost doubles the pseudo R^2. Respondents favoring an upper limit for the yearly intake of refugees are three to four times as likely to vote AfD than those who do not. This most likely includes former CDU/CSU voters who have been dissatisfied with Merkel's moderate stance on immigration. Yet, this view is also shared by voters on the far right. The nativist element in the AfD's electorate is further highlighted by voters who see immigration as a threat to German culture being almost 4.5 times more likely to vote AfD than those who do not

Table 9.4: Determinants of AfD Vote in 2017 (odds ratios)

Variable	M1	M2	M3	M4	M5	M6	M7	M8
Gender	2.33***	2.16***	1.87***	1.81**	2.23***	2.08***	2.33***	2.43***
(1=male)	(0.42)	(0.39)	(0.35)	(0.36)	(0.48)	(0.44)	(0.51)	(0.55)
Age group								
30 to 44	2.38**	2.41**	2.37**	2.35*	2.74**	2.67**	2.92**	2.98**
	(0.73)	(0.74)	(0.74)	(0.79)	(1.02)	(0.99)	(1.12)	(1.17)
45 to 59	2.26**	2.50**	2.24**	2.58**	2.19*	2.17*	2.30*	2.17*
	(0.66)	(0.74)	(0.67)	(0.84)	(0.77)	(0.77)	(0.84)	(0.81)
60+	1.42	1.64	1.19	1.42	1.21	1.15	1.38	1.29
	(0.43)	(0.50)	(0.38)	(0.48)	(0.44)	(0.42)	(0.51)	(0.49)
Identifying as religious								
Not very		0.53*	0.46**	0.49**	0.55*	0.46**	0.61	0.57
		(0.13)	(0.12)	(0.13)	(0.16)	(0.13)	(0.18)	(0.18)
Somewhat		0.45***	0.38***	0.38***	0.38***	0.34***	0.45**	0.45**
		(0.09)	(0.08)	(0.08)	(0.09)	(0.08)	(0.11)	(0.11)
Very		0.26***	0.18***	0.19***	0.21***	0.18***	0.25**	0.24***
		(0.10)	(0.07)	(0.08)	(0.09)	(0.07)	(0.11)	(0.10)
Against SSM			3.69***	3.72***	2.49***	2.49***	2.41***	2.33***
			(0.74)	(0.77)	(0.56)	(0.56)	(0.56)	(0.55)
Merkel not CDU values				3.54***	3.31***	3.14***	2.55***	2.34**
				(0.78)	(0.85)	(0.80)	(0.68)	(0.64)
Upper Limit					3.85***	4.59***	3.89***	3.45***
					(1.20)	(1.39)	(1.23)	(1.12)
Fear of Refugee Crisis								
2					0.55		0.66	0.66
					(0.40)		(0.49)	(0.49)
3					0.62		0.70	0.71
					(0.43)		(0.50)	(0.51)
4					1.23		1.32	1.23
					(0.73)		(0.79)	(0.75)
5					1.84		1.81	1.44
					(1.06)		(1.06)	(0.85)
6					2.38		2.53	1.76
					(1.37)		(1.48)	(1.05)
7					6.02**		4.51**	2.91
					(3.41)		(2.59)	(1.71)
Cultural Threat						4.49***		
						(0.92)		
Economically Worse Off							1.49	1.39
							(0.39)	(0.37)
Dissatisfied with Democracy							3.60***	3.24***
							(0.76)	(0.70)
Socialism is a Good Idea								2.51***
								(0.57)
Pseudo R^2	0.03	0.06	0.10	0.13	0.25	0.26	0.29	0.31
N	1,908	1,894	1,854	1,802	1,772	1,768	1,764	1,759

Source: GLES 2017 Postelection Cross-Section dataset. Results are odds ratios for a logistic regression (standard errors in parentheses), rounded to two decimal places. Independent variables are categorical, with smallest value as reference category. $^{*}p_z < 0.05$; $^{**} p_z < 0.01$; $^{***} p_z < 0.001$.

share this view. Moreover, respondents who say that the refugee crisis scares them a lot are substantially and significantly more likely to be AfD voters than those who are not at all scared by it. While including these variables in the same model may make us expect multicollinearity, tests indicate that the level of multicollinearity is very low (for the full model, the mean VIF equals 1.18; 1.38 for upper limit, 1.46 for fear of refugee crisis). We may thus be looking at a quite different electorate–one more conservative and one more nativist in nature.

Interestingly, the effect of feeling very scared of the refugee crisis disappears when we control for pro-socialist attitudes. The odds of respondents who consider socialism a good idea that has only been poorly implemented to vote AfD are more than twice as high as those of people who disagree with this statement. This correlation underscores the heterogeneity of the party's support base and likely reflects the losses of the Left Party to the AfD in eastern Germany.

Finally, AfD voters are characterized by a sense of dissatisfaction. This dissatisfaction is not rooted in a negative development of their own economic situation as the respective effect is undistinguishable from zero. It echoes previous findings on the limited explanatory power of the modernization loser thesis for explaining AfD vote.[53] Instead, being dissatisfied with the way democracy has been realized in Germany makes people more likely to vote AfD. These results are robust to including sampling weights to correct for the oversampling in eastern Germany, as Table 9.5 in the Appendix demonstrates.

The AfD's electoral basis therefore corresponds to the findings presented above regarding the transformation of its programmatic platform. It may have started as an alternative for social and fiscal conservatives but has transformed into a populist radical right party, attracting support from social conservatives, anti-establishment, and nativist as well as far-left voters.

The Importance of Holding the Party Together

The AfD's track record of internal conflicts and splits casts doubts on whether it will succeed in holding the strange coalition together that has been the basis of its electoral success. Initially, the AfD seemed to be in relatively good shape to establish itself as a serious challenger to the Christian Democrats. For a new party, the AfD could rely on an impressive amount of resources and organization.[54] Moreover, the party's initiators Lucke, Gauland, and Adam had all a CDU background. They attracted other former Christian Democrats with an expertise on economic issues like Gerd Robanus and Joachim Starbatty.[55] They also gained the support of Hans-Olaf Henkel who had been president of the Federation of German Industry. Together, they appealed to two distinct groups of discontented Christian Democrats. While Lucke and Henkel wooed market-liberal voters, Adam, Frauke Petry, and Gauland reached out to social conservatives.[56]

Nevertheless, defecting to the AfD quickly became an unappealing option for dissatisfied Christian Democrats as the AfD disintegrated into factional competition. Lucke and his supporters, while agreeing to the diversification of the party's program beyond Euroscepticism, wanted to continue emphasizing the AfD's economic positions and prepare it for joining governing coalitions. In contrast, the group around Gauland and Petry envisioned the AfD as a populist radical right and relational anti-system party.[57]

The AfD proved unable to integrate these competing positions within its organization, which resulted in the party's first split in 2015. Many economic liberals and moderate conservatives had already been leaving the AfD since 2014 as the internal balance of power was shifting toward Petry and Gauland. After Petry was elected party leader at the AfD's national congress in May 2015, Lucke and most members of his faction broke away from the AfD. They founded the Alliance for Progress and Renewal (ALFA), which was later renamed into Liberal Conservative Reformers (LKR), and adopted a program that placed it between the Christian Democrats and the AfD on the socioeconomic and sociocultural dimension.[58]

The split, however, did not put an end to the infights within the AfD, which underlines that it has so far lacked essential mechanisms to resolve internal conflicts. Conflicts emerged between a group behind Petry, promoting more national-conservative positions, and proponents of a far-right course, including Gauland and Björn Höcke. Again, many moderate members, whereby moderate now designated the group behind Petry, left the AfD. In addition, numerous MPs defected from the party's group in many state parliaments, including in Baden-Württemberg, Saxony, Saxony-Anhalt, Mecklenburg-West Pomerania, and North Rhine-Westphalia.[59]

A second party split ultimately occurred only three days after the 2017 federal election. At a press conference together with Gauland and the AfD's top candidate for the election, Alice Weidel, Petry, who had won her constituency seat, suddenly declared that she would not join the AfD Bundestag group.[60] Shortly thereafter, she and other members left the AfD and formed a new party, called the Blue Party (Die Blaue Partei).[61]

Recently, the AfD has also experienced the first break-away on its far right. Criticizing Gauland and Weidel for downplaying the AfD's nativism to prevent Germany's Federal Office for the Protection of the Constitution from investigating the party, André Poggenburg, former AfD leader in Saxony-Anhalt, formed the Awakening of German Patriots.[62]

Thus, the AfD has lost large parts of its initial membership and split three times in the six years of its existence. Given its internal instability, it seems questionable whether it will succeed in consolidating the heterogeneous electoral basis that was responsible for the party's surge in the 2017 federal election.

Conclusion

In conclusion, it would be too simplistic to consider the AfD a primary threat to the Christian Democrats. The latter are therefore best advised to not dramatically alter their profile. This article has come to this conclusion by analyzing the development of the AfD's programmatic platform, its electoral basis in the 2017 election and its internal integrative strength (or rather the lack thereof).

Indeed, the AfD was only in its beginnings a conservative challenger to the Christian Democrats. Very quickly after its formation, it started moving toward the populist radical right. Fiscal and social conservatism were thereby sidelined by authoritarianism, populism and nativism. This programmatic transformation was reflected in an electoral basis that is best described as a coalition of strange bedfellows. On the one hand, the CDU/CSU did lose ground to the AfD. The latter has attracted support from voters in the 2017 election who express socially conservative views and regard Merkel as not representing traditional CDU values. On the other hand, however, the AfD gained importantly from almost all parties and, in particular, from other minor parties, including those on the far right, and the Left Party. In the literature on party competition and voting behavior, such a heterogeneous support coalition has often been characteristic of populist radical right parties.[63]

Yet, the refugee issue blurs the boundary between these groups. Opposition to Merkel's refugee policies has been widely shared by many conservative Christian Democrats. The strong correlation between support for an upper limit for the yearly intake of refugees and AfD vote in 2017 thus seems to primarily concern the CDU/CSU. While the latter most likely lost many voters to the AfD because of this issue, AfD voters are also more likely to consider immigration in general as a threat to German culture which points toward Cas Mudde's conceptualization of nativism.[64] In combination with the nonreligious, anti-establishment, and pro-socialist attitudes found to affect the odds of voting AfD, we can therefore conclude that the AfD electorate is not simply flesh from the flesh of the Christian Democrats. Instead, it also upholds views associated with the radical right and left.[65]

Finally, the AfD's track record of internal conflicts and splits has shown that the party has so far been unable to integrate these different positions within its ranks. After the ordoliberal and conservative faction around Bernd Lucke had left the AfD in 2015, another conflict between a national-conservative and a far-right faction erupted. The former around Frauke Petry broke away from the AfD shortly after the 2017 Bundestag election. The tension between different views on how far to the right the AfD should be has also led to fissions within the AfD's parliamentary groups in the German state parliaments and recently to yet another break-away. Given its inability to mediate between competing positions, the party does not appear to be well-equipped to maintain its support base.

Hence, demands to move the CDU/CSU to the right to fight off the AfD does not sufficiently consider the complexity of the AfD's platform, electorate, and internal factionalism. Giving into such demands now that Merkel has announced to not run again in 2021 may entail a similar fate for the German Christian Democrats as the one suffered by the SPD when confronting the Left Party in the early 2000s or by other European center-right parties in the face of a radical challenger. They tried to accommodate more extreme positions but failed to stop the rise of their respective rivals.[66] The result was, in many cases, a decline from which these parties have not yet recovered. Future research would benefit from analyzing the trajectory of the AfD and CDU/CSU in such comparative terms.

Matthias Dilling is a Departmental Lecturer at the University of Oxford. His research is on comparative politics with a particular focus on party politics in Europe. E-mail: matthias.dilling@politics.ox.ac.uk

Notes

1. Michael Geiss, "Beschlossen und Beschwiegen," *Die Zeit*, 14 July 2011, 3; Heribert Prantl, "Kanzlerin des Ungefähren," *Süddeutsche Zeitung*, 17 May 2010, available at http://www.sueddeutsche.de/politik/cdu-parteitag-kanzlerin-des-ungefaehren-1.792349, accessed 11 March 2018; Volker Rensing, *Die Kanzlermaschine. Wie die CDU funktioniert* (Freiburg, 2013), 149.
2. Simon Franzmann, "Von AfD zu ALFA. Die Entwicklung zur Spaltung", *MIP* 22 (2016): 23–37, here 27–28, 34.
3. Compare Noam Gidron, "Many ways to be right. The unbundling of European mass attitudes and partisan asymmetries across the ideological divide," (PhD diss., Harvard University, Cambridge, 2016).
4. See, for example, Downs' seminal study. Anthony Downs, *An Economic Theory of Democracy* (New York, 1957).
5. Kai Arzheimer and Elisabeth Carter, "Political opportunity structures and right-wing extremist party success," *European Journal of Political Research* 45, no. 3 (2006): 419–443, here 438–439; Matt Golder, "Far Right Parties in Europe," *Annual Review of Political Science* 19 (2016): 477–497, here 478; Cas Mudde, *Populist radical right parties in Europe* (Cambridge, 2007), 229.
6. "Tillich will CDU nach rechts rücken", *Die Welt*, 30 September 2017; available at https://www.welt.de/newsticker/dpa_nt/infoline_nt/brennpunkte_nt/article169194793/Tillich-will-CDU-nach-rechts-ruecken.html, accessed 11 March 2018; "Kauder will nicht nach rechts rücken," *Der Spiegel*, 5 October 2017; available at http://www.spiegel.de/politik/deutschland/cdu-fraktionschef-volker-kauder-lehnt-rechtsruck-ab-a-1171314.html, accessed 11 March 2018.
7. Bonnie M. Meguid, "Competition between unequals: The role of mainstream party strategy in niche party success," *American Political Science Review* 99, no. 3 (2005): 347–359, here 348, 350, 356.
8. I thank Stathis Kalyvas for pointing me toward this terminology.
9. Geiss (see note 1), 3; Prantl (see note 1); Rensing (see note 1), 149.
10. Marc Debus and Jochen Müller, "The programmatic development of CDU and CSU since Reunification. Incentives and constraints for changing policy positions in the German multi-level system," *German Politics* 22, no. 1–2 (2013): 151–171, here 161–162, 167; Petra Hemmelmann, *Der Kompass der CDU. Analyse der Grundsatz- und Wahlprogramme von Adenauer bis Merkel* (Wiesbaden, 2017), here 334–342.
11. Jan Dams, Carsten Dierig and Nikolaus Doll, "Die schleichende 'Sozialdemokratisierung der CDU,'" *Die Welt*, 25 October 2016; available at https://www.welt.de/wirtschaft/article158994860/Die-schleichende-Sozialdemokratisierung-der-CDU.html, accessed 11 March 2018.
12. Clay Clemens, "Modernization or disorientation? Policy change in Merkel's CDU," *German Politics* 18, no. 2 (2009): 121–139, here: 132–134; Hemmelmann (see note 8), 403–416; Joyce Marie Mushaben, "Wir schaffen das! Angela Merkel and the European Refugee Crisis," *German Politics* 26, no. 4 (2017): 516–533, here 517–518.
13. Franzmann (see note 2), 27–28, 34.
14. Rüdiger Schmitt-Beck, "Euro-Kritik, Wirtschaftspessimismus und Einwanderungsskepsis. Hintergründe des Beinah-Wahlerfolges der Alternative für Deutschland (AfD) bei der Bundestagswahl 2013," *Zeitschrift für Parlamentsfragen* 45, no. 1 (2014): 94–112, here 95–97; Franzmann (see note 2), 27, 34.
15. Schmitt-Beck (see note 14), 96–97; Robert Grimm, "The rise of the German Eurosceptic party Alternative für Deutschland, between ordoliberal critique and popular anxiety," *International Political Science Review* 36, no. 3 (2015): 264–278, here 265–266.
16. Simon Franzmann, "Calling the ghost of populism. The AfD's strategic and tactical agendas until the EP election 2014," *German Politics* 25, no. 4 (2016): 457–479, here 465–466.

17. Alternative für Deutschland, "Programm für Deutschland. Das Grundsatzprogramm der Alternative für Deutschland," available at https://www.afd.de/grundsatzprogramm, accessed 21 February 2018, 15–22, 67, 74, 76; Alternative für Deutschland, "Programm für Deutschland. Wahlprogramm der Alternative für Deutschland für die Wahl zum Deutschen Bundestag am 24. September 2017;" available at https://www.afd.de/wahlprogramm/, accessed 21 February 2018, 7, 12, 14, 50–51, 53, 69.
18. AfD "Grundsatzprogramm" (see note 17), 30–32, 36–37, 40–41, 44; AfD "Wahlprogramm" (see note 17), 37–40, 51, 56.
19. AfD "Grundsatzprogramm" (see note 17), 25, 52-54, 56, 83; AfD "Wahlprogramm" (see note 17), 19, 24–25, 43–44, 63, 66.
20. Mushaben (see note 12), 529.
21. Schäuble quoted in ibid.
22. Mudde (see note 5), 22–31.
23. Rüdiger Schmitt-Beck, "The 'Alternative für Deutschland in the electorate'. Between single-issue and right-wing populist party," *German Politics* 26, no. 1 (2017): 124–148, here 140.
24. Grimm (see note 15), 273; Schmitt-Beck (see note 21), 140.
25. Grimm (see note 15), 273.
26. Mudde (see note 5), 23.
27. AfD "Grundsatzprogramm" (see note 17), 26.
28. AfD "Wahlprogramm" (see note 17), 23-24.
29. Simon Franzmann, "Die Programmatik von ALFA in Abgrenzung zur AfD. Droht Deutschland eine Spirale des Populismus?" *MIP* 22 (2016): 38–51, here 42.
30. Giovanni Capoccia, "Anti-system parties. A conceptual reassessment," *Journal of Theoretical Politics* 14, no. 1 (2002): 9–35, here 15.
31. Mudde (see note 5), 23.
32. AfD "Grundsatzprogramm" (see note 17), 6, 8, 11, 12, 14, 24, 47, 49, 54–55, 58, 64, 75, 79, 81.
33. AfD "Wahlprogramm" (see note 17), 8-10, 40–41, 45, 53.
34. Mudde (see note 5), 19.
35. AfD "Grundsatzprogramm" (see note 17), 47–49, 59–61, 63; AfD "Wahlprogramm" (see note 17), 28–29.
36. AfD "Grundsatzprogramm" (see note 17), 59–60; AfD "Wahlprogramm" (see note 17), 28, 30.
37. AfD "Grundsatzprogramm" (see note 17), 59–60; AfD "Wahlprogramm" (see note 17), 30.
38. AfD "Grundsatzprogramm" (see note 17), 58–59, 60–61, 63; AfD "Wahlprogramm" (see note 17), 29–30.
39. AfD "Grundsatzprogramm" (see note 17), 59; AfD "Wahlprogramm" (see note 17), 31.
40. AfD "Wahlprogramm" (see note 17), 28, 31.
41. AfD "Grundsatzprogramm" (see note 17), 48–50; AfD "Wahlprogramm" (see note 17), 33–35, 45.
42. AfD "Wahlprogramm" (see note 17), 28.
43. Ibid., 28.
44. Ibid., 37.
45. Ibid., 37.
46. Ibid., 37.
47. Viola Neu and Sabine Pokorny, "Bundestagswahl in Deutschland am 24. September 2017," Konrad-Adenauer-Stiftung, September 2017, 16–17.
48. Sigrid Roßteutscher, Harald Schoen, Rüdiger Schmitt-Beck, Bernhard Weßels, Christof Wolf, Aiko Wagner, "Nachwahl-Querschnitt (GLES 2017)," GESIS Datenarchiv, Cologne: ZA6801 Datenfile Version 1.0.0, doi: 10.4232/1.12954.
49. Gary King and Langche Zeng, "Logistic Regression in Rare Events Data," *Political Analysis* 9, no. 2 (2001): 137–163, here 157.
50. Mudde (see note 5), 23, 31; Golder (see note 5), 478.

51. Holger Lengfeld, “Die ‘Alternative für Deutschland’: eine Partei für Modernisierungsverlierer?” *Kölner Zeitschrift für Soziologie und Sozialpsychologie* 69 (2017): 209–232, here 224; Schmitt-Beck (see note 14), 104.
52. Compare to Viola Neu, “Die Mitglieder der CDU,” Konrad-Adenauer-Stiftung, 2007, here 41.
53. Lengfeld (see note 51).
54. Oskar Niedermayer, “Eine neue Konkurentin im Parteiensystem? Die Alternative für Deutschland” in *Die Parteien nach der Bundestagswahl*, ed. Oskar Niedermayer (Wiesbaden, 2015): 175–208, here 173–184.
55. Grimm (see note 15), 266.
56. Franzmann (see note 2), 34.
57. Ibid., 31, 34–35.
58. Ibid., 32–34.
59. Rüdiger Soldt, “Spaltung der AfD-Fraktion,” *Frankfurter Allgemeine Zeitung*, 5 July 2016, available at http://www.faz.net/aktuell/politik/inland/spaltung-der-afd-fraktion-im-landtag-baden-wuerttemberg-14325303.html, accessed 11 March 2018; Stefan Tomik, “Das sind die AfD-Abtrünnigen,” *Frankfurter Allgemeine Zeitung*, 14 November 2017, available at http://www.faz.net/aktuell/politik/inland/nicht-nur-frauke-petry-das-sind-die-afd-abtruennigen-15259984.html, accessed 11 March 2018; “AfD-Abgeordneter will zur CDU wechseln,” *MDR Sachsen-Anhalt*, available at https://www.mdr.de/sachsen-anhalt/landespolitik/afd-abgeordneter-jens-diederichs-tritt-aus-landtagsfraktion-aus-100.html, accessed 21 February 2018; “Landtagsfraktion der AfD zerbricht,” *Die Zeit*, 25 September 2017, available at http://www.zeit.de/politik/deutschland/2017-09/mecklenburg-vorpommern-afd-spaltung-neue-fraktion, accessed 11 March 2018.
60. “Erst verlässt sie die Fraktion, dann die Bundespressekonferenz,” *Die Welt*, 25 September 2017, available at https://www.welt.de/politik/deutschland/article168998281/Erst-verlaesst-sie-die-Fraktion-dann-die-Bundespressekonferenz.html, accessed 11 March 2018.
61. “Bundeswahlleiter bestätigt Gründung einer Blauen Partei,” *Die Zeit*, 11 October 2017, available at http://www.zeit.de/politik/deutschland/2017-10/frauke-petry-die-blaue-partei-afd-bundeswahlleiter, accessed 11 March 2018.
62. Michael Lühmann, "Angriff von rechts," Die Zeit (italic), 11 January 2019, available at https://www.zeit.de/politik/2019-01/andre-poggenburg-afd-abspaltung-rechtsruck-ostdeutschland, accessed 04 February 2019.
63. See Mudde (see note 5), 227–229; Golder (see note 48), 489–490.
64. Mudde (see note 5), 22.
65. See for a recent analysis that further investigates the complexity of the AfD electorate in 2017, Michael A. Hansen and Jonathan Olsen, "Flesh of the same flesh. A study of voters for the Alternative for Germany (AfD) in the 2017 Federal Election," *German Politics* 28, no. 1 (2018): 1-19.
66. Compare, for example, Meguid (see note 7), 356.

Appendix

Table 9.5: Determinants of AfD Vote in 2017 (odds ratios, weighted data)

Variable	M1	M2	M3	M4	M5	M6	M7	M8
Gender	2.36***	2.14***	1.83**	1.71**	2.03***	1.89**	2.12***	2.19***
(1=male)	(0.44)	(0.40)	(0.35)	(0.34)	(0.44)	(0.41)	(0.47)	(0.49)
Age group								
30 to 44	2.67**	2.76**	2.76**	2.66**	3.08**	3.06**	3.32**	3.36**
	(0.85)	(0.88)	(0.87)	(0.92)	(1.25)	(1.23)	(1.41)	(1.48)
45 to 59	2.41**	2.78***	2.48**	2.77**	2.30*	2.31*	2.41*	2.25
	(0.74)	(0.85)	(0.76)	(0.94)	(0.91)	(0.90)	(0.97)	(0.95)
60+	1.41	1.71	1.21	1.41	1.15	1.13	1.33	1.25
	(0.45)	(0.54)	(0.40)	(0.50)	(0.46)	(0.46)	(0.55)	(0.53)
Identifying as religious								
Not very		0.57*	0.49**	0.52*	0.56	0.48*	0.63	0.61
		(0.14)	(0.13)	(0.14)	(0.17)	(0.15)	(0.20)	(0.20)
Somewhat		0.41***	0.35***	0.34***	0.33***	0.28***	0.37***	0.36***
		(0.08)	(0.08)	(0.08)	(0.08)	(0.07)	(0.09)	(0.09)
Very		0.26***	0.18***	0.19***	0.19***	0.16***	0.23**	0.22***
		(0.10)	(0.07)	(0.08)	(0.08)	(0.07)	(0.11)	(0.10)
Against SSM			4.00***	3.95***	2.52***	2.50***	2.38***	2.26**
			(0.85)	(0.87)	(0.62)	(0.60)	(0.59)	(0.57)
Merkel not CDU values				3.93***	3.81***	3.37***	3.02***	2.67***
				(0.89)	(1.04)	(0.88)	(0.81)	(0.74)
Upper Limit					4.36***	5.22***	4.17***	3.62***
					(1.45)	(1.65)	(1.38)	(1.22)
Fear of Refugee Crisis								
2					0.40		0.49	0.52
					(0.31)		(0.38)	(0.38)
3					0.51		0.57	0.61
					(0.37)		(0.43)	(0.44)
4					1.04		1.11	1.06
					(0.63)		(0.68)	(0.61)
5					1.85		1.82	1.50
					(1.11)		(1.11)	(0.87)
6					2.31		2.48	1.82
					(1.39)		(1.51)	(1.07)
7					5.59**		4.29*	2.82
					(3.33)		(2.59)	(1.67)
Cultural Threat						4.85***		
						(1.04)		
Economically Worse Off							1.56	1.46
							(0.44)	(0.42)
Dissatisfied with Democracy							3.83***	3.39***
							(0.84)	(0.76)
Socialism is a Good Idea								2.64***
								(0.61)
Pseudo R^2	0.04	0.06	0.11	0.14	0.27	0.28	0.32	0.34
N	1,908	1,894	1,854	1,802	1,772	1,768	1,764	1,759

Source: GLES 2017 Postelection Cross-Section dataset. Results are robust odds ratios for a logistic regression (robust standard errors in parentheses), rounded to two decimal places. Sampling weights are included to correct for the oversampling in eastern Germany. Independent variables are categorical, with smallest value as reference category. $^{*}p_Z < 0.05$; $^{**} p_Z < 0.01$; $^{***} p_Z < 0.001$.

··· Chapter 10 ···

THE AFD AND THE END OF CONTAINMENT IN GERMANY?

David Art

The federal elections of 2017 brought a radical right party into parliament for the first time in postwar Germany. This fact alone would have made the rise of the Alternative for Germany (AfD) the central storyline in elections that ultimately returned Angela Merkel (Christian Democratic Union, CDU) as chancellor and led to yet another grand coalition with the Social Democratic Party (SPD). But, the AfD did not merely clear the 5 percent hurdle required for representation: it soared over it on its way to amassing 12.6 percent of the national vote and ninety-four seats in the Bundestag. Thus, for the first time in several decades, observers of German politics are tasked not with explaining the enduring weakness of the German radical right, but rather with accounting for a historic electoral breakthrough. And with the AfD now technically the largest opposition party in the Bundestag, there is a very real possibility that it—unlike past radical right parties in Germany—might become a permanent force. If so, the consequences for both Germany and Europe would be dramatic.

In this article, I argue that the rise of the AfD is not terribly puzzling, even if it is unprecedented. Within the last seven years, Chancellor Angela Merkel has taken two enormous political decisions in response to two monumental international challenges, each of which virtually ensured some form of political backlash from the far right. First, her eventual rescue of the Eurozone during the sovereign debt crisis created the AfD. Second, her decision to allow a million refugees into Germany led both to the AfD's radicalization and to its electoral takeoff. Thus, one way of looking at the rise of the AfD is that it was a direct product of Merkel's policies, or policy missteps, depending on one's point of view.

Notes for this section can be found on page 221.

That there is a clear and compelling explanation for the AfD's breakthrough does not make its occurrence any less significant. One of the defining features of postwar German politics has been the irrelevance of the radical right at the federal level. It is worth reflecting—as I do in the first section of this article—on how this result has been achieved. I argue that Germany represents the exemplar of the containment of the radical right. Whereas other states in Europe have normalized the radical right since it re-emerged in the 1980s, the sustained mobilization of German political parties, the media, and civil society against anti-immigrant parties has, to date, been very effective. The second section analyzes how two international shocks—and Merkel's response to them—allowed the radical right to flourish in spite of the continuation of containment. Rather than writing off the AfD as simply the product of Merkel's actions, I offer a different reading of events: the chancellor was able to take such profound decisions precisely because the radical right was, at the time she took them, of little political consequence. Moreover, she did so cognizant of the fact that stabilizing the Eurozone and opening Germany to one million refugees would provide an opening for the radical right. Her bet—if one could call it that—was that Germany would rise to both challenges without producing a powerful and sustainable nativist movement in the process. One view is that Merkel's wager was wrong, and that Germany is moving toward a seven-party system with a radical right party being a permanent player. The third section of this article considers this possibility, but ultimately concludes that the AfD is more likely headed along the same trajectory as other radical right parties in postwar Germany.

Containment and Normalization

Since the rise of the radical right in the 1980s, European states and societies have adopted two basic responses to it. The first is what I have referred to previously as containment, and I follow that terminology here. The second is normalization, which I consider an improvement upon the concept of "contagion" that I initially posed as the alternative to containment.[1]

I use the term containment cognizant of its Cold War associations, and admit up-front that any analogy with the U.S.'s early foreign policy toward communism internationally will be imperfect.[2] For whereas the doctrine of the containment of the USSR had an original theoretician—George Kennan—who outlined a set of specific policies that the U.S. largely followed, the containment of the European radical right had no master architect, and the dynamics of this strategy developed over time. It was also not a universal European response, as many other West European states normalized the radical right and no state in Central and Eastern Europe, with the exception of the Czech Republic, has adopted the containment strategy.[3] Nevertheless, putting aside this and other problems with the historical analogy, the drawing of sharp lines against an adversary to provoke its collapse from within–the core of principle of containment–describes both U.S. grand strategy during the Cold War and one possible democratic response to the politics of nativism.

The containment of the European radical right includes a political, a civil society, and a public discourse component. The clearest political manifestation of containment is the *cordon-sanitaire* (or the policy of *Ausgrenzung* in Germany), which at the minimum involves explicit agreements to not enter into political coalitions with the radical right, and, at the maximum, means calling out the radical right as antidemocratic, racist, or otherwise morally compromised. Civic reaction against the radical right involves a significant and sustained amount of social mobilization and peaceful protest. Finally, the media contributes to containment by (a) refusing to recognize the radical right at all; (b) by consistently presenting it negatively; (c) calling its audience to action against it; or (d) some combination of (b) and (c). Those countries in Western Europe that have contained the radical right in this way include Belgium, France, Germany, Great Britain, and Sweden.

Given the enduring electoral power of the National Front in France, and to a lesser extent of the Vlaams Belang in Flanders, one cannot claim that containment has necessarily made the radical right any less attractive to a core constituency. Even in these two cases, however, it is difficult to argue that containment has been counterproductive. Marine Le Pen's percentage of the vote in the presidential elections of 2017–a year that provided close to ideal circumstances for radical right parties–was not that much greater than her father's total in 2002, or even in 1988. Thirty years of the *cordon-sanitaire* in France has rendered the National Front a strong contender for the award for the party least able to translate millions of votes into measurable policy outcomes. Members of the Front–as well as many academics–nevertheless claim that the party's influence has shifted the entire political terrain of party competition, but Jean Marie Le Pen's oft-cited quip that the parties were copying his message remains a rhetorical weapon of the weak.

Containment need not "lock-in" an electorally powerful and politically excluded radical right. More likely is that the perpetual lack of coalition options, sustained negative press, and regular social protest are powerful enough at the minimum to prevent radical right parties from growing stronger, and at the maximum leads to party implosion.[4] Until the recent elections, Germany had executed containment close to perfection. The history of every radical right party in postwar Germany– the National Democratic Party (NPD), the Republikaner, the German People's Union (DVU), the Schill Party, to name some of the most successful ones–is one of sudden rise, factional infighting, radicalization, and organizational decay.

The policy of normalization, by contrast, has led to the consolidation of the radical right in every European state that has adopted it. When other political parties cooperate and even govern with radical right parties, when civil society does not protest against it, and when important media outlets have embraced its message, the radical right has not generally wilted after riding an anti-establishment wave. Indeed, the radical right has itself become the establishment in states like Austria, Denmark, Italy, and Switzerland. The notion that radical right parties would be either ideologically tamed or electorally destroyed by government participation now seems, with the benefit of close to forty years of hindsight, terribly misguided. Furthermore, once normalization has occurred, it is probably impossible to roll back. The choice of strategies that states adopted when the radical right first appeared in the 1980s and 1990s has mattered profoundly. The Northern League in Italy and the Austrian Freedom Party thus currently find themselves in similar commanding positions to those they held in 2000.

Shocks to the System

Within the space of six years, the European Union faced two monumental challenges: the Eurozone crisis and the European refugee crisis. For the first time since the founding of the European Union, Germany played the leading role in shaping Europe's response to such massive international challenges. Putting aside the question of whether her delaying tactics ("merkeling" as they are known) contributed to the economic crisis, two points are clear: Merkel ultimately decided that there would be a Eurozone bailout and that it would be on German terms. The latter fact allowed her a fair degree of political cover, as well as a chance to reshape the institutional architecture of the Eurozone.[5] But, by violating the no-bailout clause of the Maastricht Treaty, Merkel drew the ire of Germany's ordoliberal establishment. While economists and business leaders believed they had an ally in "Frau Nein" during the winter of 2010 when Merkel steadfastly refused to renegotiate the terms of Greece's sovereign debt, her ultimate decision to sign off on a trillion dollar bailout– the first of many to Greece and other EU states–amounted to a betrayal, in the ordoliberal view, of German values and of the German constitution. Although Merkel won the political and constitutional battle, her victory came at the price of major resignations, such as Axel Weber from the Bundesbank in 2011, and a rebellion among professors of economics.

Historians will be looking at the motives and consequences of Merkel's handling of the Eurozone crisis for a long time. There can be no debate, however, that her policies–which she routinely described as *alternativlos*–led directly to the foundation of the Alternative for Germany. The AfD began as a website constructed by Bernd Lucke, Professor of Economics at the University of Hamburg, in March 2013. It was *euro*-skeptical rather than Euroskeptical, in that it wanted an orderly dissolution of the common currency but not of the European Union. The founders of the party included–in addition to the many economists–former members of the CDU (as well as of the classically liberal Free Democratic Party, FDP) and social conservative activists. Academic studies that were conducted during the AfD's first year of existence found that the party was not xenophobic. Based on an analysis of the party's manifesto and on hundreds of its online statements, one discovered no "evidence of nativism or populism in the party's manifesto, which sets it apart from most of the other new right parties in Europe."[6] Another study was more equivocal, but nevertheless concluded that "the AfD is not a right-wing populist party in itself but may be a right-wing populist movement in the making."[7]

This proved prescient, for by the 2014 European elections the party had developed a distinctly anti-immigrant profile. The 2013 Federal Elections had been a referendum on Merkel's handling of the Eurozone crisis, and while the AfD nearly surmounted the 5 percent hurdle for parliamentary representation it was difficult to see exactly how it could build on that performance with a single-issue campaign based on the return of the deutschmark. There was thus a deliberate turn toward "cultural issues," such as immigration as well as gender and family politics in the search for votes. The messaging apparently worked, for in the 2014 European Parliament elections AfD voters mentioned immigration as much as a stable currency as having motivated their choice.[8] The question of whether the AfD was nativist from the beginning, as some researchers have argued, is not as important as the fact that it had become decidedly anti-immigrant *before* the onset of the European refugee crisis in the fall of 2015.[9]

Like with her defense of the common currency, Merkel's welcome of refugees was hardly unqualified.[10] Yet, with all the criticisms and caveats, Merkel's call on the refugee crisis amounted to one of the most significant defenses of the liberal international order within the last decade. It also made every single election since then a referendum on Merkel's refugee policy. One could have hardly imagined a more favorable opportunity structure for the AfD. As the victories piled up, any chances of it moderating its central message of "Islam is not part of Germany" and returning to its original economic message quickly evaporated.

Indeed, the AfD lurched even more unmistakably rightward through some of its leaders attacks on Holocaust memory. Speaking in Dresden in January 2017, Björn Höcke lamented how "German history is handled as rotten and made to look ridiculous" and that Germans had the "mentality of a totally vanquished people." He specifically disavowed President Richard von Weizsäcker's influential 1985 speech that, among other notable elements, designated 8 May 1945 as a "day of liberation" rather than one of defeat. According to Höcke, the president gave "a speech against his own people, and not for his own people." He further noted that Germans were "the only people in the world to plant a monument of shame in the heart of their capital." His conclusion was that "these stupid politics of coming to grips with the past cripples us–we need nothing other than a 180-degree reversal on the politics of remembrance."[11]

A Seven-Party System or Just Another Wave?

Is Germany now moving toward a seven-party system that includes the radical right? Although similar predictions based on the rise of the Republikaner following German unification and the asylum crisis of the early 1990s came to naught, this time might truly be different. In addition to being in the Bundestag, the AfD is now represented in fourteen of sixteen state parliaments. Thus, in contrast to the Republikaner party, which was unable to expand beyond its base in Baden-Württemberg and Bavaria, and to parties like NPD and DVU that have shown intermittent strength in the east, the AfD is a national phenomenon. That said, when any radical right party wins over 20 percent of the vote in any state election–as the AfD did in both Saxony-Anhalt in March 2016 (24.2 percent) and in Mecklenburg-West Pomerania (20.8 percent)–such concentrations of strength further suggest the party is unlikely to be a flash in the pan.

At the same time, the history of the postwar radical right in Germany suggests another possible outcome for the AfD. An apparently irreconcilable conflict between "moderates" (those who want to avoid xenophobia and potentially form coalitions with other political parties) and the extremists (those who adopt xenophobic appeals and want to remain in permanent opposition to the existing political system) has undercut every attempt to build a party to the right of the CDU/CSU. The policy of containment paradoxically helped ensure that the extremists were always the more powerful faction in postwar Germany, as moderates were both less likely to join and more likely to quit a party that was a political and social pariah. Radicalization, organizational breakdown, and institutional decay have been the hallmarks of every postwar German radical right political party to date.[12]

There are clear signs that the AfD is on this same trajectory. Even before the refugee crisis and the AfD's anti-immigrant turn, the extremists (they would no doubt prefer the term national populists) within the AfD had outmaneuvered the moderates like Lucke. Frauke Petry, a businesswoman with no previous political experience who learned of the AfD through a political flyer from her mother, played a key role in the AfD's first major split. Petry rose quickly to become one of the AfD's three co-chairs (along with Lucke and former Christian Democrat Alexander Gauland), and her apparent willingness to publicly embrace anti-immigrant positions when neither of the other party leaders would turned her into a favorite of the party's extremist faction.

At the AfD's congress on 4 July 2015, Petry challenged Lucke for the party leadership and won by a tally of 60 percent to 38 percent. "Barely suppressing tears, Mr. Lucke slammed his laptop shut and left the stage."[13] He left the party four days later, as did four of the seven AfD members of the European Parliament. Following a long tradition among ousted moderate leaders of radical right parties, Lucke then founded his own party: the Alliance for Progress and Renewal (ALFA). None of these radical right successor parties–such as Bruno Mégret's X (National Republican Movement) in France or even the far more successful BZÖ of Jörg Haider in Austria–have ever consolidated themselves, there is little reason to believe that ALFA will prove the exception. Indeed, to date ALFA has failed to win even 1 percent of the vote in the state elections it has contested.

Petry, by contrast, enjoyed a two-year run as Germany's "first lady of populism." During the height of the refugee crisis in January 2016, she claimed that police should "if necessary" shoot at migrants seeking to enter the country illegally. She appeared alongside Marine le Pen at rallies and press conferences. Yet Petry was not particularly adept at fending off challenges from her right flank. After Höcke's attack on Germany's institutionalized Holocaust memory, Petry called him a "burden for the party" and sought to expel him from the AfD. Apparently, she lacked the political muscle to do so, and Hocke remained. At this point, the extremist wing of the party had lost confidence in Petry, for she appeared to want to turn the AfD into a possible coalition partner for the established parties. Facing a potential revolt, Petry signaled she might step down as chancellor candidate in March 2017, and then did so at the Party Congress in April 2017.

The bitter infighting within the AfD obviously did not prevent it from entering the Bundestag. Yet only one day after the September 2017 election, Petry stunned everyone by announcing she was leaving the AfD and would retain her mandate in the Bundestag as an independent. She had apparently set the wheels in motion on 17 September (one week before the election) by beginning the process of founding a new political party. She then formally announced the formation of the Blue Party in December 2017, with the aim of drawing moderates to it. Whereas the AfD's official position is that there is "no place for Islam in Germany," the Blue Party only denounces "political Islam." At this point, it remains unclear whether such a slightly less virulent form of xenophobia will have any electoral appeal.

Petry's departure from the AfD left the position of co-chairman open, and the contest at the party congress on 4 December 2017 came down to a moderate, Georg Pazderski, and a representative of the extremist wing (X), who was put on the ballot to block Pazderski. When the extremist candidate easily beat the moderate (but without sufficient votes to win), Gauland emerged as compromise candidate. Since Gauland is perceived as closer to the extremist than to the moderate wing of the party, and since Hocke appears to be the central power figure in the AfD at the moment, any chance of the AfD moderating its defining features seems remote.

I can make one prediction with absolute confidence: the AfD will be treated as a political pariah and political coalition markets will remain closed to it. There will also be symbolic protests, such as when no political party would agree to be seated, literally, next to the AfD in the Bundestag. Leading politicians in the party will face the same social environment that Petry did, and that as a profile in *Der Spiegel* argues, took a heavy toll on her:

> Sometimes it seems as though Petry is paying too high a price for her political success. She has difficulties finding an apartment, her family van was set on fire last September, and her children are bullied in school. In advance of the meeting of European right-wing populists in January, she couldn't find a hotel to accept her reservation until one did, on the condition that she wouldn't enter through the lobby. She had to arrive through the subterranean garage, like a Colombian drug kingpin.[14]

A recent case of social protest reveals the remarkable commitment of the AfD's adversaries. Shortly after Höcke described the Berlin's Monument to the Murdered Jews of Europe as a "monument of shame," a group of artists arrived in his village and began scouting it discretely. They registered a business in order to get local license plates, and then used those plates to rent the property directly next to Höcke's house. Under the cover of a tent, the artists erected a to-scale replication of a piece of the Holocaust Memorial that was different in one crucial detail: the slabs were tilted 180 degrees.

Conclusion

Writing less than three years ago, one distinguished scholar noted that "the meteoric rise of the AfD and its ability to steer clear of Nazi connotations is a very unusual and significant development."[15] As this article has argued, however, it was also short-lived. The AfD radicalized within a short period of time, and in this sense its experience mirrors other political parties to the right of the CDU that have tried to preserve enough moderation to make them potential coalition partners in government. The AfD's embrace of anti-immigration and historical revisionism ensures that it will be treated like a pariah in the Bundestag. When leading figures in the party refer to Turks as "camel drivers" and "unpatriotic rabble" who should "return to their mud huts and polygamy," their vitriol helps legitimize the strategy of containment.[16]

But, will containment still work now that the AfD is in the Bundestag, heading up important parliamentary committees, and introducing legislation on immigration and national identity at a rapid clip? Will it be effective given that the AfD is now the largest opposition party in parliament and is running ahead of the SPD in some public opinion polls in early 2018? And if the AfD consolidates its recent gains in state parliaments and reproduces its 2017 performance in the next federal elections, is the end of Germany's exceptional resistance to nativist political forces nigh?

While I would still bet on the AfD collapsing in the short to medium turn, and while Merkel has vowed to get the party out of parliament, one can no longer rule out the less rosy scenario. The consequences for German and European politics would be so dramatic that I cannot even begin to lay them out here. So instead of prognosticating further, let me close with a historical counterfactual: imagine that the radical right in postwar Germany played a role equivalent to that in Austria, Italy, or even France. Would Merkel have had the freedom of maneuver to accept a million refugees or to agree to bail out the Eurozone? Moving further back in time, would eastern enlargement of the European Union have happened at all? Would Germany have ever agreed to a single currency? Readers of this journal might possess more creativity than me, but I cannot imagine any of these monumental foreign policy choices turning out similarly in a domestic politics setting where nativism is strong and well represented. Put another way, the weakness of the German radical right has made major steps in European integration possible. Time will tell if 2017 was the year that this formula was abandoned.

David Art is Professor of Political Science at Tufts University. His field is comparative politics, with a regional focus on Europe and research interests that include extremist political parties and movements, the politics of history and memory, and comparative historical analysis in the social sciences. He is the author of *Inside the Radical Right: The Development of Anti-Immigrant Parties in Western Europe* (New York, 2011) and *The Politics of the Nazi Past in Germany and Austria* (New York, 2006). His articles have appeared in *Comparative Politics, German Politics and Society, Party Politics, Political Science Quarterly*, and *West European Politics.* Art was Co-Convenor of the European Consortium for Political Research's (ECPR) Standing Group on Extremism and Democracy from 2006–2012. E-mail: david.art@tufts.edu

Notes

1. See David Art, "The Containment of the Radical Right in Europe," *Ethnic and Racial Studies* 38, no. 8 (2015): 1347–1354.
2. John Lewis Gaddis, *Strategies of Containment* (New York, 1982).
3. Sean Hanley, "The Czech Republicans 1990–1998: A populist radical right outsider in a consolidating democracy" in, *Populism in the Europe and the Americas: Threat or Corrective for Democracy?*, ed. Cas Mudde and Cristobal Rivera Kaltwasser (New York, 2012): 68–88.
4. See David Art, *Inside the Radical Right: The Development of Anti-Immigrant Parties in Western Europe* (New York, 2011).
5. See David Art, "The German Rescue of the Eurozone: How Germany is Getting the Europe it's Always Wanted," *Political Science Quarterly* 130, no. 2 (2015): 181–212.
6. Kai Arzheimer, "The AfD: Finally a Successful Right-Wing Populist Euroskeptic Party for Germany?" *West European Politics* 38, no. 3 (2015): 535–556, here 551.
7. Nicole Berbuir, Marcel Lewandowsky, and Jasmin Siri, "The AfD and its Sympathisers: Finally a Right-Wing Populist Movement in Germany?" *German Politics* 24, no. 2 (2015): 154–178, here 173.
8. Frank Decker, "The "Alternative for Germany": Factors Behind its Emergence and Profile of a New Right-wing Populist Party," *German Politics and Society* 34, no. 2 (2016): 1–16.
9. Rudiger Schmitt-Beck, "The 'Alternative fuer Deutschland' in the Electorate: Between Single Issue and Right-Wing Populist Party," *German Politics* 26, no. 1 (2017): 124–148.
10. Maximilian Conrad and Hugrún Aðalsteinsdóttir "Understanding Germany's 'Short-Lived' Culture of Welcome," *German Politics and Society* 35, no. 4 (Winter 2017): 1–21.
11. https://www.tagesspiegel.de/politik/hoecke-rede-im-wortlaut-gemuetszustand-eines-total-besiegten-volkes/19273518.html, accessed 1 May 2018.
12. See Art (see note 5), 190–208.
13. "A Bad Time to Break Up," *The Economist*, 11 July 2015.
14. Alexander Osang, "Frauke, ich habe Angst um dich," *Der Spiegel*, 9 April 2017.
15. Arzheimer (see note 7), 540.
16. These comments were attributed to Andre Poggenburg, the leader of the AfD in the state of Saxony-Anhalt. Poggenburg stepped down following a media firestorm over his remarks. *Reuters*. 8 March 2018.

··· Chapter 11 ···

Radical Right-Wing Populists in Parliament

Examining the Alternative for Germany in European Context

Lars Rensmann

Following the long-term rise and recent electoral boost of radical-right populist parties across Europe, the Alternative für Deutschland (Alternative for Germany, AfD) became the third strongest party in the 2017 general elections for the German Bundestag. This is remarkable for several reasons. First, the postwar political and electoral resurgence of radical right and right-wing populist parties in (Western) Europe started more than three decades ago, when the French Front National celebrated a breakthrough by achieving a whopping 11.2 percent of the vote in the 1984 European elections.[1] Yet, despite some local and regional electoral breakthroughs by radical right parties, in Germany, such parties never really came close to successfully mobilizing voters nationally. Thus, Germany is now, after all, no longer an exception to the new normal of successful–or at least politically relevant–radical-right, nationalist, and authoritarian populist parties within Europe's liberal democracies.

Second, for a long time many observers had seen the electoral success of a radical right-wing (populist) party in post Holocaust Germany–the historical home base of Nazi rule–as improbable due to the country's particular legacy. This legacy seemed to largely discredit and undermine any potential broader appeal of politically organized ethnic nationalism or actors promoting radical-right ideology. No matter if this *Sonderweg* (special path) claim was valid in the past or not, it no longer holds today. To the contrary, the very transgression of established discursive boundaries–including breaking with civil standards of political discourse, "bad manners,"[2] and taboo-breaking in relation to the legacy of the Nazi crimes–seems now to be an appeal-

Notes for this section begin on page 246.

ing force for mobilization in Germany like elsewhere in Europe rather than negatively affecting electoral performance.

Third, for decades Germany provided the prime European example of failing radical- right populist parties due to organizational problems, lack of professional competence, and infighting. These problems on the supply side of politics made even regional electoral successes short-lived. Despite the fact that the AfD also massively faces internal conflicts, doubts about competence, and constant reshuffling of personnel, such issues do not seem to have hitherto hurt the party at the ballot-box.[3]

Hence, things have changed. Founded just five years ago the AfD now represents, it is argued here, the first radical right-wing (populist) party in the German parliament since the Nazi era. This caesura potentially marks a critical juncture: the beginning of a new, centrifugal and polarized era in German electoral and parliamentary politics, and the transformation of Germany's postwar political culture at large. Against this backdrop, this contribution addresses three questions: What is the ideology of the AfD as a relevant opposition party in the Bundestag? What explains the AfD's dramatic electoral rise and support? And what is the party's behavior and impact in parliament, especially with regard to interparty interactions and Germany's political culture? In answering these research questions, I situate the AfD's political ideology, electoral success, and parliamentary politics in the comparative context of the recently accelerated European-wide ascent of–especially rightist, authoritarian-nativist–populist movement-parties. The main argument advanced is that the AfD–some German particularities notwithstanding–has turned into a typical or "normalized," radical(ized) right-wing populist movement-party that expresses and fosters profound sociocultural discontent, political polarization, and a broader authoritarian-nationalist, politico-cultural "noisy counterrevolution" in and beyond parliaments across Europe. The trans-European rise of authoritarian-nativist populist parties harshly critical of societal Europeanization is thereby also part of Europeanization processes of politics.[4]

The article proceeds in three steps. First, the significant programmatic evolution of the AfD and the respective transformation of a party leadership representing these changes are reconstructed, primarily on the basis of a diachronic comparative party manifesto analysis. Examining party and electoral platforms over four years from the party's founding to the 2017 electoral campaign, the article identifies significant programmatic shifts and authoritarian-nationalist radicalization processes shaping this young and new party. This analysis of the supply side is followed, second, by a brief analysis of electoral demand–the appeal of the AfD among voters in the

2017 election–in view of survey data, and favorable conditions that may explain the AfD's rise in a comparative European context. Third, a first analysis of initial sessions of the newly constituted Bundestag follows. It indicates significant transformations of parliamentary politics and political culture in general, in which the AfD as the largest opposition party in the national parliament takes an active role. It points to disruptive populist strategies, centrifugal polarization trends and parliamentary shifts which are, too, reflective of European political developments.

From a Euroskeptic to a European Radical Right-Wing Populist Party? The Political and Programmatic Evolution of the AfD on its Way to National Parliament

To grasp and explain the rise as well as the parliamentary and politico-cultural significance of the AfD in German and European context, it is important to understand its nature and position in the party spectrum, especially in terms of the party's programmatic outlook and its underlying ideological core. Defining the party and typologically situating it in a particular party family is not just a relevant scholarly endeavor as such. It is also a necessary condition to evaluate the potential scope of the changes in the party system, and in political culture at large, which the electoral success of a certain new party may indicate or foster. Recent party research has hereby paid particular attention to the supply side:[5] the active ideological and organizational role of parties as agents of public opinion formation and as intermediaries shaping their own political fate and their voter mobilization capacities.[6]

Most research on political parties looks at four criteria to classify and typologize parties: their programmatic profile and political ideology; historical origins; organizational structures and formation; and the structure of its electorate and members, i.e., the demand side.[7] From the perspective of party system research, the AfD can therefore be analyzed, understood, and classified in several ways. I suggest, however, that the ideological core to which a party is attached and that is expressed in shared programmatic goals, platforms, and public statements by party leaders, is still the single most important criterion to assess the character of a party.[8] It also provides the most meaningful way to place a party in a party family and party typology. This applies to the AfD as well, which–like other new parties before–claims to challenge established parties and ideological divisions. The key supply side variable overshadowing others is the ideological core and the evolving programmatic profile, which in the case of the AfD are closely aligned with organizational and leadership changes and with a strong effort to distance the party from its still young historical origins.[9]

With regard to the AfD, many scholars and publicists have hereby observed some continuities, but also a profound ideological and programmatic transformation of the party within the relatively short span of five years.[10] Yet the precise nature and conceptualization of this ideological shift, which I argue has major implications for classifying this party, deserves closer scrutiny. It points to a change from a conservative protest party initially driven by one single issue–opposition to the Eurozone–to an authoritarian-nativist, radical right-wing populist movement-party gradually further radicalizing. This transformation is also reflected in the dramatic turnover rate in the party's leadership and parallel changes of the party's organization. After briefly reconstructing its origins, organizational development, and programmatic evolution, the AfD's platform changes will be evaluated more specifically in order to assess the current political ideology and character of the biggest opposition party in the Bundestag.

The AfD's Origins, Organizational Development, and Programmatic Evolution

The AfD was initially founded in April 2013 as a self-identified "liberal-conservative" protest party primarily seeking to offer an alternative to policies of the center-right, governing catch-all party Christian Democratic Union (CDU) led by chairwoman and chancellor Angela Merkel.[11] As Frank Decker points out, new parties tend to either emerge from within society or after a split from an existing party. In the AfD's case, "many of its former and current leading figures used to call the center-right camp (CDU and FDP) their home, albeit failing to ever make it past its 'second row.'"[12]

The new party's primary focus, however, was a very specific issue: an economic critique of the common currency of the Euro and an ordoliberal protest of Germany's membership in the Eurozone. As Oskar Niedermayer has shown, even though the new party immediately received 4.7 percent in the 2013 general election (and came close to entering the Bundestag only five months after its official founding), the origins of this party can be traced back to 2010.[13] This is the year when the Merkel government decided to provide large-scale financial support to Greece in the context of the country's sovereign debt crisis as a "last option" to save the Eurozone and Greece's membership in it. In opposition to the often declared *Alternativlosigkeit* (lack of alternatives) toward this policy, economics professor Bernd Lucke initiated a so-called "plenary of economists" opposing Merkel's policies in support of the Euro–presumably purely based on economic arguments.[14] In response to the 2012 European Stability Mechanism (ESM), the group led by

Lucke subsequently formed the loose, nonpartisan alliance Bündnis Bürgerwille (Alliance Citizens' Will) and then the Wahlalternative 2013 (Electoral Alternative 2013) before founding the AfD as a party in the spring of 2013.[15] It could build on an existing elite network. Lucke was one of nominally three chairpersons, yet the best-known face of the party.[16]

Even though the "citizens' will" rhetoric sounded populist, the initial leadership by no means pretended to be anti-elite but they styled themselves as part of Germany's elite: as economic experts with alternative, superior knowledge. Moreover, Lucke and other AfD leaders offered a consistent "official" rejection of extremism and the populism label and presented themselves as a right-wing liberal force.[17] Yet, to be sure, the party assembled a heterogeneous group of citizens displaying popular discontent with government policies. From the beginning it thereby created openings to the nativist right.[18] Since its inception, the AfD was charged with being right-wing populist and promoting Deutsche-Mark nationalism due to its call to leave the Eurozone and reinstitute the D-Mark. Futhermore, as Torsten Oppelland points out, posters against welfare migration already displayed nativist outreach. The party slogan *Mut zur Wahrheit* (Courage to Tell the Truth) suggested in a populist fashion that the established democratic parties in parliament "would lie to the people."[19] From the beginning, the AfD has also displayed some organizational features of a movement-party that tries to distance itself from "traditional" party politics in practice and substance. In so doing, it has also been reaching out, albeit initially in a subtle way, to a growing, initially partly diffuse discontent with mainstream politics and policies–a discontent that finds expression in a new type of politically active, engaged and enraged segment of *Wutbürger* (angry citizens).[20] A year after its founding, the new party had a first series of electoral successes. It entered the European Parliament, winning 7.1 percent of the vote, and consecutively joined several regional Landtage, thus becoming a relevant parliamentary actor.[21] The rising political force soon no longer primarily focused on the Euro crisis. Meanwhile, following increasing success, the AfD attracted all kinds of new enraged citizens as members and voters.[22]

In light of this success and expansion, a conflict about the future political direction and programmatic orientation broke out at the beginning of 2015. This first inner-party crisis and subsequent infighting ultimately represented a first turning point in the party's development, leading to a split. At the national party assembly in July of that year, Frauke Petry, one of the three original chairpersons representing the nationalist wing of the party, turned into the AfD's new face. Until the end of 2017, she then served as speaker alongside economics professor Jörg Meuthen, until the end of 2017 also state chairman in Baden-Württemberg and now leading the party in the European Parliament.

Substantively, the conflict erupted over the party's relationship to the unfolding migration crisis, Islam and cultural identity–and in particular to the new East German anti-Muslim and nationalist protest movement PEGIDA (Patriotic Europeans Against the Islamization of the Occident). PEGIDA successfully mobilized thousands of East German citizens in street protest against refugees, immigrants, "Islamization," and an alleged *Lügenpresse* (lying press) supposedly manipulating and fabricating public opinion on these issues.[23] Petry and especially East German party leaders, like the radical right-wing state chairman of Thuringia, Björn Höcke, argued that it is important to address the political discontent of PEGIDA supporters and "civic protest movements" (as stated in the so-called Erfurt Resolution initiated by Höcke, which attacked the Lucke leadership for staying away from the protest movement and for conforming to "established political business").[24] By contrast, Lucke and his supporters had first criticized PEGIDA's unmitigated xenophobia and then, in their *Weckruf 2015* (Wake-up Call 2015), charged inner-party opponents with integrating radical forces forming an antisystem, nationalist "fundamental opposition."[25] Defeated in this conflict about leadership and direction, Lucke and his supporters subsequently left the party (and with them around 20 percent of party members). The defeat of the Lucke wing signaled a critical juncture and an interrelated, three-fold development: (1) a significant departure from the party's origins; (2) a replacement of the initial, dominant party leadership alongside an organizational change from an "economic expert party" to a movement-party against "the corrupt elite;" and, (3) a programmatic and ideological "right-wing nationalist turn" or "radicalization" of the party (to be further examined here).[26]

Following double-digit electoral performances in West and East German Länder elections in 2016 under Petry's leadership, the party experienced its second crisis in the prelude to the 2017 Bundestag election. Even though Petry had celebrated electoral successes and managed to build transnational cooperation with other rightist-populist parties in Europe, now it was Petry's turn to be challenged from a more radical nationalist right. To prevent a further extreme right drift, Petry–replicating the right-wing populist Front National leader Marine Le Pen acting against the most extreme actors in her party–intended to exclude the radical nationalist Höcke from the party. Speaking in front of the party youth organization Junge Alternative in January 2017, the latter had attacked the Holocaust memorial and called for a "180 degree change in national memorial policies."[27] Petry failed in this attempt, as Höcke experienced vast support from the rank and file and among other key leaders like Alexander Gauland and Meuthen. With her attempt to contain fundamental antisystem opposition, she was ultimately side-lined in the party and its 2017 general electoral campaign.[28]

This second party crisis thus represents another right-wing radicalization. Thomas Oppelland, to be sure, suggests that the two candidates for the 2017 federal election now co-leading the AfD's Bundestag delegation, Gauland and Alice Weidel, did not signal another right-wing turn. Oppelland argues that Weidel represents an "economically liberal and pragmatic" wing of the party.[29] Both politicians, however, are known for harsh and radical anti-immigrant statements, agitating fiercely against minorities, and promoting ethnic nationalism, as well as supporting keeping the radical rightist Höcke in the party.[30] As I analyze below, the leadership crisis, change, and radicalization had once again no demonstrable negative electoral repercussions for the AfD.[31]

Alongside the party leadership, goals, and programmatic orientation, the party organization has also been profoundly transformed since its founding. On the one hand, the party has become more organized, though leadership positions are still floating, behind-closed doors compromises dominate the decision-making, and there are questions about transparency and inner-party democracy. On the other hand, the party has also increasingly become a (radical right) movement-party.[32] This is expressed in strengthened outreach towards PEGIDA and other right-wing nationalist milieus, including the so-called "identitarian movement" of young radical nationalists and the nationalist monthly *Compact*.[33]

The AfD's Political Ideology on the Road to Parliament: Evaluating Campaign Platforms from 2013 to the 2017 Bundestag Election

As indicated, identifying the ideological core is the arguably most important task to define the character and nature of a political party. To empirically assess and conceptualize the ideological core does not only allow one to define the party and situate it in a particular party family.[34] This endeavor is also significant if one wants to evaluate its electoral success and political impact. As sociopolitical actors and intermediaries between state and society, however, parties and their ideology can evolve and transform over time. This is particularly relevant in the case of new parties entering political competition, which often still develop their political ideology and objectives. As we have seen, programmatic and ideological shifts, indicating that the party at large is still in flux, are strikingly evident in the AfD's first five years and on the road to their electoral success in the 2017 Bundestag election. The initial single-issue, partly euroskeptic outlook and the earlier fragile "fusion of economically liberal and socially conservative/nationalist positions" were soon challenged.[35]

Examining party and electoral platforms over four years from the party's founding to the 2017 electoral campaign, this sections identifies the specific shifts towards a comprehensive rightist-nativist radicalization, as initially diagnosed by Decker in 2016.[36] The systematic comparison between the early 2013 electoral platform for the Bundestag election and the slightly broader 2014 platform for the European elections, on the one hand, and, on the other hand, the 2017 platform for the Bundestag election confirms a specific, partly drastic shift of programmatic objectives. This indicates a profound change in the ideological core, i.e., the political ideology that keeps the party together.[37]

The early platforms are clearly dominated by one issue: Euro policies and the Eurozone monetary union.[38] The topic of the sovereign debt crisis and Germany's financial transfers to Greece and investments in the Eurozone, to be sure, were also the prevailing subjects of German political debates in the early 2010s and thus of broad popular concern.

The 2013 electoral platform consists hereby of only four pages. It laments the "failure of the Treaty of Maastricht" and declares three main objectives: First and foremost, Germany should leave the Eurozone, which de facto implies that the common currency should be abandoned altogether.[39] Second, the AfD asks to give up any European financial debt and "reliability community." And third, more diffusely, the AfD demands an institutional shift of governing and decision-making competences from the European level back to the level of the nation state.[40] It remains unclear what this was supposed to specifically entail but the AfD "decidedly rejects a transfer union or even a centralized European state."[41] The early AfD, however, accepts the "shared cultural heritage of Europe" and supports a common European market: "We support a Europe of sovereign states with a common market. We want to live together in friendship and as good neighbors."[42] While the Eurozone is viewed as an external threat to Germany's stability and welfare, the early AfD does not oppose European integration in principle.

Other topics are mentioned but marginal in the short 2013 program. Among the other issues, the "rule of law and democracy" takes the most prominent spot. The party "unconditionally" supports the rule of law and "strengthened democratic civil rights." It supports debating "unconventional opinions" as long as they are not in violation of the constitution.[43] Fiscal and budget policies, secure pensions, family, education, and energy policies are also briefly addressed.[44] "Integration policy," referring to immigrants and immigration, is limited to a short final section. It claims that "Germany needs qualified immigrants interested in integrating into society," and advocates for an "immigration law according to the Canadian model."[45] Traces of right-wing populism or anti-immigrant rhetoric can be detected because the AfD opposes "disorderly immigration into our welfare system," while the platform insists that "those who are really politically persecuted should find asylum in Germany. Treating humans with dignity also means that asylum-seekers can work here."[46] Despite the emphasis on the sovereign nation state, neither explicit ethnic nationalism (i.e., giving priority to ethnic nationals, anti-immigrant rhetoric), nor authoritarianism (i.e., supporting unchecked political authority and opposition to constitutional liberal democracy), nor populism (i.e. dividing society into "the good people" and "the corrupt elite") are ideological features of the program.[47] In other words, the key ideological elements of radical right-wing populism are absent.[48]

Entering party politics as a "single-issue" movement,[49] Robert Grimm argues that the initial AfD should be classified as a "partially Eurosceptic party" pursuing an ordoliberal policy critique of the common currency that is ultimately "anti-Euro" but "pro-European."[50] If interpreting the AfD as "pro-European" may be pushing it, the analysis of the platform points to what Paul Taggart and Aleks Szczerbiak classify as a qualified, "soft Euroskepticism" focused on particular institutional aspects and policy areas of the EU (as opposed to "hard Euroskepticism" fully rejecting European integration, as expressed by parties like UKIP).[51]

The subsequent platform for the 2014 European elections is a considerably expanded document. While its dominant topic remains the same, the platform now reaches out to anti-immigrant views by calling for stricter immigration rules because of "an overtaxing of the welfare budget and the erosion of the welfare state."[52] Until then, the AfD had avoided to attack the rights of immigrants, asylum-seekers, and religious minorities.[53] The anti-immigrant rhetoric also took prominence in platforms for East and West German Länder elections and began to overshadow the Eurozone issue.

The electoral platform for the 2017 Bundestag election, then, reads drastically different from the first party platform. Sixty-eight pages long, it is divided into fifteen chapters and thus also substantially longer than previous ones. The AfD thereby no longer presents itself as a single-issue party. While unspecific in most policy areas, it provides sufficient material to analyze the current political core ideology of the AfD.[54] In 2017, the core ideological elements of European radical right-wing populist parties, such as the French Front National, the Dutch PVV or the Italian Lega, feature prominently, that is: xenophobic, ethnic nationalism or nativism combined with hardened anti-immigrant (and antirefugee) rhetoric against "the others" (a horizontal dichotomy); political authoritarianism combined with an illiberal opposition to individual rights entitlements; and populism, which can be understood with Cas Mudde and Cristobal Rovira Kaltwasser as a "thin-centered ideology" that claims to express the *volonté generale* of the "silent majority," thereby promoting a culturally biased, antipluralistic idea of "the good people" allegedly oppressed by a "corrupt elite" (a vertical dichotomy).[55]

In so far as a single issue dominates most other policy domains, it is now migration. The 2017 platform is, first of all, a program of an anti-immigrant, nativist, and ethnic-nationalist party. Several sections of the platform start with, or are overshadowed by, the migration issue. From chapter 1 onwards, the party attacks the allegedly "illegal" refugee policies of the government.[56] Chapter 4 discusses domestic security, and begins with a call for enforcing "expulsion, deportation and expatriation."[57] Among other things, the platform claims that "the majority of organized crime is committed by foreigners."[58] Immigrants and refugees hereby appear mostly as "criminal foreigners." The following chapter 5 focuses exclusively on migration, asylum, and national borders. The AfD demands that our "borders must be closed immediately" for there to be "no more immigration into the welfare systems."[59] The party insists that "every immigrant has to adapt to the new home country, not the other way around."[60] The horizontal dichotomy between "us" (the Germans) and "them" (the others, who allegedly do not belong) is thereby a constitutive feature of the platform, while it is in part unclear who classifies as "foreign" or "immigrant" and who exactly "they" are.

Rejecting the very idea of an immigrant society, the AfD calls for a full ethnic-nationalist return to the German *ius sanguinis,* the *Abstammungsprinzip*—the "ancestry" or "blood" principle for acquiring citizenship, which dates back to 1913 but was adjusted in the 2000 immigration reform.[61] Ethnonationalist codes and innuendo can be detected throughout the platform, in statements such as: "We want our descendants to inherit a country still recognizable as our Germany."[62] Chapter 6 focuses exclusively on "Islam in conflict with our free and democratic constitutional order."[63] This is one of the few sections where we find unambiguously positive references to the existing system of liberal democracy, namely in contrast "with Islam:" "In the spread of Islam and the presence of over 5 million Muslims, the AfD sees a great danger to our state, our society and our value order."[64] Chapter 8 addresses education policy, yet a key focus is once again on consequences of "mass immigration," while the AfD suggest that there should be "no more special privileges for Muslims at our schools."[65] Chapter 9 deals with German culture and identity and the media. The section strongly advocates against "multiculturalism," while chapter 11, dedicated to welfare policy, (wrongly) identifies immigrants as a major cause for welfare state regress in Germany.[66] Finally, even the subject of animal protection, addressed in chapter 15, is exclusively directed against religious minorities. It is limited to a call for a (with some exceptions already existing) ban on *Schächten*, i.e., animal slaughtering according to Jewish or Islamic rites, rather than addressing actual problems such as factory farming.[67] Such programmatic statements are supplemented with provocations against cultural diversity and immigration by the AfD on social media or by party leaders like deputy chairman Gauland, who said about the black German national football team star player Jérôme Boateng that he may be appreciated for his performance on the field but people would "not want someone like Boateng as a neighbor."[68]

Second, the 2017 AfD platform features political authoritarianism. The AfD hereby combines nativist nostalgia and anti-immigrant views with a law and order rhetoric and the presumed need to "restore" the protection of the country.[69] The AfD advocates a "cluster of defensive and restrictive measures to prevent the further destruction of European values governing the community of enlightened citizens" in response to an allegedly "already existing cultural struggle between the Occident and Islam as a doctrine of salvation and bearer of cultural traditions."[70] The AfD's political vision seems to point to a socially cohesive, illiberal order, exhibiting an antipluralistic understanding of society strictly controlled by authorities. It features arch-conservative elements, such as antifeminist rhetoric against "gender research" coupled with the opposition to several social value liberalizations, and calls for returning to a "classical" family structure.[71] Add to this programmatic statements before and after the election expressing great admiration for the Putin regime, for which no other electorate expresses stronger sympathy than AfD voters, while the AfD's youth organization Young Alternative is in official partnership with the youth organization of Putin's United Russia.[72] The praised Russian political system under Putin epitomizes the combination of ethnic nationalism and illiberal authoritarianism while strongly opposing pluralism, freedom of speech, and human, civil, or LGBTQ+ rights. Similarly, AfD leaders admire the authoritarian populist (and ethnonationalist) regime of Viktor Orbán in Hungary. Prominent AfD politician Beatrix von Storch celebrated Orbán's electoral success in 2018 as "a bad day for the EU, a good one for Europe."[73]

Third, the platform employs populism throughout, understood as a "thin-centered ideology" operating with a vertical dichotomy between the "people" cheated by "the corrupt elite." The latter term is not used explicitly in the program. Yet, generalizing negative statements about the political elite are ubiquitous, such as: "today's politicians exploit the state."[74] Politicians are contrasted to "the people," which "has to become sovereign again,"[75] assuming that it has lost its sovereignty vis-à-vis the "elite" and "others." The will of the people and "people's sovereignty" are supposed to be restored, alongside the "restoration" of a "lawful state."[76] In this spirit, the AfD also advocates constitutional reform along populist lines, such as more direct democracy and referenda according to the "Swiss model."[77] Meanwhile, Euroskepticism remains present but it no longer forms a central part of the platform, and the critique of the Eurozone is limited to four pages–though the policy proposal to reinstitute the D-Mark remains consistent.

In sum, the AfD's electoral platform for the 2017 general election shows the core ideological features of xenophobic nationalism, authoritarianism, and populism that overshadow specific issues or policies, and which are typical for European radical right-wing populist parties. This distinct ideological profile is also anchored in transnational collaborations, embodied in the "Europe of Nations and Freedom" in the European Parliament and beyond. There are, as is common among radical-right and nationalist parties, some specific national ideologemes. In the case of the AfD, this includes the nationalist downplaying of the Holocaust and German atrocities. Deputy leader Gauland claims: "If the French are rightly proud of their emperor and the Britons of Nelson and Churchill, we have the right to be proud of the achievements of the German soldiers in two world wars."[78]

While the AfD increasingly represents radical right views, promotes radical-right state-level chairmen like Höcke and has even recruited former neo-Nazis now working for the party,[79] the party's 2017 platform also defends civil liberties and constitutional democracy. It, thus, cannot be classified as radical or extreme right without qualifications. Nevertheless, our comparative and diachronic platform analysis, in addition to public statements by a changing leadership regime and the party's social media feed, confirms and extends Decker's radicalization thesis to the 2017 Bundestag electoral campaign and beyond: the AfD has transformed from a largely single issue protest party against the Euro, which sought to challenge existing left-right distinctions and could have replaced the FDP in the party system if it had reinforced its moderate-centrist wing, to a typical European radical right-wing populist party displaying an increasingly open flank to the extreme right. Arzheimer's earlier analysis, according to which the AfD has no nativist objectives and is thus not right-wing populist, is by now obsolete.[80]

Political Opportunity Structures, Electoral Appeal, and the 2017 Bundestag Vote in European Context: What Drives the Success of the AfD?

Given the history of "centripetal" German democratic party competition, at least on the national level open-ended radicalization processes tended to be punished at the ballot box. This effect even survived the fragmentation and pluralization of the party system since unification. So why was the AfD eventually catapulted into German national parliament as the biggest opposition party–even though it suffered from massive intra-party conflicts and increasingly radicalized?

In search for an explanation of the AfD's popularity and road to German national parliament, it needs to be remembered that an array of old and new, refashioned radical right or right-wing populist parties already had entered state (Länder) parliaments since the 1980s–in most cases, to be sure, only to dramatically lose electoral support in subsequent elections. In West Germany there were first the Republikaner in Berlin and Baden-Württemberg in the 1980s and 1990s, then the Schill Partei "PRO," which scored an impressive 19.4 percent in Hamburg in 2001; while in post-unification East Germany different, more extreme right parties, the Deutsche Volksunion (German People's Union, DVU) and the neo-Nazi party Nationaldemokratische Partei Deutschland (National Democratic Party of Germany, NPD), celebrated electoral successes that carried them into various state legislatures from 1998 onwards.[81] Thus, radical right successes have been fluctuating–in particular due to disorganized actors, in-fighting, and a lack of effective electoral mobilization and consolidation. But, electoral demand for these parties has been more and more frequently mirrored in turnout since the late 1980s, and especially since German unification. This points to a long-underestimated pool of potential radical-right voters in Germany who have time and again been successfully mobilized on the level of state elections. Such a pool has already for years resonated in more consistent electoral performances in other European countries, including neighboring Austria, Switzerland, Belgium, France, Poland, and the Netherlands. Both in diachronic national and in comparative European perspective, the national success of a German radical-right populist party therefore does not come out of nowhere. Rather, the AfD's breakthrough seems to at least temporarily overcome a long-term disequilibrium between demand and (effective) supply on the level of national elections and parliamentary representation. In so doing, it also indicates a German "normalization" catching up with a broad and lasting European trend.[82]

Social research and survey data point to a set of four explanatory factors engendering the rise of radical right-wing populist parties like the AfD–and of the AfD as a radicalized right-populist party acting in fundamental opposition.[83] Insights into voting behavior and attitudes can hereby be linked to transformed politico-cultural opportunity structures and other causes benefitting the AfD. They point, on the one hand, to a long lingering potential on the electoral demand side for deep-seated discontent with contemporary postethnic liberal democracy, including its dominant norms, procedures, and policy-making. On the other hand, they mark a rapidly changing German political landscape, party competition, and political/discursive culture–changes largely in sync with European-wide developments–according to which radicalizations are no longer negatively sanctioned by voters but may reinforce electoral success.

First, support for the AfD can be viewed in context of a far-reaching, "noisy" authoritarian-nativist counterrevolution directed against "liberal," postmaterial social value change and present-day liberal democracy, a sensed loss of national or cultural identity, and the postethnic cosmopolitanization that has transformed Germany into a pluralistic immigrant society.[84] Core voters of the AfD frustrated by mainstream parties accuse the allegedly "corrupt elite" of advancing these processes. Mirroring a transnational trend, AfD supporters put on display long lingering, deep-seated sociocultural conflicts–or a hardened major cleavage–over social values and cultural identity among German and European voters, framed in binary opposition between the "pure people" vs. "the elite/immigrants."

A majority of AfD voters show strongly nationalist, anti-immigrant and culturally exclusionary attitudes–if not radical-right worldviews–previously not translated into respective electoral turnout. Strikingly, although 55 percent of AfD voters think that the party does not sufficiently distance itself from extreme right positions, according to Infratest Dimap exit polls at the 2017 Bundestag election only 14 percent of AfD voters want Germany to be *weltoffen*, that is: tolerant, cosmopolitan and open-minded country–in opposition to the majority of voters of all other parliamentary parties.[85] In a 2016 representative phone survey of 1,004 respondents conducted by the University of Hamburg, a majority of AfD sympathizers (59 percent) claim that "Jewish influence is big," as opposed to 16 percent of sympathizers of other relevant parties supporting this claim. Meanwhile, 36 percent of AfD voters long for a "leader [*Führer*] who governs Germany with a strong hand" (in opposition to 7 percent of supporters of the other parties), and 40 percent of AfD supporters believe that Nazism "also had good sides," in contrast to 6 percent of supporters of other parties.[86] Anti-immigration is hereby the overwhelming issue mobilizing AfD voters. For 92 percent of AfD voters in the 2017 general election the party "primarily serves the purpose to change Germany's refugee policies," and 96 percent support that the party "wants to more strongly restrict the immigration of refugees."[87]

These data point to a persistent, yet previously not politically represented authoritarian-nationalist potential in society that is now mobilized in a politico-cultural revolt against liberal democracy, globalization, immigrants, and "the elite." This revolt constitutes the core of the AfD, as it does for similar parties elsewhere in Europe.[88] The core constituency, which forms the party base, also drives the party's radicalization. A German and postcommunist particularity consists of a significant East-West divide: although the AfD is far from being just an eastern German phenomenon, here it is now the second strongest party with a 21.9 percent share of the general vote (western Germany: 10.7 percent). With 27.0 percent, it is the strongest party in Saxony–ahead of the governing CDU (in a small village like Dorfchemnitz, the party received up to 47.4 percent).[89] This drastic difference points to an ongoing East-West divide among voters and in the party system. In particular, this suggests that there are unmastered authoritarian politico-cultural legacies among segments of the East German electorate who are not at ease with Western, liberal-democratic immigrant society.[90]

Second, the authoritarian cultural revolt is arguably aggravated by structural economic grievances, and relative or subjective social deprivation. While AfD support mostly cuts across social strata and other demographic divisions like age, there is a noticeable gender gap–in 2017, 16 percent of male and 9 percent of female voters opted for the AfD–in addition to relevant social class and educational variables. Only 7 percent of voters holding a university degree voted for the party, as opposed 14-17 percent with the lowest educational degrees.[91] According to Infratest Dimap, 21 percent of workers and 21 percent of the unemployed support the party at the ballot-box (in the latter group, the AfD is the second strongest party, only 2 percent behind the Social Democrats).[92] Recruited from both mainstream parties and the group of nonvoters, these results may point to factors of socioeconomic, material insecurity affecting lower and lower middle classes in German society and reinforcing politico-cultural discontent. The former is caused by massive, politically produced welfare state regress since the 1990s, stagnating wages, the "precarization" of labor, and overall rapidly growing economic class divisions. For many citizens, the visible transfer of wealth from the poor to the well-to-do and the lack of accessible prosperity accelerates a sense of socioeconomic frustration–of being left behind and cheated. "The cheated masses are dimly aware," argue Max Horkheimer and Theodor Adorno, that liberal society's promise of universal justice and equality "remains a lie as long as classes exist."[93] Material insecurity, relative social deprivation, and economic grievances tend to reinforce existing projections, stereotypes, and reified ideologies in society. Widespread popular resentments may target "the elite," "the immigrants," or "the Jews" also as the personified "causes" of what is experienced as an aggravated social malaise. The reified blame for negatively experienced socioeconomic and cultural change against which authoritarian-nativist populists mobilize, and which they identify with "the elite" and "the others," has arguably been reinforced by catch-all parties' actual long-term socioeconomic policy shifts. In particular center-left, social democratic parties have electorally suffered from endorsing neoliberal welfare state regress that eroded socioeconomic security in society (and benefitted the economic elite) while promoting more inclusive socio-cultural values and immigration policies. In Germany, this shift is epitomized by the Schröder government (1998-2005), which implemented neoliberal "Hartz IV" reforms alongside overdue immigration reform. The space hereby created points to an emerging new "winning formula" for right-wing populists: combining cultural discontent and previously largely unrepresented authoritarian-nationalist social values with the objective of restoring welfare policies for "the (ethnic) people" largely abandoned by centrist catch-all parties.

This emerging winning formula has been, third, facilitated and emboldened by drastic transformations of the patterns and conditions of the public sphere in an age of social media. The growth of fake news, "uncivil" and "postfactual" discourses through social media in Germany, Europe and around the globe have polarized public perceptions and attitudes in recent years, whereby public debate is more and more shaped by what David Roberts calls "tribal epistemology:" information is evaluated based not on common standards of evidence but on whether it supports one's (political) tribe's values and goals. Public resentments against minorities have hereby also become increasingly "normalized," and the boundaries of socially accepted public and political discourse, of "what can be said," have eroded.[94] Challenging civil standards and rules of political discourse as well as aggressively displaying "bad manners," populists have both fueled, and flourished in, self-immunized, radically polarized communicative environments. Breaking rules and taboos has been part of the populists' attraction. In the German context, this entails the popular wish to break alleged "taboos" in relation to Holocaust memory and the legacy of the Nazi crimes. Radical views and provocations are thus no longer necessarily disadvantageous but often viewed as "courageous" and can work in populists' favor in a rapidly transforming political culture–changes which were fertilized by long existing politico-cultural milieus and media of the "New Right."[95] Rather than diminishing the AfD's appeal, the party's ongoing radicalization has thereby been reinforced by initial electoral successes through which the party became attractive for a large pool of authoritarian-nativist members and voters.

Fourth, the increased demand for and success of the AfD can be partly attributed to specific political developments, including actual party crises and policy failures. In addition to deliberate welfare state regress and failed policies creating a profound housing crisis, Germany has been largely unprepared to meet the heightened, dramatically politicized migration challenge of 2015. Established parties largely failed to find coherent responses tackling problems and societal conflicts, creating a political opening for an anti-immigrant party. Political opportunity structures have hereby been generally more favorable for new parties challenging existing parties. The gradually progressing erosion of party attachment and identification among increasingly volatile parts of European electorates has also helped the AfD's successful electoral mobilization, which benefits from the fact that a majority of its sympathizers feel frustrated with established parties.[96]

European Right-Wing Populists in Parliament: The AfD as a Radical Parliamentary Opposition Party

Against this backdrop of ideological changes and factors that have helped generate support for a radicalized AfD, we can better measure the party representatives' behavior in parliament and analyze its causes. This allows us, in turn, to better understand the AfD's strategic objectives in parliament and, in particular, the party's impact on German parliamentary politics and political culture at large–in national as well as comparative transnational perspective.

As indicated, German radical-right parties which had been elected into state legislatures often collapsed in subsequent elections. They were punished by voters for infighting, scandals, and political amateurism in office.[97] In the European context, several radical-right parties joined the German parties' fate. But, many European counterparts could also hold on to, and have recently been able to expand, their parliamentary representation–despite or because of strong ideological views, often paired with a lack of specific policy competences. Over the years, several successful right-wing populist parties have even joined democratic governments as junior partners (e.g. the FPÖ in Austria or the Lega Nord in Italy), or govern by themselves (e.g., FIDESZ in Hungary or PiS in Poland).

The initially widely shared prediction that institutional mechanisms would exert control and constraint over authoritarian-nationalist populist parties has seen at best mixed support. There has been a dominant expectation among scholars and commentators that these parties would either be "tamed" in their policy positions, or simply fail when challenged to engage in developing serious parliamentary work and specific policy alternatives beyond ideological iterations or populist rhetoric–which would in either case weaken these parties' political impact and future electoral appeal. This effect has been expected to especially apply when these parties govern and thus have to actively participate in the complexities of policy-making, as this is likely to alienate disillusioned voters attracted by simple or authoritarian solutions unattainable under conditions of liberal democracy. Findings on the political impact of these parties' parliamentary representation on government policies, party systems, and public discourse, however, yield mixed results. European rightist populist parties' electoral fortunes following years in public office also vary widely. Some governing parties could consolidate successes while upholding radical ideological positions and having significant direct or indirect effects on policy regimes and public debates, especially on immigration.[98]

In the case of the AfD, based on an analysis of motions and speeches in the first year in the Bundestag, we can detect initial indicators for assessing the party's strategic orientation and performance as parliamentary actors, as well as its impact on policy-making, parliamentary debate, and political culture. Following three years of parliamentary presence on the regional/state level across the republic and in the European Parliament, the first year of the AfD as an opposition party in the newly constituted Bundestag indicates firstly that the AfD tries to partly portray itself as a "normal" parliamentary force. Yet, while it is advancing many motions and proposed bills, the party actually shows little interest in active committee work, the policy-making process, or parliamentary debate on specific issues over optimal policy solutions.[99] Neither are there any signs that the diagnosed ideological radicalization towards a distinctly right-wing populist, European anti-immigrant and nativist movement-party is tamed in parliament–even though many proposals seem, superficially, close to mainstream positions and sometimes address "real or apparent common ground with other parties' positions, to make their proposals look conventional."[100] Virtually all of the AfD MPs' contributions center around the limited repertoire of four campaign topics–anti-establishment rhetoric, Muslims and refugees (often framed as "Islamic invasion"), cultural/national identity, and Euroskepticism–whereby there seems to be little interest in direct, active policy-making.[101]

In fact, secondly, the AfD seems primarily interested in utilizing the national parliament as stage for continuous campaigning, antagonistic and aggressive rhetoric directed against immigrants and those not considered "real Germans." Respective speeches often employ fake facts and "alternative" news fitting the ideological outlook. Remaining in a constant, disruptive protest mode, the party shows contempt for "the establishment," "the political elite," and other elected representatives by which the AfD is allegedly victimized. Disrupting regular parliamentary politics and procedures seems both strategy and goal, as the AfD appears to enjoy its role as "pariah party."[102]

In so doing, thirdly, debates in parliament indicate that the AfD extends the process of political polarization to parliamentary politics. With its radical provocations, the AfD affects, so it seems, the dynamics of inter-party politics and political communication patterns in the Bundestag as a whole.[103] There is a noticeable impact on the interaction among parties (including a drastically increased intensity of ad hominem attacks, verbal aggressions, and screaming). Challenging the very rules and procedures of parliamentary democracy, the party advances thereby both the erosion of civil discourse, i.e., of the boundaries of "what can be said" in parliament, and anti-parliamentarism, i.e., opposition to and contempt for the institution as a central tenet of liberal democracy. This fits to the AfD's increasingly fundamental opposition and advocacy for radical societal change.

Anna Sauerbrey suggests that the AfD generally follows a "triple strategy" of pretending to be a normal conservative party proposing bills in parliament, provoking controversy, and "self-victimization."[104] In order to act as a serious parliamentary force, AfD representatives want to be seen as working in relevant committees and introduce or co-sponsor many bills in which they at times employ positions previously adopted by the governing CDU or other parties. All of their proposals fail to pass. Yet, the goal is not getting them passed but proposing legislation, says the AfD's parliamentary coordinator Bernd Baumann, "so that everybody knows what we stand for, to put our ideas on the top of Germany's political agenda."[105] Moreover, even within this "normality" or "normalization" strategy, which seeks to make the AfD appear as a respectable actor, the party betrays its xenophobic, nationalistic, and authoritarian core. Proposed bills often evoke notions such as "German soil" or "dominant foreign cultures."[106] The "normalization" strategy is generally accompanied and often overshadowed by the interlinked strategies of provocation and self-victimization: the AfD makes xenophobic/nationalist, authoritarian or populist statements radically challenging civil societal norms and, once criticized, portrays itself as the victim of "political correctness," subjected to "opinion dictatorship" and infringement upon free speech.

In addition to what Sauerbrey suggests, these strategies–advancing a radical right-wing, fundamentalist opposition and crying foul when being criticized for it–do not only take place outside of the parliament but also very much within its walls.[107] For instance, MP Nicole Höchst recently used the parliamentary stage to lament the "systematic discrimination of men," the "so-called religion" Islam, and the alleged creation of an "Islamicized federal state Germany in a centrally governed Islamic Europe."[108] Another significant example is the parliamentary debate on the German-Turkish journalist Deniz Yücel, initiated by the AfD. Yücel, who works for the conservative daily *Die Welt,* had just been released from a Turkish prison after being arrested by the Erdogan regime for one year without specific charges when the AfD's parliamentary delegation head Weidel, still often portrayed as "moderate," claimed on Twitter: "If the media report today that the 'German journalist' Yücel was released, this is two fake news in one sentence." Weidel explains that for her Yücel is neither German nor a journalist, and that this "'journalist' who hates our country...should not have German citizenship."[109] The statement reveals both an autocratic, illiberal understanding of government ready to deprive citizenship from journalists with whom one disagrees, and apparently a notion of citizenship restricting it to those who are marked as ethnic Germans. Subsequently, the AfD used the parliament to propose a motion urging the German government to publicly condemn and express disapproval of Yücel's prior work, arguing he was "anti-German."[110] In the heated parliamentary debate that ensued, senior Green Party MP Cem Özdemir called the AfD's proposal an attack on press freedom which also demonstrates that some "members of parliament are racist." The AfD measure was voted down by a large majority of parliamentarians.[111]

Recent public addresses by parliamentary representatives and AfD leaders confirm the previously diagnosed radicalization process towards fundamentalist, nativist, and authoritarian opposition since the party entered national parliament. These speeches also support the hypothesis that the party primarily seeks to promote an antagonistic system opposition against current liberal democracy, and thereby changes inter-party interactions in parliament by means of constant polarization. Targeting its competitors in parliament to advance the party's ideology and using parliament as a stage to provoke leaves little space for actual policy debate. At a regional party assembly in Braunschweig, for instance, the AfD's federal co-chairman

Meuthen, like Weidel long perceived as part of the party's more "moderate" wing and initially critical of antisemitism within the AfD, harshly attacked competing parties. Employing classical ethnonationalistic and antisemitic tropes reminiscent of what Victor Klemperer called *Lingua Tertii Imperii*, Meuthen accused the Green Party of being "crypto-communist decomposers of the fatherland." Meuthen defamed all parliamentary parties apart from the AfD collectively as a "filthy left-red-green-black-yellow party cartel abolishing Germany." Calling the AfD "the last evolutionary chance to preserve our homeland," Meuthen's opposition no longer seems to exclude revolutionary options, as *Die Welt* comments.[112]

The strategies the AfD has so far employed in parliament–the ideological fundamentalist opposition the AfD displays alongside provocations and self-victimization and the less consistent strategic attempt to appear as a "normal" right-wing conservative actor engaging in parliamentary work, submitting proposals, and participating in committees–are largely reflective of other right-wing populist parties in the national and European context.[113] In this sense, too, the AfD appears now as a "normalized," Europeanized right-wing populist party that acts similar to, and has apparently learned from, parliamentary actors like the PVV in the Netherlands or the Front National in France. They also primarily use parliaments as a stage for agenda-setting, protest, provocation and self-vicitimization, and ideological purity rather than constructive involvement in legislative processes. Defying expectations to become more moderate, the AfD–following many European counterparts–has in many ways accelerated its provocations and strategic polarization since it entered parliament–with no noticeable negative effect in terms of popularity or electability, as the AfD continues to do well in polls while stirring controversies.[114]

The direct legislative impact of the AfD is so far negligible. Yet its effects on the way parties communicate and discuss policy may be considerably more significant. The indirect impact on policy-making may also be relevant–as expressed in hardened positions on immigration, integration, and national identity today especially pushed by the CSU and parts of the CDU, and more generally in relation to the conditions of fact-based policy-making. Like elsewhere in Europe, there is a potentially transformative impact on the politico-cultural environment in which politics and public debate operate. The AfD's constant polarizations and attempts to provoke, challenge, and tear down civil discursive boundaries in the most important political institution of a parliamentary democracy are likely to have long-term effects on democratic political culture in Germany. These effects, to be sure, are yet to be systematically researched and tested again in future studies.

The Alternative for Germany in the Bundestag: A Partially European(ized) Phenomenon

The analyses of the party's ideological profile, electoral mobilization and voters, and strategies in parliament have demonstrated that the AfD has become the first radical right-wing (populist) party in the German parliament since the Nazi era. For that reason alone, the 2017 elections and nineteenth Bundestag stand out, potentially signifying a new era in Europe that has now also arrived in Germany with full force. The examination of electoral platforms since its founding shows that the AfD has transformed from a single issue, anti-Euro party to a typical radical right-wing populist party elected into parliaments across Europe–with an identifiable hardened ideological core of xenophobic nationalism, authoritarianism, and populism. In the process, views presented in platforms and by leaders, even formerly more moderate ones, radicalized and gained votes by doing so. While Gideon Botsch rightly argues that the AfD is not yet programmatically an antisystem extreme right party,[115] it can be classified as a radical right populist party that displays an increasing openness to overt extreme right and racist views, tropes and agitation. It already points, in the words of Hajo Funke, to "a republic far removed from the standards of rule of law and liberal democracy."[116]

Although the AfD retains some specific German features in its political ideology, the party expresses and aggressively advances a deep-seated transnational "noisy counterrevolution" that is currently shaking up party systems, parliaments, and political cultures in Europe. The party primarily articulates a revolt directed against social value change, sociocultural diversity and immigration, "the elite," and "the others." In this regard as well the AfD in the Bundestag can be understood as a (partially) European(ized) politico-cultural phenomenon. The party is influenced by transnational models, predecessors, and new crossnational political dynamics in which it now takes part. This entails building trans-European party alliances and ties to illiberal regimes in Russia and Hungary. The trans-European rise of new authoritarian-nativist populist parties like the AfD, which display hard Euroskepticism, is thereby also part of the Europeanization (and globalization) processes of politics taking shape within national political arenas.[117] Considering that in many European countries such parties have for years consolidated their success, parliamentary presence, and space in party systems, this represents a "German normalization" of sorts: authoritarian-nativist voters in Germany and in other European societies feel now better democratically represented, although the parties themselves work at destabilizing liberal democracy and its constitutional order.[118]

This "normalization," however, is also part of a European process of normalizing resentment against "the elite" and "the others"–immigrants, refugees, Muslims, Jews–in public discourse, whereby such "uncivil" norm transgressions have gained traction and social acceptability with unforeseen consequences for democratic political cultures. In fact, such transgressions help explain part of radical right-wing populist parties' appeal. Consequently, these parties seem less concerned with appearing sufficiently moderate in order not to limit their electoral appeal, as often in the past. Rather, they tend to deliberately provoke and often radically break with dominant societal norms, values, and the allegedly manufactured "opinion dictatorship" in European liberal democracies.

While mobilizing different fractions of discontent, AfD voters and members largely support the party's programmatic turn. The radicalization of the party and the seemingly "taboo-breaking" authoritarian transgressions of dominant civil norms by the party leadership show no negative effects on party support (even though more than half of its supporters wish that the party distances itself from the extreme right). This is also in sync with European trends. Data from surveys and voting patterns suggest that in a recently transformed political-communicative environment such polarizing political behavior is rewarded by a considerable share of voters–rather than diminishing a party's appeal. Initial electoral success and illiberal, right-wing political radicalization seem in fact, intertwined and mutually reinforcing factors of the AfD's political development into a radical right populist movement-party in parliament; electoral breakthrough attracted a large group of formerly unrepresented members as well as disillusioned (non)voters to the party, which changed accordingly.

The AfD is thereby both a national actor advancing, and a symptom of, a European-wide and Europeanized centrifugal trend among voters and parties. First and foremost, this trend points to deep-seated conflicts over social values, democracy, and cultural identity among European voters, publicly expressed in a changed environment of political communication. In particular, these conflicts are engendered by widespread discontent among volatile parts of the European electorates longing for a politico-cultural counterrevolution and representing a persistent, yet previously not politically articulated authoritarian-nativist potential in society. Boosted by transnationally proliferating fake news, tribal epistemologies, and the erosion of discursive boundaries on social media across Europe, parties like the AfD benefit from new political opportunities in increasingly destabilized, fragmented, and polarized European party systems. These parties also point to actual transnational European policy crises and failures that have eroded trust in parties and institutions, ranging from increased levels of economic insecurity or terrorism to the partly mismanaged migration challenge. Across Europe, the failures and policy shifts of catch-all parties have added to more favorable conditions for right-wing populists. The combination of policy failures by established or mainstream parties, including deliberate welfare state regress, and a hitherto unrepresented but significant anti-cosmopolitan, antiliberal cultural counter-revolution points to a newly emerging winning formula for these populists: linking culturally exclusive, authoritarian-nationalist social values to the goal of restoring the old (ethnic) welfare state policies largely abandoned by center-left social democratic parties. There are, to be sure, some specific German conditions contributing to the AfD's strength. For instance, support for the AfD is overall considerably stronger in the eastern German regions. This indicates the continuous relevance of postcommunist, authoritarian legacies and the persistence of an East-West politico-cultural divide also mirrored in the party system and likewise reflected in Eastern Europe.

Rather than being tamed through institutional integration and parliamentary cooperation, the initial analysis presented here indicates that the AfD acts primarily as a radical right, fundamental opposition party in parliament that defies expectations of conventional party behavior. It was shown that the AfD follows the strategic paths of other European radical right parties holding public office. They use parliaments foremost as a stage for anti-establishment protest, continuous campaigning in line with ideological purity, proposing authoritarian measures, and hostile rhetoric against "the elite," immigrants, or those not considered "real citizens." Primarily, the AfD utilizes the parliament to communicate their ideology and protest, giving its supporters, who are frustrated with established parties, the sense that their voice is being heard.

AfD MPs hereby often employ postfactual claims. They also seem to envision a society markedly different from today's, based on a socially cohesive and illiberal order. Even though the AfD at times tries to behave as a "normal" parliamentary party proposing bills and following procedures, it shows little interest in legislative processes and policy-making debates seeking to resolve complex policy problems. Instead, the party's MPs frequently display contempt for or bully other parliamentarians, the parliament as a democratic institution, and Germany's constitutional liberal democracy. Portraying itself as a victim while using verbal aggressions against others, the party's antagonistic stance and strategy thereby further foster the accelerated process of politico-cultural polarization: they extend it to the parliamentary stage. Considering that at least in the short term the AfD's ideological self-immunization from facts and policy-making does not seem to undermine the support among its voters, the AfD, like similar populist actors in parliaments across Europe, is unlikely to be tamed by parliamentary institutional mechanisms in the future.

In comparative perspective and for competing democratic parties, this raises the question what institutional or politico-cultural responses would be effective to counter the right-wing populist winning formula, presence, and strategies in parliament. Although further research on impact and effects is needed, the party's programmatic evolution towards European radical right-wing populism and the electoral support of the AfD's radicalization make it likely, however, that the party continues to take part in transforming German politics and debate, in and beyond the Bundestag, and German political culture at large.

Lars Rensmann, PhD, is Professor of European Politics and Society at the University of Groningen, the Netherlands, where he also serves as the Chair of the Department of European Languages and Cultures and leads the Chair Group European Politics and Society at the Centre of International Relations Research (CIRR). Previously, he served as the Chair of the Department of Political Science and International Affairs at John Cabot University in Rome, Italy and as Assistant Professor of Political Science at the University of Michigan at Ann Arbor. Recent publications include *Rage and Revolt: Authoritarian Populism and Illiberal Democracy in Our Time* (forthcoming); *The Politics of Unreason: The Frankfurt School and the Origins of Modern Antisemitism* (Albany, 2017). Email: l.p.rensmann@rug.nl

Notes

1. Until then, only the postfascist Movimento Sociale Italiano had a steady presence in West European party systems. The radical right had been thoroughly discredited and electorally successful in the aftermath of Nazi and fascist regimes and the political terror with which they reigned in Europe. See Lars Rensman, "The New Politics of Prejudice: Comparative Perspectives on Extreme Right Parties in European Democracies," *German Politics & Society* 21, no.4 (2003): 93–123.
2. Benjamin Moffitt and Simon Tormey isolate the display of "bad manners" as one of three constitutive, shared features of populist politics, alongside the appeal to "the people" and a crisis/threat discourse. See Benjamin Moffitt and Simon Tormey, "Rethinking Populism: Politics, Mediatisation and Political Style," *Political Studies,* 62, no.2 (2014): 381–397, here 392–393.
3. See Frank Decker, "The 'Alternative for Germany': Factors behind its Emergence and Profile of a New Right-Wing Populist Party," *German Politics and Society* 34, no.2 (2016): 1–15. A consistent majority of AfD shows little trust in the party's problem-solving competences; see for instance Dietmar Neuerer, "AfD-Wähler halten ihre eigene Partei für inkompetent," *Handelsblatt,* 22 November 2016; available at http://www.handelsblatt.

com/politik/deutschland/umfrage-zur-afd-in-ost-laendern-studie-afd-anhaenger-gehen-bei-rechtsruck-ihrer-partei-mit/14876894-2.html, accessed 5 August 2018.

4. Lars Rensmann, "The Noisy Counter-Revolution: Understanding the Cultural Conditions and Dynamics of Populist Politics in Europe in the Digital Age," *Politics and Governance* 5, no. 4 (2017): 123–135. On the European comparative study of radical right-wing, authoritarian populist parties as a transnational phenomenon see below and, among others, Cas Mudde, *Populist Radical Right Parties* (Cambridge, 2007); Sarah de Lange, "New Alliances: Why Mainstream Parties Govern with Radical Right-Wing Populist Parties," *Political Studies* 60, no.4 (2012): 899–918.
5. On this, see especially Cas Mudde, *The Ideology of the Extreme Right* (Manchester, 2003) and Mudde (see note 4).
6. See David Art, *Inside the Radical Right: The Development of Anti-Immigrant Parties in Western Europe* (Cambridge, 2011); Linda Bos and Wouter van der Brug, "Public Images of Leaders of Anti-immigration Parties: Perceptions of Legitimacy and Effectiveness," *Party Politics* 16, no. 6 (2010): 777–799.
7. A fifth criterion, emphasized by Paul Lucardie and by Frank Decker, looks at a party's goals and functions in the political system. It is less commonly accepted. Insofar as this presumed criterion points to generic goals such as seeking public office or mobilizing votes, which tend to apply to all parties and thus hardly serve as distinguishing criteria; insofar as this criterion refers to the party's relationship to the political system (e.g., anti-system opposition to constitutional democracy), it is part of any analysis and typology of the ideological core (e.g., centrist, moderate, radical, extreme/system opposition). On party typologies see Paul Lucardie, "Zur Typologie der politischen Parteien" in *Handbuch der politischen Parteien*, ed. Frank Decker and Viola Neu (Bonn, 2013), 61–76; Angelo Panebianco, *Political Parties. Organization and Power* (Cambridge, 1988); Richard S. Katz and Peter Mair, "Changing Models of Party Organization and Party Democracy. The Emergence of the Cartel Party," *Party Politics* 1, no. 1 (1995), 5–28; Frank Decker, "Politische Parteien: Begriff und Typologien," *Bundeszentrale für politische Bildung (bpb)*, 7 November 2014; available at http://www.bpb.de/politik/grundfragen/parteien-in-deutschland/42045/begriff-und-typologien, accessed 5 August 2018.
8. Parties, as social organizations and political intermediaries, are not static entities but subject to change. Especially new parties often transform considerably and redefine their goals and ideology in their formation years and early years of existence.
9. For excellent first overviews see Thomas Oppelland, "Alternative für Deutschland (AfD)," Bundeszentrale für politische Bildung, ed., *Dossier Parteien in Deutschland* (Bonn, 2018), 115–125; Decker (see note 3); Florian Hartleb, *Die Stunde der Populisten* (Schwalbach, 2017); and in European comparative context, Kai Hirschmann, *Der Aufstieg des Nationalpopulismus: Wie westliche Gesellschaften polarisiert werden* (Bonn, 2017), 137–145.
10. See David Bebnowski, *Die Alternative fur Deutschland. Aufstieg und gesellschaftliche Reprasentanz einer rechten populistischen Partei* (Wiesbaden, 2015); Justus Bender, *Was will die AfD? Eine Partei verandert Deutschland* (Muunich, 2017); Alexander Häusler and Rainer Roeser, "Die 'Alternative für Deutschland': eine Antwort auf die rechtspopulistische Lücke?" in *Strategien der extremen Rechten: Hintergründe–Analysen–Antworten*, ed., Stephan Braun, Alexander Geisler, Martin Gerster (Wiesbaden, 2015). Alexander Häusler, *Die Alternative für Deutschland. Programmatik, Entwicklung und politische Verortung* (Wiesbaden, 2016).
11. See Kai Arzheimer, "The AfD: Finally a Successful Right-wing Populist Eurosceptic party for Germany?" *West European Politics*, 38, no.3 (2015): 535–556.
12. Decker (see note 3), 3.
13. Oskar Niedermayer, "Die Wahlerschaft der AfD. Wer ist sie, woher kommt sie und wie weit rechts steht sie?" *Zeitschrift fur Parlamentsfragen* 47, no.2 (2016): 267–284, here 177. See also Oppelland (see note 9), 115.
14. Oppelland (see note 9), 116.
15. Decker (see note 3), 2.
16. Oppelland (see note 10), 116; Decker (see note 3), 3.

17. Decker (see note 3), 13.
18. Christoph Kopke and Alexander Lorenz show that the AfD can be seen as the CDU/CSU's right-wing split-off. However, some parts of the AfD were from the beginning recruited from the so-called New Right (part of the milieu of Alexander Gauland, who is one of the few AfD leaders who were with the party from the beginning and represents continuity) or extreme right fringe parties such as the Bund freier Bürger (BFB). See Christoph Kopke and Alexander Lorenz, "Zwischen konservativem Nationalpopulismus und fundamentaloppositioneller Bewegung: Das aktuelle Profil der AfD in Brandenburg" in *AfD und FPÖ: Antisemitismus, völkischer Nationalismus und Geschlechterbilder*, ed. Stephan Grigat (Baden-Baden, 2017), 79–100, here 80–81.
19. Oppelland (see note 9), 116.
20. Karl-Rudolf Korte, Claus Leggewie, and Marcel Lewandowsky, "Partei am Scheideweg: Die Alternative der AfD," *Blätter für deutsche und internationale Politik* 60, no.6 (2015): 59–67; Alexander Häusler and Rainer Roeser: *Die rechten 'Mut'-Bürger: Entstehung, Entwicklung, Personal & Positionen der "Alternative für Deutschland"* (Hamburg, 2015).
21. Decker (see note 3), 2.
22. Oppelland (see note 9), 116.
23. The *Lügenpresse* (lying press) claim, defaming "the media" and suggesting a media conspiracy, is an antisemitic trope. Even though PEGIDA uses some coded language, culturalist discourse, and speaks of Europeans rather than ethnic German nationalism, neo-Nazis and the organized extreme right are present at these marches. The PEGIDA leadership makes little effort to distance itself from these political forces, and racist hate speech is common during PEGIDA demonstrations. Höcke participated in and supports these marches and ties to PEGIDA. On PEGIDA as a radical right, nativist xenophobic movement see Hajo Funke, *Von Wutburgern und Brandstiftern. AfD, Pegida, Gewaltnetze* (Berlin, 2016). On the history and legacy of the *Abendland* (occident) discourse in Germany since Oswald Spengler and the "Conservative Revolution" of the 1920s, see Volker Weiß, *Die autoritäre Revolte: Die Neue Rechte und der Untergang des Abendlandes* (Stuttgart, 2017), 155–186.
24. The most extreme right wing of the party openly calls for an ethnic nationalist party orientation and a coalition with PEGIDA. See "Erfurt Resolution;" available at http://derfluegel.de/erfurterresolution.pdf, accessed 20 March 2016. On the "Erfurt Resolution" see also Oppelland (see note 9),117; and Marc Grimm and Bodo Kahmann, "AfD und Judenbild: Eine Partie im Spannungsfeld von Antisemitismus, Schuldabwehr und instrumenteller Israelsolidarität" in Grigat, (see note 18) 41-59, here 43–45.
25. Grundungsaufruf "Weckruf 2015;" available at http://www.weckruf2015.de/gruendungsaufruf, accessed 12 July 2016. Members of the "wake-up call" overwhelmingly supported the establishment of a new euroskeptic party under Lucke's leadership; see Decker (see note 3), 9; see also Oppelland (see note 9), 117.
26. The "radicalization of the AfD" in 2015 was first analyzed by Decker (see note 3), 14; see also Oppelland (see note 9), 118.
27. Quoted in Reiner Burger, "Immer mit der Waffenruhe," *Frankfurter Allgemeine Zeitung*, 27 February 2017, 4.
28. Petry and her supporters left the party after the general election, just as Lucke and his supporters did two years before.
29. Oppelland (see note 9), 119.
30. While Gauland has long been known for radical, "taboo-breaking" claims transgressing the boundaries of civil discourse in Germany (which has not diminished his appeal among the AfD electorate and the party's rank and file), Weidel is not liberal or pragmatic either. Among many other things, Weidel is known for harsh anti-immigrant statements and led the AfD's ethnic-nationalist attacks on the German-Turkish journalist Deniz Yücel.
31. The AfD's partly chaotic organization and leadership, which is reflective of many other and previous radical right parties in Germany and Europe, is also crystallized in the fight over an affiliated party foundation/think tank (in Germany, it is common for every

elected party to have such an institution). The Desiderius Erasmus Foundation was the first and primary candidate, but the conservative intellectual Konrad Adam lasted only four months as chairman before he was voted out of office. Three other organizations and different chairmen compete for the status as the AfD's affiliate foundation now. See Markus Wehner, Eckart Lohse and Justus Bender, "AfD plant parteinahe Gustav-Stresemann-Stiftung," *Frankfurter Allgemeine Zeitung,* 19 December 2017.

32. See Kopke and Lorenz (see note 18), p. 94.
33. Since 2015, regional and national ties have evolved to the monthly run by Jürgen Elsässer, which asked its readers to vote for the AfD and is currently the most relevant publication in the German-speaking world promoting and publishing reactionary ideas, including anti-Americanism, nationalism, conspiracy myths, sexism, and racism, as well as unbridled enthusiasm for the Putin regime. See Kopke and Lorenz (see note 18), 81.
34. See Mudde (see note 5).
35. Decker (see note 3), 2.
36. Decker (see note 3), 14. The significant programmatic and ideological evolution of the AfD, reflected in the respective transformation of the party leadership representing is reconstructed primarily on the basis of a diachronic comparative party manifesto analysis. Key statements by party leaders are also taken into account as relevant forms of political expression signifying, if uncontested, the ideological profile of a party, especially in times of changing forms of political communication.
37. For previous analyses of platform developments before the election see also Joel Rosenfelder, "Die Programmatik der AfD: Inwiefern hat sie sich von einer primär euroskeptischen zu einer rechtspopulistischen Partei entwickelt?" *Zeitschrift für Parlamentsfragen* 48, no.1 (2017): 123–140.
38. AfD Wahlprogramm Bundestagswahl 2013, Parteitagsbeschluss, 14 April 2013.
39. AfD Wahlprogramm Bundestagswahl 2013, 1: "We offer an alternative to the government's policies and demand an ordered dissolution of the Euro currency zone. Reinstituting the D-Mark must not be a taboo."
40. Niedermayer (see note 13), 191. See also Marcel Lewandowsky, "Rechtspopulismus in Deutschland. Eine empirische Einordnung der Parteien zur Bundestagswahl 2013," *Politische Vierteljahresschrift,* 57, no.2 (2016): 1–36.
41. AfD Wahlprogramm Bundestagswahl 2013, 1.
42. Ibid.
43. Ibid., 2.
44. Ibid., 3-4.
45. Ibid., 4.
46. Ibid. Hence, any clear programmatic right-wing populist or radical right direction is missing here.
47. On these features see Mudde (see note 4); Lars Rensmann (see note 4), 124–126.
48. For an instructive analysis of the 2013 program, see Charly Castelein, *Die Alternative für Deutschland: Heute noch eine euroskeptische Partei?* BA Thesis, University of Groningen, 2017.
49. Robert Grimm, "The Rise of the German Euroskeptic Party Alternative für Deutschland: Between Ordoliberal Critique and Popular Anxiety," *International Political Science Review* 36, no. 3 (2015): 264–278, here 272.
50. Ibid., 266.
51. Paul Taggart and Aleks Szczerbiak, *Opposing Europe? The Comparative Party Politics of Euroscepticism* (Oxford, 2008), 7. Following Pieper et al. and their more differentiated categorizations, it can be argued that a utilitarian (soft) Euroskepticism prevailed in the AfD of 2013. Morten Pieper, Stefan Haußner and Michael Kaeding, "Die Vermessung des Euroskeptizismus der Alternative für Deutschland (AfD) im Frühjahr 2014" in *Die Europawahl 2014,* ed. Michael Kaeding and Niko Switek (Wiesbaden, 2015), 149–160, here 152.
52. AfD Programm Europawahl 2014, 15.
53. See Niedermayer (see note 13), 195.

54. AfD Wahlprogramm Bundestagswahl 2017, "Programm für die Wahl zum deutschen Bundestag am 24. September 2017. Leitantrag der Bundesprogrammkommission zum Bundesparteitag am 22./23.04.2017 in Köln;" available at https://www.alternativefuer.de/leitantrag-wahlprogramm/, accessed 5 August 2018.
55. On these conceptualizations see Rensmann (see note 4), 124–126. On populism, see Cas Mudde and Cristóbal Rovira Kaltwasser, *Populism: A Very Short Introduction* (Oxford, 2017),1–20. Under Petry's leadership, the AfD also fostered a European-wide cooperation with these other farright or radical-right populist parties in early 2017. Radical-right populist parties have recently also reinforced their crossnational organizational and political ties in the European Parliament and beyond. The political group "Europe of Nations and Freedom" in the EP, launched in 2015, prominently includes the AfD, Geert Wilders' single-member party Partij voor de Vrijheit (PVV) from the Netherlands, the Front National (FN) from France, the Lega Nord from Italy and the Austrian Freedom Party (FPÖ) and Vlaams Belang (VB) from Belgium. Several of these actors also expressed support for U.S. President Donald Trump whose success they explicitly see as a model. See Simon Shuster, "Europe's far right leaders unite at dawn of the Trump era," *Time*; available at, http://time.com/4643051/donald-trump-european-union-koblenz/, accessed 5 April 2018].
56. AfD Wahlprogramm Bundestagswahl 2017 (see note 54),7.
57. Ibid., 21.
58. Ibid., 22.
59. Ibid., 26.
60. Ibid., 29.
61. Ibid., 29.
62. Ibid., 25. The Lega Nord, one of the AfD's partners in the political group "Europe of Nations and Freedom" in the EP, is more explicit in its racist, ethnonationalist claims. For instance, Attilo Fontana, the Lega's elected president of the Lombardy region, recently said: "We need to decide whether or not our ethnic group, our white race, our society should continue to exist or be wiped out." Quoted in Roger Cohen, "Risotto from Sri Lanka is Just as Good," *The New York Times,* 6 April 2018,; available at https://www.nytimes.com/2018/04/06/opinion/italy-immigration.html, accessed 6 April 2018.
63. AfD Wahlprogramm Bundestagswahl 2017 (see note 54), 30.
64. Ibid., 31. The selective defense of liberalism, civil rights, and also women's rights in relation to Muslim immigration contradicts the AfD's otherwise ambiguous relationship to liberalism and civil rights. Against gender equality and gay rights, the AfD posits the "classical family" as "role model" and an "institution supportive of the state" because "only the family can produce the state's people as a carrier of sovereignty." (40) This "selective liberalism" as part of an "existential cultural struggle" follows the model of Geert Wilders' one-man party PVV, which on the one hand views Islam as a threat to Dutch liberalism and liberties, and on the other hand nostalgically promotes a return to the Netherlands of 1850. See Koen Vossen, *The Power of Populism: Geert Wilders and the Party for Freedom in the Netherlands* (London, 2016); and Chris Klomp, "Pechtold: Minder aandacht besteden aan circusklanten zoals Baudet," *Algemeen Dagblad,* 30 December 2017; available at https://www.ad.nl/binnenland/pechtold-minder-aandacht-besteden-aan-circusklanten-zoals-baudet~a3e17f99/, accessed 12 April 2018.
65. AfD Wahlprogramm Bundestagswahl 2017 (see note 54), 39.
66. Ibid., 49.
67. Ibid., 66. Some empirical animal research even suggests that *Schächtung* is a more humane way of animal slaughtering but the AfD platform does not discuss such factual findings.
68. See "AfD provokes anger with racist comments about German national team player," *Deutsche Welle,* 29 May 2016; available at http://www.dw.com/en/afd-provokes-anger-with-racist-comments-about-german-national-team-player-boateng/a-19291393, accessed 2 April 2018.
69. AfD Wahlprogramm Bundestagswahl 2017 (see note 54), 25.
70. Ibid., 42.

71. Ibid., 35. On the AfD's antifeminist gender politics, see Juliane Lang, "Feindbild Feminismus: Familien- und Geschlechterpolitik in der AfD" in Grigat (See note 18), 61–78.
72. Melanie Amann and Pavel Lokshin, "German Populists Forge Ties with Russia," *Der Spiegel*, 27 April 2016; available at http://www.spiegel.de/international/germany/german-populists-forge-deeper-ties-with-russia-a-1089562.html, accessed 7 April 2018. 81percent of AfD supporters, more than supporters of any other party represented in the German parliament, support a political rapprochement towards Russia. See Cornelia Karin Hendrich, "Mehrheit der Deutschen wünscht sich politische Annäherung an Russland," *Die Welt*, 17 March 2018 available at https://www.welt.de/politik/ausland/article174648662/WELT-Trend-Mehrheit-der-Deutschen-wuenscht-politische-Annaeherung-an-Russland.html, accessed 5 April 2018.
73. "Orban siegt bei Wahl in Ungarn," *Frankfurter Allgemeine Zeitung*, 9 April 2018; available at http://www.faz.net/agenturmeldungen/dpa/orban-siegt-bei-wahl-in-ungarn-15533097.html, accessed 10 April 2018.
74. AfD Wahlprogramm Bundestagswahl 2017 (see note 54), 8.
75. Ibid., 7.
76. Ibid., 7.
77. Ibid., 9.
78. "AfD co-founder says Germans should be proud of its second world war soldiers," *The Guardian*, 14 September 2017; available at https://www.theguardian.com/world/2017/sep/14/afd-co-founder-alexander-gauland-says-germany-needs-to-reclaim-its-history, accessed 5 April 2018.
79. "Ehemaliger Rechtsextremer," *Frankfurter Allgemeine Zeitung*, 10 April 2018, 5.
80. See Arzheimer (see note 11), 546.
81. Only in 1967, fifty years ago in the old Bundesrepublik, the NPD gained 4.3 percent and once came close to entering the national parliament but felt short of doing so thanks to the exceptionally high 5 percent threshold in German electoral law designed to do exactly that: keep extremist parties out of the Bundestag.
82. On the previous disequilibrium in the German party system, see Lars Rensmann, "Volatile Counter-Cosmopolitans: Understanding the Electoral Performance of Radical Right Parties in Eastern Germany and Poland," *German Politics and Society* 30, no.2 (2012): 64–102.
83. Hereby we assume with Rooduijn, van der Brug and de Lange that populist discontent is both cause and consequence of the rise of populist parties, which are also agents fueling discontent by exposing their supporters to populist messages. Electoral demand should not be viewed as the explanatory causal mechanism but rather as part of an interactive dynamic between demand, supply, and politico-cultural opportunity structures in relation to party competition and political communication. See Matthijs Rooduijn, Wouter van der Brug, and Sarah L. de Lange, "Expressing or fueling discontent? The relationship between populist voting and political discontent," *Electoral Studies* 43, no.3 (2016), 32–40.
84. Lars Rensmann, "The Reluctant Cosmopolitanization of European Party Politics: The Case of Germany," *German Politics and Society* 32, no.2 (2014): 59–85.
85. See Sebastian Dalkowski, "Der typische AfD-Wäler: Arbeiter, männlich, ostdeutsch," *Rheinische Post Online*, 26 September 2017; available at http://www.rp-online.de/politik/deutschland/bundestagswahl/wer-waehlt-afd-umfragen-geben-hinweise-auf-den-typischen-afd-waehler-aid-1.7104621, accessed 30 March 2018.
86. Quoted in Dietmar Neuerer, "Viele AfD-Wähler sehen Nazi-Zeit positiv," *Handelsblatt*, 24 November 2016; available at http://www.handelsblatt.com/politik/deutschland/umfrage-unter-hamburger-waehlern-viele-afd-waehler-sehen-nazi-zeit-positiv/14888776-all.html, accessed 5 April 2018.
87. See http://wahl.tagesschau.de/wahlen/2017-09-24-BT-DE/umfrage-afd.shtml, accessed 5 August 2018.
88. Ronald Inglehart and Pippa Norris, "Trump and the Populist Authoritarian Parties: The *Silent Revolution* in Reverse," *Perspectives on Politics* 15, no. 2 (2017): 443–454.

89. Franz Rohleder and Florian Naumann, "Bundestagswahl 2017," *Merkur,* 21 November 2017; available at https://www.merkur.de/politik/bundestagswahl-2017-endergebnis-und-ergebnisse-aus-allen-bundeslaendern-zr-7408963.html, accessed 22 November 2017.
90. See Lars Rensmann, "Mind the Gap: Explaining Unified Germany's Divided Party System," *European View* 8, no. 2 (2009): 271–283.
91. Matthias Kolb, "Sechs Grafiken, die den Erfolg der AfD erklären,“ *Süddeutsche Zeitung,* 25 September 2017; available at http://www.sueddeutsche.de/politik/afd-bei-bundestagswahl-sechs-grafiken-die-den-erfolg-der-afd-erklaeren-1.3681714, accessed 26 September 2017.
92. See note 87.
93. Max Horkheimer and Theodor W. Adorno, *Dialectic of Enlightenment: Philosophical Fragments* (Stanford, 2002), 141.
94. David Roberts, "Donald Trump and the Rise of Tribal Epistemology," *Vox,* 19 May 2017; available at https://www.vox.com/policy-and-politics/2017/3/22/14762030/donald-trump-tribal-epistemology, accessed 16 August 2018; Lars Rensmann, *Demokratie und Judenbild* (Wiesbaden, 2004), 78.
95. See Roger Woods, *Germany's New Right as Culture and Politics* (Basingstoke, 2007); Samuel Salzborn, *Angriff der Antidemokraten: die völkische Rebellion der Neuen Rechten* (Weinheim, 2017).
96. See Nicole Berbuir, Marcel Lewandowsky and Jasmin Siri, "The AfD and its Sympathisers: Finally a Right-Wing Populist Movement in Germany?" *German Politics,* 24, no.2 (2015): 154–178.
97. See Rensmann (see note 82), 88–92.
98. On the impact of populist parties in government see Daniele Albertazzi and Duncan MacDonnell, *Populists in Power* (London, 2015).
99. For a first in-depth analysis of the AfD's parliamentary performance on the level of state legislatures see Benno Hafeneger, Hannah Jestädt, Lisa-Marie Klose and Philine Lewek, eds., *AfD in Parlamenten: Themen, Strategien, Akteure* (Schwalbach/Taunus, 2018).
100. Anna Sauerbrey, "Populists in your Parliament," *The New York Times: International Edition,* 15 March 2018, 10.
101. To be sure, the AfD pressures the government on its signature issues, most importantly "national identity" and calls to restrict migration, to which especially the Christian Social Union (CSU) seems to be responsive.
102. Joost van Spanje, *Controlling the Electoral Marketplace: How Established Parties Ward Off Competition* (Basingstoke, 2017), 37–66.
103. As Gauland programmatically declares: "if you want to have war in parliament, you can have war."
104. Sauerbrey (see note 100).
105. Quoted in ibid.
106. Quoted in ibid.
107. Ibid.
108. "AfD-Frau Höchst hält wirre Rede im Bundestag,“ *Huffington Post,* 1 March 2018; available at https://www.huffingtonpost.de/entry/afd-frau-hochst-halt-wirre-rede-gegen-die-gleichberechtigung_de_5a97b0d7e4b09c872bb1406e, accessed 1 March 2018.
109. Alice Weidel, Twitter, 17 February, 2018; available at https://twitter.com/alice_weidel/status/964818818878107648?lang=en, accessed 10 April 2018.
110. Quoted in Guy Chazan, "AfD turns up the heat in Germany's Bundestag," *Financial Times,* 3 April 2018; available at https://www.ft.com/content/5a9d5fc0-2d17-11e8-9b4b-bc4b9f08f381, accessed 3 April 2018.
111. Quoted in "Germany: Pot, abortion and Deniz Yücel top marathon debate day in Bundestag," *Deutsche Welle,* 22 February 2018; available at http://www.dw.com/en/germany-pot-abortion-and-deniz-yücel-top-marathon-debate-day-in-bundestag/a-42704715, accessed 10 April 2018.
112. Quoted in Matthias Kamann, "Die undurchschaubare Agedna der neuen AfD-Chefin," *Die Welt,* 8 April 2018; available at https://www.welt.de/politik/deutschland/article

175271196/Dana-Guth-Undurchschaubare-Agenda-von-Niedersachsens-AfD-Chefin. html, accessed 8 April 2018. Along these lines of extreme right rhetoric, a political Ash Wednesdat (*Politischer Aschermittwoch*) speech by André Poggenburg, who served as state chairman of Saxony-Anhalt since 2016, defamed Turkish-German citizens as "camel drivers" who should "go off to where they belong; far, far away beyond the Bosporus to their mud huts and polygamy." The racist speech evoked nation-wide public criticism, but Poggenburg received only mild warnings and a limited formal censure from the AfD's national party headquarters, although he was subsequently forced to resign as chair of the twenty-two- member AfD party group in the Landtag following inner-party power quarrels. Quoted in "German Turks plan to sue far-right AfD for 'camel driver' slur," *Reuters,* 15 February 2018' available at https://www.reuters.com/article/us-germany-afd/german-turks-plan-to-sue-far-right-afd-for-camel-driver-slur-idUSKCN1FZ2GH, accessed 15 February 2018.

113. See Simon Otjes and Tom Louwerse, "Populists in Parliament: Comparing Left-Wing and Right-Wing Populism in the Netherlands," *Political Studies* 63, no.1 (2015): 60–79.
114. Recent surveys since the AfD entered parliament see the party gaining support and at over 15 percent; See https://www.wahlrecht.de/umfragen/, accessed 13 May, 2018.
115. Gideon Botsch, *Wahre Demokratie und Volksgemeinschaft. Ideologie und Programmatik der NPD und ihres rechtsextremen Umfelds* (Wiesbaden, 2016), 75.
116. See Funke (see note 23), 73. The party is thus less ideologically "thin-centered" and less flexible on issues than Alexander Hausler observed two years ago. See Alexander Hausler, "Die AfD–eine rechtspopulistische "Bewegungspartei?" in *Neue soziale Bewegung von rechts? Zukunftsangste, Abstieg der Mitte, Ressentiments*, ed. Alexander Hausler and Fabian Virchow (Hamburg, 2016), 42–51.
117. Thomas Risse, *A Community of Europeans? Transnational Identities and Public Spheres* (Ithaca, 2010).
118. The AfD expresses and mobilizes some particular German radical right ideological features and issues, such as relativizing Nazism and German crimes during the Holocaust or downplaying the crimes of the Wehrmacht, in order to exculpate tainted German nationalism and rehabilitate German national identity. Notwithstanding some occasional pro-Israel rhetoric, "secondary antisemitism" and conspiracy myths, which are often antisemitic in nature, are also especially present in the party and among its voters. Meuthen's notion that groups are working to "decompose" the "fatherland" is in itself an antisemitic trope originating in, and tied to, the specific history of German nationalism and antisemitism. On this issue, see also Grimm and Kahmann (see note 24), and Samuel Salzborn in this issue.

··· Chapter 12 ···

ANTISEMITISM IN THE "ALTERNATIVE FOR GERMANY" PARTY

Samuel Salzborn

The relatively new party known as the Alternative for Germany (Alternative für Deutschland, AfD) and its relationship to right-wing extremism has been the subject of a great deal of intensive discussion among political and social scientists. While one stream of research focusses primarily on the strategic aspects of the AfD, such as its populist rhetoric and use of social media, another devotes more attention to the worldview of the AfD, and its increasing radicalization from a right-wing conservative party to a right-wing extremist one:

> In the beginning, the AfD leadership tried to maintain a clear separation from anti-constitutional right-wing extremism. This has since changed. Today, the overall impression is that the AfD is on the threshold of becoming a "nationalist opposition." It appears that a large part of the party is pushing to go a step further.[1]

It has become undeniable that the AfD has now adopted large parts of the far-right tradition, including racism and *völkisch* nationalism (a form of ethnonationalism) as central components within an ideology of inequality, alongside nationalist protectionism and anti-EU economic positions, an emphatic rejection of parliamentarianism and representative democracy, and a long-standing antifeminism and hostility towards gender equality.

Nevertheless, there has been somewhat less attention paid to the AfD's handling of the Nazi past and its relationship to antisemitism. This might be because the party has avoided officially espousing anti-Israeli views, and at times even seems to view Israel as a strategic ally for its own anti-Muslim racism, which is ultimately aimed at blocking migration to Europe. But beyond its cultivated media image, there exist a number of antisemitic

---

Notes for this section begin on page 271.

stances within the AfD that will be the subject of this investigation. In the case of the AfD, antisemitism can be attested on various levels.

Antisemitism can be generally understood as combining a worldview and an emotional zeal, and thus a specific way of thinking and feeling.[2] Antisemitism involves both an inability and an unwillingness to think abstractly and to feel concretely; these two aspects are swapped in antisemitism, so that one thinks only concretely but feels abstractly. Furthermore, antisemitic resentments have been expressed in certain distinct forms that have appeared again and again throughout history, in particular: a religious/anti-Judaic antisemitism; an ethnonationalist/racist one; a guilt-deflecting one; an anti-Israel one; and an Arab/Islamist one. With regard to the AfD, it is primarily the ethnonationalist/racist and guilt-deflecting forms of antisemitism that are involved.

Here, it will be shown how antisemitism has been gradually taking hold in the AfD, thereby demonstrating that the AfD is shifting from a party for antisemites into an antisemitic party. The argument here is that the party has been transforming itself step by step over the course of its general radicalization. It began with the tacit toleration of antisemitic positions. Then came the first antisemitic incidents (such as the case of Wolfgang Gedeon, discussed below), which were downplayed along with denials of any antisemitism. The next step involved occasionally attempted expulsions from the party and their ultimate failure, meaning that party members who had come under fire for their antisemitic stances were not expelled after all. As a result, there was a slowly increasing tolerance for publicly expressed antisemitic positions—right up into the party's leadership ranks. It became publicly apparent that antisemitism not only goes unpunished in the AfD, it is now routinely tolerated and sometimes even accepted. This demonstrates a long-term evolution from a party for antisemites into an antisemitic party—although the final step has not been taken (yet), namely insertion into the party platform. The policy plank debates described at the end of this article, however, show that this step is also under development. While internal efforts to curtail this shift do still occasionally emerge, there are many indications suggesting that this development, especially when seen in light of Germany's history of right-wing extremism, is no longer a question of "if," but "when."

The Bedrock of Antisemitism: The Ideology of the *Volksgemeinschaft*

An important starting point for the formulation of antisemitic positions within the AfD lies in its conception of society, which is strongly influenced by the ideology of Germany's "New Right" (*Neue Rechte*), thus drawing upon Nazism's intellectual forefathers from the Weimar period, an ideological heritage that has informed the (West) German "New Right" from the 1970s until today.[3] Here, the main goal is to present the *völkisch* ("folkish," but with ethnonationalist connotations) terminology of these forerunners as not being genuinely antidemocratic. If one can make the Nazi heritage seem harmless, then it becomes possible to take its associated concepts like the *Volksgemeinschaft* (ethnonational community) and resurrect it in public speech, before then striving to make it a reality–even as the totalitarian instrument of coercion and repression that it actually is.

This project is exemplified by two attempts to rehabilitate Nazi terms–here specifically *Volksgemeinschaft* and *völkisch*–and detach such words from their antidemocratic background, while maintaining a cover of naiveté that is certainly staged. On 24 December 2015, the AfD of Saxony-Anhalt wished its Facebook audience a "contemplative and peaceful Christmas," while also calling upon them to think about "shared values" and "responsibility for the *Volksgemeinschaft*."[4] Responding to criticism of this word choice, the local head of the AfD in Sachsen-Anhalt, André Poggenburg, wrote that apparently "certain entirely unproblematic and even highly positive terms are not supposed to be used" today.[5] A few months later, the national party head at the time, Frauke Petry, sang from the same songbook when she wanted to rehabilitate the word *völkisch* in September 2016, asserting that this Nazi term needed to put back in a positive light.[6]

With these efforts, the AfD is effectively trying to ignore the fact that the *Volksgemeinschaft* term is historically and inextricably tied to Nazism.[7] But, even if one retreated to the excuse of historical naiveté, the term is in itself untenable within a democracy: combining *Volk* with *Gemeinschaft* produces a twofold exclusion, one that can only be interpreted ethnically, and never democratically (*Volk* corresponds to "folk," but variously means people, nation, or ethnonation, while *Gemeinschaft* means "community.")[8] The *Volk*, as an alternative to the civic conception of "nation," is not defined by rational, democratic criteria such as the subjective will (i.e., deciding to belong–or not), but instead by pre-political aspects, such as the fiction of a collective's ostensibly shared descent. And the *Gemeinschaft*, if used in this way, is conceptually opposite to the *Gesellschaft* (society), namely a form of association that is open, plural, accepting of contradictions, and ultimately voluntary.[9] In contrast, the *Volksgemeinschaft* stands only for coercion, one that is repressive and totalitarian towards both the included and the excluded. This is why the notion is inherently incompatible with the ideas of democracy. The concept of the *Volksgemeinschaft* is not only profoundly antidemocratic due to political and historical reasons, but is also inimical to democracy in terms of its fundamental incompatibility with Germany's modern constitution, as confirmed in early 2017 by the country's highest tribunal, the Federal Constitutional Court: "This political concept violates the human dignity of all those who do not belong to the ethnic *Volksgemeinschaft*, and is incompatible with the constitution's principle of democracy."[10]

This highlighting of the *Volksgemeinschaft* by the AfD is a direct reflection of *völkisch* thinking,[11] and it is no accident that Petry had likewise tried to rehabilitate the word *völkisch* itself, which lies at the heart of far-right thought. The "*völkisch Volk*" (i.e., an ethnonationally defined body politic) is the countermodel to the democratic nation: whereas the democratic nation makes all citizens into political subjects, regardless of their cultural, religious, or ethnic self-ascriptions, the *völkisch Volk* demands the exclusion of all persons who do not belong to the ostensible ethnic homogeneity of the collective–at least according to pre-political criteria, meaning ones that are entirely accidental and without any conscious choice by the subject, and yet are considered paramount by an outside observer. The political subject of the democratic nation is the *demos*, while the *völkisch Volk* takes the *ethnos* as the foundation of its political conception. The real and already existing *demos* is to be transformed according to the premises of ethnopolitics into an *ethnos*, whereby the belief in a *völkisch* collective identity is to be consolidated through an ethnicization process "in which originally irrelevant constituent aspects are *gradually transformed into significant constituent characteristics*, in order to create a separate social group."[12]

Through this ethnicization process, the *völkisch* vision strives to transform the *Gesellschaft* into the *Gemeinschaft*, so that the plurality of interests is replaced by the monolith of identity, rational thought by direct action, processes of conflict by irrefutable destiny, the legitimate opponent by the mortal enemy, and the argument by the battle. This terminological embracing of the *Volksgemeinschaft* and of *völkisch* thought is thus tied to a rejection of the modern civic conception of the nation, which is not guided by the political principle of the *ethnos*, but that of the *demos*.[13]

The AfD and Antisemitism

Public opinion surveys conducted over recent decades have shown that Germany's overall populace has consistently included around one-fifth who are antisemites and one-quarter who are racists.[14] While these percentages may fluctuate here and there, this discriminatory antiliberal baseline has remained stable. Not all of these people, however, are organized neo-Nazis: while some may join far-right organizations, and others might openly sympathize with right-wing parties, most are outwardly politically inconspicuous in their everyday lives, precisely because they do not see themselves as far right and would strongly reject such a label for themselves. In today's Germany, such people prefer to present themselves as simply "concerned citizens," despite actually having racist, *völkisch*, and nationalist attitudes, with a disdain for rational thought, equal rights, and the heritage of the Enlightenment.

These are very much people who are socially well integrated, mostly from the lower-to-middling middle class, often with an academic education, not infrequently male and with a solid income, but nonetheless with considerable irrational fears. Their attitudes are hard right but they do not want to admit it, so they invent labels enabling a self-image that is as far away as possible from the analytically objective ascription of "right-wing extremist."

Before the emergence of the AfD, it had been difficult for this clientele to find a political home. In terms of available options, the political system offered either openly neo-Nazi parties, such as the National Democratic Party of Germany (Nationaldemokratische Partei Deutschlands, NPD) and the German People's Union (Deutsche Volksunion), or else the traditional conservative parties, which tried to distance themselves from the far right, regardless of whether for genuinely ideological reasons or purely strategic ones. There was no party that united the full range of discriminatory and antiliberal resentments while also consistently refusing a far-right label.[15] With the departure of several prominent members in the summer of 2015, the last fragments of the AfD's conservative veneer have long since flaked away, although it still maintains the image of a party that should not entirely be classified as far-right—also as a result of the media's excessively mild treatment of it.[16]

The AfD is thus a manifestation of modern Germany's political system that is only somewhat comparable to the other populist-oriented movements operating on the right-wing fringes of other European countries.[17] Perhaps the closest comparison would be to the Freedom Party of Austria (Freiheitliche Partei Österreichs), a far-right party with a strongly populist public image that has long established itself as a force for antidemocrats within Austria's democratic system.[18] This desire to express essentially Nazi positions without being called a far-right extremist is particularly pronounced in Germany, a country where most have never explored the question of their own grandparents' complicity in the Nazi regime, even now.[19] In fact, perpetrators have often been recast as victims in German family memories, as seen when children and/or grandchildren remember their parents and/or grandparents as victims; they do so precisely because they lack detailed knowledge about the Nazi past and the Shoah (or choose to have none), and furthermore see their own parents and/or grandparents as the victims of surveillance, state terror, war, bombing, and imprisonment, as has been demonstrated in the family biography study conducted by Harald Welzer, Sabine Moller, and Karoline Tschuggnall.[20] Since Nazi perpetrators have been morally condemned as "bad" and "evil" by the descendent generations, the latter have recast their own parents and/or grandparents as victims of Nazism, and even as resistance fighters against it. Historical studies, however, have shown that the fraction of those who actually gave assistance to potential victims of Nazism was only around 0.3 percent, which would mean around two hundred thousand persons in a population of seventy million.[21] This makes it entirely impossible that even a small fraction of all those claiming a story of victimhood or resistance for their families could be anywhere close to reality.

Another aspect that is specific to the AfD and its success among a certain segment of society, namely those who may be socially and economically embedded in the middle class but nonetheless adhere to far-right views, is the desire to defend one's own prosperity at all costs, a prosperity that is always felt to be inadequate. This racist segment of the middle class seems to have subconsciously sensed that the source of their prosperity was not simply the postwar achievements of the grandparents' generation, a foundational myth known as the *Wirtschaftswunder* (economic miracle.) Here, the argument is very much about feelings: feelings of grievance, feelings of neglect, feelings of inferiority. Of course, these are not necessarily present in each and every AfD voter, but they nonetheless characterize the general sentiment shared by many, a sentiment that is not based on any realistic assessment of actual achievements (and indeed also weaknesses), but on a one-sided overestimation of one's own achievements–and thereby also an underestimation of those of others In fact, the main origin of their own privileged position, which the AfD would defend by proxy through its *völkisch* and racist slogans (i.e., "We prefer bikinis to burkas"), was historically the astounding willingness of the Allies to give the Germans a second chance, even after the evils of Nazism and the mass murder of Europe's Jews. There is also another, much deeper sense in which the source of Germany's prosperity lay beyond its borders, as emphasized by migration researchers who point out that "without guest workers, the German economic miracle would not have been possible at all."[22] Furthermore, the guest workers were essential for sustaining the boom.

But, admitting this would not only highlight one's own inabilities, it would also open a back door allowing the question of family complicities during the Nazi era to be put back on the agenda. Indeed, there exists a deeply conflicted relationship between these two levels of German history:

> Unlike the history of victimhood during the Second World War, the history of Nazism and its crimes is inserted by very few Germans into the personal context of themselves and their families. Factual history is perceived as an abstract one, and is also to be remembered as this abstract history … Our official remembrance does not pester us with all too personal questions about individual or familial involvement. It leaves us in peace and no longer jolts us. And it also does not call upon young people to confront this very personal past, since the actual culprit generation is barely still breathing.[23]

The AfD is tied to the perceived promise of being able to avoid both of these things and offers a space for projecting one's own alternative narratives about them. This cannot actually work in sociopsychological terms, however, leading to an increasing aggressiveness and readiness for violence in the radicalized milieu represented by the AfD as a party and by Pegida as a street movement (PEGIDA is an acronym translating as Patriotic Europeans Against the Islamization of the Occident).[24] This is because what is being evaded is the burden of German family histories, the latter of which is denied and projected onto others, causing one to seek it out in others and persecute them even more brutally.

Deflection of the Nazi Past and the Desire for Collective Blamelessness

Therefore, the deflection of the Nazi past cannot be sociopsychologically separated from the *völkisch* and racist stances seen in today's right-wing discourse. This handling of Nazi history is exemplified by a long interview that Alexander Gauland, a leading figure in the AfD, gave to the weekly newspaper *Die Zeit* in April 2016. During this discussion, Gauland was asked to explain an expression he had used in another setting, "Sittengesetz des Volkes" (moral law of the *Volk*,) which needed defending. Here he answered:

> It is the thing from which a *Volk* has developed, from history and tradition, from upheavals. You could also replace this expression with the word "identity," and this identity is defended much more strongly by other *Völker* [the plural of *Volk*]. Of course, this has to do with Auschwitz. I was recently in Auschwitz for the first time, when I realized that it was no longer grabbing me, unlike during my visit to Buchenwald. It's like a frozen horror. When you see all the hair, the brushes, and the suitcases, you suddenly get the feeling that this is petrified, it doesn't speak anymore. I believe that Auschwitz, also as a symbol, has destroyed much within us.[25]

Of course, the immediate and obvious question was whether it was not in fact the Germans "who destroyed something there," which was the follow-up question promptly posed by Bernd Ulrich and Matthias Geis, the journalists conducting the interview. Here, Gauland responded:

> That's correct, but much more was ruined at the same time. The Nazis touched upon many things that suddenly can no longer be said, due to their touch. The national pride felt by every Englishman and Frenchman is intensely called into question among ourselves, according to the idea: Are we actually allowed to still say this?[26]

Here too, the interviewers followed up with the obvious objection that "outside of German history, there has been no crime like Auschwitz." On this point (and Gauland was obsessively fixated on Nazism throughout the interview, even when it was not necessarily addressed, such as when he answered the question about the "moral law of the *Volk*" by bringing up Nazism and Auschwitz without any need), he replied with: "Yes. Hitler destroyed much more than cities and human beings, he broke the spine of the Germans, to a great extent."[27]

What Gauland apparently meant with this metaphor was that the actual "victims" of Nazism were the Germans, and that this victimhood also goes far beyond the issue of Nazism: in this view, it was ultimately because of Hitler that an assertive and self-confident German politics was no longer possible–and with this embodiment in the person of Hitler, any responsibility for the Shoah on the part of the German people was also denied. This interview is highly revealing of the AfD self-image in relationship to Nazism, not only in terms of explicit statements, but also in regards to subconscious motivations, which speak here through Gauland's comments–thereby making apparent without self-editing that the AfD is virtually obsessed with Nazism, and for a long time has simply been better at disguising the revisionist implications of this, more so than the openly neo-Nazi NPD, for example.

This denial of German responsibility for Nazism, as expressed through Gauland's attempts to absolve German guiltiness (including his own) in both historical and political terms, is tied to the desire for a German collective guiltlessness, and the fiction of German victimhood in this situation. According to this, it was not that the Germans did something, but that something that was done to them, in a rhetorical trick achieved by separating Hitler–as the personal embodiment of evil and Nazism–from his people, so that guilt can be expatriated and denied. In Gauland's worldview, it seems that there are no more perpetrators, except for Hitler and perhaps a few leading Nazis.

Regardless of whether intentionally or not, this ignores the fact that the Nazi regime enjoyed great approval among the German populace, and that the vast majority of Germans were either actively or passively involved in the mass extermination of Europe's Jews, be it through direct participation in confiscations, plundering, denunciations, executions, deportations, etc., through looking away and not resisting, through the spreading of antisemitic and racist sentiments, through refusing to speak about Nazi crimes, or through profiting from forced labor and the "Aryanization" of property and jobs. And this also ignores the fact that the reason why this *völkisch* ethnopolicy and antisemitic extermination policy could be implemented to such a monstrous extent was precisely because there existed a very wide-reaching consensus between the Nazi leadership and the German populace.

Gauland's conception of history is based on a positive self-identification with the German nation, so that "being German" is not subjected to interrogation, nor does a critical examination of German history's negative sides take place. Here, any feelings of ambivalence are either very limited or completely nonexistent–instead, there is only the desire to highlight and exaggerate whatever is seen as positive. This was also seen in early 2017 with the AfD parliamentary group in Baden-Württemberg, when it called for the elimination of local state funding for a concentration camp memorial and tried to justify this with the need for a "balanced culture of remembrance," while also repudiating "a one-sided focus on the dark chapters of history and a suppression of our historical achievements." The goal, according to the AfD, is a "positive self-identification with Germany and our history."[28] Beyond that, there was also a proposal that grants for visiting "memorials to Nazi wrongdoings" should be dedicated instead to visiting "significant sites of German history."[29]

On the federal level as well, the current party platform of the AfD explicitly downplays the objective historical reality of German responsibility for Nazism and the Shoah, so that the general push towards historical revisionism has even become an official plank in the federal party's platform: "The current narrowing of the German culture of remembrance to the time of National Socialism is to be broken up in favor of an expanded historical view that also includes the positive, identity-building aspects of German history."[30] This identifying with the German nation lies at the heart of this world view. Gauland's intervention into the politics of memory is thus also an attempt to suggest that Germans in general are victims of Nazism. The remarkable thing about this act of self-projection is the indirectly expressed desire to claim the status of the victim, which often seems like a badge of honor in public debates–and this despite the fact that every victim of violence would prefer to have never suffered this, since actually being a victim is anything but desirable. This victim envy in the context of Nazism is then expressed through the belief that Jews are somehow trying to profit from the Nazi past, a notion that has been documented through numerous empirical studies.[31]

It is thus about deflecting feelings of inferiority and guilt by projecting not only one's own sullied state on the Jews, but also one's envy of their accomplishments and successes, be they real or imagined. Here, on the path taken by the AfD towards openly invoking central components of Nazi ideology, the whitewashing of the Nazi past has been not simply a minor detour, but in fact the primary route. Gauland's historical revisionism was then further escalated in January 2017 by Björn Höcke, the AfD parliamentary leader in Thuringia's state assembly, when he similarly took up the myth of the German victim and tried to whitewash history, but now tied this to an antisemitic stance that also included a brazen threat of violence against the modern German republic.

During a speech at a Dresden event organized by the Young Alternative for Germany (the AfD's youth organization), Höcke declared that the bombing of Dresden had been a "war crime" and that "even today, it is not possible for us to mourn our own victims" (which is simply a barefaced lie, considering the ubiquitous war memorials across Germany, including the commemoration of the flight and expulsion of Germans in the wake of World War II, manifested in countless dedicated sites and thoroughly anchored in the official culture of remembrance: besides the countless memorials in almost every German cemetery, there are also numerous commemoration sites not only in larger localities, but also smaller ones, with extensive information on the topics of flight and expulsion). He thereby called for a "turnaround in remembrance policy" to highlight the "magnificent achievements of our forebears" and called the Holocaust Memorial in Berlin a "memorial of shame," one that the German *Volk* had "planted ... in the heart of its capital."[32] Here, Höcke added an explicit threat: "The AfD is the last revolutionary chance, the last peaceful one, for our Fatherland."[33]

Höcke's speech reflects the real substance of assertions like the ones expressed by Gauland, and clearly demonstrates how a historically revisionist antisemitism is combined with an ahistorical, anti-factual belief in a German victim identity. Here, in creating a historical facade or "cover identity," the still dominant strategy is to cultivate the myth of collective guiltlessness: the goal is to talk about "German victims" without actually mentioning Nazism.[34] The historical context is meant to disappear, so that we forget how German ethnopolicy and extermination schemes ultimately led to the bombing of German cities and the mass resettlement of German populations; such connections are redacted from memory, without ever being subjected to serious reflection in public discourse. Constantly imagined accusations of German collective guilt, a concept that never actually guided the policy conduct of the Allies and their associates, are met with an interpretation of history aimed at creating precisely the opposite: the myth of German collective guiltlessness.[35]

This was shown very clearly by a speech that Gauland gave in September 2017, in which he tried to completely reverse perpetrator/victim roles by denying the criminality of the Wehrmacht, a central institution in Germany's antisemitic war of extermination, believing it had been unfairly singled out; but he conveniently forgets that the Wehrmacht was quite unlike the Allied armies, which had not conducted a war of extermination, but had instead prevented the Wehrmacht from murdering even more people. According to Gauland, if the British can be proud of Churchill and the French of Napoleon, then "we have the right to be proud of the achievements of German soldiers from two world wars." He furthermore stated that "there is no longer a need to reproach us for these twelve years. They no longer pertain to our identity. This is why we also have the right to take back not only our country, but also our past."[36]

The fact of having followed in Nazism a doctrine that promised special privileges to Germans above all other people, and of having projected one's own aggressions upon fellow human beings and thus made them into "subhumans," did not lead to a sense of shame among the vast majority of Germans after the war, but instead to the childish excuse of having "only" followed the leader. As already highlighted by Alexander and Margarete Mitscherlich, this explains:

> the tendency of many Germans to take on the role of innocent victim after the war. Each individual feels the disappointment of his own desires for protection and direction; he has been misled, seduced, abandoned, and finally expelled and condemned, although he had only been obedient, as commanded by the citizen's first duty.[37]

This childish attitude not only "forgets" the historical facts, it also inverts the perpetrator/victim roles in one's own favor: an act of destruction and extermination is indeed regretted, but only in regards to one's own position and desires. Gauland encapsulates this with just a few sentences in his cited interview, while Höcke conveys the same idea in his cited speech, yet expressing it even more clearly than Gauland and combining his revisionist stance with an explicit threat of violence.

The deflection of German culpability and the denial of the Nazi past, as already seen right after the end of World War II, thus goes together with an almost ritualistic cultivation of personal guiltlessness and personal victimhood. If this myth of German collective guiltlessness is now being reactivated by the AfD, however, then the implications of this go far beyond the politics of memory. After all, if one manages to minimize or entirely jettison Nazism by making its terminology and worldview seem acceptable and by freeing its central geopolitical and ethnopolitical ideas from the Nazi context, then it becomes possible to once again pursue the implementation of concepts like the ethnonationally oppressive *Volksgemeinschaft*. And it is precisely here that one finds the deeper meaning behind the instrumentalization of German history by the AfD: whoever manages to excise Nazism from memory can then implement Nazi ideas without being seen as a Nazi or right-wing extremist. This is exactly why so many in the AfD have been unwilling to recognize the clearly, explicitly, and unmistakably articulated antisemitism of Wolfgang Gedeon as such: because accepting the obvious would have meant a real roadblock to the entire political program of the AfD.

The Tip of Many Icebergs: The Gedeon Affair and Deep-Rooted Antisemitism

The originating circumstances of the Gedeon affair can be quickly summarized: Wolfgang Gedeon became a member of the Baden-Württemberg state legislature for the AfD in the spring of 2016, and had previously expressed extensive, indisputably antisemitic sentiments in his writings. For any German legislator, this in itself was already a scandal. But the even bigger scandal was how the AfD dealt with the Gedeon affair–and it is the party's handling of this that offers greater insights into antisemitism in the AfD, more so than what is found in Gedeon's words alone. The party's reaction makes it clear how deeply rooted antisemitic sentiments are in the AfD, and why, despite having not been an explicitly antisemitic party in terms of its official platform so far, it is nonetheless undeniably a party for antisemites.

What did Gedeon write? In one book, he described revisionist neo-Nazis like Horst Mahler, Ernst Zündel, and David Irving as "dissidents," and took the view that in the courts, "the Zionist influence is manifesting itself in a limiting of free speech."[38] According to Gedeon, the Jews are working towards the "enslavement of humanity within a messianic empire of the Jews," with the goal of "Judaizing the Christian religion and Zionizing the politics of the West."[39] He further claimed:

> Just as Islam is the external foe, the Talmudic ghetto Jews were the internal foe of the Christian Occident ... As the political centre of power shifted during the twentieth century from Europe to the U.S.,

> Judaism, in its secular Zionist form, became a decisively powerful and influential factor in Western politics … The previous internal foe of the Occident is now a dominating power in the West, and the previous external foe of the Occident, namely Islam, has overrun the borders through mass migration and penetrated deeply into Western societies, and is reshaping them in many ways.[40]

The situation is fairly straightforward so far–but then the party and its leaders began desperately casting around for experts who could speak about Gedeon in their stead, before the AfD parliamentary group in Baden-Württemberg's state legislature finally underwent a (purely cosmetic) schism in July 2016. The central question plaguing federal party leader Petry and her colleagues was: did Gedeon's words actually constitute antisemitism? With the desperate search for outside experts to answer this question in the party's stead, one might well be tempted to discount this as simply a rhetorical strategy.[41] But, it makes more sense to take the party's actions seriously here, and to make it accountable for this. After all, it is evident that Gedeon had made clearly and unmistakably antisemitic statements, drawing upon numerous aspects of common antisemitic tropes. The fact that AfD members could seriously ask whether Gedeon's utterances were even antisemitic at all shows that they clearly did not find the content of his statements to be problematic, instead wanting an outside referee to make an evaluation for them. Here it is clear that they must find at least parts of Gedeon's world view acceptable–there is no other plausible explanation.

This handling of the affair shows two things. Firstly, the AfD wanted to farm out all responsibility for the conduct of its members, purely so that it would not have to scare any of them away–in this case, Gedeon might at worst have been ruled an antisemite by some member of academia (which is more or less reviled anyway by the AfD and its followers), but this verdict would not have come from the party itself. Secondly, antisemitism is deeply rooted in the AfD, with the party attracting antisemites like a magnet. After all, if the party is unable to see antisemitism even in a case like Gedeon's, then where does antisemitism actually begin in AfD eyes? Only with the onset of mass murder?

When AfD members refuse to acknowledge antisemitism for what it is, they do so because they are either unwilling to admit sharing antisemitic opinions themselves, or unwilling to hold antisemites accountable for their words, as has also been demonstrated by many other cases–and in no case has the AfD ever admitted, officially and unambiguously, that antisemitism was involved. Instead, the AfD has failed to distance itself from such ideas, which is why Gedeon is only one tip of the increasingly visible icebergs of antisemitism within the AfD.

The cases of antisemitism in the AfD have become so numerous that the usual right-wing strategy of shrugging them off as isolated incidents has lost all substance. For example, Gunnar Baumgart, who was a local AfD politician from the town of Bad Münder (near Hanover), was already defending the neo-Nazi revisionists and Holocaust deniers Ernst Zündel, Germar Rudolf, and Fred Leuchter back in 2015, and posted a Facebook link to an article claiming that "not a single Jew" had died from "Zyklon B or in the gas chambers." He further stated that "if I had children, they would not attend history lessons in Germany." After several criminal charges were filed against him, he said he wanted to resign from the AfD, "in order to deflect any damage to the party."[42]

Antisemitic sentiments have also been expressed by other AfD officeholders.[43] For example, Peter Ziemann, local state-level treasurer of the AfD in Hesse, ranted in 2013 about "satanic elements in the financial oligopoly" and "cover organizations organized by Freemasons," harking back to common themes in antisemitic conspiracy theory.[44] Or Jan-Ulrich Weiss, an AfD local state-level politician in Brandenburg who reposted an ostensible quote from British investment banker Jacob Rothschild, saying "we control … the media … and your government."[45] Or Gottfried Klasen, an elected AfD county assembly member in northern Hesse who claimed that the Central Council of Jews in Germany possessed "political opinion-making hegemony and political control over Germany."[46] And Höcke, the AfD parliamentary party leader in Thuringia's state legislature defended prolific neo-Nazi activist Ursula Haverbeck when he spoke at an AfD rally in the city of Gera in late October 2016–soon after her latest of many criminal convictions for Holocaust denial.[47]

After the national elections of September 2017, Germany's federal parliament was joined by AfD politician Wilhelm von Gottberg, who had previously spent almost two decades as head of the Homeland Association of East Prussia (Landsmannschaft Ostpreussen, a right-wing reactionary group), and has since failed to unequivocally repudiate the front-page article he wrote for the far-right newspaper *Das Ostpreussenblatt* in 2001, in which he included comments doubting the Holocaust. Here, he approvingly cited an Italian neofascist who stated that the "propaganda steamroller" has not weakened over the years, but is strengthening instead, so that "the Holocaust must remain a mythos, a dogma, exempt from all free historical discussion."[48] Back in 2003, Gottberg had also defended Martin Hohmann, a member of the federal parliament who gave an antisemitic speech in October 2003 and was consequently thrown out of the parliamentary group of the CDU/CSU (Christian Democratic Union and its Bavarian sister party, the Christian Social Union), and then out of the CDU altogether. In his speech, Hohmann had tried to downplay German responsibility for Nazi crimes, while also accusing Jews of "perpetratorship" in terms of the October Revolution in Russia. Hohmann has since returned to the federal parliament, this time sitting for the AfD.

During the Berlin municipal election campaign of 2016, Hugh Bronson, deputy head of the local AfD, made his worldview clear when he trivialized the Shoah in his tweet: "Extremes are typically German. Like with people on trains, it's either Auschwitz or Refugees Welcome. Both are wrong!"[49] Meanwhile, Kay Nerstheimer, the AfD politician who won a seat representing the district of Lichtenberg I at the same election, repeated a conspiracy theory that the "powers" behind the First and Second World Wars were now trying to start a third one, while also denigrating the modern German state as a "Federal German Trust Company headquartered in Frankfurt," thus adding a financial conspiracy theory as well.[50] The fact that Nerstheimer was excluded from the AfD parliamentary group upon its establishment in Berlin's state legislature is no more than a cosmetic ruse, just like what was seen in Baden-Württemberg's state legislature with the schism of its AfD parliamentary group, orchestrated to effectively stifle media criticism of antisemitism in the AfD, but then rescinded again just a few months later in October 2016.

As for Wolfgang Gedeon himself, it seems he was entirely unmoved by the public criticism of his words, and simply added fuel to the fire when he responded to an article in *Die Zeit* that analyzed his antisemitic comments, written by a scholar working at the Center for Research on Antisemitism at Berlin's Technical University.[51] Gedeon demanded to know "from what non-state actors" this center receives its financing, as "this would certainly interest a few readers."[52] Here, Gedeon does not really want an answer to his question: for him it is enough to simply make an insinuation, thus utilizing the common antisemitic strategy of suggesting a conspiracy without naming any specifics. And within the now reunited AfD parliamentary group in Baden-Württemberg's state legislature, there are once again elected members who do not see any antisemitism in the statements of Gedeon, now sitting as an independent, and continue to support him.[53] By November 2017, he was being invited to participate in AfD committees as a "parliamentary guest."

It is with increasing frequency and clarity that antisemitic beliefs are manifesting themselves in openly antisemitic statements, as shown by the examples seen so far. In its handling of the Höcke affair, the AfD took a fateful step in January 2017, when its leadership ultimately decided not to expel him after his revisionist and antisemitic speech, thereby granting him their political backing. As it was put in *Der Spiegel*, the AfD has thereby lost all "democratic accountability;" furthermore, "it has become a party for Nazis and their followers. And whoever votes for them must now know: you are one as well."[54] This appraisal of AfD voters as equivalent to Nazis is shared by sixty-two per cent of all German citizens, according to a survey conducted by the Forsa Institute.[55]

Conclusion

It is simply a matter of time before a party for antisemites ultimately becomes a decidedly antisemitic party. This trajectory is demonstrated by the obsessive efforts seen within the AfD to revive positive feelings for Nazi terms like *Volksgemeinschaft* and *völkisch*: not only does this incorporate the ethnonationalist and antisemitic extermination policy of the German *Volksgemeinschaft*, these words also have a historical reality in the implementation of this extermination. The *völkisch* worldview represents the essential foundation of German antisemitism–and of the Nazi regime's antisemitic extermination program.

Furthermore, the evolution of the AfD since its foundation has demonstrated a steady radicalization towards the far right, so that classical conservative stances, let alone liberal ones, no longer exist at all in the AfD today, with the latest party infighting clearly about personal dominance and not about any real differences in political agenda. Even now, nobody of rank and influence in the AfD has ever publicly acknowledged, clearly and unequivocally, that representatives like Gedeon and Höcke had been plainly antisemitic in their statements. Debates within the party are focused only on whether such statements might damage the party's image–and so are only strategic in nature. The same thing applies to the lip service paid to Israel by the AfD. Its support is not based on fighting antisemitism–which the AfD clearly propagates in its treatment of the Nazi past, its inversion of perpetrator/victim roles, and its glorification of criminal institutions like the Wehrmacht. The AfD only wants to use Israel, firstly to deflect accusations of antisemitism by exploiting the notion that whoever is pro-Israel could not possibly be antisemitic, and secondly to find strategic allies in its fight against Muslim immigration.

Nevertheless, even the supposedly pro-Israel stance of the AfD has now become largely a myth, one based mostly on statements by politicians who have since left the AfD. More recently, during its 2017 federal party convention in Cologne, a motion to consider a clause entitled "strengthening German-Israeli friendship" for inclusion in its federal election platform failed to pass; in a speech against further considering this proposal, it was argued that there existed a problem with Israeli "war criminals."[56] A few months later, the leading AfD figure Gauland even questioned whether the championing of Israel's right to exist, long an element of Germany's national consensus, is actually in Germany's "national interest."[57]

In order to understand the party's true nature and its progression towards right-wing extremism, one cannot overlook the antisemitism that has become an established fixture in the worldview of the AfD. It would clearly prefer to downplay the antisemitism displayed by many of its members and officials, since acknowledgement of this would remove the last obstacle to recognizing the AfD as simply one more of the many far-right parties that have emerged in Germany's postwar history–with the only difference being that the AfD has managed to profit from the middle-class image of its early phase, thus allowing it to achieve double-digit results in the federal elections of 2017, making it the first far-right party to enter the German parliament since the end of the Nazi era. For the development of the AfD, the result of a representative opinion poll is particularly enlightening. The renowned Allensbach Institute for Demoskopie has shown in June 2018 how common antisemitism is among supporters of the AfD: 55 percent of the supporters of the AfD agree with the statement: "Jews have too much influence in the world."[58] Compared with the other German parties, the approval in any other party is a maximum of 20 percent. The results show that antisemitism not only unites the officials of the party, but also its supporters.

Prof. Dr. Samuel Salzborn is a Visiting Professor for Research on Antisemitism at the Center for Research on Antisemitism (ZfA) at the Technical University of Berlin, and a Senior Fellow at the Centre for Analysis of the Radical Right (CARR). He received his doctorate in 2004 from the University of Cologne and habilitated at the University of Giessen in 2009. He has also been a Research Fellow at the Hebrew University of Jerusalem, a Visiting Lecturer at the University of Economics in Prague, and a Visiting Professor at the University of Marburg. Email: salzborn@tu-berlin.de

Notes

1. Christoph Kopke and Alexander Lorenz, "Auf dem Weg in die 'Nationale Opposition?,'" *vorgänge: Zeitschrift für Bürgerrechte und Gesellschaftspolitik*, no. 216 (2016): 15–28, here 24.
2. For a closer look at this, see Samuel Salzborn, *Antisemitismus als negative Leitidee der Moderne: Sozialwissenschaftliche Theorien im Vergleich* (Frankfurt, 2010).
3. See Samuel Salzborn, "Renaissance of the New Right in Germany? A Discussion of New Right Elements in German Right-wing Extremism Today," *German Politics and Society* 34, no. 2 (2016): 36–63.
4. Quoted in Patrick Gensing, "Die AfD und die 'Volksgemeinschaft,'" *tagesschau.de*, 29 December 2015.
5. Quoted in ibid.
6. See Beat Balzli and Matthias Kamann, "Petry will den Begriff 'völkisch' positiv besetzen," *Die Welt Online*, 11 September 2016.
7. See Markus Brunner, Jan Lohl, Rolf Pohl, and Sebastian Winter, ed., *Volksgemeinschaft, Täterschaft und Antisemitismus: Beiträge zur psychoanalytischen Sozialpsychologie des Nationalsozialismus und seiner Nachwirkungen* (Giessen, 2011); Dietmar von Reeken and Malte Thiessen, ed., *"Volksgemeinschaft" als soziale Praxis: Neue Forschungen zur NS-Gesellschaft vor Ort* (Paderborn, 2013); Detlef Schmiechen-Ackermann, ed., *"Volksgemeinschaft": Mythos, wirkungsmächtige soziale Verheißung oder soziale Realität im Dritten Reich?* (Paderborn, 2012); Peter Schyga, *Über die Volksgemeinschaft der Deutschen: Begriff und historische Wirklichkeit jenseits historiografischer Gegenwartsmoden* (Baden-Baden, 2015); Michael Wildt, *Hitler's Volksgemeinschaft and the Dynamics of Racial Exclusion* (New York, 2012).
8. See Samuel Salzborn, *Ethnisierung der Politik: Theorie und Geschichte des Volksgruppenrechts in Europa* (Frankfurt, 2005).
9. See Samuel Salzborn, *Demokratie: Theorien, Formen, Entwicklungen* (Baden-Baden, 2012).
10. Bundesverfassungsgericht, "Urteil des Zweiten Senats vom 17. Januar 2017: 2 BvB 1/13–Rn. (1-1010);" available at www.bverfg.de/e/bs20170117_2bvb000113.html, accessed 20 January 2017.
11. See Uwe Puschner and G. Ulrich Grossmann, ed., *Völkisch und national: Zur Aktualität alter Denkmuster im 21. Jahrhundert* (Darmstadt, 2009).
12. Wolf-Dietrich Bukow, "Soziogenese ethnischer Minoritäten," *Das Argument*, no. 181 (1990): 422–426, here 423 (emphasis in original).
13. See Anthony D. Smith, *National Identity* (London, 1991), 8.
14. See Wilhelm Heitmeyer, ed., *Deutsche Zustände*, 10 vols. (Frankfurt 2002-2011).
15. On the party's early history, see David Bebnowski, *Die Alternative für Deutschland: Aufstieg und gesellschaftliche Repräsentanz einer rechten populistischen Partei* (Wiesbaden, 2015); Sebastian Friedrich, *Der Aufstieg der AfD: Neokonservative Mobilmachung in Deutschland* (Berlin, 2015); Alexander Häusler and Rainer Roeser, *Die rechten "Mut"-Bürger: Entstehung, Entwicklung, Personal und Positionen der Alternative für Deutschland* (Hamburg, 2015); Andreas Kemper, *Rechte Euro-Rebellion: Alternative für Deutschland und Zivile Koalition e.V.* (Münster, 2013).
16. See Samuel Salzborn, *Angriff der Antidemokraten: Die völkische Rebellion der Neuen Rechten* (Weinheim, 2016).
17. See Frank Decker, Bernd Henningsen, and Kjetil Jakobsen, eds., *Rechtspopulismus und Rechtsextremismus in Europa: Die Herausforderung der Zivilgesellschaft durch alte Ideologien und neue Medien* (Baden-Baden, 2015); Ralf Melzer and Sebastian Serafin, ed., *Right-wing Extremism in Europe: Country Analyses, Counter-Strategies and Labor-Market Oriented Exit Strategies* (Berlin, 2013).
18. See Anton Pelinka, "Die FPÖ in der vergleichenden Parteienforschung: Zur typologischen Einordnung der Freiheitlichen Partei Österreichs," *Österreichische Zeitschrift für Politikwissenschaft* 31, no. 3 (2002): 281–299; Heribert Schiedel, *Der Rechte Rand: Extremistische Gesinnungen in unserer Gesellschaft* (Vienna, 2007).

19. See Jan Lohl, *Gefühlserbschaft und Rechtsextremismus: Eine sozialpsychologische Studie zur Generationengeschichte des Nationalsozialismus* (Giessen, 2010); Ingrid Peisker, *Vergangenheit, die nicht vergeht: Eine psychoanalytische Zeitdiagnose zur Auseinandersetzung mit dem Nationalsozialismus* (Giessen, 2005).
20. Harald Welzer, Sabine Moller, and Karoline Tschuggnall, *"Opa war kein Nazi": Nationalsozialismus und Holocaust im Familiengedächtnis* (Frankfurt, 2002).
21. See Jana Hensel, "Opa war kein Held," *Die Zeit Online*, 3 March 2018.
22. Thomas K. Bauer, "Einwanderung ist kein Minusgeschäft (Interview)," *Die Zeit Online*, 21 October 2010. See also Klaus J. Bade and Jochen Oltmer, *Normalfall Migration: Deutschland im 20. und frühen 21. Jahrhundert* (Bonn, 2004).
23. Hensel (see note 21).
24. See Kai Arzheimer, "The AfD: Finally a Successful Right-Wing Populist Eurosceptic Party for Germany?," *West European Politics* 38, no. 3 (2015), 535–556; Hans Vorländer, Maik Herold, and Steven Schäller, *PEGIDA: Entwicklung, Zusammensetzung und Deutung einer Empörungsbewegung* (Wiesbaden, 2016).
25. Alexander Gauland, "Hitler hat den Deutschen das Rückgrat gebrochen (Interview)," *Die Zeit*, 14 April 2016.
26. Ibid.
27. Ibid.
28. Alternative für Deutschland Landtagsfraktion Baden-Württemberg, "Pressemitteilung 'Gedenkstätte Gurs,'" 23 January 2017.
29. Quoted in Roland Muschel, "AfD will Fördergelder für Gurs-Gedenkstätte streichen," *Badische Zeitung*, 21 January 2017.
30. Alternative für Deutschland, *Programm für Deutschland: Das Grundsatzprogramm der Alternative für Deutschland* (Stuttgart, 2016), 48.
31. See Samuel Salzborn, *Antisemitismus: Geschichte, Theorie, Empirie* (Baden-Baden, 2014).
32. Björn Höcke, "Vollständiges Transkript der Rede vom 17. Januar 2017 im Ballhaus Watzke, Dresden im Rahmen der Veranstaltungsreihe 'Dresdner Gespräche' organisiert vom Jugendverband der Alternative für Deutschland, der 'Jungen Alternative;'" available at http://pastebin.com/jQujwe89, accessed 19 January 2017.
33. Ibid.
34. On the concept of "cover identity" (*Deckidentität*), see Elisabeth Brainin, Vera Ligeti, and Samy Teicher, *Vom Gedanken zur Tat: Zur Psychoanalyse des Antisemitismus* (Frankfurt, 1993), 64.
35. On the fiction of collective German guilt, see Norbert Frei, "Von deutscher Erfindungskraft oder: Die Kollektivschuldthese in der Nachkriegszeit," *Rechtshistorisches Journal* 16 (1997): 621–634.
36. Quoted in "Gauland fordert 'Stolz' auf deutsche Soldaten," *Frankfurter Allgemeine Zeitung online*, 14 September 2017.
37. Alexander Mitscherlich and Margarete Mitscherlich, *Die Unfähigkeit zu trauern: Grundlagen kollektiven Verhaltens* (Munich, 1980), 53–54.
38. Quoted in Hans-W. Saure and Anton Maegerle, "Skandal um antisemitisches Buch von W. Gedeon," *Bild*, 1 June 2016.
39. Quoted in Justus Bender and Rüdiger Soldt, "Im Eiferer-Modus gegen Juden," *Frankfurter Allgemeine Zeitung*, 4 June 2016.
40. Quoted in ibid.
41. On the search for outside experts, see Martin Krauss, "Rechtspopulisten halbiert. AfD spaltet sich wegen Umgang mit Antisemiten," *Jüdische Allgemeine*, 6 July 2016.
42. Quoted in Jens Rathmann and Thomas Thimm, "Vorwurf der Volksverhetzung," *Hannoversche Allgemeine*, 13 August 2015.
43. See also Jan Riebe, "Wie antisemitisch ist die AfD?," *Netz-gegen-Nazis.de*, 10 May 2016.
44. Quoted in Armin Pfahl-Traughber, "AfD: Antisemiten finden Durchlass; Es ist kein Zufall, dass in der 'Alternative für Deutschland' ständig judenfeindliche Skandale auftauchen," *Jüdische Allgemeine*, 9 June 2016.

45. Quoted in ibid.
46. Quoted in Carsten Meyer and Joachim F. Tornau, "Antisemit in der AfD," *blick nach rechts*, 25 July 2016.
47. See Knut Krohn, "Höcke verteidigt Holocaust-Leugnerin," *Stuttgarter Zeitung*, 22 November 2016.
48. Quoted in "AfD-Politiker lehnte Distanzierung von Holocaustzitat ab," *Die Zeit online*, 15 March 2017.
49. Quoted in Frederik Bombosch, "Auschwitz-Vergleich: Berliner AfD-Vize Hugh Bronson relativiert Shoah," *Berliner Zeitung*, 16 September 2016.
50. Quoted in Oliver Das Gupta, "AfD-Abgeordneter schmäht Flüchtlinge als 'widerliches Gewürm,'" *Süddeutsche Zeitung Online*, 20 September 2016.
51. See Marcus Funck, "Wolfgang Gedeon: Wie antisemitisch ist dieser AfD-Politiker?," *Die Zeit*, 11 August 2016.
52. Wolfgang Gedeon, "Zur Kritik von Marcus Funck in der Zeit;" available at www.wolfgang-gedeon.de/2016/09/zur-kritik-von-marcus-funck-in-der-zeit/, accessed 17 September 2016.
53. See Rüdiger Soldt, "Unangemessene Formen," *Frankfurter Allgemeine Zeitung*, 16 November 2016.
54. Stefan Kuzmany, "Höcke darf in der AfD bleiben: Partei für Nazis und Mitläufer," *Spiegel Online*, 23 January 2017.
55. See "Nazi-Ideologie in der AfD," *Stern*, 25 January 2017.
56. See Benjamin Steinitz and Daniel Poensgen, "Die AfD im Spannungsfeld zwischen Relativierung und Instrumentalisierung des Antisemitismus," *rechtsaussen.berlin*, November 2017.
57. See "Gauland bringt kritische Sätze über Israels Existenzrecht," *Berliner Kurier*, 25 September 2017.
58. See Thomas Petersen, "Wie antisemitisch ist Deutschland?" *Frankfurter Allgemeine Zeitung*, 20 June 2018.

··· Chapter 13 ···

GERMANY'S AUSSENPOLIK AFTER THE ELECTION

Stephen F. Szabo

The main consequence of the 2017 Bundestag election has been its impact on the stability and reliability of Germany as a foreign policy actor. The emergence of a seven-party system is likely to be a factor for at least the next four to eight years and this will make managing a coalition government more difficult than at any time since the stabilization of the Federal Republic's foreign policy in 1955, when West Germany entered NATO. This comes at a time of great instability in Germany's strategic environment and the consequent need for more–not less– German leadership. The presence of a right-wing extremist party, the Alternative for Germany (AfD) as the largest opposition party in the Bundestag is an entirely new and unpredictable factor. The weakening of Chancellor Angela Merkel's position and the anticipation that she will leave office during or at the end of this term have made the weakening of Germany's leadership role in Europe and especially on Russia policy more likely. While many in Germany welcome this lowering of expectations,[1] it comes at a time when there is a leadership deficit in Europe and Germany is the most important power in the region.

The Electorate and German Foreign Policy

The outcome of the 2017 election and the almost half year it took afterwards to form a government was not the intention of the German electorate. Post elections polls found that the public believed the Christian Democrats (CDU/CSU) to be the most competent party in foreign policy with 48 percent choosing them compared to 21 percent favoring the Social Democrats (SPD)

Notes for this section begin on page 286.

and 17 percent the AfD. Confidence in Angela Merkel's leadership was also substantial with 56 percent preferring her to be chancellor compared to only 34 percent favoring Martin Schulz, the Social Democrats' chancellor candidate. Voters believed she was by far the most competent in understanding the issues.[2] The election, however, was not about foreign policy in the classic sense but was dominated by a foreign policy issue, namely refugees and the presence of foreigners in Germany. When asked what problems those polled found as most important in the election, 44 percent listed refugees and foreigners, 24 percent pensions, 16 percent social inequality, 9 percent criminality or domestic security, and 8 percent unemployment. On the key issue of which party was most competent to deal with refugees and asylum seekers, 35 percent listed the CDU/CSU, 19 percent AfD, and 15 percent the SPD. On what voters saw as a related issue–criminality and domestic security–40 percent chose the AfD, 34 percent the CDU/CSU, and only 11 percent the SPD. The AfD mobilized nonvoters in large numbers but also gained from those who had voted for the Christian Democrats (accounting for 21 percent of the AfD vote), while the SPD lost 10 percent of their previous voters to the new right party.[3]

A poll conducted in November 2017 by the Körber Foundation also indicated the continuing saliency of this complex of issues with 56 percent of those polled favoring limiting the number of refugees in Germany and 59 percent supporting European Union aid to African states for border protection to reduce migration, even if those states were known to commit human rights abuses.[4] The same poll found that refugees were listed as the most important challenge currently facing German foreign policy, with 26 percent listing it compared to 19 percent choosing relations with the U.S./Trump and 17 percent relations with Turkey/Erdogan. A large majority (69 percent) stated that they were strongly or very strongly interested in German foreign policy with 52 percent wanting Germany to become more involved in international crises. The areas of international engagement which this group selected were ensuring the security of Germany and its allies (71 percent), protecting the environment and the climate (67 percent), protecting human rights (64 percent) and regulating and reducing illegal immigration to Germany (54 percent).[5]

The New GroKo Government: Unruly and Unpredictable

The grand coalition (Grosse Koalition or GroKo) government which finally emerged after over five months of negotiations and one failed attempt to form a Jamaica coalition (of CDU/CSU, FDP and Greens based on the parties' colors corresponding to the flag of that country), found the Social Democrats in a stronger position than its electoral results would have indicated. Although the SPD received a third fewer votes than the Christian Democrats, it ended up with five ministries including the Finance, Foreign and Labor Ministries. The CSU came away with Interior, important on domestic security and refugees and Transportation. The CDU kept the Chancellery, but has only the Defense, Economics, Health, Education, and Agriculture portfolios.

This constellation means that Chancellor Merkel enters what will be her final term in office greatly weakened in the foreign policy area. She will no longer have her key national security advisor, Christoph Heusgen, who moved to the UN as German ambassador. His successor as director of the important Abteilung 2 in the Chancellery, Jan Hecker, was a surprise appointment. A former federal judge, Hecker has little foreign policy experience and has not served in the Foreign Office. He worked with the chancellor as her refugee coordinator since October 2015 on the wide range of issues surrounding the refugee crisis, including the agreement with Turkey. Merkel has also lost Wolfgang Schäuble as Finance Minister and Thomas de Maziere, who played a key role for her at Defense and then as interior minister. Her chief of staff, Peter Altmaier, moves to the Economics Ministry. Finally, her appointment of Annegret Kramp-Karrenbauer to be the general secretary of the CDU is clearly meant to pave her way as Merkel's successor, while the appointment of Jens Spahn, a clear critic and rival, to the Health Ministry sets up the beginning of a succession struggle which will further dilute her authority. The fact that the party forced the Spahn appointment on the chancellor indicates her weakened position.

The role of the chancellor in foreign policy has been one of largely setting policy guidelines and then coordinating policy in the cabinet. As Josef Janning noted: "A lot of foreign policy is made in the chancellery. That is always the case when you are dealing with chancellors who have passed their first term in office. Chancellors tend to take on more and more of the issues relating to European and international affairs."[6] However, ministers under the *Resortsprinzip* have a great deal of autonomy once the policy guidelines are set, an autonomy strengthened by the importance of the professional civil service in each ministry. This principle of ministerial competence combined with the constraints of the coalition agreement and the fact that five of the ministers in this cabinet are Social Democrats and two are from the CSU means that her role will be limited to a few issues that she deems vital, the so called *Chefsachen.* In addition, she has a very small staff dealing with foreign and security policy (less than twenty-five all told in the key Abteilung 2). In the previous government, the chancellor played a central role on refugee policy, Russia, Europe and the Eurozone, and Transatlantic relations. The extent that she can continue to control these areas will be greatly limited in her final term.

As Horst Seehofer's first statement as interior minister on Muslims not belonging in Germany and the response of the Social Democratic ministers indicates, cabinet members seem to fear Merkel less and are more worried about their own constituencies.[7] In Seehofer's case, the upcoming Bavarian state election in October 2018 and the threat to the Christian Social Union's dominance in that state posed by the rise of the Alternative for Germany is regarded as more important than maintaining cabinet unity. Seehofer is following the example of the agriculture minister in the former government, Christian Schmidt, also of the CSU, who went against cabinet discipline in agreeing to renew an EU license for a contentious weed killer, illustrating Merkel's weakness even then. [8]

New Foreign Minister Heiko Maas, served as justice minister in the previous government. He is a newcomer to foreign policy with no known positions on key issues and will rely on the extensive and competent network of German diplomats in the Foreign Office. He is well known and respected in the SPD and will work closely with Olaf Scholz, the finance minister. Another important foreign policy ministry, Defense, remains with Ursula von der Leyen of the CDU, who will be a candidate to succeed Merkel and who will want to keep a high profile. Whether she will be able to do so in a politically unpopular portfolio will be a major question and she starts her new term under the shadow of a scathing report from the Parliamentary Commissioner for the Bundeswehr, Hans Peter Bartels (SPD), which laid out her failures to address major deficiencies in equipment, training, and personnel in the armed forces. Economics Minister Altmaier, will play an important role in two foreign policy related areas–trade and energy. His closeness to the chancellor from his time as her chief of staff, combined with the centrality of trade to Germany's foreign policy will give him a central role. He traveled to Washington in March 2018 just days after being sworn in to deal with the issue of the Trump tariffs on steel and aluminum.

The Foreign Policy Agenda

The final Merkel government is facing the greatest upheaval in German foreign policy since reunification with all its major pillars under great strain. The *Westbindung*, which has anchored German foreign policy since 1949 resting on the twin pillars of NATO and the European Union, are now challenged both in the United States and within Europe. The legacy of *Ostpolitik* and of engagement with Russia is now under the greatest stress since the Euromissile debate of the 1980s given Russia's actions since its seizure of Crimea. Germany's role as the world's greatest export nation is now threatened by the rise of protectionism, not the least from the architect of the postwar liberal economic order, the United States. Demands for and concerns about Germany's leadership role in the West are at the highest level in the postwar German experience.

While Germany does not regard itself as a regional hegemon and continues to be reluctant as being seen as Europe's indispensable power, it has taken the lead on eurozone stabilization, Russia, EU refugee and energy policies during the previous GroKo. Its agenda will have to focus on European policy and the Franco-German relationship including the issue of populism, the rise of illiberal governments in Europe, and the implications of Brexit. In addition, relations with Russia, Turkey, the United States and Transatlantic relations will demand German policy responses.

Europe and the Franco-German Relationship

The Körber Foundation poll asked Germans which partnership the future priority for Germany's defense policy should be and 88 percent chose that with the European states to only 9 percent selecting the U.S. France was selected by 63 percent as Germany's most important partner, followed by the U.S. at 43 percent. This poll also found that close to a third support Germany playing a more dominant role in the EU, while only 15 percent thought it was too dominant. Nevertheless, 59 percent believed that the EU was not on the right track, and 54 percent opposed the creation of a European minister of finance. [9]

The coalition agreement with the SPD stands in stark contrast on European policy from the one which would have emerged from the Jamaica negotiations. The Free Democrat's (FDP) leader, Christian Lindner, had taken a tough line on the Eurozone, rejecting a common budget and calling for the exit of Greece from the euro. FDP voters along with those supporting the AfD and the CSU are clearly more euroskeptical and would have pulled Merkel toward a tougher line on the eurozone and on EU budget negotiations. Lindner, made it clear that any Eurozone reform that entailed major fiscal transfers as part of a Eurozone budget and cost Germany money would be "a line in the sand." Before the election, newly elected French President Emmanuel Macron had said "If Merkel is tied to the Liberals then I am dead."[10]

Now the prospect for some movement on both Franco-German relations and the Eurozone are improved with the SPD pushing through a pro EU position in the coalition agreement. This agreement begins with a rousing defense of the importance of Europe to Germany and the need to strengthen EU institutions against antiliberal tendencies. It singles out the importance of the Franco-German relationship to the European renewal. "The renewal of the EU can only be accomplished if Germany and France work for it together with their entire power."[11] While these generalities will have to be given substance by the new government, however, its support for the EU's Permanent Structured Cooperation (PESCO) initiative in defense is clear.

While Macron supports creating a Eurozone budget, appointing a European finance minister, and establishing a European Monetary Fund, the GroKo agreement is less clear on financial policy calling for fiscal controls, economic cooperation, and the fight against tax evasion and tax avoidance. It supports the idea of a European Monetary Fund which is responsible to national parliaments but makes no mention of a European finance minister. The SPD leadership is closer to the Macron view than is the chancellor. Merkel favors a small monetary fund to support structural reform in Eurozone countries, but the German public has been wary of such attempts, arguing they would encourage fiscally irresponsible behavior–a fear enhanced by the 2018 Italian elections which produced a victory for anti-European parties. The decision over the appointment of the new head of the European Central Bank (ECB) in 2019 will be an indicator of the future of Eurozone policy. If Jens Weidmann, the head of the Bundesbank, is pushed by the German government it will conflict with Macron's desire for a more relaxed approach on monetary policy. "German's priority for the ECB is a change in policy rather than personnel. German savers hate low interest rates, while the broader economic and political establishment denounces the banks euro 2.3 trillion quantitative easing program."[12] Merkel's first trip in her fourth term was to Paris where she was met with both hope and skepticism that Germany will take the bold steps called for by the French president. At her meeting with Macron she stated: "I know that you have waited a long time but our coalition deal… is a response to France's demands."[13]

The role of the AfD as the main opposition party in the Bundestag as well as the euroskeptical views of the CSU will make a major European initiative unlikely, except in the areas of border security and counterterrorism. Macron's focus on border security and counterterrorism measures and his crackdown on immigrants have broad appeal among the CSU and the CDU.

Given that there is a CSU minister of the interior, Macron should find an ally in Berlin. All this portends a tougher position on immigration and asylum within the EU in light also of the new Austrian government and trends in Italy and other EU member states, but less than Macron has asked for on the Eurozone.

While the coalition agreement makes a strong statement in favor of an open Europe, the election results have placed in question Germany's role as leader of the liberal order. As many European and American media reactions show, the sense from outside of Germany is that of a "normalized Germany" that is not that different from the rest of the West. Anne Applebaum in her column concluded:

> Germany now becomes one of a team of countries fighting similar problems, rather than a disinterested outsider. The leading political minds of the richest country in Europe are now forced to focus with a good deal more urgency on calming the anti-immigrant, anti-EU emotions in their own country, instead of just denouncing it in others. This is important, because German policy–on refugees, money and much else–is itself the source of some of these emotions, or at least that's how many perceive it. Finally, Germany will be forced to confront these issues at home. So yes, Merkel keeps her job, but that job just got harder.[14]

The reaction in Poland has also made the point that Merkel remains vulnerable about the refugee issue and both Stephen Bannon and Viktor Orban supported the winning euroskeptical parties in the Italian election. Partnership with Poland is singled out in the coalition agreement, which proposes intensifying contacts without mentioning the state of democracy in that country. The acting German government had already warned Poland about the violation of the rule of law and supported the EU Commission's actions against it for not accepting asylum seekers. The problem of democratic backsliding in Central Europe will be a divisive one for the new government given the close ties of the CSU to populist leaders in Poland and Hungary and the presence of AfD in the Bundestag. Here is an arena where Foreign Minister Maas may make a difference as he has been an outspoken defender of the liberal order at home including his efforts as justice minister to impose tough hate speech laws on social media sites and his criticism of the German far right.

On Brexit, the GroKo agreement states that it regrets the United Kingdom's decision to leave the European Union and wants to keep a good relationship with Britain after its departure. All the parties in the coalition want a good relationship with the UK after Brexit but not at the cost of "cherry picking" or a la carte options for that country. They will also support a policy of that carries some pain for the UK to discourage other EU members from following suit. German industry is more concerned about a viable European single market than it is about its investments in Britain and is hoping to benefit from the outmigration of eastern Europeans from the UK to Germany. Frankfurt is also vying to replace London as Europe's premier financial center.[15] Still, the loss of the UK as an EU member poses a budget shortfall in Brussels that will have to be covered in part by Germany. Berlin also loses a strong ally regarding its desire to promote liberalization of EU markets.

Russia

It was noteworthy that Russian efforts to affect the outcome of the German election were not very apparent or successful. On the one hand, there is some evidence of efforts in eastern Germany to help the AfD, as well as to influence the 2 million Russian speakers in Germany. This may have had some impact in the east where the AfD came in as the second party with almost a quarter of the votes. On the other hand, Putin already had several sympathetic partners in Germany. Except for the CDU and the Greens, all the other parties are either soft on Russia or are willing enablers of Putin (the Left Party and the AfD). The CSU has been urging the end of sanctions and the SPD has promoted the Nord Stream 2 gas pipeline between Germany and Russia. During the election campaign, FDP leader Lindner made a remarkable statement calling the Crimea annexation a permanent provisional situation and signaling a move away from the Minsk 2 agreement on Ukraine. The Greens have been very critical of Russia and Putin, but with the SPD once again in the government, the line on Russia is likely to soften. The controversial Nord Stream 2 project received approval from the caretaker government in January 2018 to begin construction in German territorial waters. Merkel's spokesman has repeated the position that this is "a purely commercial project," and it will proceed under the new government.[16]

The coalition agreement's statements on Russia do not reveal much new in German policy, reiterating that the Russian violation of Ukrainian sovereignty damaged the European peace order and requires "attentiveness and resilience." It repeats the SPD position of the importance of cooperation with Russia to Germany and to European security. While the Russian market has waned in importance for Germany, Russia still supplies about 35 percent of German oil and gas and a substantial Russia business lobby exists in Berlin. Its most prominent member is former Chancellor Gerhard Schröder who heads the board of the Russian gas concern, Rosneft, and is a major figure in promoting Russian interests within the SPD including the Nord Stream 2 gas pipeline. Merkel had to take the extraordinary step of declining to impose sanctions on Schröder for his work with the Russians.[17]

The massive decline of confidence in the Trump Administration and in the United States more generally has resulted in a new relativization of Russia and America among many Germans. The Körber Foundation's "Berlin Pulse" poll taken at the end of 2017 found that 78 percent of Germans polled believed that Germany should cooperate more with Russia, while the figure for cooperating more with the U.S. was 56 percent. Only 11 percent, however, felt Russia was a first or second most important partner for Germany, while 43 percent regarded the U.S. as one of Germany's two most important partners.[18] That said, the German public finds Putin more reliable than Trump. A poll taken in February 2018 found that although Germans assessed the prospect of Putin's re-election as Russian president as bad, only 53 percent found his policies cause for great or some worry. Meanwhile, 82 percent had similar worries about Donald Trump.[19]

Given the centrality of Chancellor Merkel's leadership both in Germany and in Europe on Russia policy and the great uncertainty of the Trump policies on Russia, a weakening of Merkel's position on Russia will have decisive consequences for how the West responds to a recently re-elected President Putin whose aggressive foreign and defense policies are widely supported in Russia.

Turkey

The German public has an overwhelmingly negative view of contemporary Turkey. A Pew/Körber poll conducted in late 2017 found that relations with Turkey ranked only behind refugees and relations with the United States as the greatest challenge facing German foreign policy. Turkey ranked lowest in trust of eight countries (at 2 percent) among Germany's most important partners. Three-fourths of Germans polled believed that EU accession talks with Turkey should be broken off, and by a margin of 75 percent to 19 percent believed that Germany should adopt a hard position toward Turkey on the refugee agreement, even if it jeopardizes the deal.[20] Polls taken earlier in 2017 produced similar findings.[21] In a poll taken by the German broadcaster ARD in 2017, only 11 percent of those polled held out any hope "that the German-Turkish relationship will improve in the next years," while 57 percent believed the chances to be small, and 30 percent very small.[22]

Germany's relations with Turkey hit an all-time low during the Merkel's third term as chancellor. The legacy of twelve years of Merkel's Turkey policy has been characterized as one "without concept or strategy or if there is a strategic element it concerns preserving the power and party political interests of the Chancellor."[23] Merkel has shifted from an emphasis on democratic values and human rights to a purely realist concern about stemming the flow of refugees, and has alternated between a policy of confrontation and appeasement.[24] The coalition agreement text on Turkey indicates German policy on Turkey is on hold until after the Turkish elections of 2018 due to the backsliding of democracy in Turkey,

> Turkey is an important partner of Germany and neighbor to the EU, with which we have a variety of relations. Therefore, we have a special interest in a good relationship to Turkey. The state of democracy, the rule of law, and human rights in Turkey has been worsening for a long period. Therefore, we are not willing to close any chapters in accession negotiations or open new ones. Visa liberalization or an expansion of the customs union will only be possible once Turkey fulfills the necessary preconditions.[25]

Merkel in her "Statement of Government Policy," which opened her term in March 2018, took a strong position on the Turkish offensive against the Kurds in the Afrin region of Syria, calling it "unacceptable" and that "we condemn it in the sharpest terms." The Social Democrats for both foreign policy and domestic political concerns are more open to keeping the door to Turkey's membership in the EU open than are the Christian Democrats, but the continuing violation of democratic norms and the rule of law in Turkey make any movement in Berlin unlikely until after the 2018 presidential election in Turkey. The new government understands that it cannot ignore Turkey and must take a long-term approach with the idea that Turkey policy must be more than an Erdogan policy.[26] Given its population of over 3 million Germans of Turkish origin and its economic relationship with Turkey, Germany cannot take a view that Turkey is lost. Amanda Sloat in her study of the West's relationship with Turkey outlined three policy options for the future: abandonment, transactionalism, and engagement.[27] Germany does not have the option of abandonment and is currently pursuing elements of transactionalism and engagement with the hope that over the long term, engagement will return as the dominant approach. A common Transatlantic approach along these lines seems to be the best long-term approach, with transactionalism as the medium-term bridge. As Kemal Kirişci has persuasively argued, "continuing to engage Turkey rather than abandoning it is of paramount importance. ... [I]t is important that both the EU and the United States continue to support the process in Turkey to keep its EU membership prospects alive, whatever the challenges might be."[28]

Transatlantic Relations

Donald Trump is deeply unpopular with the German public and the Social Democrats ran against him in their campaign. Merkel has been conscious of avoiding the kind of rhetoric that led to a split during the Bush-Schröder years over Iraq. During the campaign, she avoided demonizing Trump as the SPD did, and it did not cost her votes. She understands the German interest in a relationship that is the ultimate guarantee of German security and in which Germany has a major economic stake. Even more than is the case with Turkey, Germany cannot afford a major break with Washington. The German public understands this well. Although it deeply distrusts the American president, it sees the U.S. as Germany's second most important partner after France (63 percent, U.S. 43 percent and Russia only 11 percent). As mentioned above, in that same poll, however, 78 percent want to see more cooperation with Russia with only 56 percent wanted to do the same with the United States.[29] At the same time, Germany is less able to criticize Trump on human rights and immigration given the rise of anti-immigrant and (arguably) antidemocratic forces in Germany. This goes with the view that a less extraordinary Germany may be less vocal on these issues.

Given Germany's heavy dependence on exports and the emergence of the American market as the largest for Germany, trade and an open international economic order are as existential as the nuclear issue to Germany. Economics Minister Altmaier's first foreign trip was to Washington to argue against protectionist policies. The Transatlantic Trade and Investment Partnership, (TTIP) is probably dead as a formal agreement, but there will be efforts to at least stabilize the trade relationship with Washington and to protect German investments there. Germany also needs the United States to balance Chinese efforts to take over key German firms and to shape the international system in its image.[30]

On defense spending, the SPD ran against the Merkel pledge to increase outlays to 2 percent of GDP as a form of kowtowing to Trump. The coalition agreement makes some vague statement about increasing defense spending, but links these increases euro for euro to increases in development assistance. The CDU has kept the Defense Ministry with von der Leyen remaining as minister, but she was immediately confronted with a scathing report on the poor state of the Bundeswehr and of its equipment from the SPD Parliamentary Commissioner for the Bundeswehr, Hans Peter Bartels.[31] Germany will have to take defense more seriously as both the chancellor and outgoing Foreign Minister Sigmar Gabriel have made the point that the changes in America's European policies go beyond Trump. The efforts to work with France on a more European defense effort along with the NATO framework nations approach will continue and German troops will remain part of the NATO stabilization force in the Baltics. Germany will also enhance its efforts in cybersecurity.

In its overall approach toward the United States, continuity and buying time will come at the subnational level and in civil society with an important role for outreach to governors, mayors, the private sector, academia, think tanks and foundations in keeping things going at the working level until the national political level stabilizes. The German-American relationship is one with a wide base and not one only centered in Berlin and Washington.[32]

Conclusion

Overall the implications of Merkel 4.0 for German foreign policy are not promising. Germany will not take on the leadership role many in the West would like to see. It is likely to be even less decisive than before given the many splits within the coalition and the beginning of a succession struggle to replace an increasingly lame duck chancellor. This is very bad news for a West which seems to be collapsing from within while it faces a hostile Russia, a predatory China, and an unstable southern neighborhood. Germany has proved to be a good partner, but one that has an underdeveloped sense of leadership or of offering public goods in its role as Europe's leading power. It continues to have a small strategic elite and lacks a strategic culture needed for its new and dangerous environment. It has proved an effective geoeconomic power, but has yet to grasp what it means to be more than that.

Merkel 4.0 is likely to be a transitional and unruly government which will bridge the end of the Merkel era and the start of a new one led by a new generation of leaders. It is instructive that those members of the CDU and the SPD least happy with the new GroKo are the youngest members. As representatives from new generations now lead Austria, France, and Italy, Germany is not far behind. Although the cabinet has an average age of 51.2–seven years older than the average for the general population–it does contain a few more younger faces, women, and perhaps some new energy. The entry into the cabinet of Julia Klöckner and Jens Spahn from the CDU and Franziska Giffey of the SPD are indicators of this coming change. The question is whether Germany and Europe have the time to wait for these new leaders.

Dr. Stephen F. Szabo is currently a Senior Fellow at the American Institute for Contemporary German Studies and Adjunct Lecturer in European Studies at SAIS, Johns Hopkins University. He has published widely on European and German politics and foreign policies, including. *The Successor Generation: International Perspectives of Postwar Europeans* (Boston, 1983), *The Diplomacy of German Unification* (New York, 1992), *Parting Ways: The Crisis in the German-American Relationship* (Washington, 2004), and *Germany, Russia and the Rise of Geo-Economics* (London, 2015). E-mail: sfszabo1@gmail.com

Notes

1. Rick Noack, "Germany won't become the 'leader of the free world' after all, and the Germans don't mind," *The Washington Post,* 21 February 2018; available at https://www.washingtonpost.com/news/worldviews/wp/2018/02/21/germany-wont-become-the-leader-of-the-free-world-after-all-and-germans-dont-mind/?utm_term=.36437892d159, accessed 17 April 2018.
2. The data are from the election analysis of Forschungsgruppe Wahlen E.V., "Bundestagswahl 24 September 2017;" available at http://www.forschungsgruppe.de/Aktuelles/Wahlanalyse_Bundestagswahl/Newsl_Bund_170928.pdf, accessed 17 April 2018.
3. All these data are taken from the Forschungsgruppe Wahlen (see note 2).
4. Körber Foundation, "The Berlin Pulse 2017: German Foreign Policy in Perspective," 38; available at https://www.koerber-stiftung.de/fileadmin/user_upload/koerber-stiftung/redaktion/berliner-forum-aussenpolitik/pdf/2017/The-Berlin-Pulse.pdf, accessed 17 April 2018.
5. Ibid., 33.
6. Quoted in Tobias Buck, "SPD ousts Gabriel from German cabinet," *The Financial Times,* 9 March 2018.
7. "German ministers respond to Horst Seehofer's Islam comments," *Deutsche Welle,* 17 March 2018; available at http://www.dw.com/en/german-ministers-respond-to-horst-seehofers-islam-comments/a-43017955, accessed 17 April 2018.
8. Matthew Karnitschnig, "Germany goes Rogue," *Politico,* 6 December 2017; available at https://www.politico.eu/article/glyphosate-christian-schmidt-decision-angela-merkel-germany-goes-rogue/, accessed 17 April 2018.
9. "The Berlin Pulse" (see note 4), 36, 37.
10. See Matthias Matthijs and Erik Jones, "This Was the Worst Possible German Election for Europe," *Foreign Policy.com,* 26 September 2017; available at https://foreignpolicy.com/2017/09/26/this-was-the-worst-possible-german-election-for-europe/, accessed 17 April 2018.
11. The agreement can be found at: "Ein neuer Aufbruch für Europa Eine neue Dynamik für Deutschland Ein neuer Zusammenhalt für unser Land Koalitionsvertrag zwischen CDU, CSU und SPD," Berlin, 7 February 2018, 152–153; available at https://www.ndr.de/nachrichten/koalitionsvertrag228.pdf, accessed 17 April 2018.
12. Claire Jones and Cuy Chazan, "Germany wary of nominating Weidmann as head of ECB," *The Financial Times,* 8 March 2018.
13. Anne Sylvaine Chassany, Guy Chazan, and Mehreen Khan, "Macron pushes Merkel hard on eurozone reform," *The Financial Times,* 17/18 March 2018.
14. Anne Applebaum, "The German election gives the country a reality check," *The Washington Post,* 24 September 2017; available at https://www.washingtonpost.com/news/global-

opinions/wp/2017/09/24/germanys-election-gives-the-country-a-reality-check/?utm_term =.da82cfbbb7c1, accessed 17 April 2018.

15. Eric Langenbacher, "*Tschüss*, Perfidious Albion: German Reactions to Brexit," *German Politics and Society* 35, no. 3 (2017): 69–85: Christian Odendahl, "Germany's Biggest Brexit Boon: Immigrants," *Politico* 18 December 2017; available at https://www.politico.eu/article/opinion-germanys-biggest-brexit-boon-migration/, accessed 17 April 2018.
16. Andrew Rettman," Germany still backs Russia gas pipeline," *EU Observer,* 5 March 2018; available at https://euobserver.com/energy/141204, accessed 17 April 2018.
17. "Regierung lehnt sanktionen gegen Schröder ab," *Frankfurter Allgemeine Zeitung*, 19 March 2018; available at http://www.faz.net/aktuell/wirtschaft/bundesregierung-lehnt-sanktionen-gegen-gerhard-schroeder-ab-15501618.html, accessed 17 April 2018.
18. The Berlin Pulse (see note 4), 33, 34.
19. Forschungsgruppe Wahlen, *Politbarometer,* March 2018; available at http://www.forschungsgruppe.de/Aktuelles/Politbarometer/, accessed 17 April 2018.
20. "The Berlin Pulse" (see note 4), 33–40.
21. Ellen Ehni, "84 Prozent gegen Türkei in der EU," ARD-DeutschlandTrend, 7 September 2017; available at https://www.tagesschau.de/inland/deutschlandtrend-909.html, accessed 17 April 2018.
22. "Infratest Dimap," ARD-DeutschlandTrend, June 2017), 13; available at https://www.infratest-dimap.de/fileadmin/user_upload/dt1706_bericht.pdf, accessed 17 April 2018.
23. Rosa Burc and Burak Copur, "Deutsche Türkeipolitik unter Merkel: eine Kritische Bilanz," Institut Français des Relations Internationales, Paris, September 2017, 25.
24. For a detailed account of the development of Merkel's policy, including interviews with the key players both in Germany and the EU, see Robin Alexander, *Die Getriebenen: Merkel und die Flüchtlingspolitik: Report aus dem Innern der Macht* (Munich, 2017).
25. Ein neuer Aufbruch (see note 11), 152–153.
26. Juliane Schäuble and Christian Böhme, "Deutschland sollte weniger über Erdogan reden," *Der Tagesspiegel,* 28 January 2018; available at http://www.tagesspiegel.de/politik/swp-chef-volker-perthes-deutschland-sollte-weniger-ueber-erdogan-reden/20899564.html, accessed 17 April 2018.
27. Amanda Sloat, "The West's Turkey Conundrum," Brookings Institution, Washington, February 2018, 14; available at https://www.brookings.edu/wp-content/uploads/2018/02/fp_20180212_west_turkey_conundrum.pdf, accessed 17 April 2018.
28. Kemal Kiri ci, *Turkey and the West: Fault Lines in a Troubled Alliance* (Washington, 2017), 192-193. For a treatment of the German relationship with Turkey see, Stephen F. Szabo, "Germany and Turkey: The Unavoidable Partnership," Brookings Institution, Washington, March 2018.
29. The Berlin Pulse (see note 4), 34.
30. Liz Alderman, "Wary of China, Europe and Others Push Back on Foreign Takeovers," *The New York Times*, 15 March 2018; available at https://www.nytimes.com/2018/03/15/business/china-europe-canada-australia-deals.html, accessed 17 April 2018; Francois Godement and Abegael Vasselier, "China at the Gates: A new power audit of EU-China relations," European Council on Foreign Relations, London, December 2017; available at http://www.ecfr.eu/page/-/China_Power_Audit.pdf, accessed 17 April 2018.
31. "Germany's lack of military readiness 'dramatic,' says Bundeswehr commissioner," *Deutsche Welle*, 2 February 2018; available at http://www.dw.com/en/germanys-lack-of-military-readiness-dramatic-says-bundeswehr-commissioner/a-42663215, accessed 17 April 2018.
32. See Frederik Bozo et al., "Suspicious Minds: U.S.-German Relations in the Trump Era," Transatlantic Academy, Washington, 2017; available at http://www.transatlanticacademy.org/sites/default/files/publications/Suspicious_Minds_Final_0.pdf, accessed 17 April 2018.

··· Chapter 14 ···

Germany's Role in the EU-27 Leadership Constellation after Brexit

Christian Schweiger

Throughout the past decade, the European Union has witnessed substantial and multiple crises. The 2008 global financial crisis was followed by the triple banking, economic, and sovereign debt crisis in selected Eurozone (and non-Eurozone) countries. Ultimately, the crisis posed a systemic risk to the future of the single currency, which required political management. Under the conditions of the crisis, Germany moved into the position of the EU's leadership hegemon. Initially, this was widely welcomed as none of the other larger member states was able to exercise the role of economic stabilizer in the Eurozone in the way Berlin could on the basis of Germany's economic and financial power resources, which prevailed even at the time of the financial crisis. The uncompromising leadership style that was adopted by German Chancellor Angela Merkel in the management of both the Eurozone and the subsequent migration crisis, nevertheless became increasingly contested. Most of all, German leadership contributed towards the deepening of the EU's lingering legitimacy problem. This is reflected by the dwindling levels of trust in EU-level institutions and policies, as well as the growing support for euroskeptic populist parties on the far left and far right of the political spectrum in many member states. The peak of this development was the decision of the majority of British voters to leave the EU in the June 2016 referendum.

Brexit, hence, confronts the EU with the unprecedented situation of having to face the first instance of disintegration, after a period of more six decades of continuous European integration. The major risk associated with this development is that Brexit may turn out not to be an isolated event, but as the tipping point towards the wider disintegration and ultimately the

Notes for this section begin on page 301.

breakup of the EU. This article critically examines Germany's role in the partial disintegration of the EU and its potential contribution towards stabilizing the European project after Brexit. The analysis adopts a liberal intergovernmentalist perspective that is most suitable to theoretically frame the obvious tendency of a new focus on domestic economic and political interests in the EU under adverse external crisis conditions.

The EU's Multiple Crises and the Declining Fortunes of Germany's Leadership

The Global Financial Crisis and the Eurozone Crisis

The dramatic events which unfolded in the EU and the Eurozone after the onset of the global financial crisis in 2008 swiftly forced the then still relatively inexperienced German Chancellor Merkel to abandon the traditional leadership avoidance reflex that had characterized Germany's postwar European policy.[1] The traditional German approach of acting in close multilateral consultation with European partners, in particular with France, was failing at a time when none of the other five largest member states was able to match Berlin's economic and political standing. France's political influence, which had been in the wane for some time due to the weakness of the French economy, was diminished further by the financial crisis. The sluggish growth of the French economy received a further setback and the ailing French public finances were heavily burdened by the need to recapitalize French banks that had been severely affected by sovereign risk. French President Nicolas Sarkozy was consequently confronted with deepening budgetary problems and the lingering risk that France would follow the economies of Southern Europe in losing its positive credit rating.[2] Ultimately, this left France in the position of Germany's unequal junior partner, moving from an initially active policy phase during which Sarkozy tried to set the agenda of collective European action in the form of a stimulus package and Eurobonds,[3] towards a reactive follower of Germany's increasingly dominant leadership. The resulting presentation of the Eurozone crisis policy responses as part of the "Merkozy" leadership duo represented an unequal revival of the formerly relatively balanced Franco-German axis.[4] France had turned into a junior partner whose role was reduced to rubber-stamping predominantly German ordoliberal policies and granting them broader legitimacy through the usual joint Franco-German public presentation.[5]

The United Kingdom faced similar problems because the financial crisis had pushed it into an almost existential crisis of its banking sector. For the

British Labour government led by Gordon Brown, the recapitalization of major UK-based banks, such as HBOS, the Royal Bank of Scotland, and Lloyds TSB, hence became the priority. There was consequently little interest on the British part to actively support Germany in the management of the Eurozone crisis. Brown prioritized the reform of the global regulatory framework over European efforts to stabilize the financial industry.[6] His Conservative successor, David Cameron, refocused his efforts on resolving the growing British budget deficit, which had emerged because of the massive financial efforts to rescue British banks. After 2010, the British government hence adopted a predominantly domestic perspective that prioritized budgetary austerity and the revitalization of the culture of credit-driven "privatized Keynesianism."[7] As disciples of Margaret Thatcher's free-market economic doctrines, Cameron and George Osborne, his chancellor of the exchequer, followed the neoliberal path-dependent culture of the new finance-driven liberal economy, which Thatcher had established in the 1980s.[8] An essential feature of the British liberal economy is the deep-seated skepticism towards the transfer of regulatory authority to supranational institutions, particularly on the EU level. Cameron consequently pursued a strategy that was orientated towards legally determining the UK's permanent differentiation from the deepening political integration in the Eurozone. Cameron's goal was to ensure that the UK would remain a "permanent outsider" from the deepening of political coordination in the Eurozone.[9] For this purpose, he demanded the renegotiation of the British EU membership terms that he had laid out in his 2013 Bloomberg speech. In that speech, Cameron emphasized the need to secure a permanent opt-out from deeper political integration in the EU, particularly in relation to financial supervision, without being discriminated against in terms of overall EU decision-making:

> [There is] a real choice between leaving or being part of a new settlement in which Britain shapes and respects the rules of the single market but is protected by fair safeguards, and free of the spurious regulation which damages Europe's competitiveness.[10]

Cameron had previously vetoed the inclusion of the Fiscal Compact into the EU's legal acquis, which Merkel and Sarkozy proposed at the EU summit in Brussels on 8 December 2011. Despite the strong focus of the British government on domestic austerity, Cameron could not accept the imposition of an EU-wide budgetary rule that strengthened the supervisory competences of the European Commission through the reversal of the qualified majority voting rule on excessive deficits. In practice, this meant that the Commission no longer required a qualified majority vote (QMV) mandate from the

Council before it can implement an excessive deficit procedure (EDP) against a member state. The Council can only reverse this by qualified majority. If it chooses not to act the member state remains under the EDP until the Commission decides otherwise.[11] Cameron justified the veto of the Fiscal Compact by emphasizing that Merkel and Sarkozy had not convinced him that non-Eurozone countries would be granted "adequate safeguards" against protecting the UK's economic interests in the Single Market in what he characterized as "a treaty within a treaty."[12] The British veto illustrated the lack of the spirit of collective solidarity and the renewed focus on national economic interests under the adverse conditions of the financial crisis and the subsequent Eurozone sovereign debt crisis.

Cameron's European diplomacy was, hence, a classic example from the rulebook of Andrew Moravcsik's liberal intergovernmentalism. Moravcsik emphasized that states play two-level games between their rational domestic economic interests and the collective bargaining with other member states on the EU institutional level.[13] Progress is most likely when member states consider the deepening of economic interdependence favorably, as was the case during the negotiations for the Single European Act in the mid 1980s. Then, the three leading players in the European Community–France, Germany, and the UK–had corresponding interests in speeding up market liberalization to enhance their domestic economic competitiveness and boost the job market.[14] In contrast, the financial crisis reinforced existing differences in the comparative economic advantage of individual economies in the EU. In this respect, the laissez-faire deregulatory culture of the British liberal market economy was most at odds with Germany's ordoliberal approach that emphasized the need to turn the eurozone into a "stability union" based on enhanced supervisory and regulatory powers for EU-level institutions.[15] Both London and Berlin came under increasing pressure from domestic constituencies to defend their strategic economic interests in the management of the crisis based on conflicting values. The conflicting value systems and resulting pressures from domestic constituencies explain why the establishment of a viable consensus for British-German cooperation in resolving the Eurozone crisis turned out to be impossible.[16]

In contrast to the UK, the larger Southern European member states Italy and Spain did not choose to isolate themselves from the EU's leadership. They had already increasingly been marginalized even before the crisis took hold due to growing domestic economic and political instability. The debate on the EU's inherent center-periphery divide emphasizes that since the 1980s enlargement of the European Community, an economically weak periphery has emerged, which is strongly economically and financially dependent on the richer core group of Northern countries.[17] It has been argued that within the EU, Germany established itself as the leader of the Eurozone "empire" that financed growth in Southern Europe through credit-driven demand, inflated real estate bubbles, which, in turn, buttressed its own position as the leading export nation.[18]

As such, the Southern European countries had become part of the EU's economic periphery, a status that was greatly reinforced by the effects of the Eurozone crisis.[19] As a consequence, they already entered the crisis with limited and weakening political influence as peripheral countries that became, at least in part, dependent on the institutionalized financial support provided under the European Financial Stability Facility (EFSF) and the subsequent European Stability Mechanism (ESM), established through Germany's initiative.[20] This further deepened the peripheral status of the region. As unstable crisis countries, Italy and Spain were destined to (reluctantly) follow rather than to contribute to Germany's leadership.

The Central-Eastern European (CEE) periphery of the EU, which had traditionally kept close economic and relations with Germany, was in a stronger position. Poland had managed to steer clear of recession during the financial crisis.[21] This was the most prominent example of the growing economic competitiveness of the Central-Eastern European region, which nevertheless has remained strongly dependent on foreign direct investment, especially from German industry. This "externally financed growth model"[22] explains why even Poland–as the leading player in the region–took a rather passive approach and considered it to be mainly Germany's responsibility to determine the parameters of crisis management. In the words of Polish foreign minister Radoslaw Sikorski: "I fear German power less than I am beginning to fear German inactivity."[23] The initially strong support of the CEE member states for German leadership stemmed from their principal support for Germany's ordoliberal stability policy that most of them had internalized during the postcommunist process of economic transition. The fact that the Eurozone continuously enlarged eastward after 2007, during the peak of its systemic crisis, reflected the efforts that the new EU member states had made in preparing themselves for the adoption of the Euro. The resulting focus on budgetary sustainability and economic stability by CEE governments stood in stark contrast to what they regarded as the fiscal irresponsibility of their Southern European counterparts.[24] The insistence of German Chancellor Merkel and Finance Minister Wolfgang Schäuble on fiscal consolidation through austerity and greater political surveillance was, hence, strongly welcome by the CEEs as long as Germany acted as an economic stabilizer that firmly rejected calls from France and the European Commission to collectivize the sovereign debt problems in the Eurozone.

During the initial phase of the crisis, the Merkel government could consequently count on the CEE governments to support the German concept of turning the Eurozone into a stability union. Germany lost its strategic advantage of having obtained a supportive "followership" for its Eurozone rescue strategy once it entered the phase of institutionalizing financial support for the crisis countries.[25] Slovakia joined the Eurozone in 2009, at a time when the initially reluctant Merkel government started to realize the inevitability of collective European action. Until then, Slovakia had been a predominantly passive policy-taker that made efforts to swiftly integrate into the EU's acquis and to join the Eurozone core. As Greece slid ever deeper into its domestic sovereign debt crisis in 2010 and threatened to undermine the long-term stability of the Euro, the German government conceded that the country needed collective support from the Eurozone countries. The financial support packages that were initiated in May 2010 were subsequently constantly expanded and initially administered by the temporary European Financial Stability Facility. The EFSF was created upon the initiative of German Finance Minister Schäuble, who was adamant to avoid that the financial stabilization of Greece would be exclusively managed by the International Monetary Fund (IMF). The Slovakian center-right government of Prime Minister Ivta Radicova threatened to withhold its allocated share of euro 80 billion in financial support for Greece under the EFSF by arguing that Slovakia could not support Greece's "irresponsible" fiscal behavior.[26]

This was the first sign that Germany was losing CEE support for acting as the Eurozone's (semi-) hegemonial economic stabilizer, a role it had initially adopted reluctantly but progressively more determinedly. Apart from Germany's economic strength, the basis for the country's hegemony in the Eurozone was built on its ability to distribute significant financial resources, but, crucially, also the ability of Berlin to gain majority consensus for its ordoliberal political preferences.[27] The latter component started to crumble when the Merkel government became increasingly self-confident and assertive in implementing its policy agenda as one for which there would be no alternative. Germany was subsequently considered less and less as the benign economic stabilizer and increasingly as an uncompromising hegemonial implementer of its domestic political interests.[28]

On the one hand, the Merkel-Schäuble approach to the Eurozone crisis managed to avoid the collapse of the Euro and the breakup of the Eurozone. On the other hand, because of the uncompromising insistence on transferring Germany's *Stabilitätskultur* to the Eurozone level on the basis of newly institutionalized mechanisms of collective financial liability and surveillance, unprecedented and profound divisions emerged between the core and the periphery, both inside and outside of the Eurozone.[29] It is obvious that the uncompromising defense of these preferences stemmed from Germany's domestic political constituency that became increasingly concerned about Merkel's willingness to enter into mechanisms of collective responsibility for fiscal matters.[30] Based on Moravcsik's approach, it can be observed that Germany's waning leadership fortunes in the Eurozone originate from the increasing mismatch between the federalist stability culture approach of the Merkel government and demands for maintaining sovereign national decision-making in the EU periphery. German ordoliberalism lost attractiveness not just within the Eurozone, where the South-Eastern European crisis countries were aching under the bitter medicine of austerity. It also became less of a rational choice for the outside periphery, as the CEE member states inside and outside the Eurozone moved closer to the British view of differentiation.[31]

This reflects the changing nature of national preferences that governments respond to by altering their stance on intergovernmental bargains in order to avoid losing support from their domestic constituency, in particular from powerful interest groups.[32] In this case, changing preferences produced a noticeable shift from the initial strong support for German leadership in the Eurozone that started to weaken the bargaining position of the Merkel government in the EU.

The Migration Crisis

The mismatch between German national preferences, as they were defined by the Merkel government, and those of other member states became even more evident during the substantial migration crisis which took the EU by surprise in the summer of 2015. Southern European member states, particularly the Italian government led by Mario Renzi, had repeatedly tried to warn the rest of the EU of a rapidly increasing number of migrants, but were widely ignored before the big influx occurred.[33] In the summer of 2015, the numbers peaked, predominantly due to the deteriorating situation of Syria's civil war. Chancellor Merkel responded personally by unilaterally declaring that the EU had a "moral imperative" to adopt a liberal stance towards the large number of asylum seekers. This approach was not coordinated with the rest of the EU. Consequently, it was widely considered as a move that encouraged more refugees and other migrants to make their way into Europe. Particularly the countries along the Balkan route, which most of the refugees had taken, were deeply concerned of an escalating crisis that the German government seemed to want to manage with an uncoordinated open border approach. Hungary responded with an equally unilateral sealing off its borders that effectively closed the Balkan route. Subsequently, Merkel's demands for the implementation of binding EU-wide refugee quotas resulted in an unprecedented diplomatic clash between Berlin and the Visegrád group (the Czech Republic, Hungary, Poland, and Slovakia) that uniformly rejected the quotas. The V4 countries issued a joint statement on 4 September 2015 in which they categorically rejected mandatory refugee quotas as "unacceptable."[34]

In spite of the firm opposition from the countries that had traditionally been the strongest supporters of Germany's European diplomacy, the Merkel government managed to obtain a majority EU Council decision to implement the refugee quotas. This, once again, showed the hegemonial status Germany had acquired since the onset of the Eurozone crisis. Even under adverse conditions of growing ideological opposition, German diplomacy still managed to achieve results by pulling the lever of its financial resources. Berlin was also helped by the failure of the emergence of alternative coalitions of interests among other members states that could have effectively undermined Germany's leadership. The circumstances of the EU Council decision on the refugee quotas were documented by various sources as an instance where the Merkel government adopted a similarly uncompromising diplomacy as it did during the Eurozone crisis. Just as the South-Eastern Europeans were confronted with unequivocal demands to implement austerity and structural reforms, the CEE countries faced what was described as "passive aggressive" bullying by government representatives from the region.[35] This time, Merkel and her ministers insisted on pushing through the refugee quotas by qualified majority voting, even though migration from outside the EU is a sensitive issue for the CEE members. The attempts of the Merkel government to impose its own liberal cultural stance on migration on the profoundly skeptical CEE neighbors ultimately resulted in reuniting the formerly internally divided Visegrád Group around the issue.

More recently, the V4 has also managed to attract wider support within the region, including from Austria, where the new center-right government of Chancellor Sebastian Kurz has declared its intention to engage in the V4 cooperation with the aim of strengthening the counterweight to Germany's approach. The V4 has therefore been transformed from a relatively weak form of cooperation towards a "potent political block in the EU, a new power factor, which now has to be taken into account."[36] In the face of the relatively uncooperative stance of the last Merkel government towards the CEE concerns on the issue of migration, the V4 risks becoming a vehicle for growing discontent with Germany's leadership in the EU periphery more generally. This development must no longer be ignored if the Merkel is serious about making the EU more effective and less divided after Brexit.

Brexit and the Risk of Wider Disintegration

Germany's European diplomacy also played a substantial role in the domestic debate in the run up to the British referendum on EU membership on 23 June 2016 that resulted in the decision of a slim majority of British voters to leave. The UK has been uneasy about its membership ever since it first joined the European Economic Community (EEC) in 1973. This was mainly the result of the mismatch between the British conception of the purpose of the EEC as predominantly a free trade area and the Franco-German vision of parallel economic and deepening political integration.[37] Particularly since the era of Conservative Prime Minister Margaret Thatcher, engagement in the European Community was increasingly considered in the British domestic debate as a process resulting in the loss of national economic and political sovereignty.[38] As outlined earlier the deepening of political coordination and the creation of new EU-level institutions in response to the Eurozone sovereign debt crisis, such as the European Stability Mechanism (ESM) and the Eurozone Banking Union, reinforced the underlying profound British concerns about a new drive towards deeper political integration under German leadership. Hence, the Cameron government adopted a strategy of containment through the renegotiation of the UK's membership conditions, which ultimately backfired. During the brief renegotiations between November 2015 and February 2016, Cameron managed to successfully push through the majority of his demands for differentiation from the Eurozone core. Most noticeably, this included the legal opt-out from the principle of "ever closer union" and the guarantee not to have to participate in Eurozone regulatory mechanisms. Even on the increasingly contentious domestic issue of the freedom of movement, Cameron secured concessions from the EU-27 that would have allowed his government to impose a four-year ban on access to welfare benefits for new migrants from other EU member states.[39]

The subsequent public referendum on EU membership held in June 2016 illustrated the mismatch between the rational choice approach of Cameron and the increasingly irrational domestic British debate. Cameron had argued that he had secured binding safeguards to protect the UK's economic and national interests. On that basis, he wanted to convince the British public that he had won the "best of both worlds" by allowing the country to continue to benefit from economic cooperation within the single market without having to join the Eurozone or deeper political cooperation on issues such as border controls, defense and budgetary matters. Britain would hence be able to stay "in the parts of Europe that work for us, and out of those that don't."[40] Cameron assumed that the majority of British voters would follow his advice rather than to opt for the irrational "leap in the dark" of leaving the EU, as he branded it.[41]

This was a profound misjudgment as the domestic public debate on EU membership in Britain had turned increasingly irrational in the wake of the financial crisis. The "Vote Leave" campaign spearheaded by Cameron's main rival within the Conservative Party, former London Mayor Boris Johnson, was able to exploit the widespread concerns about the loss of sovereignty and the perception that migration to the UK from within and from outside the EU would result in growing economic and social pressures.[42] The predominantly euroskeptic British tabloid media and the increasingly popular euroskeptic UK Independence Party (UKIP), led by populist Nigel Farage, had laid the ground for Johnson's "Vote Leave" campaign, which successfully countered Cameron's rational choice approach with the slogan "Take Back Control." Cameron had assumed that his offer of maintaining membership of the EU under different conditions would appeal to the British public. The reality was however that the majority of his domestic constituency had paramount concerns about remaining in an EU that–from their perspective–had changed fundamentally under German leadership. In the end, 51.9 percent of voters rejected Cameron's argument that their country would be strengthened if it continued to pool its sovereignty inside the EU. All regions supported this view, apart from Scotland, London, and Northern Ireland. Opposition to the government's perspective was particularly strong in Northern English regions, where it came close to 60 percent.[43]

The outcome of the British referendum on EU membership, therefore, represented the situation that Moravcsik's liberal intergovernmentalist approach had characterized as one where the "principal-agent relationship between social pressures and state policies is tight."[44] In this case, Moravcsik's prediction applies that domestic constituencies are unlikely to support supranational policy coordination and the pooling of sovereignty if there is a notion that unilateral policies can be cost-effectively adjusted to counteract negative effects. This is even more so the case if powerful vested interests amongst the domestic constituency advocate such unilateralism because they see little benefit for themselves in enhancing cooperation: "Powerful groups disadvantaged by co-operation will seek to obstruct government policy, even where such policies generate net gains for society as a whole."[45] In the UK, the strong euroskeptic lobby within the Conservative Party, UKIP, and in the (partly foreign-owned) media represent such a constituency,[46] the political determination and public support of which grew substantially as the EU's multi-level system of governance became ever more complex.[47]

Merkel's European diplomacy, which increased the complexity of the EU's multi-level governance through the introduction of new coordinating governance mechanisms and institutions, substantially contributed to this development. Most of all, however, her uncompromising stance on migration turned out to be the tipping point in the British domestic political debate on EU membership. After the summer of 2015 and the prospect of binding refugee quotas being introduced, the calls for taking back control from "Brussels" from British euroskeptics found an ever more fertile breeding ground among the British electorate. The leadership style of the German government that ignored these domestic sentiments in the UK (and in other member states) consequently contributed its fair share to the first instance of EU disintegration now developing. As Anthony Glees points out in his summary of the background to the Brexit decision:

> Merkel's politics of going-it-alone and her demands concerning other countries made Germany appear as the "bully" of Europe, as many critics and mudslingers had already portrayed the country for a long time … In the autumn of 2015, not a few Europeans for the first time considered Germany as a real threat to their security and their political culture. Nowhere was this as strongly the case as it was in the United Kingdom.[48]

Conclusion: Can Germany Rebuild an Inclusive Political Agenda for the EU?

Although the UK had a long-standing troubled relationship with the concept of European integration, Brexit was not inevitable. In the end, it is the result of a mixture between adverse external circumstances and the particular historical-institutional features of the UK's domestic polity. The likely prospect that the third largest member state and one of the most vibrant economies will leave the EU at some point between 2019 and 2021 nevertheless also has its roots in the ever more unilateral political constellation created by the Eurozone, under which German hegemony emerged.

This poses a major risk for the future of the EU, as the failure to achieve a more inclusive political agenda and a more cooperative multilateral leadership agenda presents the realistic prospect of eventual wider disintegration beyond Brexit. The domestic constituencies particularly in the Central-Eastern European member states are turning progressively more euroskeptic, which to a substantial extent is occurring in response to the perceived political peripheralization under Germany's top-down leadership approach.[49] If the populist wave that has started to take hold in parts of the EU's periphery cannot be halted and spreads further, disintegration of the EU beyond Brexit is very likely to occur.

Since the start of the official exit negotiations between the British government and the EU Commission in March 2018, the remaining twenty-seven member states have remained relatively united in presenting a joint negotiation position. This unity over Brexit can nevertheless not conceal the fact that the negotiations have shown how difficult, time-consuming, and costly the disassociation of an existing member state turns out to be in practice. Most importantly, however, the EU has recently witnessed a lack of direction as Germany faced a prolonged period of domestic political instability following the national elections on 24 September 2017. The elections showed a sharp decline in Merkel's domestic political fortunes, which was reflected by her failed attempt to form a new Jamaica government coalition with the Free Democrats (FDP) and the Green Party. The renewal of the grand coalition with the Social Democrats (SPD) returns Germany's domestic politics to at least moderate stability. It remains to be seen if the politically weakened Merkel will be able to revive Germany's waning clout in the EU. Much will depend on if Merkel can build a more inclusive agenda for the EU in cooperation with French president Macron, whose domestic political standing has declined substantially. Merkel faces difficult choices as she is now under dual pressure from the rising domestic political fortunes of the right-wing populist and euroskeptic Alternative for Germany (AfD) and the growing euroskepticism in the EU. If Merkel teams up with Macron in pushing towards political union in the Eurozone, this would present the AfD with an issue that it will be able to exploit significantly to its own political advantage at the 2019 regional and European Parliament elections and most of all the next national election. As the SPD has once again joined Merkel in government, the AfD is currently already the largest opposition party in the German Bundestag. As such, it is able to define the opposition agenda to the government, including a focus on limiting migration and the rejecting any moves towards implementing collective financial responsibility for the Eurozone.[50]

If the AfD becomes a permanent political force in Germany's domestic politics and even manages to move into second place by overtaking the ever less popular SPD at the next national election, Germany's former role as stabilizer would change substantially. In the long run, it could "move from asset to liability in the EU" and enhance the likelihood of disintegration rather than preventing it.[51]

The fourth Merkel government therefore needs to work with Macron to rebuild political consensus within the member states and also between the EU core and periphery. Building a bridge towards the Southern and Central-

Eastern periphery needs to include a thorough and open engagement with the political and economic reasons for their increasing skepticism towards the EU. In the case of the CEE region, the tendency towards authoritarian democratic backsliding needs to be countered by bringing these countries back from the political periphery. Cooperation with the enlarged Visegrád Group, including Austria and especially with Poland as part of a revived Weimar Triangle, will be indispensable for this purpose.

There are some hopeful signs that a new phase of cooperation between the German-Franco core and the CEE periphery could indeed be built. The V4 group have recently issued a statement on their vision for the future of the EU that is orientated towards ensuring "unity in diversity" through greater democratic accountability in the EU's decision-making procedures by strengthening the role of the European Council and the equal representation of all member states on all institutional levels. Migration policy remains the most contentious issue as the V4 stand firm in their opposition to distribution quotas and instead focus on the protection of the EU's external borders.[52] The new SPD Foreign Minister Heiko Maas emphasized in his inaugural statement at the Foreign Office that the future of the EU can only be built in cooperation with Central-Eastern European partners. During his first visit in Poland, Maas called for avoiding a permanent rift between Eastern and Western Europe and emphasized that Poland remained a "central partner" for Germany in the EU.[53] This was echoed by Merkel during her first visit to Warsaw since her reappointment as chancellor. During the press conference with Polish Prime Minister Mateusz Morawiecki on 19 March 2018, Merkel highlighted that the revival of the Weimar triangle cooperation with Poland and France was part of her new government's coalition agreement: "… The whole government wants to nourish and strengthen the good, neighborly relations."[54]

On the other hand, the fourth Merkel government seems to be adamant to continue the ordoliberal approach in its economic policies, which does not bear well for the reform of the Eurozone. The Social Democratic Finance Minister Olaf Scholz repeatedly emphasized his intention to continue the policy of his predecessor, Wolfgang Schäuble, of promoting the "black zero" approach of strictly balanced budgets for the Eurozone.[55] In practice, this means maintaining a strict austerity course for countries with sovereign debt problems, including France. At the same time the black zero approach makes it unlikely that Germany will increase its share of European security. The risk remains, therefore, that during Merkel's fourth term, the weakened chancellor will continue to exercise German European policy predominantly through the lens of domestic politics. For the Eurozone, this would mean more of the same and an unwillingness to seriously engage with the reform proposals of French president Macron.[56] For the EU itself, the risk is that Germany will continue to hamper the demands for a more integrated defense and security policy, supported by substantially strengthened capabilities.[57]

To prevent the ultimate disintegration of the EU, Germany's European policy needs to transform itself from Merkel's hegemonial and domestically orientated "self-righteousness"[58] in the management of the Eurozone and the migration crisis towards an inclusive and cooperative multilateral approach that is most of all orientated towards consensus. If Merkel is able to achieve this during her fourth and possibly final term as chancellor, it will not only define the assessment of her record in government, but it will also determine the fate of the European project and the future of the EU.

Christian Schweiger is Visiting Professor, Chair for Comparative European Governance Systems in the Institute for Political Science, Chemnitz University of Technology. Previously he was Associate Professor in Government in the School of Government and International Affairs at Durham University in the United Kingdom. His research concentrates on the comparative study of political systems, economies, and welfare states of the member states of the European Union (particularly the UK, Germany, and transformation in the CEE countries), the political economy of the EU single market, economic globalization and transatlantic relations. His most recent publications include the jointly edited collection with José M. Magone and Brigid Laffan *Core-periphery Relations in the European Union: Power and conflict in a dualist political economy* (New York, 2016), the monograph *Exploring the EU's Legitimacy Crisis: The Dark Heart of Europe* (Cheltenham, 2016) and the jointly edited collection with Anna Visvizi *Central and Eastern Europe in the EU: Challenges and Perspectives Under Crisis Conditions* (New York, 2018). E-mail: christian.schweiger@phil.tu-chemnitz.de

Notes

1. Simon Bulmer, "Shaping the Rules? The Constitutive Politics of the European Union and German Power' in *Tamed Power: Germany in* Europe, ed. Peter J. Katzenstein (Ithaca, 1997), 49–79, here 51.
2. Jean-François Jamet "France: Lowering the Barriers to Growth" in *From Reform to Growth: Managing the Economic Crisis in Europe*, ed. Vit Novotný (Brussels, 2013), 175–200, here 190.
3. Christian Schweiger, *Exploring the EU's Legitimacy Crisis: The Dark Heart of Europe* (Cheltenham, 2016), 107.

4. W.E. Paterson, "Germany and the European Union" in *Developments in German Politics 4*, ed. Stephen Padgett and William E. Paterson (Basingstoke, 2014), 166–187, here 181.
5. Jörg Bibow, "On the Franco-German euro contradictions and ultimate euro battleground", *Contributions to Political Economy* 37, nos. 609–629 (2013): 128.
6. Gordon Brown, *Beyond the Crash: Overcoming the First Crisis of Globalisation* (London, 2010), 239.
7. Colin Crouch "Privatised Keynesianism: An Unacknowledged Policy Regime," *British Journal of Politics and International Relations* 11 (2009): 382–399, here 390.
8. Andrew Gamble, "The United Kingdom: The Triumph of Fiscal Realism?" in *The Consequences of the Global Financial Crisis: The Rhetoric of Reform and Regulation*, ed. Wyn Grant and Graham K. Wilson (Oxford, 2014), 34–50, here 46.
9. Nicolai von Ondarza, "Core Europe vs. Europe à la carte" in *Drifting Towards the Exit? Taking Stock of Britain's EU Membership*, ed. Christian Schweiger (Augsburg, 2015), 52–70, here 66–67.
10. David Cameron, "EU Speech at Bloomberg," London, 23 January 2013; available at https://www.gov.uk/government/speeches/eu-speech-at-bloomberg, accessed 6 March 2018.
11. Christian Schweiger, "The EU *Fiscal Compact*: Differentiated *Spillover* Effects under Crisis Conditions," *Perspectives on European Politics and Society* 15, no. 3 (2014): 293–304, here 301.
12. Ian Traynor, Nicholas Watt, David Gow, and Patrick Wintour, "David Cameron blocks EU treaty with veto, casting Britain adrift in Europe," *The* Guardian, 9 December 2011, available at https://www.theguardian.com/world/2011/dec/09/david-cameron-blocks-eu-treaty, accessed 6 March 2018.
13. Andrew Moravcsik, "Preferences and Power in the European Community: A Liberal Intergovernmentalist Approach," *Journal of Common Market Studies* 31, no. 4 (1993): 473–524, here 480.
14. Andrew Moravcsik, "Negotiating the Single European Act: National Interests and Conventional Statecraft in the European Community," *International Organization* 45, no. 1 (1991): 19–56.
15. Franz-Josef Meiers, *Germany's Role in the Euro Crisis: Berlin's Quest for a More Perfect Monetary Union* (London, 2015), 18.
16. Andrew Moravcsik "Taking Preferences Seriously: A Liberal Theory of International Politics," *International Organization* 51, no.4 (1997): 513–553, here 528.
17. Kenneth Dyson and Angelos Sepos, "Differentiated Integration as a Design Principle and as a Tool in the Political Management of European Integration" in *Which Europe? The Politics of Differentiated Integration*, ed. Kenneth Dyson and Angelos Sepos (Basingstoke, 2010), 3–23.
18. Angelos Sepos, "The Centre-Periphery Divide in the Eurocrisis: A Theoretical Approach" in *Core-Periphery Relations in the European Union: Power and Conflict in a Dualist Political Economy*, ed. José M. Magone, Brigid Laffan, and Christian Schweiger (Abingdon, 2016), 35–36, here 43.
19. Bela Galgoczi, "The Southern and Eastern Peripheries of Europe: Is Convergence a Lost Cause?" in Magone et al. (see note 18), 130–146, here 134.
20. Christian Schweiger, *The EU and the Global Financial Crisis: New Varieties of Capitalism* (Cheltenham, 2014), 168.
21. Maciej Duszczyk, "Poland under Economic Crisis Conditions," *Perspectives on European Politics and Society* 15, no. 3 (2014): 370–384.
22. Bela Galgozi, "Boom and Bust in Central and Eastern Europe: Lessons in the Sustainability of an Eternally Financed Growth Model," *Journal of Contemporary European Research* 5, no.4 (2009): 614–625.
23. Radek Sikorski, "Poland and the Future of the European Union", German Council on Foreign Relations, Berlin, 28 November 2011; available at http://www.mfa.gov.pl/resource/33ce6061-ec12-4da1-a145-01e2995c6302:JCR, accessed 14 March 2018.

24. Tim Haughton, "Central and Eastern Europe: The Sacrifices of Solidarity, the Discomfort of Diversity, and the Vexations of Vulnerabilities" in *The European Union in* Crisis, ed. Desmond Dinan, Neill Nugent and William E. Paterson (London, 2017), 253–265, here 258.
25. Vladimir Handl and William E. Paterson, "The Continuing Relevance of Germany's Engine for CEE and the EU," *Communist and Post-Communist Studies* 46 (2013): 327–337, here 333.
26. "Slovakia's Revolt against Solidarity," *The Economist* 13 August 2010; available at https://www.economist.com/blogs/easternapproaches/2010/08/slovakia_and_greece, accessed 14 March 2018.
27. Simon Bulmer and William E. Paterson, "Germany as the EU's Reluctant Hegemon? Of Economic Strength and Political Constraints," *Journal of European Public Policy* 20, no. 10 (2013): 1387–1405, here 1390.
28. Simon Bulmer "Germany and the Eurozone Crisis: Between Hegemony and Domestic Politics," *Western European Politics* 37, no. 6 (2014): 1244–1263, here 1249.
29. Hans Kundani, *The Paradox of German Power* (London, 2014), 112.
30. Luigi Bonatti and Andrea Fracasso, "The German Model and the European Crisis," *Journal of Common Market Studies* 51, no. 6 (2013): 1023–1039, here 1034.
31. Christian Schweiger, Frank Markovic, and Tomas A. Nagy, "The Dire Straits of Brexit: Potential Implications for the EU, UK and the V4," *European Public Affairs,* 19 February 2016; available at http://www.europeanpublicaffairs.eu/the-dire-straits-of-brexit-potential-implications-for-the-eu-uk-and-the-v4/, accessed 20 March 2018.
32. Andrew Moravcsik, "The New Liberalism" in *The Oxford Handbook of International Relations,* ed. Christian Reus-Smit and Duncan Snidal (Oxford, 2008), 234–254.
33. "Mediterranean migrant deaths: EU faces renewed pressure," BBC News, 28 April 2015; available at http://www.bbc.com/news/world-europe-32376082, accessed 20 March 2018.
34. Visegrád Group, "Joint Statement of the Heads of Governments of the Visegrád Group of Countries," Prague, 4 September 2015; available at http://www.visegradgroup.eu/calendar/2015/joint-statement-of-the-150904, accessed 20 March 2018.
35. Duncan Robinson and Henry Foy, "Migrants Crisis Sets Germany at Odds with Neighbours to the East," *Financial Times,* 17 September 2015; available at https://www.ft.com/content/09ffbc28-5d46-11e5-a28b-50226830d644, accessed 20 March 2018.
36. Boris Kálnoky, "Entfremdung von Deutschland–Die Kanzlerin hat die Osteuropäer vor den Kopf gestoßen" in *Merkel: Eine kritische Bilanz,* 6th edition, ed. Philip Plickert (Munich, 2017), 209–215, here 215.
37. Robert Cooper, "Britain and Europe," *International Affairs,* 88, no. 6 (2012): 1191–1203.
38. Simon Usherwood, "Britain and Europe: A Model of Permanent Crisis?" in *The European Union in Crisis: Explorations in Representation and Democratic Legitimacy,* ed. Kyriakos N. Demetriou (London, 2015), 3–14, here 6.
39. Lee McGowan and David Phinnemore, "The UK: Membership in Crisis" in Dinan et al. (see note 24), 77–99, here 86–87.
40. David Cameron, "Prime Minister's Statement on EU Renegotiation," House of Commons, London, 3 February 2016; available at https://www.gov.uk/government/speeches/prime-ministers-statement-on-eu-renegotiation-3-february-2016, accessed 20 March 2018.
41. David Cameron "2016 Speech on the EU Referendum," Eastleigh, 23 May 2016; available at http://www.ukpol.co.uk/david-cameron-2016-speech-on-the-eu-referendum/, accessed 21 March 2018.
42. Harold D. Clarke, Matthew Goodwin, and Paul Whiteley, "Why Britain Voted for Brexit: An Individual-Level Analysis of the 2016 Referendum Vote" 70, no. 3 (2017): 439–464.
43. Electoral Commission, "EU Referendum Results;" available at https://www.electoralcommission.org.uk/find-information-by-subject/elections-and-referendums/past-elections-and-referendums/eu-referendum/electorate-and-count-information, accessed 20 March 2018.
44. Moravcsik (see note 13), 485.

45. Ibid., 487.
46. David Baker and Pauline Schnapper, *Britain and the Crisis of the European Union* (Basingstoke, 2015), 82–84.
47. David Sanders, "The Reluctant Europeans: Britain and the EU, 1952–2014" in Schweiger (see note 9), 9–37, here 28.
48. Antony Glees, "Bye-bye Britain–Wie Angela Merkel den Ausschlag zum Brexit gab" in Plickert (see note 36), 199–208, here 204.
49. "Illiberal Central Europe: Big, Bad Visegrad," The Economist, 28 January 2016; available at https://www.economist.com/news/europe/21689629-migration-crisis-has-given-unsettling-new-direction-old-alliance-big-bad-visegrad, accessed 20 March 2018.
50. Alternative für Deutschland, "Raus aus dem Euro;" available at https://www.afd.de/wp-content/uploads/sites/111/2018/01/AfD_Bund_Flyer_8-Seiter_Euro_01-18_RZ_FLY.pdf, accessed 20 March 2018.
51. Simon Bulmer and William E. Paterson, "Germany and the Crisis: Asset or Liabilty" in Dinan et al. (see note 24), 212–232, here 230; Douglas Webber, "Can the EU Survive?" in Dinan et al. (see note 24), 336–359, here 354.
52. Visegrád Group, "V4 Statement on the Future of Europe," 26 January 2018; available at http://www.visegradgroup.eu/calendar/2018/v4-statement-on-the, accessed 20 March 2018.
53. Auswärtiges Amt, "Den Zusammenhalt in Europa stärken: Außenminister Maas in Warschau," 15 March 2018; available at https://www.auswaertiges-amt.de/de/aussenpolitik/laender/polen-node/-/1787140, accessed 20 March 2018.
54. Angela Merkel, "Pressekonferenz von Bundeskanzlerin Merkel und dem polnischen Ministerpräsidenten Morawiecki," 19 March 2018; available at https://www.bundeskanzlerin.de/Content/DE/Mitschrift/Pressekonferenzen/2018/03/2018-03-19-pk-merkel-morawiecki.html, accessed 20 March 2018.
55. Guy Chazan, "Scholz vows to follow Schäuble path as Germany's finance chief," 12 March 2018; available at https://www.ft.com/content/e74ff27c-2608-11e8-b27e-cc62a39d57a0, accessed 22 March 2018.
56. Sophia Besch and Christian Odendahl, "The Good European? Why Germany's Policy Ambitions Must Match Its Power," Centre for European Reform, London, February 2018, 10; available at https://www.cer.eu/publications/archive/policy-brief/2018/good-european-why-germanys-policy-ambitions-must-match-its, accessed 20 March 2018.
57. Hans Kundnani, "The New Parameters of German Foreign Policy," *Transatlantic Academy Paper Series* no. 3 (2017): 10–11.
58. Wolfgang Streeck, "Scenario for a Wonderful Tomorrow," *London Review of Books* 38, no. 7 (2016): 7–10; available at https://wolfgangstreeck.com/2016/03/29/scenario-for-a-wonderful-tomorrow/, accessed 20 March 2018.

··· EPILOGUE ···

MOVING BEYOND MERKEL

Eric Langenbacher

It bears repeating that perhaps the most striking aspect of this political moment is a disjunction between the disruption in the political system and the economic and social situation. Crime has decreased to a twenty-five-year low.[1] Unemployment–long the bugaboo of German politics–is hovering around 4 to 5 percent and approached a record low below 4 percent at one point in 2018; there is a budgetary surplus (and no new public borrowing for four straight years); the debt-to-GDP ratio has declined from over 80 percent in 2010 to just above 60 percent today. Growth rates are respectable despite all the uncertainty (sanctions against Russia, Trump, and Brexit); and there is increased personal and public consumption, buoyed by wage increases. The economy has been doing well for almost as long as most people can remember. Although there was some worrying news in late 2018 and early 2019 especially in the automotive sector and from within the eurozone, most predictions are merely for a slowdown in growth to a still-decent 1.5 percent.[2] The coalition partners are contemplating some kind of tax cut as a stimulating response. Certainly, the declinist funk that the country was stuck in around the turn of the millennium is largely forgotten.

Admittedly, there are parts of the country, especially in eastern Germany and some rural western regions, where prosperity has been more elusive. Poverty has increased in some segments of the population (especially among Germans with a migration background), and income and wealth inequality has grown. Affordable housing is a pervasive concern particularly in many of the most dynamic regions like Munich, Frankfurt, and Berlin. But, these factors do not really explain the political upheavals of the last two years, nor support for the AfD. Indeed, the typical (right-

Notes for this section begin on page 310.

populist) protest voter is not economically down and out, but is rather obsessed with inchoate fears about his (only sometimes her) social and cultural status. Sometimes I even think that voting for populists today is a bizarre kind of luxury good that is only possible when most of the typical economic and political concerns are allayed.

Moreover, the rise of German influence and power in Europe and beyond over the last fifteen years surely (surreptitiously) warms the heart of many Germans. The men's national team even won the 2014 World Cup of soccer–although had a horrible tournament in Russia in summer 2018. From a different angle, Merkel and Germany were almost universally lauded by liberals and the left the world over for the decision to admit refugees in 2015. People even spoke about Merkel deserving the Nobel Peace Prize. After Obama left office, many proclaimed her the leader of the free world.[3] In 2015, she was even voted *Time Magazine* Person of the Year, only the fourth German to be so honored (the others were Hitler in 1938, Adenauer in 1953, and Brandt in 1970). The country has rarely, perhaps never, been held in such high international esteem. *The Washington Post* even ran a column by George Will in January 2019 entitled "Today's Germany is the best Germany the world has seen."[4]

All of this should have made German voters ecstatic and ensured a landslide victory for Merkel, who has presided over all of this. But, voters can be fickle and the political context can change suddenly–domestically and internationally. In fact, only one admittedly momentous policy decision likely created this political situation. Still riding the wave of her stunning 2013 electoral victory, Merkel was gravely wounded by her migration policy decision in summer 2015 and has never really recovered. One could argue that this policy shift was responsible for the rise of the AfD–just as some have (partially) blamed Merkel for the Brexit referendum decision in 2016 and increasingly xenophobic and authoritarian governments in eastern Europe.[5] Interestingly, this was an unusually bold and risky decision for the chancellor–yet one that she characteristically justified with the pithy phrase "wir schaffen das" (we'll get it done). Many believe that the lack of a more robust justification for this momentous policy shift exacerbated the political damage. A more general fatigue with her leadership and centrist governments also set in.

In the end, it was not a controversial policy, poor economic performance, lack of popularity in the electorate, or a scandal that brought her down. Rather, like so many other politicians Merkel succumbed to internal party criticism after lackluster election results–first at the 2017 Bundestag election and then in October 2018 in Bavaria and Hesse. As discussed above, an unprecedented three-way race to replace her as CDU party leader resulted in Merkel loyalist Annegret Kramp-Karrenbauer narrowly winning in early December 2018 over old-boy favorite Fredrich Merz. Despite her victory, it is not preordained that Kramp-Karrenbauer will be able to re-unify the party and win elections like before. Then again, Merkel was relatively unknown when she took over the CDU in 1998-2000–similar to Theresa May and Emmanuel Macron before their speedy ascents in 2016 and 2017.

Despite Merkel's efforts to secure her legacy, it could be a political bloodbath within the CDU after she steps down fully. Will Merkel loyalists eventually win the internal power struggle and continue with a centrist (even center-left) social democratic-ish agenda and profile? Or will those who think the party needs to return to the (center) right prevail? Can AfD voters be brought back into the fold even with a move rightwards? These issues are incredibly difficult to traverse. Thus, there might be a good reason for the party not to ditch Merkel as chancellor just yet–and actually to hold out until the next elections loom in 2021. Many might actually wish for a period in opposition (just like the SPD has been fantasizing about for years) to hammer out these differences–quite challenging when one is governing seemingly in perpetuity as the responsible "adult" in the room. Therefore, it is quite possible that Merkel will last until at least 2020. There is some speculation that she will step aside at the two-year midterm review of the current coalition government. A transfer of power to a new leader will ensure that this individual will have some experience with the top job and can develop a bit of incumbency advantage before the fall 2021 election. But, if the Social Democrats pull out of the grand coalition (as some predict if they do poorly in the European Parliamentary elections in May and then later in 2019 in several eastern states) and early elections take place, all bets are off. The internal party drama that Merkel has stanched for fifteen years will come with a vengeance.

For a long time, Germans seemed to prefer Merkel's pragmatic, no-drama style. The old Helmut Schmidt quote–"if you have a vision, you go to the doctor–has been frequently trotted out.[6] On that note, Schmidt, who had taken on a witty, elder statesman role, was the second legendary chancellor to have died in the last legislative period in December 2015 at the age of ninety-six. But, it appears that many German voters are yearning for a different type of leader–for someone who can articulate a joint project or a goal to which the country can aspire.[7] For these reasons, the pragmatic Kamp-Karrenbauer may face an uphill battle consolidating her position in the party and resonating with the broader electorate. On a final note, Merkel's exit from political life is typical–deliberate, planned, gradual, on her own terms, and lacking any unnecessary drama and emotion.

Internationally, almost immediately after his election in 2017, French President Macron seized the international initiative from Merkel with his grand plans for EU reform, catching the Germans flat-footed. External attention, however, has been devoted to more pressing day-to-day concerns such as the Brexit mess, the next EU budget (without the British contribution), combatting populists, elections to the European Parliament in late May 2019, and then selecting the new Commission. The weakness and instability of the current coalition government and the upheaval surrounding Merkel's departure, have ensured that nothing ambitious will likely be done at the EU level in the immediate future. This surely pleases many Germans (and other Europeans) who have little to negative interest in the more ambitious reformist proposals, especially Eurozone deepening. But, this also means that certain Eurozone vulnerabilities that Macron was trying to address will persist, perhaps generating more crises in the future. Indeed, in late 2018, the Eurozone was embroiled in a serious budget dispute with the Italian government, which had the potential to quickly destabilize the still-fragile Eurozone.[8]

More generally, the post Cold War world is seemingly coming to an end. The unipolar moment of unquestioned U.S. and western hegemony has passed. Multipolar competition is back and major powers like China, Russia, and Turkey are entrenching authoritarian systems and trying to export their models abroad. Who will carry the banner of liberal democracy and collective defense forward, especially with Trump leading the United States? Indeed, one of Germany's most fraught external relationship is currently with the U.S. Much of this is due to the erratic leadership of the current president. The Germans understand acutely how much they have to lose especially economically if Trump's "America first" trade policy continues. And the U.S. government is continuing to apply pressure. U.S. Ambassador Richard Grenell ("little Trump") has actively intervened in domestic German affairs, stating that he intends to strengthen European conservatives and sending a letter to German companies in January 2019, threatening sanctions if they continue to engage in the Nordstream 2 gas pipeline from Russia to western Europe.[9]

These tensions explain why the German government has embarked on an unprecedented Deutschlandjahr (Germany Year), a quintessential soft-power charm offensive through the end of 2019 centered on the slogan "Wunderbar Together."[10] Previous "years of friendship" took place in countries like China, India, and Mexico–doing one in the U.S. is a mark of how poor the current Transatlantic relationship is.[11] Interestingly, the programming is focusing in particular on the "heartland" away from the cosmopolitan coasts and major cities and is highlighting the economic contributions that German companies make to the United States. Yet, given the apparent depth of Trump's animus to Germany specifically,[12] improvements are unlikely until he leaves office. How much lasting damage Trump has done to Germany's reputation among average Americans and to the Transatlantic relationship more generally is one of the biggest open questions.[13]

In recent years, Germany has been quite adept at leading from behind, often in a reactive, last-minute manner. Perhaps leaders have not had the opportunity for a more proactive, vision-defining foreign policy. Merkel's tenure will likely be remembered as one of almost constant crisis-management, with a string of crises–the financial crisis and recession, Euro crisis, Syria, Crimea/Ukraine, migration, Brexit, Trump–the responses to which have dominated the political agenda. One might add that the chancellor has managed the crises well enough, even if full resolution was often elusive. Moreover, Merkel also consolidated past policy successes (labor market reforms), upheld entrenched policy traditions such as minimizing debt and maintaining price stability, and pushed through various institutional reforms (federalism). This is to say, that in many respects she really was an effective and inherently conservative leader. She has never been an ideological, grand-strategy, or big-idea person. "Thank goodness" many would say. But, I do think we are at a point where a new common project is needed.

Germany under Merkel has not had to fully embrace the status and the responsibilities that its increase in power and influence have generated over the last two decades. It has been content as a trading state, a "geoeconomic power" using its soft power to advance its interests.[14] The country has not been forced to decide to take on a larger role or to fulfill the expectations many have of it–expectations that have if anything mounted as the international situation worsens. But, this moment of reckoning cannot be denied much longer. Trump's America is seemingly in full retreat from much of the world and could be entering a phase of long-term decline. After Brexit, Britain will be even less visible on the continent and globally. French strength is still more of a possibility and is contingent on Macron being able to follow through on his increasingly divisive domestic reform agenda. In fact, his power ebbed by late 2018 and early 2019 in the face of the "gilets jaunes" (yellow vest) protests, which forced him to backtrack on several domestic reforms and diverted attention from the EU level.[15] Will Germany under a new leader fill the void? Can it? Or will it keep treading water and wait for Trump to leave and France to rise again? But, even the latter scenario assumes that the status quo ante can be re-established–probably an overly optimistic hope.[16]

The present moment is a critical juncture akin to 1989-1991. Indeed, at the point in February 2018 when people marked the fact that more time had elapsed since the Berlin Wall fell than it was actually up, former U.S. Ambassador John Kornblum observed that German history has worked in twenty to thirty-year phases. Thus, the post Wall era is winding down and the post-post Wall period will soon begin.[17] What will Germany do in this new era? One thing is, however, certain: Merkel–chancellor for thirteen years, party leader for eighteen–is not the leader to preside over this new moment. Her era was successful in so many ways, but it is now essentially over. We must wait to see how new leaders like Kramp-Karrenbauer will traverse these perpetually stormy waters and what kind of Germany will result.

Notes

1. https://www.politico.eu/article/germany-crime-rate-lowest-since-1992/, accessed 13 January 2019.
2. https://www.bloomberg.com/opinion/articles/2019-01-08/germany-isn-t-floundering-despite-the-industrial-production-data, accessed 8 January 2019.
3. http://www.independent.co.uk/voices/angela-merkel-donald-trump-democracy-freedom-of-press-a7556986.html, accessed 4 February 2018.
4. https://www.washingtonpost.com/opinions/global-opinions/todays-germany-is-the-best-germany-the-world-has-seen/2019/01/04/abe0b138-0f8f-11e9-84fc-d58c33d6c8c7_story.html?utm_term=.11777dcaadd4, accessed 13 January 2019.
5. http://www.spiegel.de/international/europe/brexit-is-merkel-to-blame-a-1100303.html; http://www.nationalreview.com/corner/437075/brexit-german-leadership-aghast-brexit-it-helped-cause; accessed 20 August 2017.
6. http://www.sueddeutsche.de/politik/zitate-von-helmut-schmidt-wer-eine-vision-hat-der-soll-zum-arzt-gehen-1.2729860, accessed 3 February 2018.
7. https://www.nytimes.com/2018/02/02/opinion/millennials-germany-politics-merkel.html?action=click&pgtype=Homepage&clickSource=story-heading&module=opinion-c-col-right-region®ion=opinion-c-col-right-region&WT.nav=opinion-c-col-right-region, accessed 2 February 2018.
8. https://www.nytimes.com/2018/12/05/opinion/eu-italy-debt-crisis.html?action=click&module=Opinion&pgtype=Homepage, accessed 5 December 2018.
9. http://www.spiegel.de/international/world/u-s-ambassador-richard-grenell-is-isolated-in-berlin-a-1247610.html; https://www.bloomberg.com/news/articles/2019-01-14/merkel-ally-pushes-back-on-trump-envoy-s-russian-pipeline-threat, accessed 14 January 2019.
10. https://wunderbartogether.org/, accessed 4 December 2018.
11. https://www.dw.com/en/a-germany-year-in-the-us-opening-up-the-conversation/a-45215380, accessed 4 December 2018.

12. https://www.politico.eu/article/donald-trump-angela-merkel-germany-nato-why-germany-trumps-strange-fixation-vexes-experts/; https://www.newyorker.com/magazine/2018/12/24/how-trump-made-war-on-angela-merkel-and-europe, accessed 14 January 2019.
13. Eric Langenbacher and Ruth Witlinger, "The End of Memory? German-American Relations under Donald Trump," *German Politics* 27, no. 2 (2018): 174-192.
14. Hans Kundnani, *The Paradox of German Power* (New York, 2015).
15. https://www.nytimes.com/2018/12/04/world/europe/france-fuel-tax-yellow-vests.html?action=click&module=Top%20Stories&pgtype=Homepage, accessed 4 December 2018.
16. https://www.nytimes.com/2018/11/30/opinion/europe-america-foreign-policy-trump.html?rref=collection%2Fbyline%2Fivan-krastev&action=click&contentCollection=undefined®ion=stream&module=stream_unit&version=latest&contentPlacement=1&pgtype=collection, accessed 4 December 2018.
17. https://www.economist.com/blogs/kaffeeklatsch/2018/02/28-years-two-months-and-27-days?cid1=cust/ddnew/email/n/n/2018025n/owned/n/n/ddnew/n/n/n/nna/Daily_Dispatch/email&etear=dailydispatch, accessed 5 February 2018.

Index

www.ingramcontent.com/pod-product-compliance
Lightning Source LLC
Chambersburg PA
CBHW070908030426
42336CB00014BA/2335
9781789202656